Builders of the Third Reich

Builders of the Third Reich

The Organisation Todt and Nazi Forced Labour

Charles Dick

BLOOMSBURY ACADEMIC
LONDON • NEW YORK • OXFORD • NEW DELHI • SYDNEY

BLOOMSBURY ACADEMIC
Bloomsbury Publishing Plc
50 Bedford Square, London, WC1B 3DP, UK
1385 Broadway, New York, NY 10018, USA
29 Earlsfort Terrace, Dublin 2, Ireland

BLOOMSBURY, BLOOMSBURY ACADEMIC and the Diana logo are trademarks
of Bloomsbury Publishing Plc

First published in Great Britain 2021
Paperback edition first published 2022

Copyright © Charles Dick, 2021

Charles Dick has asserted his right under the Copyright, Designs and Patents Act,
1988, to be identified as Author of this work.

Cover image: An armband for NCOs of the Organisation Todt © INTERFOTO / Alamy

All rights reserved. No part of this publication may be reproduced or
transmitted in any form or by any means, electronic or mechanical, including
photocopying, recording, or any information storage or retrieval system,
without prior permission in writing from the publishers.

Bloomsbury Publishing Plc does not have any control over, or responsibility for,
any third-party websites referred to or in this book. All internet addresses given
in this book were correct at the time of going to press. The author and publisher
regret any inconvenience caused if addresses have changed or sites have
ceased to exist, but can accept no responsibility for any such changes.

A catalogue record for this book is available from the British Library.

Library of Congress Cataloging-in-Publication Data
Names: Dick, Charles, author.
Title: Builders of the Third Reich : the Organisation Todt and Nazi forced labour / Charles Dick.
Other titles: Organisation Todt and Nazi forced labour
Description: London ; New York : Bloomsbury Academic, [2020] |
Includes bibliographical references and index.
Identifiers: LCCN 2020029970 (print) | LCCN 2020029971 (ebook) |
ISBN 9781350182660 (hardback) | ISBN 9781350182677 (ebook) | ISBN 9781350182684 (epub)
Subjects: LCSH: Organisation Todt (Germany)–History. | World War,
1939–1945–Engineering and construction. | Engineering–Germany–History–20th century. |
World War, 1939–1945–Conscript labor–Europe. | World War, 1939–1945–Prisoners and prisons,
German. | Forced labor–Europe–History–20th century. | Slave labor–Europe–History–20th century. |
Forced labor–Europe–History–20th century. | Germany–History–1933–1945.
Classification: LCC D795.G3 D53 2020 (print) | LCC D795.G3 (ebook) | DDC 940.54/05–dc23
LC record available at https://lccn.loc.gov/2020029970
LC ebook record available at https://lccn.loc.gov/2020029971

ISBN: HB: 978-1-3501-8266-0
        PB: 978-1-3503-3705-3
        ePDF: 978-1-3501-8267-7
        eBook: 978-1-3501-8268-4

Typeset by Integra Software Services Pvt. Ltd.

To find out more about our authors and books visit www.bloomsbury.com
and sign up for our newsletters.

Contents

Acknowledgements	vii
List of abbreviations	viii
Introduction	1

1	The Organisation Todt in Hitler's empire	15
	The Organisation Todt under Todt	17
	The Organisation Todt under Speer	25
	Organisation Todt operations	33
	Organisation Todt transitions	46
2	Plunder in Europe	51
	The business of slave labour under the Organisation Todt	52
	The Organisation Todt in Nazi-occupied Europe	60
	The Organisation Todt in the Greater Reich	70
	Hitler and the Organisation Todt	77
3	The Organisation Todt in the Nazi system	81
	The Organisation Todt and the SS	84
	The Organisation Todt and industry	91
	The Organisation Todt and the Wehrmacht	95
	The Organisation Todt and the Nazi party	99
	Key players in slave labour	103
4	Slave labourers under the Organisation Todt	105
	Hard labour under the Organisation Todt	108
	Organisation Todt control over camps	110
	Nazi racial hierarchies	133
	Types of labour	147
	Women under the Organisation Todt	152
	Violence in the camps	158

5	Engineers as slave drivers	161
	The Organisation Todt in Radoskowice	163
	Nazi war criminals and the Organisation Todt	172
	Managing the Organisation Todt	176
	Organisation Todt perpetrators	186
	Flight from reality	190

Conclusion 193

Notes 199
Appendix: Organisation Todt ranks with Army equivalents 240
Bibliography 241
Index 254

Acknowledgements

This book is based on my PhD gained at Birkbeck College, London, and I should like to thank many people for helping me in my studies there. My first big debt of gratitude is to my doctoral supervisor, Nikolaus Wachsmann, for his wisdom and kindness in guiding me towards completion of the work. I am also deeply grateful to Christian Goeschel, Jan Rüger, Orlando Figes, David Feldman, Jessica Reinisch, Julia Laite, Jerry White, Hilary Sapire and John Arnold for their advice and unfailing encouragement throughout my history studies at the college. I extend special thanks to Richard Overy and Chris Dillon for their generous advice and support, as well as to Christine Schmidt of the Wiener Library in London for her organisation of seminars and patient help in searches of the International Tracing Service database. I am grateful, too, to Ruth Bettina Birn for her generous assistance and suggestions, and to Felix Römer of the German Historical Institute in London for his advice during conferences there. Among the numerous people who assisted me in my research in various archives, I should like to thank Jon Barstad of the National Archives of Norway in Oslo for his expert guidance. I am grateful to the dedicated staff at the Bundesarchiv branches in Ludwigsburg, Berlin and Freiburg, as well as to the Institut für Zeitgeschichte in Munich and the Zwangsarbeit 1939–1945 archive. My thanks go out also to many former Reuters colleagues for inspirational discussions during lengthy country walks over the years. Finally, I owe an incalculable debt to my family for their love and support during this whole enterprise.

Abbreviations

AEL	Arbeitserziehungslager (work education camp)
Baltöl	Baltische Öl GmbH (Baltic Oil Company)
BA/MA	Bundesarchiv/Militärarchiv, Freiburg
BArchB	Bundesarchiv Berlin
BArchL	Bundesarchiv Ludwigsburg
DAF	Deutsche Arbeitsfront (German Labour Front)
DESt	Deutsche Erd- und Steinwerke GmbH (German Earth and Stone Works)
Dipl. Ing.	Diplomingenieur (qualified engineer)
Dr. Ing.	Doktor Ingenieur (doctor of engineering)
GBBau	Generalbevollmächtigter für die Regelung der Bauwirtschaft (general plenipotentiary for the regulation of the construction industry)
Gestapo	Geheime Staatspolizei (Secret State Police)
HLSL	Harvard Law School Library, Nuremberg Trials Project
HSSPF	Höhere SS und Polizeiführer (Higher SS and police leader)
IfZ	Institut für Zeitgeschichte, Munich
IKL	Inspektion der Konzentrationslager (Inspectorate of Concentration Camps)
IMT	Trial of the Major War Criminals before the International Military Tribunal
ITS	International Tracing Service
IWM	Imperial War Museum, London
KDAI	Kampfbund deutscher Architekten und Ingenieure (Action Group of German Architects and Engineers)

NMT	Trials of War Criminals before the Nuernberg Military Tribunals
Nordag	Nordische Aluminium AG (Nordic Aluminium Company)
NSBDT	Nationalsozialistischer Bund deutscher Technik (National Socialist League of German Technology)
NSDAP	Nationalsozialistische deutsche Arbeiterpartei (National Socialist German Workers' Party)
NSKK	Nationalsozialistisches Kraftfahrkorps (National Socialist Motor Corps)
OT	Organisation Todt
POW	prisoner of war
RAD	Reichsarbeitsdienst (Reich Labour Service)
RM	Reichsmark
RSHA	Reichssicherheitshauptamt (Reich Security Head Office)
SA	Sturmabteilung (Storm Detachment)
SD	Sicherheitsdienst (Security Service)
SS	Schutzstaffel (Protection Squadron)
TNA	The National Archives of the UK
WVHA	Wirtschafts-Verwaltungshauptamt (SS Economic and Administrative Head Office)

Introduction

Uroš Majstorović arrived by ship in Nazi-occupied Norway in 1942 in time for winter. He was one of more than 116,000 foreign slave labourers transported there during the Second World War, of whom more than 18,000 died.[1] He endured extreme hard labour, innumerable beatings and near-starvation under a regime he later described as 'pure terror'.[2]

Majstorović, a Serb from Croatia then aged 22, reached Ørlandet labour camp around the end of November.[3] Here he and other prisoners worked day and night in appalling conditions to build a big underground complex and coastal battery to guard the sea approaches to Trondheim. This city was to have been grandly redesigned as a home for 250,000 Germans and act as the most northerly naval base in Hitler's empire.[4] Situated about 500 km below the Arctic Circle on Norway's west coast, Majstorović's camp was one of at least 460 set up throughout the country.[5]

Exhaustion, illness, starvation and fatal beatings and shootings were common causes of death among the foreign prisoners across Norway. Slave labourers infested with lice died in typhus epidemics. Pitifully insufficient rations led to cases of cannibalism.[6] Freezing to death and amputations due to frostbite were most frequent in the Arctic north, where temperatures in winter fell to minus 30 degrees C or below.[7] In summer the Nazi occupiers took advantage of the polar 'midnight sun' and forced prisoners to work in shifts around the clock.

In Majstorović's camp, just like elsewhere in the country, prisoners wore wooden clogs and clothes that were utterly inadequate for the bitter winter weather and subzero temperatures. Majstorović said the first six months were the worst.[8] He estimated the camp held up to 500 prisoners, and a post-war investigation reported that 160 of these inmates had died.[9] Among the victims were three hanged for escape attempts.[10] 'They were hanged and we had to march by them, so that all could see what might happen to them,' recalled Majstorović.[11]

After the German defeat, the organisation that first guarded and ran the camp was condemned by a British investigation into war crimes in Norway for its 'inhuman use of slave labour'.[12] But the name of this organisation was not among those that gained global notoriety after the war as Nazi enforcers of terror under the Third Reich, such as the SS, the SA and the Gestapo. It was the Organisation Todt.

The brutal role played by this paramilitary force in the Third Reich's exploitation of millions of foreign workers has received scant attention. It has either been concealed by apologists for the Nazi (National Socialist German Workers' Party – NSDAP) slave-labour programme,[13] treated marginally in scholarly works on the Third Reich or otherwise confined to studies in German of specific camps.[14] As for works in English, no in-depth history of the Organisation Todt (OT) exists.

Yet Hitler enlisted the OT's brightest stars – the leading lights of the nation's engineers and architects – to build the empire of his dreams. Whether it was military fortifications in wartime or grand imperial cities in peacetime after the imagined final victory, the dictator turned to his loyal favourites in the organisation to design and create them. Specialising in large-scale construction tasks, the Organisation Todt was formed in 1938 and grew to command a labour force of around 1.5 million.[15] It was headed by two successive armaments ministers: the first was its founder, Fritz Todt, and the second was Albert Speer. The Organisation Todt was therefore at the heart of the Nazi system and a power ranking alongside the SS (Schutzstaffel – Protection Squadron), the Wehrmacht and the Nazi Party. Its uniform included swastika armbands, although it was not a party organisation and answered directly to Hitler. High-ranking SS and SA (Sturmabteilung – Storm Detachment) officers, including Todt himself, held key positions. OT construction experts oversaw vast building programmes throughout German-occupied Europe, being deployed from the Arctic Circle to the Balkans and deep into what the Third Reich termed its eastern *Lebensraum* (living space). In the final year of the war the OT gained control of all military construction in the Reich, and played a big part in gargantuan projects like the relocation of vital German industries underground to protect them from Allied bombing.

Hitler called the OT 'the greatest construction organisation of all time', commissioning it directly to oversee works he considered vital to the Third Reich's war effort.[16] Germany's dictator was not the only one to express such praise. British intelligence credited the OT in 1945 with having carried out in little over five years 'the most impressive building programme since Roman times'.[17] OT operations mainly relied in wartime on Germany's slave-labour system, which was the largest such exploitation of foreign labour since the end of the transatlantic African slave trade in the nineteenth century.[18]

In the conflicts of the nineteenth and twentieth centuries, prisoners of war (POWs) and civilians were not put to work by their captors on a large scale until the First World War but the extent of this practice in the Second World War was unprecedented. Both Germany and its Axis ally, Japan, flouted international law with their establishment of huge forced-labour systems.[19] Japan put millions of civilians to work in Korea, China and occupied areas of Southeast Asia. One million Korean men and women and at least 40,000 Chinese were deported to Japan.[20] The Japanese forced both POWs and civilians to work on tasks like transport links, similar to those the OT undertook in Europe for Hitler's regime. Of the 60,000 predominantly British, Australian and Dutch POWs who worked under abysmal conditions on the 420 km Burma–Thailand railway between November 1942 and October 1943, more than 12,000 died. About 60,000 also perished out of 300,000 Asian labourers conscripted by the Japanese for the 'death railway'.[21]

Under the German slave-labour programme in Europe, millions of civilians, POWs, Jews, *Ostarbeiter* (eastern workers) and other workers from Nazi-occupied territories lost their lives.[22] While no exact figures exist for deaths of foreign workers, an estimated 2.7 million died in the Greater Reich alone out of more than 13.5 million.[23] Yet this was only part of the story, since these calculations excluded millions of slave labourers in German-occupied territories like the former Soviet Union. Hundreds of thousands were deported to third countries, where they worked above all for the OT.[24]

Nazi dependence on foreign workers

Hitler's Third Reich became so reliant on its foreign workforce that by autumn 1941, after the Wehrmacht's invasion of the Soviet Union, there was no turning back. Many millions of foreigners were harnessed into what became an increasingly violent and lethal system. The vast scale of the Nazi programme contrasted with Germany's more limited use of forced labour in the First World War.[25] Foreign workers probably never made up more than 10 per cent of all employees in Germany during the 1914–18 conflict. In the next global conflagration, though, more than a quarter of all workers in the Reich consisted of foreigners by mid-1944.[26] Up to half the workforce in the country's munitions factories were foreign nationals, and they constituted about one-third of all employees in the metal, chemical, construction and mining industries. Nearly half of all employees in agriculture were foreigners.[27]

This foreign labour force fell into three main categories: civilians, POWs and concentration-camp inmates. The biggest group was civilians, numbering about 8.4 million in the Greater Reich from 1939 to 1945. The next largest was prisoners of war, totalling 4.6 million, followed by 1.7 million concentration-camp inmates and *Arbeitsjuden* (working Jews).[28] The sum of these three figures, purged of 'double counting', amounted to more than 13.5 million foreign labourers.[29]

Soviet prisoners of war and concentration-camp prisoners suffered most deaths among foreign slave labourers in the Greater Reich, while death rates among civilians were significantly lower. Estimating death tolls among the three main groups of foreign workers is fraught with difficulties, not least because civilians who were too sick to work were transported back home. West European prisoners of war, such as French and Belgians, ranked relatively highly under the Nazi racist code and were also sent home if unfit to work. Nevertheless, the number of prisoners of war estimated to have died is around 1.1 million, the number of civilians 0.5 million and the number of concentration-camp inmates and *Arbeitsjuden* 1.1 million.[30]

While these figures starkly underline the extent of the Nazi slave-labour system and its murderous nature, they do not convey the breadth of conditions experienced by the foreign workers. At one extreme, a non-Jewish, non-Slavic civilian engineer, working in Germany or elsewhere in West Europe up to around 1942, could benefit from reasonable wages and conditions; at the other, a Jewish ghetto inmate would suffer unrelenting brutality and the torment of hard labour before being murdered in an extermination camp. The complexity and scale of the Nazi slave-labour system meant there were no neat chronological divisions. Although 1942 marked something of a turning point, after which conditions for foreign workers became increasingly harsh, Polish workers were deported to Germany and generally suffered brutal treatment virtually from the start of the war. Poles were vilified under Nazi racist ideology, but the practical application of this ideology was not always uniform. As a rule, the fate of slave labourers depended on their ethnic origin, meaning that Jews and Soviet prisoners of war suffered the harshest of conditions, being ranked lowest on the Nazi racial scale. Others closer to the 'Aryan' ideal, such as West Europeans, could expect more favourable treatment. All the same, there were exceptions. Nazi racist goals were not always ruthlessly pursued in practice as war progressed, displaying what has been termed an 'erosion of the ideological'.[31] Evidence of significantly lower death rates among prisoners on the bottom rung of Nazi racial categories, compared to groups in 'higher' classifications in some satellite camps, has forced an adjustment to established thinking.

Among many other issues related to Nazi slave labour, this book examines how camps were managed and who controlled them. Levels and categories of violence suffered by camp inmates are also investigated. Further analysis concerns types of labour that prisoners were compelled to perform and treatment of women in the camps.[32]

The role of the Organisation Todt

So how did the Organisation Todt fit into the Nazi system? One way of starting to answer this question is to examine the verdict handed down by the Nuremberg Tribunal on the OT's most prominent war criminal, Albert Speer. Having taken over on Fritz Todt's death in 1942, Speer had been armaments minister and OT chief until Germany's defeat, and was therefore tried at Nuremberg with other major Nazi figures. He was sentenced to twenty years for war crimes and crimes against humanity relating to slave labour. The tribunal referred to Speer's role as head of the OT in its judgment, and one of the counts in the indictment listed the OT as an organisation for which civilians in Nazi-occupied territories were compelled to work.[33] Speer defended himself before the tribunal by saying he saw his job as a 'technical task'.[34] This was an assessment the tribunal rejected with its guilty verdict.

Although the Nuremberg Tribunal referred explicitly to 'slave labor' as a Nazi war crime in its indictment and throughout its proceedings, controversy has surrounded the use of this term by historians after the war. Opponents of the 'slave' label view it as euphemistic, arguing that the fate of concentration-camp prisoners, in particular, was worse than slavery. On the other hand, leading historians have advanced convincing arguments in favour of employing the word 'slave'. The term is valid for most foreign workers or German Jews overseen by the OT. Even opponents of the term 'slave' agree it applied to millions of civilian labourers in the German-occupied eastern territories, large numbers of whom toiled under the OT. Survivors of labour and concentration camps, including those who worked under the OT, have described themselves as having been 'slaves'. There were many shades of grey between slave labourers and voluntary, paid foreign workers within the Nazi system, as already indicated. The term 'forced labourers' is used in this book to describe non-Slavic, non-Jewish foreign labourers who were compelled to work but paid a meaningful wage.[35]

The OT was one of four major German entities exploiting forced and slave labour during the Third Reich; the three others were the SS, the Wehrmacht and industry. Of the four, the OT was most successful at cooperating simultaneously with all the others. This was largely because the mutual benefits for the OT and its partners in using slave labour were closely matched. Although this collaboration with partners was the hallmark of OT practice in running slave-labour projects, the organisation also ran work camps by itself with its own guards across occupied Europe.

The OT grew out of Fritz Todt's pre-war development of Germany's motorway network and the Westwall defence line. As it expanded, the organisation shifted from an early practice of seeking voluntary paid workers to one of coercion and increasing dependence on prisoners of war and concentration-camp inmates. Its tasks spanned a very wide range, covering the Atlantic Wall coastal defence line stretching from Norway to the Franco–Spanish frontier, road and rail links in occupied territories, armaments production including V1 and V2 rockets, large-scale energy and mining projects to exploit captured sources of raw materials, and a huge operation to move key German armaments factories and industrial plants underground to protect them from Allied bombing. This last task included subterranean factories which Hitler commissioned the OT to build; they were to produce Messerschmitt Me-262 planes, which at the time were the world's first operational jet fighters.

The OT's job of building underground fighter-plane factories, roads and railways required enormous resources. It involved tackling such rugged terrain as the mountains and fjords of Norway and the vast expanses of the Soviet Union. Freight transport across Norway was essential to the Third Reich as a secure land route for Swedish iron ore, which represented more than 80 per cent of German imports of this vital commodity in 1940.[36] In the Soviet Union, the Caucasus oilfields were a principal objective after Hitler's 1941 invasion, and the OT oversaw Jewish and other slave labourers involved in the huge task of building transport links. The OT also took a leading role in an energy project at the SS-run Vaivara concentration camp in the Baltics. The shale-oil project in Estonia, one of the world's richest sources of such fuel, was especially valued by Hitler as he fretted about Germany's vulnerability to Allied air strikes on Romanian oilfields and the failure to win the Caucasus fields in the course of the war. The OT was one of the main employers at the shale-oil plant, together with Baltische Öl GmbH (Baltöl), a subsidiary of Kontinentale Öl AG. Both of these concerns came within the sphere of Carl Krauch, Germany's chemical industry supremo and chief executive of the mammoth chemical combine IG Farben.[37] The OT and Baltöl used Soviet prisoners of war and Jewish and other slave labourers for tasks such as the production of oil from shale, building a railway, construction work, forestry and assembly of cement-clad naval mines.[38]

Prisoners laboured under various overseers, including the SS, the Wehrmacht and the OT, and spoke of high death rates and harsh conditions.[39] The OT was also deeply involved in the Third Reich's exploitation of raw materials in the Balkans, particularly the Bor copper mine in Yugoslavia.[40] In the core of the Reich itself, meanwhile, the OT took over all military construction and a host of major underground and other building projects in the final year of the war as German forces were driven back by the Allies.

Under the Third Reich, conditions and death rates tended to worsen in the labour camps as the war progressed, although there were exceptions. The trend towards a bleaker outlook for prisoners accelerated after Hitler's invasion of Russia in mid-1941 and the OT joined the SS, the Wehrmacht and industry in exploiting Soviet POWs and civilians as slave labourers. In the core of the Reich, Nazi slave-labour policy see-sawed on the use of Jews, up to 6 million of whom died in the Holocaust. German Jewish men and women compelled to work in the Reich reached a peak of 51,000–53,000 in the summer of 1941, but they were subsequently deported to ghettos and extermination camps. After the last expulsions in spring 1943 the Reich was declared 'Jew-free', although Nazi policy on the issue was later reversed.[41] In 1944 Jewish labour was again used in the Reich for projects like the construction of the 'bomb-proof' underground factories for the Messerschmitt jet fighter planes. At Kaufering and the 'Mühldorf ring', two sets of Dachau satellite camps whose prisoners were forced to undertake this task under the SS and OT, around half of more than 38,000 inmates perished.[42]

Foreign workers deported to Norway were predominantly Soviet POWs, but included Serbs like Majstorović, whose fate is outlined at the start of this chapter. Out of more than 116,000 Soviet labourers, Yugoslav prisoners and Poles sent there, at least 18,400 died.[43] The British investigation into war crimes in Norway singled out one notorious Arctic complex of up to thirty camps, known as Strafgefangenenlager Nord (SGL Nord), where treatment of prisoners was especially brutal and death rates were high. Strikingly, the camp inmates were mostly German criminals, although there were some foreigners.[44] SGL Nord was run by the German Justice Ministry, while the OT supervised all work done by the prisoners. West German prosecutors launched a post-war investigation into the camp complex regarding maltreatment of Czechoslovak former inmates, but no trial resulted.[45]

Camp survivors in general tell of acts of murderous brutality by OT guards and of hunger, sickness and torment. Because OT overseers drove slave labourers ever harder at the work sites and often provided pitifully inadequate rations and shelter, they bear a heavy responsibility for the high prisoner death toll. Most deaths in labour camps, other than those caused by physical violence, typically resulted from abuses for which the OT was responsible.[46] It was the OT which generally set the exhausting pace of work and provided inadequate rations, medical care, shelter and work clothes, thus causing deaths through extreme hard labour, malnutrition, sickness and exposure. These were the biggest killers in the slave-labour and concentration camps, with the important exclusion of the gas chambers in death camps such as Auschwitz-Birkenau and Majdanek.[47]

The Organisation Todt below the radar?

In view of the importance Hitler attached to the Organisation Todt and its prominent part in supervising slave labour, how has it largely escaped the otherwise scrupulously intent gaze of historians of Nazism? One explanation is that, apart from the regime's political and military leaders, the SS attracted much of the attention of post-war prosecutors investigating mass murder and genocide before the major trials at Nuremberg and elsewhere. While OT guards had routinely practised lethal violence against prisoners too, trials were rare.

Another explanation for the OT's low historical profile is the length of time slave labour took to become a focus of debate. Interest within Germany on slave labour using the country's concentration-camp prisoners was barely aroused until the 1980s. Since then, much has been published on the satellite camps that mushroomed from 1942 to place labourers closer to worksites, such as factories producing armaments.[48] Parent concentration camps were often too far away. The OT's role, though, has been marginalised in this literature. Its real level of involvement was further shrouded by tortuous negotiations over the issue of compensation for the victims, which continued for decades after the war because the negotiations specifically excluded any payout to millions of POWs, one of the biggest sources of OT slave labour.[49] But whether overseen by the OT, army engineers or the SS, prisoners of war were routinely subjected to barbarous treatment. Red Army soldiers seized after Hitler's invasion of the Soviet Union suffered horribly even before the Führer's decision in October 1941 to use them as workers in the Reich. Two million Soviet prisoners of war had died in captivity by February 1942, out of 3.35 million. Their treatment reflected Nazi racist ideology vilifying Slavs as subhuman (*Untermenschen*). A further 1.3 million had died by the end of the conflict, many of them having been worked to death.[50]

The OT has also evaded attention because historians have tended to focus on slave labour within the Reich, where statistics are more precise and German interest most intense, rather than in the Nazi-occupied territories across Europe. Yet these areas of foreign conquest were precisely where the OT mostly operated. In the former Soviet Union, for instance, the OT's labour force numbered around 400,000 after a major expansion at the start of summer 1942. For short periods it reached 800,000, more than the combined total of inmates in all Germany's concentration camps registered in mid-January 1945.[51] The OT partially withdrew into Germany's core only during the last year of the war, when its workforce in the Reich grew by September 1944 to more than 835,000.[52]

The OT possessed one further quality which was perhaps its most effective camouflage: it defied easy classification. No official decree was ever issued announcing the OT's founding. Instead, the German public first heard the name Organisation Todt from Hitler's lips when he addressed a Nazi Party rally in Nuremberg in 1938.[53] The OT had existed for almost five years before its functions were set out in 1943 in German law.

'Ordinary Men' of the Organisation Todt

For all the reasons listed, public awareness of the part played by the Organisation Todt under the Third Reich has remained minimal decades after the Second World War. The aim of this book is thus to set out the evidence reflecting the OT's true role in the Nazi slave-labour programme. This entails a fundamental reappraisal of the organisation to present a more balanced and complete picture of how it operated and flourished within the Third Reich. Five main themes are explored: firstly, the theme of empire and how the OT participated in Hitler's imperial plans; secondly, the OT's involvement in the plunder of Europe and the organisation's important role in Germany's war economy; thirdly, the OT's cooperation and rivalry with its slave-labour partners, the SS, the Wehrmacht and industry; fourthly, OT violence in the camps; and fifthly, OT perpetrators and how they fitted into the wider group of Nazi war criminals.

The first theme of empire and Hitler's vision of how the OT should help bring some of his imperial notions to life has so far been insufficiently explored. Huge OT operations were conducted across Nazi-occupied Europe to construct defence lines and transport links designed to buttress Hitler's domination of the continent. The dictator's fantasies regarding imperial cities rested on his engineers and personal architects like Todt and Speer, as well as on OT construction teams in places like Trondheim, in the area where Majstorović worked. The OT's leading figures were therefore among those helping to fashion and realise Hitler's dreams. Was it Hitler's own ambitions to be an architect, expressed in *Mein Kampf*, which made the OT elite his natural choice to create and design infrastructure and cities for his empire?[54]

The second theme, regarding OT participation in securing the spoils of Europe for the Third Reich to drive the country's war economy, has also attracted limited attention from historians. The organisation was, however, a key player in extracting raw materials and exploiting foreign labourers across the continent, to help secure occupied Europe and ensure sufficient resources for the manufacture and operation of Germany's weapons, tanks, ships and warplanes.[55]

Exploration of the third theme of OT cooperation and competition with its slave-labour partners necessitates a major reassessment to reflect the OT's true place in Germany's power structure. The OT was a vital partner in overseeing the Nazi slave-labour programme alongside the SS, the Wehrmacht and industry. Insufficient emphasis has previously been placed by researchers on Speer's role as leader of the OT, which was spelled out in numerous decrees issued by Hitler. The dictator repeatedly chose the OT to carry out projects of the highest priority.[56] Speer himself implemented policy decisions in his capacity as OT chief, a position which also afforded him exceptionally detailed knowledge of how so many were worked to death under the slave-labour programme.[57] Since Speer and the OT worked so closely with the SS, the relationship between the two organisations deserves sharper focus. Comparison between the activities of the OT and the construction arm of the SS Economic and Administrative Head Office (Wirtschafts-Verwaltungshauptamt – WVHA) is especially valuable.[58] Were members of the OT influenced by the culture of violence practised by the SS? Was belief in Nazi ideology as important to OT personnel as it was to the SS?

The fourth theme of OT violence in camps, where the organisation collaborated with the SS, the Wehrmacht and industry, reveals the plight of slave labourers under the Third Reich's yoke. This book's investigation into OT violence gives the organisation's foreign workers a voice, drawing on an extensive collection of often harrowing accounts by former camp inmates. The labour-camp survivors describe how it was not just SS and Wehrmacht guards who routinely practised lethal physical violence; OT staff also shot or beat slave labourers to death. Apart from these killings, though, many prisoners lost their lives through extreme hard labour, lack of food or inadequate shelter and healthcare, which were precisely the areas where the OT bore responsibility. It was the OT which generally drove slave labourers to toil harder at work sites and failed to provide basic needs for prisoners on projects it supervised, causing high death rates. The apparent breakdown of frontiers between various types of violence in the brutal and chaotic environment of the camps is also scrutinised to evaluate how useful are the terms traditionally employed to define categories of violence.

The fifth theme of OT perpetrators and Nazi war criminals in general explores the important question of what motivated OT personnel. What were the circumstances under which some OT overseers of slave labourers carried out war crimes? Speer's case has come under intense scrutiny, but comparatively little research has been carried out into other perpetrators in the OT. This book investigates how staff operated across occupied Europe, and how much leeway they possessed to act independently. SS officers, as well as leaders of Hitler's regime and the German armed forces, have been extensively analysed by historians,[59] who have frequently sought to discern the motives of perpetrators they saw as 'ordinary' men.[60] OT staff, however, perhaps deserved this label more than any other group of Nazi war criminals. These were not soldiers or policemen, let alone units of the SS or SD (Sicherheitsdienst – SS security service) execution squads formed to commit mass murder. They were builders and engineers, whose ranks included a significant number of SS and SA officers, but whose organisation was created not to kill an enemy or implement Nazi racist policy resulting in genocide, but to perform the everyday work of construction. How did it come about, then, that OT engineers, architects and building-site foremen became Hitler's slave drivers? Why did they kill prisoners by shootings, beatings and murderous hard labour and neglect, when their job was to construct buildings, bridges and bunkers?

Sources

The main sources for historical analysis are OT records and correspondence. While Wehrmacht and Waffen-SS documents were more methodically destroyed, the OT's own records at the German Federal archive in Berlin do still suffer from considerable gaps. Many OT records that have survived can be found in institutions in formerly German-occupied countries, such as Norway's National Archives in Oslo, which have yielded significant material for this study. Some holes in OT records can be bridged by referring to alternatives, such as Allied documents, post-war criminal investigations, German industry files and the accounts of former slave labourers. The German Federal archives in Berlin, its military section in Freiburg and the records in Ludwigsburg of German legal investigations into suspects from the Nazi era have all proved rich sources for this research. The Institut für Zeitgeschichte (IfZ) in Munich is also an invaluable resource that has provided much material for this book, including details from Nazi Party files and post-war statements to Allied interrogators by Speer and other senior OT personnel.

Other important sources of original documents include the National Archives in London. A very detailed British intelligence report on the OT specifically excludes slave labour provided by Soviet prisoners of war, but is otherwise wide-ranging.[61] Blinkered by the conflicting political interests of the Western Allies and Stalin,[62] it provides an important contemporary insight into the workings of the OT. The intelligence file, dated March 1945 and entitled 'Handbook of the Organisation Todt (OT)', comprises nearly 500 pages.

Several of the OT's slave-labour projects led to a limited number of post-war trials, some of which were held within a few years of the end of the war and provided detailed information on individual defendants. Apart from the trial of Speer, others included the 'Mühldorf ring' case. This involved an architect favoured by Hitler and an intense rival of Speer's, OT regional chief Hermann Giesler, who was initially sentenced to life imprisonment before his term was reduced. Another trial concerned crimes in Norway, including at the Ørlandet camp holding prisoners such as Majstorović.[63] The wider subject of post-war trials is analysed later in this book, with particular reference to the relatively few proceedings involving OT personnel.

For the perspective of slave labourers, the International Tracing Service (ITS) has provided important material on the fate of individuals during the war and its aftermath, including details on Kaufering and OT activities in Nazi-occupied territories.[64] Accounts by former slave labourers are also held in archives such as Zwangsarbeit 1939–1945: Erinnerungen und Geschichte.[65] This is an online database of nearly 600 former forced or slave labourers from twenty-six countries, who were interviewed in 2005–6 as part of a project which grew out of an initiative by Germany's government and industry to pay compensation to victims of National Socialism.[66] Apart from such archives, former slave labourers have described their own experiences in published accounts of life in the labour camps.[67]

Finally there are the books written by Speer himself, which by their nature as a version of events from a convicted war criminal must be treated with extreme caution.[68] His comments in his memoirs reveal the bitterness of his conflict with SA Brigadeführer Xaver Dorsch, his second-in-command in the OT. Their dispute reached a climax when Hitler ignored Speer to commission Dorsch in 1944 to build underground factories for fighter planes, for which the OT deputy chief was to exploit slave labourers, including 100,000 Hungarian Jews.[69] Evidence of crimes committed at one of the factory sites was heard during the Mühldorf case, when the court in Dachau convicted Giesler and others.[70] Dorsch never faced trial.[71]

Historians have thoroughly analysed Speer's post-war accounts, which can shed some light on the organisation he headed before his imprisonment in Spandau.[72] However, Speer wove a web of deceit in portraying himself at Nuremberg and in his memoirs as disinterested in politics and engrossed in his 'technical' work. The truth about the head of the OT was quite different: Hitler's loyal henchman was a co-enforcer of Nazi racist policy who made pacts with the SS and drove slave labourers to their deaths.[73]

The book's framework around five central ideas, as outlined, allows a thematic rather than rigidly chronological approach to examining the development of the Organisation Todt. A chapter is devoted to each theme before the concluding chapter. The OT grew to become one of Hitler's key agencies, and the dictator turned to the organisation with increasing urgency as military setbacks multiplied during the Second World War. Works he commissioned the OT to undertake culminated in projects to move vital war industries underground to protect them from Allied bombing. The OT had already shown itself to be both efficient and flexible in completing monumental feats of engineering. Like other forces of the Third Reich, though, the OT was transformed by war, and acted ever more ruthlessly to try to fulfil the Führer's commands.

1

The Organisation Todt in Hitler's empire

On the road to war, Hitler entrusted Fritz Todt and Albert Speer with two tasks at the core of his future empire: the dictator chose Todt to mastermind the construction of the Third Reich's motorway network, destined to radiate out into conquered territory, and instructed Speer to begin rebuilding Berlin as an imperial capital, to be renamed 'Germania'.[1] Hitler put Todt in charge of building the *Autobahnen* in 1933, just months after he became chancellor. He then appointed Speer to realise his vision for Germania on 30 January 1937, the fourth anniversary of his accession to power. In both instances he chose men who would go on to serve in succession as his armaments ministers and leaders of what became known as the Organisation Todt (OT). This labour force grew out of Todt's motorway-building concern, and Hitler publicly named it for the first time in 1938. This was while its engineers were building the Westwall, known as the Siegfried Line to Germany's wartime foes, just over a year before the Second World War started with the Wehrmacht's invasion of Poland.

The projects to create the motorways and Germania reflected Hitler's megalomania and craving for all things gargantuan. They also demonstrated his reliance on the workforce of engineers and construction specialists created by Todt, which began on the motorways, largely transferred to the Westwall and then absorbed the builders of Germania during the war.[2] From an improvised group of around 350,000 German workers in the run-up to the twentieth century's bloodiest conflict, the Organisation Todt metamorphosed in wartime into a 1.5-million-strong agency mostly composed of foreign slave labourers,[3] including Jews and Slavs vilified under the Nazi racist code. Germans made up less than a quarter of the force. As Hitler's imperial designs grew following initial military successes, so did the OT's geographical reach. By 1940 the OT had started motorway networks to link Klagenfurt to Trondheim and Calais to Warsaw, with a route later planned as far as Moscow. Development of the railways was to include the introduction of double-decker trains travelling at up to 200 kilometres per hour, taking 600 passengers per carriage from Munich to

Rostov-on-Don. Hitler instructed Munich rail authorities to make the necessary changes to the main station, whose hall was to have required the largest steel-frame structure in the world. As for the city of Germania, Hitler's obsession with buildings which would outdo rival colonial powers was its hallmark. A triumphal arch would dwarf its Parisian counterpart, and the main north–south and east–west roads were to have been more than 100 metres wide. A massive domed hall next to the Führer's palace would accommodate 180,000 people, while a neighbouring square was designed for events attended by a million.[4] On seeing a model of the planned city, Propaganda Minister Joseph Goebbels commented admiringly: 'Incomparably monumental. The Führer is raising a memorial to himself in stone.'[5]

The imperial capital of Germania was the biggest of five 'leader cities' (*Führerstädte*) to be redeveloped at great cost under plans reaching into peacetime after an imagined Nazi final victory. The other cities in this elite group were Nuremberg, Hamburg, Munich and Linz, earmarked for the grandest rebuilding under plans which, to a lesser extent, included almost all of Germany's major cities. The Baltic seaside spa of Prora, on the island of Rügen, was to have become the world's largest resort, with 75 kilometres of beach and facilities for 14 million German holidaymakers a year. Although German military setbacks from late 1941 onwards meant most of these long-term schemes were never realised, they covered not just the core of the Reich but the occupied territories of Europe. The Norwegian city of Trondheim was to have been turned into a settlement for more than a quarter of a million Germans, protected by a naval base which Hitler claimed would have made Singapore look like 'mere child's play'. In Eastern Europe the dictator instructed that new German urban developments should be modelled on the Fatherland's medieval towns, such as Regensburg or Heidelberg. They would have been ringed at a distance of 30–40 kilometres by model settlements built for the German rural population, with imposing public buildings and fast road links.[6]

The significance of the OT's involvement in this chilling imperial vision, under which the lives of the local East European population counted for virtually nothing, was twofold: building was Hitler's passion, and this was the area where the OT excelled. Hitler's imperial goals were central to the operations of the Organisation Todt, which was deployed almost exclusively in Nazi-occupied territory for most of the war and relied heavily on slave labour. In choosing Todt and Speer to construct the Third Reich's highways and the colossal buildings of metropolitan Berlin, even before he appointed them as successive armaments ministers, Hitler entrusted these two men with components of his imperial design that he especially prized. What he required were edifices and feats of technology designed to proclaim German power and his own to the world.

The dictator relied on Todt and Speer to fashion these symbols of imperial might, while hundreds of thousands of OT staff and foreign labourers built defence lines and transport links to defend conquered territories up to their furthest frontiers. For Hitler, the OT was an instrument of conquest and occupation. The bonds that developed between himself, Todt and Speer boosted the profile of the organisation, which became tightly woven into his dreams of empire, architecture and German technological prowess. To understand how the OT spread its network through German-occupied Europe and came to dominate all construction in the Reich in the final year of the war, the structure and aims of the organisation itself need to be investigated. Professional and academic qualifications of around 1,400 OT personnel are analysed in this chapter to assess the backgrounds of senior staff. Investigation of the remarkable expansion of the OT should start, though, with an assessment of the contribution of its two successive leaders. Hitler respected Todt, valuing his loyalty and competence; he delighted in discussing architecture with the much younger Speer, who was thirty-one when put in charge of rebuilding Berlin. Hitler's relationships with Todt and Speer are examined in turn, contrasting the two OT chiefs' individual styles of leadership and gauging their separate efforts to realise Hitler's imperial ambitions.

The Organisation Todt under Todt

Todt and his large workforce had been constructing motorways for five years before Hitler named the 'Organisation Todt' in public for the first time. The dictator's decision, proclaimed at the Nazi Party's Nuremberg rally in September 1938, represented an extraordinary honour for a man who had become one of his closest confidants.[7] It recognised Hitler's favourite civil engineer in a way normally reserved for the Führer alone. The leader of the Third Reich was the figurehead of the Hitler Jugend, but Fritz Todt became one of the few in the Nazi elite deemed worthy of having a national organisation bearing his name.[8] This accolade reflected the strength of the bond between the two men, first forged during the building of the *Autobahnen* and the Westwall.

Hitler's impatience with the army led him to choose Todt's labour force to complete the Westwall. Frustrated by the slow pace of army engineers, Hitler ordered Todt to take over building the fortifications facing France's Maginot Line in May 1938. The dictator saw the Westwall as essential to secure Germany's western flank before his grab for Czechoslovakia, but concluded that the army was not up to the job.[9] He derided army understanding of the required bunker strength and the power of modern weapons as 'shocking'. Hitler later declared that, if he had left it to the army alone, the Westwall would 'still not have been ready in ten years'. It was thanks to the Organisation Todt, he said, that the whole project had got under way and progress had been made.[10] The dictator foresaw two possible outcomes: Europe would either be under German leadership or fall victim to 'Bolshevism'. He would rather not have to build the Westwall, but the more intensely the Third Reich looked to the East, the more it needed to guard itself against the West, where France, its First World War enemy, was viewed as the threat.

Like many OT operations, the Westwall was a massive undertaking, measuring about 600 kilometres in length and up to 50 kilometres in depth.[11] Its construction required 350,000 OT workers, 90,000 of the army's fortification engineers and 100,000 from the Reich Labour Service (Reichsarbeitsdienst – RAD).[12] Todt set up his headquarters in Wiesbaden for what became a round-the-clock operation. He used his excellent contacts with industry to enlist the expertise and manpower of about 1,000 firms,[13] as well as Nazi Party resources such as the National Socialist Motor Corps (Nationalsozialistisches Kraftfahrkorps – NSKK) to provide the fleets of trucks and other transport needed. It was this kind of improvisation and ingenuity that inspired Hitler's faith in Todt and his workforce.

When Hitler came to power, Todt was forty-two and possessed impeccable political credentials for becoming part of the regime. He had joined the Nazi Party as early as January 1923, gaining the very low membership number of 2465, and the SA in 1931. Like Hitler, he had served in the armed forces in the First World War, having been forced to interrupt his engineering studies to do so. He had joined the army in 1914 and transferred to the air force in 1916. He was wounded and received the Iron Cross. After the war he returned to college and gained his engineering diploma in Karlsruhe before eventually going on to obtain the higher qualification of doctor of engineering in Munich in 1931. On acquiring his initial qualification in Karlsruhe, Todt worked in industry, gathering experience which was to prove exceptionally useful in building up contacts with firms which would later be hired by the OT to carry out its gigantic construction and engineering projects. Some of Todt's colleagues from his time with the Munich road-building firm Sager and Woerner from 1921 to 1933 held senior posts under him in the OT, including his deputy, Xaver Dorsch.[14]

It was while he was working for Sager and Woerner that Todt wrote to the NSDAP in Munich in response to an appeal in the party's publication, the

Völkischer Beobachter, and offered his services as an engineer, suggesting ways to make technical and administrative savings in building the Reich's highways.[15] The party's favourable response brought an invitation for him to join the newly formed Kampfbund deutscher Architekten und Ingenieure (KDAI – Action Group of German Architects and Engineers) as head of its section for civil engineers. In December 1932 Todt wrote a forty-nine-page report entitled 'Road-building and Road Administration', which set out for the party leadership what he viewed as a way to combat Germany's high unemployment and provide a motorway network with considerable military potential. He estimated that an army of 300,000 men could be transported during just two nights of driving on these highways from the east to the west of the Reich. Hitler was said to have been delighted when the report was presented to him, and Todt's appointment as overseer of the construction of the Reich's motorways followed soon after Hitler's appointment as chancellor.[16]

After Todt went on to oversee construction of the Westwall, he revealed a ruthless streak in his character when problems arose. Long shifts and hard labour, sometimes under fire after the war began, sparked protests among the workers and Todt, fearing delays, resorted to harsher methods to ensure the pace did not slacken.[17] He acted swiftly to crush opposition among his workers (at that time predominantly German). The measures he took to punish OT Westwall workers guilty of mostly minor offences included detention and 're-education' in Hinzert camp, led from October 1939 by a future commandant of Buchenwald concentration camp, SS-Sturmbannführer Hermann Pister. Since 1938 the OT had used police detention centres to incarcerate alleged offenders from the *Autobahnen* and Westwall workforces as a means of ensuring labourers quickly returned to work, typically after three weeks of 're-education'. When Pister started work with Todt as part of the SS security staff on Germany's western frontier, he was given OT funding to convert disused barrack camps into detention centres designed to reform any 'work-shy' OT labourers on the Westwall and the motorways. The project was fully supported by the local Gestapo (Geheime Staatspolizei – Secret State Police). Hinzert and three other SS special detention units quickly came to resemble small-scale concentration camps, despite Todt's express instruction that they should not do so. The head of the OT was nevertheless said by Pister to have been very satisfied with an increase in productivity among his labour gangs. When the OT shifted manpower into occupied France following the Wehrmacht's May 1940 western offensive, the SS at first regarded Hinzert as having lost its reason for existence. On Himmler's order, however, it continued to operate and was brought under the SS Inspectorate of Concentration Camps (Inspektion der Konzentrationslager – IKL) in July 1940. Hinzert was deemed in its initial phase to have been so successful that it became a model for experiments with police detention centres elsewhere. The Gestapo, whose acts of terror against political opponents earned them a fearsome reputation, also detained tens of thousands of German and foreign workers for non-political, labour-related offences in around 200 'work education camps' (*Arbeitserziehungslager* – AEL) around the Reich.[18]

In a report covering his time in charge of Hinzert, Pister said the camp's average total of 600–700 prisoners could be put to work on the Westwall and other sites and their SS guards could ensure 'maximum work performance', combining punishment with productive labour at the same time as relieving the load on the prison system. He bragged that initially reluctant firms had become eager to use his prisoners, whose productivity was twice or three times as high as that of other labourers.[19] The concept of re-education or reform of offenders was much favoured by Pister. He believed that his German 'boarders' (*Zöglinge*) in the Hinzert special camp could be reintegrated into society and turned into useful members of the community. He relied on traditional techniques based on military-style camp life, strict discipline and extreme hard labour.[20]

Todt was proud of his organisation's links with the SS and recommended Pister to Himmler, whose SS controlled the concentration camps, as a 'good leader of men'. Todt was himself an *SA-Obergruppenführer* and committed National Socialist, having been a Hitler loyalist from the movement's earliest days. In an exchange with Himmler in October 1941 about SS members working for the OT, he argued that about seventy such SS officers should keep the field-grey uniforms worn by the Waffen-SS, 'for I have always considered it right that it should be indicated by means of the uniform, also, that the OT's leadership developed strongly from party structures'.[21] The OT became a paramilitary organisation in wartime, forming its own armed Schutzkommando guard unit, but was never a Nazi Party offshoot like the SS or SA and came instead directly under Hitler. However, many engineers and architects in the higher echelons of the organisation were members of the SS or the SA. As a decorated First World War air force veteran, military duty was also a quality Todt wished to promote in the OT. In a message to OT personnel after Germany's assault on Poland at the start of the Second World War he congratulated his team on building the Westwall.

> With the outbreak of war, we have handed over our work with proud confidence to the German soldier. We are convinced that the Westwall, manned by German soldiers, will fulfil its task. The Führer has ordered that the Organisation Todt should remain in existence as a fortifications organisation and continue working

... In a state of war, every individual, whether worker, employer or construction engineer, even if he does not wear a uniform, is no longer a civilian in his outlook, but a soldier.[22]

In such exhortations to militarism, alongside his enthusiastic support for the inclusion of the SS in OT ranks, Todt seemed to suggest that the 'worker soldiers' of the Organisation Todt should march in step not only with the army but also with Nazi Party paramilitaries, like the 'political soldiers' of the SS.[23]

Todt's 'Engineers of the Future'

As the most powerful engineer in the Third Reich after Hitler became chancellor in 1933, Todt worked from the outset to promote his vision for technology's place in National Socialist society.[24] Although Nazi technology in fact culminated in a desperate search for 'wonder weapons' to reverse military failures, as well as the mechanised horror of Auschwitz, Todt believed in an idealised symbiosis between man, machine and nature. He personified the 'reactionary modernist' element of Nazi ideology,[25] although pressures of war forced him to compromise and focus on more urgent priorities, such as armaments production. He saw the creation of an *Autobahnen* network as an 'artistic task' and believed: 'Real engineers and real artists are related in nature. A class of creatively gifted people.'[26]

Todt used two institutions in particular to educate and politicise members of his profession: the main Nazi engineering association, the NSBDT (Nationalsozialistischer Bund deutscher Technik – National Socialist League of German Technology), which he led from 1934, and the Plassenburg political school for engineers. 'Technopolitical' training courses for German engineers began at Plassenburg in June 1937, and the 'Reich Castle of Technology' in Lower Bavaria became the symbol of the new Nazi technology. It was set up on the pattern of other Nazi 'order castles' (*Ordensburgen*), and Todt saw the role of the Plassenburg as creating the National Socialist engineer corps of the future. He regarded its 'educational task' as 'the cultivation, promotion and heightening of the National Socialist attitude'.[27] Todt saw himself as loyal to both party and profession, and in 1937 membership of the highly efficient NSBDT stood at 37 per cent of Germany's 220,000 engineers. Of the 81,000 NSBDT members in 1937, 27 per cent were NSDAP members, a figure Todt judged 'serviceably good'.[28] In the same year, Todt's first four-day technopolitical course was held for engineers in Plassenburg Castle. Reflecting the militaristic values of Nazism, participants marched from the train station to the castle, the old Franconian seat of the Hohenzollerns, performed morning gymnastics, slept in barrack-style quarters and wore uniforms. The main themes laid down by Todt for the ideological indoctrination of course members were technical knowledge, political attitude, personal values for leadership and physical training. Even after the outbreak of war forced Todt to shift resources swiftly to armaments production, he insisted at Plassenburg that the engineer's role belonged on a lofty plane in the field of human endeavour. The fusion of wartime necessities and Todt's interpretation of a link between technology and culture was reflected in an address to architects at Plassenburg Castle in August 1940. On the one hand, Germany's *Autobahnen* needed to be extended to enable Panzer divisions to deploy swiftly in a Reich which had already tripled in size. On the other, Todt waxed lyrical about Germany's motorway construction representing an activity on an elevated plane, in the same way as the ancient Greeks still held the Olympic Games and fostered science and art in wartime 'because they did not want to do without this higher measure of human activity'.[29]

Such a combination of ideas may have prompted Hitler to praise Todt in September 1936, during his motorway-building programme, as his 'most faithful idealist and at the same time most level-headed realist'.[30] Todt was a character full of contradictions, and his achievements did not all flow from single-minded ambition. Although he was a man whose praise of Hitler could at times be sycophantic, he was also renowned as one who would not shrink from telling the dictator unpalatable truths.[31] So he would display one side of his nature when he lauded what he saw as the Führer's exceptional talents.

> The great monuments of our time can only be built as long as Adolf Hitler, the Führer of our people and architectural genius, remains among us. It often takes a thousand years before another great man comes, and the ensuing thousand years live off that which was achieved in the time of such a man.[32]

But the same loyal servant of Hitler repeatedly confronted the dictator to argue that a military victory in Germany's war against the Soviet Union, commenced in mid-1941, was unattainable and a political solution should be sought. Speer described Todt as being very dispirited after a trip to the Eastern battlefront, saying the armaments minister 'didn't think we could possibly win the war there'. Speer tried to reassure him about the strength of the German soldier, but Todt replied: 'You are young. You still have illusions.'[33] On 29 November 1941, Todt delivered his most emphatic statement to Hitler on the hopelessness of the war in the East at the Reich Chancellery, declaring in the presence of Field-Marshal Walther von Brauchitsch: 'This war can no longer be won by military means.' When the dictator asked him what was the alternative, Todt replied that the conflict should be ended politically. The industrialist Walter Rohland, a board member of the giant Vereinigte Stahlwerke whom Todt had enlisted in his campaign to increase armaments production, also believed the war was impossible to win and said Todt repeatedly had discussions with Hitler on the issue in January 1942.[34] Historians have speculated that Todt may have paid for his straight talking with his life when he died in a plane crash on 8 February 1942 following a discussion with Hitler on the evening of 7 February at the dictator's headquarters at Rastenburg.[35] These talks went on late into the night, but no detailed record of the discussion was made. Speer, who had arrived in Rastenburg from Ukraine, then met with Hitler after Todt retired to bed. Speer's discussions with Hitler on his plans for rebuilding Berlin continued into the early hours, so he decided to alter his travel arrangements for 8 February. He had originally accepted Todt's offer of a seat on the plane returning to Berlin, but left word that he had changed his mind. Hence instead of being on the doomed aircraft, Speer was woken by a phone call shortly after 8.00 am telling him about the crash: the converted Heinkel 111 had plunged to earth and burst into flames, and there were no survivors. Rohland believed Todt was the target of an SS assassination, although the evidence does not support his accusation. The mystery of the crash of the twin-engined plane will therefore probably remain unsolved.[36]

Hitler respected Todt for his realism and ability to get things done. His loyal engineer refused to stoop to the constant political intrigues and lavish excess typical among Hitler's entourage: Todt had a modest house in the Berchtesgaden area, on the Obersalzberg in the Bavarian Alps, where Hitler and members of the Third Reich's elite had residences. The dictator therefore treated him differently to less-favoured members of the regime's inner circle, always ready to receive him or talk by telephone instead of communicating by formal letter. Until Todt's death he was among Hitler's closest confidants, together with Hermann Göring, the dictator's official deputy, and General Wilhelm Keitel, the Führer's unquestioningly loyal head of the German High Command.[37] Todt's high standing was reflected in the titles and responsibilities awarded to him: he became armaments minister in March 1940,[38] and after he was appointed general inspector for water and energy the following year only the vain and ambitious Göring had amassed more state and party posts.[39] It was Göring, though, who had added to Todt's powers in 1938 with an appointment that was to have crucial implications for the OT's use of slave labour; then Hitler's official deputy, Göring installed Todt as general plenipotentiary for the regulation of the construction industry, which in wartime extended its control into German-occupied territories and authorised regional OT leaders to use forced or slave labour. This developed into the mass exploitation of prisoners of war, Jews and civilians performing extreme hard labour under lethally harsh conditions.[40] Todt was determined the OT should exploit foreign labour, declaring that every German OT 'frontline worker' (*Frontarbeiter*) 'must become foreman for 50 foreign workers'.[41]

In the Reich, around 3,300 kilometres of *Autobahnen* had been built by the start of the war, and Todt was for a time prepared to concentrate foreign workers on this task, while the Wehrmacht still appeared invincible. In 1940 he demanded and received the first 10,000 prisoners of war to work on further extension of the road network. Jews were also put to work in large numbers. However, after the invasion of Russia Todt ordered a stop to the motorway programme in the winter of 1941, and the prisoners of war were switched to work on armaments production. Speer applauded these decisions by Todt when he took over in 1942.[42]

Increasing armaments production had become a central focus of Germany's war effort after Todt's appointment as head of the new Armaments Ministry. Reflecting the strong support he received from German industry, Krupp's chief weapons designer, Erich Müller, had lobbied Hitler in favour of Todt's appointment.[43] Todt actively sought an alliance with big business to improve armaments production and formed committees overseeing various sectors, with Müller in charge of one for guns and artillery. Munitions production figures surged, and Hitler gave Todt sole credit for Germany's success in boosting armaments in his victory speech in the summer of 1940 following the invasion and defeat of France.[44] It was Todt who paved the way for an eventual 'armaments miracle', falsely claimed by Speer as all his own achievement. After German armaments production doubled in the first half of 1940, Todt argued the following year, against the background of setbacks in the Russia campaign, that the 'Blitzkrieg economy' should be abandoned and preparation be made instead for a long war. Although Todt's attempts to persuade Hitler of the futility of war with the Soviet Union ultimately failed, he was successful in winning the dictator over on armaments production. By the end of January 1942, just over a week before his death, his recommendations were before Hitler; these would lead to the Armaments Ministry being given central control over military production. Powers that Speer claimed he had won from Hitler early in his appointment had in fact already been bestowed by the dictator on Todt.[45] The OT, meanwhile, underwent dramatic change when Speer took charge in February 1942.

The Organisation Todt under Speer

Snow was falling as Speer, wearing his OT uniform, addressed staff in the courtyard of the Armaments Ministry less than a week after Todt's death and pledged to continue their deceased leader's work, asking for their trust and cooperation.[46] As an architect rather than a civil engineer, and a man with no military background, he must have been aware he needed to win over sceptics who valued the qualities that Todt had possessed and which were missing in him. Speer later recalled that he was at first staggered by the weight of responsibilities being placed upon him, viewing Hitler's choice of him as Todt's successor in all his posts as reckless because of his lack of expertise.[47] A 1945 British intelligence report said there was a 'decided temptation' to describe Todt in more favourable terms than Speer. Todt 'had the true technician's ability of adapting the method of execution to the nature of the operation', although Speer was 'obviously ... a skilled politician'.[48]

Speer came, like Todt, from a wealthy middle-class family in the southwestern region of Baden, having been born in Mannheim in 1905. He studied architecture in Munich and Berlin, where Heinrich Tessenow, a distinguished architect who made his reputation during the Weimar Republic, appointed Speer his assistant at the age of twenty-three. Speer joined the Nazi Party and the SA in 1931, then the SS in the following year.[49] Speer wrote in a post-war memoir that he certainly appreciated qualities he saw in his predecessor, and believed Hitler's feelings towards Todt reflected 'respect, bordering on reverence'. His own view of Todt was that he was 'irreplaceable' and 'one of the very few modest, unassertive personalities in the government, a man you could rely on, and who steered clear of all the intrigues'.[50] This retrospective praise contrasts with what Speer said of Todt during the war. Speer tried to shift the blame on to Todt when it became clear in the final months of the war that his own extravagant claims about German 'miracle weapons' and higher armaments production were false. In a report in January 1945, he said the mistake had been that Germany was not fully armed by 1941 at the latest, the year before he took office, when Todt was still armaments minister.[51]

Speer owed much to Todt's groundwork, but some of his predecessor's legacy proved dangerous. An 'old guard' led by Todt's deputy, the experienced engineer Xaver Dorsch, turned out to be a constant thorn in Speer's side. They were markedly unwilling to pledge their support, and eventually turned dramatically against him. Dorsch was five years older than Speer and had joined the Nazi Party in February 1929.[52] Todt met Dorsch while working for Sager and Woerner, which later won contracts for OT projects in the Reich and in occupied Europe.[53] After Todt became armaments minister in March 1940 and OT work on the Westwall wound down, he put Dorsch in charge of OT headquarters in Berlin.[54] Speer retained Dorsch, but his OT deputy was a central figure in a political crisis in 1944 during which Speer threatened to resign.[55] Speer prevailed, but the clash reflected fault-lines running between the successive leaderships of Todt and Speer. It was also a prime example of how Speer's rivals could use the OT to come close to bringing about his downfall. Nevertheless, some key members of Todt's team went on to be promoted under Speer. Examples included Karl Otto Saur, Todt's deputy in the Nazi-controlled Office (later Central Office) for Technology, and Willi Henne, a high-ranking SS officer who had played a leading role under Todt in the building of the Westwall. Saur, pugnacious and ambitious, went on to replace Speer in Hitler's favour, and the dictator's last 'will and testament', written before his suicide, named Saur as armaments minister.[56]

Seeking to show his commitment to the organisation which Todt created, Speer made a highly significant gesture as soon as he was appointed its new leader: he announced the incorporation into the OT of his team originally assigned to rebuild Berlin, known as 'Construction Staff Speer'.[57] This team made up a sizeable proportion of the OT workers; with the inclusion of Speer's transport and other units, these numbered 98,000 by the start of October 1941.[58] Speer's move underlined what was to be his guiding policy principle as the new minister and leader of the OT: the concentration of all available resources on the war effort. Within a month of his appointment he told a meeting of *Gauleiter*, the Nazi Party's powerful regional chiefs, that all activities not essential to the war effort were being postponed. 'Increasing efficiency in the factories is chiefly a technical and economic matter. It is therefore ... only the task of the Party and its organisations to be active in this area if I think it necessary.'[59]

Speer's readiness to confront party stalwarts created enemies, but the man Hitler praised as having 'tremendous organisational talent' managed in the first weeks of office to restructure not only the OT but his Armaments Ministry as well.[60] Speer reorganised the OT into seven task groups responsible for areas across Nazi-occupied Europe and called them *Einsatzgruppen*, the same name given to the squads who committed mass murder in shootings in Eastern Europe.[61] In an important early victory over a rival which bolstered OT operations and increased the responsibilities of his men in occupied East Europe, Speer managed to outmanoeuvre Alfred Rosenberg, minister for the East. He did this by securing control for the OT of all technical operations in the occupied Eastern territories, wresting it away from Rosenberg.[62] As a result, the highly qualified engineers heading the various OT regions in Nazi-occupied Europe received wider powers, which were boosted even further in the final year of the war on the OT's partial return to the Greater Reich.

Speer also restructured his ministry's administration to direct armaments production under a scheme Todt had initiated. It broadly involved dividing armaments into the various weapons systems and creating committees to be in charge of each section, with 'rings' attached. The committees came under Saur as head of the Technical Office. Walther Schieber, a high-ranking official in the Armaments Ministry, was in charge of the 'rings', headed by executives of Germany's major industrial concerns. Under the system, the Armaments Ministry would set targets, leaving industry to ensure these were met. Speer called the new organisational principle 'self-responsibility of industry', a notion echoing Todt's idea of allowing private industry to take decisions independently within set parameters. Speer, as head of Central Planning, managed the supply of raw materials, and his aim was to control the entire war economy. In September 1943 he took a giant step towards that goal when Hitler issued his Decree for the Concentration of the Wartime Economy, which broadened Speer's authority. Speer's Ministry for Armaments and Ammunition was renamed to reflect his new responsibilities, becoming the Ministry for Armaments and War Production.[63]

Speer was a linchpin of the Nazi war effort, although he tried to reinvent his past after the war by emphasising his work as Hitler's architect and telling Allied interrogators and the Nuremberg Tribunal that his role was merely 'technical'. The tribunal sentenced Speer to twenty years for his exploitation of slave labourers but spared him his life, rejecting a Soviet demand that he should hang.[64] Researchers have since gathered significant evidence not made available to the tribunal at the time,[65] including Speer's eviction from their Berlin homes of thousands of Jews who were subsequently murdered by late 1942, as well as his involvement in an extension of Auschwitz death camp which became known in the SS as 'Professor Speer's special programme'.[66]

Evidence directly relevant to the OT, which has recently been brought to light against Speer, is also damning. Shortly before Speer's 'Germania' force was formally integrated into the OT, he established a group of 30,000 engineers and construction specialists who were switched to the occupied East, cooperating with the OT on tasks exploiting mostly Jews forced to work in murderous conditions. The Speer Construction Staff East (Baustab Speer-Ostbau), formed with Hitler's agreement in January 1942, was deployed in Ukraine and the southern sector of the Eastern front. Speer's force worked with the OT and the

SS on projects such as a strategic highway through Ukraine known as DG IV (Durchgangsstraße IV, or Transit Road IV).⁶⁷ Another example which makes a mockery of Speer's post-war denials of responsibility involves his request to Himmler for concentration-camp inmates to perform hard labour for the OT on the Atlantic Wall, since not enough labourers were available in France and elsewhere in the occupied West. In February 1944, writing from his sickbed while being treated in hospital, Speer said a camp and the necessary guards were ready to receive 6,500 prisoners, with resources soon expected to be available for 1,000 more. In addition, he requested at least 10,000 prisoners to work above all in chemical plants in Upper Silesia, pointing out to Himmler that the provision of labour would be relatively simple since Auschwitz was in the region.⁶⁸

These examples show that Speer enthusiastically exploited slave labourers in the same way as Todt. The difference was that Todt openly advocated slave labour and tied it to Nazi ideology; by contrast, Speer was less of an ideologue, but this did not cause him to view foreign workers differently. He personally witnessed the infernal conditions for slave labourers at the site of the gigantic SS-run underground V2 rocket factory at Mittelbau-Dora. Speer praised the SS officer in charge, Hans Kammler, commending him for the 'near-impossible' speed with which he had built the plant, 'which has no equal anywhere in Europe'.⁶⁹ Just as in the rocket programme, consequences were grim for slave labourers under a scheme Speer headed to boost aircraft production. The armaments initiative known as the Jägerstab (Fighter Staff) caused levels of murderous violence against foreign workers to reach new heights. 'In the case of the *Jägerstab*, the system of industrial "self-responsibility" touted first by Todt and then by Speer quite definitely mutated into dictatorship uninhibited by any rule of law or code of civilisation,' wrote historian Adam Tooze.⁷⁰

Speer's efforts to increase armaments production prompted him to make exaggerated claims. One occasion was at a meeting in October 1943 in Posen, where Himmler delivered an infamous speech on murdering Jewish women and children. Speer addressed the meeting that morning, and offered hope of technological advances in aircraft, tank, rocket and submarine manufacture.⁷¹ This rosy forecast, however, was false, and Speer's denial of reality was further demonstrated by his later insistence on the defence of the Reich to the last man. The significance of his decision was underlined by Germany's own military and civilian casualties in the latter part of the war: more people died between the end of June 1944 and Germany's final defeat than in the previous five years of conflict put together.⁷²

Both Speer and Todt worked loyally and ruthlessly under Hitler, and their relationships with the dictator were close. Hitler showered favours on Speer, including the remarkable greeting he liked to give him – 'Heil Speer!' This form of address, normally reserved for the Führer alone, reflected Hitler's frequent acknowledgements of his armaments minister's successes. However light-heartedly or condescendingly expressed, it betrayed the intensity of the dictator's relationship with Todt's successor.[73] During his interrogation after the war, Speer said: 'Up to the beginning of the war, my relations with Hitler were marked by the fanatical enthusiasm which he was bound to inspire in any artist working for him. He was an ideal patron and I was his architect in whom he had full confidence. This resulted in an intimate contact.'[74]

Hitler would seek out his armaments minister, arranging impromptu meetings with Speer to discuss the Berlin of the future. Hitler's adjutant placed late-night calls to Speer saying the Führer needed diversion. On Speer's arrival, they would discuss art, town planning or the new Reichstag building. After Speer's new office was set up adjoining the Chancellery, separated only by gardens, whenever Hitler was in Berlin he would walk across to see his architect and pore over plans for the city. One biographer wrote that Hitler saw in Speer 'not just an outstanding architect, his favourite minister and a possible successor, but also a "friend" and conceivably his only passion, however surprising the term may seem'.[75] Speer told the Nuremberg Tribunal: 'Through this predilection which Hitler had for architecture, I had a close personal contact with him. I belonged to a circle which consisted of other artists and his personal staff. If Hitler had any friends at all, I certainly would have been one of his close friends.'[76] This common bond of architecture had exceptional significance for the standing of the OT in the Third Reich's power structure. Empire and architecture, in other words the building of that empire, were rich themes running through the OT's history.

Hitler's fascination with architecture facilitated contact between the Führer and architects attracted to a large construction agency like the OT. The dictator's passion for the grand buildings of the metropoles of colonial powers, such as Paris and Rome, remained powerful to the last, even though his own ambitions as a would-be artist and architect were frustrated as a young student in Vienna. His early failure stung him, and he talked to Goebbels of making his home town of Linz into a German Budapest with an art gallery and opera house to reduce the cultural pre-eminence of Vienna, which had rejected him.[77] He gave the task of rebuilding Linz to an OT architect, Hermann Giesler, who was also in charge of Munich's facelift and a bitter rival of Speer's. Speer, in his position as the Führer's architect, later acknowledged: 'For a commission to build a great building, I would have sold my soul like Faust.'[78] Speer had the job of turning Berlin into an imperial capital in the Nazi style, and also responsibility for rebuilding Nuremberg, the venue for party rallies. Hitler adored monumental buildings, and his lust for the trappings of empire made him turn to Todt, the civil engineer, to build the infrastructure he considered necessary to fulfil his grandiose vision. The dictator boasted that the Third Reich's *Autobahnen* were his Parthenon. He also compared them to the pyramids of the pharaohs.[79]

Speer's networks

Speer's favourite architects and engineers were among those placed in top jobs in the OT when he replaced Todt. Being the consummate 'networker', Speer put his own teams in place when he changed the OT's structure, bringing the entire OT under the administration of his Armaments Ministry.[80] The OT's regional chiefs in the furthest regions of Hitler's European empire conducted their operations energetically to achieve goals which they and the staff in their task groups showed every sign of viewing as prestigious and worthwhile. Bonds within the organisation formed by a system of patronage and common experiences, such as working on the *Autobahnen* and Westwall before service in occupied Europe, were important. Both Todt and Speer fostered such ties. The system of patronage based on social and professional networks resembled practices governing appointments within the SS leadership of concentration camps in the latter half of the war. Such networks often provided the only means for ambitious members of the concentration-camp SS to succeed in their careers, and a similar system operated in the OT at high levels.

Speer possessed extraordinary skill in creating motivated teams of gifted young managers to put his plans into practice. He positioned capable engineers in critical areas in occupied Europe. One of these men was Professor Walter Brugmann, who had worked on the Nazi Party building in Nuremberg while Speer was in charge of the city's rebuilding. Brugmann became head of the OT's Russia-South region in mid-1942, an area which attracted Hitler's intense interest as the gateway to the Caucasus oilfields.[81] A year later, Brugmann accompanied Speer in an assault boat speeding over the Kerch Strait during a visit by the armaments minister to mark the OT's completion of a cable railway linking the Crimea to the Taman Peninsula. Celebrations of the OT's achievement included servings of the local delicacy – Russian caviar. Brugmann was killed in an air crash in May 1944 and, in recognition of his dedication as Speer's key local troubleshooter, the region's OT task group was named after him.[82]

Another senior OT manager under Speer working in the occupied East was Arnold Adam, who was put in charge of the infamous Transit Road IV road leading to the Caucasus. Having presided over road building carried out by Jewish and other prisoners held in camps where death rates were exceptionally high, Adam went on to oversee OT repairs in 1943 after the devastating British 'Dambuster' raid in the Ruhr region. He then became regional chief in the important northern sector known as 'Hansa' (Einsatzgruppe III) after the partial OT withdrawal into the Reich.[83]

Senior SS officers holding important jobs at OT headquarters, such as Fritz Schmelter and Alois Poschmann, are discussed in a later section, but Speer prized such officers among his team of top engineers in occupied Europe. One example was Willi Henne, whom Speer proposed for promotion within the OT, together with Brugmann, at the time of the 1944 crisis involving Dorsch.[84] Henne's career is significant because it illustrates the importance Speer attached to the OT, as well as how his views contrasted with Todt's on matters affecting SS officers serving in the OT. Henne had joined both the Nazi Party and the SS in 1933 at the age of twenty-five and was in charge of the OT's office in Wiesbaden to manage the construction of the Westwall.[85] Todt then assigned him to Norway, but it was under Speer that this ruthless and energetic chief of OT operations in Scandinavia rose to the rank of *SS-Standartenführer*. When the SS offered him a Waffen-SS rank involving temporary suspension from OT duties, Speer acted to protect the interests of both the OT and his employee, but compromised in the end to secure the important objective of keeping Henne in post. Already at full stretch in his efforts to boost arms production, Speer went to considerable lengths to intervene personally in the affair. The issues were similar to those that prompted an exchange between Todt and Himmler in 1941. The problem again revolved around SS members in the OT, and what uniform they should wear. In contrast to Todt, who favoured emphasising links with the Nazi Party, Speer succeeded in negotiating that his man should wear a specifically OT uniform. In exchanges with Himmler and senior SS officers, Speer at first opposed the temporary lifting of Henne's protection from the military draft through his attachment to the OT, which was required in order for Henne to receive a Waffen-SS rank. Writing to Himmler just over four months after taking charge of the OT, Speer argued that since many SS members served in the OT, no special measure should be introduced for Henne.[86] However, he then backed down to ensure he achieved what he wanted: the maintenance of a professionally competent and valued OT regional leader in his job. Subsequent exchanges brought agreement from Speer that Henne's bond to the OT could be briefly lifted, so that Henne could be promoted to *SS-Obersturmbannführer* of the Waffen-SS Reserve. Speer was firm, however, about Henne wearing OT uniform on his reinstatement on completion of the procedure – a condition the SS accepted.[87]

Speer's willingness to devote time and effort to protect valued individual staff earned him loyal followers whom he took with him on his meteoric rise to armaments minister and head of the OT. One of them was Rudolf Wolters, who was among Speer's three protégés placed at OT headquarters, where he needed them to monitor the danger posed by Todt's potentially rebellious old guard. The others were Gerhard Frank, who was business manager, and Erwin Bohr, chief of personnel.[88] Wolters was a fellow architect whom Speer employed on the Germania project, in the Armaments Ministry and in the OT. Wolters wrote an office journal recording Speer's work on all these tasks, and his loyalty to his former boss even extended to the safekeeping and editing of Speer's post-war memoirs smuggled out of Spandau jail. Their relationship only ruptured when Wolters, embittered by what he saw as Speer's post-war betrayal of their Nazi-era beliefs, revealed material he had excised from his record of wartime events that was highly incriminating for Speer. Some of these details related to evidence of Speer's evictions of thousands of Jews from Berlin as part of the Germania project and their 'resettlement', which meant their handover to the SS, which organised their expulsion and murder. Wolters stated that an excised passage confirmed that Speer had seized 23,765 Jewish apartments in Berlin, forcing 75,000 Jews to be 'resettled'.[89]

While Speer developed a network of loyalists, there also existed 'counter-networks' whose members harboured resentment of the OT chief. Dorsch's moves against Speer and the resistance of Todt's 'old guard' have already been described, but there were other prominent opponents. One of these was Giesler, the architect who battled with Speer for Hitler's favour and commanded two OT task groups in succession – Russia-North and Deutschland VI. Giesler had his own protégés, including Max Gimple, who served as his deputy in both those task groups.[90] Ten years younger than his mentor, Gimple had worked under Giesler after the architect was given the prestigious job of redeveloping the city of Munich in 1938. While working in Giesler's OT Russia-North task group, Gimple had a notorious collaborator, the former detention-camp leader in Auschwitz, Hans Aumeier, who was then commandant of Vaivara concentration camp in Estonia. Aumeier told Allied interrogators after the war he had been working in that area with a unit using Jewish labour. 'Working together with this unit was the OT Oberbauleitung "A", which was a part of the OT Einsatzgruppe "Russland-Nord" under the command of Oberbaudirektor Gimple.'[91]

High-level intrigues exploiting such counter-networks are examined later, but the fact that a man such as Giesler could tolerate working under his arch-rival was a measure of the relative autonomy such regional chiefs exercised. Giesler and Speer continued to display their disdain for one another in their respective post-war publications. Giesler wrote scathingly of Speer, who showed his own contempt by misspelling Giesler's name at every mention.[92]

Organisation Todt operations

The OT was transformed by the successive leaderships of Todt and Speer, as well as by dramatic changes in its role because of the initial rapid expansion and eventual collapse of Hitler's empire. OT operations were almost entirely confined to Nazi-occupied European territory for most of the war, with the core of the Reich largely out of bounds, and this made the organisation especially focused on Hitler's imperial ambitions expanded by military conquests. The OT only switched to sustained, large-scale operations within the Reich itself in 1944–5 when Allied armies forced the Wehrmacht to retreat before Germany's final collapse. Decisions taken personally by the OT's two successive leaders radically affected the organisation's structure and management, but external pressures caused by wartime developments had a massive impact. Such transformations of the structure of the OT and how the organisation evolved are now considered in more detail. This material is divided into four sections: the first covers overall structural changes and OT regional management in Europe as Hitler's empire changed shape; the second analyses high-ranking OT personnel, including senior SS officers; the third examines OT exploitation of foreign slave labourers; and the fourth analyses the status of the engineer and the OT in Nazi Germany.

Organisation Todt structures

Hitler issued a decree on 2 September 1943 which was pivotal for the OT. It legally set out the OT's functions for the first time and placed its leader, then Armaments Minister Speer, directly under the Führer. The OT had long acted as a parastatal organisation driving the slave-labour economy to boost the war effort, and signed contracts with German and foreign businesses across occupied Europe in the name of the Reich.[93] However, Hitler's act of formally making the organisation and its chief answerable only to him greatly increased the OT's power as 'an agency to carry out construction tasks of all kinds decisive for the outcome of the war'.[94] It dealt a severe blow to rivals such as the German Labour Front (Deutsche Arbeitsfront – DAF), headed by Robert Ley and subservient to the Nazi Party. Hitler's decree also formalised the inclusion of the Greater Reich in the OT's sphere of operations, although the organisation had already strayed beyond its otherwise almost complete restriction to occupied Europe. One such instance was when Hitler directed in April 1942, on Speer's suggestion, that OT technical experts be diverted to Germany's core to repair devastation caused by Allied bombing.[95] On that occasion, damage to the northern city of Lübeck prompted the move. Another case followed about a year later: tens of thousands of OT personnel were pulled back from the Atlantic Wall and other tasks following the British 'Dambuster' air raid in May 1943, which caused disastrous flooding in the Ruhr and Eder valleys in a heavily industrialised region. This mass transfer of OT workers was so great that Karl Weiß, the Paris-based OT regional chief, wrested a promise that they be replaced when he met shortly afterwards with Fritz Sauckel, the ruthless Thuringian *Gauleiter* whom Hitler made general plenipotentiary for labour mobilisation in spring 1942.[96] All the same, the need for the emergency OT task force in the Ruhr was extreme. Dorsch, the OT deputy chief, believed German military leaders were convinced at the time that the war would be lost if the damage were not quickly repaired. Despite the success of the British bombing of the Möhne and other dams, OT engineers did, in fact, work speedily to help complete the repairs within five months.[97] But these two examples of OT deployment in the core of the Reich were exceptional before Hitler's 1943 decree, which the dictator issued without bothering to wait for the views of General Wilhelm Keitel, head of the High Command of the Wehrmacht, one of the OT's closest partners.[98] Hitler's announcement paved the way for much more extensive OT operations in the Greater Reich. In June 1944 eight OT task groups were set up in that territory after German forces retreated under Allied attack. The OT engineers leading these groups had greatly increased powers, controlling day-to-day running of construction schemes in their regions. The OT's management, by then renamed OT Construction Office (Amt Bau-OT), only stepped in to direct them when the very biggest projects and labour deployment were involved.[99]

While the OT went through these changes under Todt's and then Speer's leadership, its headquarters were run by Dorsch. The administration had been moved to Berlin after work was stopped on the Westwall in the summer of 1940. Staff at the headquarters numbered about 100 in early 1941 and grew to 3,500 by April 1944, which Speer later viewed as too large and cumbersome.[100] Even before then, the OT's administration had shown itself to be ponderous and overextended, struggling to keep up to date with projects being carried out by far-flung construction teams across occupied Europe.[101]

Organisation Todt task groups in Europe

Regional OT chiefs in occupied Europe, as well as in the Greater Reich in the final year of the war, formed a highly qualified professional team supervising giant construction projects in their regions, often covering more than one country. These engineers led the core of the OT's task force on the ground, supervising specialists in charge of operations cascading through the levels of multiple construction networks down to individual building sites. Three of the original seven OT task groups covered the occupied West, North and Southwest, while four were located in the occupied East. They varied in number and name as the war progressed. One of the biggest OT projects was the Atlantic Wall, which was run by the head of Task Group West, Karl Weiß, as OT engineer in charge of France, Belgium and the Netherlands. Speer's rival, Professor Hermann Giesler, led Task Group Russia-North before being switched back to the Reich to head Task Group Deutschland VI. Another OT regional leader was Willi Henne, in charge of Norway, Denmark and (from 1943) Finland. The task group leaders (*Einsatzgruppenleiter*) were the highest-ranked OT engineers in the field, equivalent to a general in the Wehrmacht, followed by *Einsatzleiter* (major general). Under their administrative control were normally several construction networks known as *Oberbauleitungen*, each headed by a *Hauptbauleiter* or *Oberbauleiter*, respectively equivalent to colonel or lieutenant-colonel. Moving down through the ranks came *Bauleiter* (major), through various grades to *Haupttruppführer* (sergeant major) down to *OT-Meister* (corporal) and simple *OT-Mann* (private).[102]

When the OT was put on a war footing in September 1939, it was attached to the Wehrmacht as an armed forces auxiliary. The term OT *Frontarbeiter* (front worker) was introduced, and such personnel possessed a *Dienstbuch* (pay and identity book), together with the right to bear arms. German staff in the OT were either its own core employees (*OT-Eigenes Personal*) or employees of firms incorporated into the OT from industry (*Firmenangehörige*). Core staff included many civil servants from German city and regional housing and construction administrations. The OT recruited German female staff, the most notorious of whom was Dr Erika Flocken, who was convicted in 1947 of 'selecting' prisoners she deemed unfit to work to be sent to Auschwitz to be murdered. Such 'selections' of sick or exhausted labourers were normally carried out by the

SS, but Flocken performed this function at the Dachau subcamp of Mühldorf, where the OT oversaw mostly Jewish slave labourers. Flocken was sentenced to death at the Mühldorf trial, but this was commuted to life imprisonment before being later reduced.[103] Apart from physicians like Flocken, the OT employed women, some of whom wore blue uniforms, for jobs such as technical drawing, accounting, secretarial work and communications.[104]

The organisation continued to be administered by the Inspectorate General for German Roadways before OT headquarters in Berlin took over after construction of the Westwall wound down in 1940. Since the OT initially operated predominantly in German-occupied Europe, rather than in the Reich, pay for OT *Frontarbeiter* included an allowance recognising they routinely worked in areas close to the front. Once the OT partly withdrew into the Reich, what was called the Front-OT was formed under which frontline areas were remapped and conditions for these allowances reset. Instructions for this were issued in 1944 for both German and foreign business and technical staff, known as *OT-Legionäre* (legionnaires), who qualified for Front-OT membership.[105]

The OT's partnership with German industry was fundamental to its operations. Firms and their employees represented units or soldiers in what was likened to Germany's 'second army'.[106] A firm could either sign up voluntarily to work under OT administration, which was common since substantial profits could often be expected, or be conscripted, which became more widespread during the Russian campaign, especially in the winter of 1943–4.[107] Employees went to OT distribution points, such as in Berlin or Munich, where they received OT uniforms, equipment and an OT rank.[108] Firms took advantage of comparatively favourable contract terms under Todt's leadership until spring 1942, when controls were tightened up under Speer and strong emphasis was placed on maximising performance.

OT ranks were thus made up of a core staff of engineers and construction experts, plus a much wider pool of skilled employees from German industry. The latter were enrolled into the OT for the duration of their contracts, and came along with their firms' considerable resources of industrial plant and machinery. Examples of this procedure in occupied Eastern Europe included enlistment into the OT of employees from various German firms deployed in the Baltics and near Minsk, in occupied Soviet territory. Employees from the southern German construction firm of Trucksäss, based in Neu-Ulm on the River Danube, and the Berlin heavy-engineering company Heinrich Köhler included civil engineers, bricklayers, pitshaft specialists and excavator operators. They were deployed in Lithuania and on tasks linked to major shale-oil works in the region; these depended on the exploitation of Jewish and other slave labourers from Vaivara concentration camp in Estonia. The jobs they undertook were varied: building barracks and sickbays, supervising tree felling, cutting railway sleepers, building railway stations and supervising shale-oil extraction. Many employees of the Trucksäss firm were incorporated into the OT in 1941–2 under a contract the firm signed with the OT. They were summoned to Munich, where they were formally enrolled and issued with work clothes. They were joined there by staff from Austrian firms before travelling by train to their assignments in the occupied East.[109]

As for the OT operation near Minsk, this was part of a more extensive deployment in both Eastern and Western occupied Europe and in the Reich for the Köln-based road-building firm of Rom. The head of the company, Josef Peter Rom, said his firm was enlisted into the OT early in the war as an OT unit, and deployed to around ten sites at various locations in Europe. He travelled regularly to oversee all these projects, on which a total of 5,000–6,000 workers laboured – mostly foreign labourers supplied by the OT.[110] Employees of his firm in the road- and bridge-building operation at Radoskowice, near Minsk, included surveyors, construction-site foremen, machinists, cooks, truck drivers, steamroller operators and administrative accounting staff. They were enrolled in the OT in Berlin, and equipped there with OT uniforms and clothing for their work. They were also awarded OT ranks, and the head of the OT Radoskowice operation was made an OT *Haupttruppführer*. The 1942–3 operation was administered by core OT personnel in Minsk. Employees working for German firms contracted to the OT in occupied areas generally had to channel any communications through the regional OT office, rather than direct to their firms in Germany.[111]

Conditions in the early war years were incomparably better in occupied Western Europe than in the occupied East from the very start of the conflict. In France, the OT did not rely wholly on German industry and recruited staff from the occupied country's own construction firms. In general, the OT depended on skilled labour from the foreign firms more than its own core staff for building projects, confining itself to planning, coordinating and delivering material and securing additional manual labour. The OT either contracted French firms which brought their own staff and hired more locally as required, recruited workers individually or sought them through local labour offices. When the OT did employ German firms, their employees received OT uniforms and ranks, being incorporated into the organisation for the duration of the firm's contract with the OT. For local French labourers there thus appeared to be little real difference between being supervised by OT core personnel and by employees of German firms coopted into the OT, although the distinction remained clear in OT records. The head of the German firm was generally in charge of a particular construction project and received the requisite OT rank, while his subordinates received lower OT ranks according to their status in the firm and were employed on tasks as they would have been in private industry.[112]

While the influence of the OT's leaders, the broad range and urgency of its tasks and the dramatic changes in its workforce were all vital factors affecting the organisation's development, another highly significant element was a change in its administrative structure, noted earlier. This stemmed from the appointments of Todt, and then Speer, to the job of general plenipotentiary for the regulation of the construction industry (Generalbevollmächtigter für die Regelung der Bauwirtschaft – GBBau). When Göring appointed Todt to the post in 1938 the object was to improve the overburdened sector's performance. But when Speer assumed the position in February 1942, along with all Todt's other responsibilities, he took matters a step further. Speer persuaded Hitler to issue a decree in August 1942 envisaging GBBau representatives in all German-occupied territories.[113] In effect, this meant that the OT regional chiefs, the OT task group leaders, fulfilled the GBBau function. This had huge implications for the OT's use of slave labour across Europe. The arrangement suited both the German construction industry, which gained full access to the OT's extended network and resources, and the OT, which profited from the GBBau's discretionary powers and control over deployment of German building firms across Europe. Speer's takeover of all engineering and technical tasks in the occupied East meant that not only he and his top colleagues but also middle-ranking managers were given wide powers. The Wehrmacht, the Economy Ministry and others needing projects to be carried out sent their requirements to the GBBau, which set total volumes governing construction materials and labour under a quota system to marshal available resources. In this way, Todt and his successor Speer not only planned construction projects in the occupied territories, but also carried them out via the OT.[114]

Organisation Todt engineers: ardent Nazis or apolitical technocrats?

Far afield in Hitler's empire, how did OT core personnel behave in conquered foreign lands, where they were an integral part of the Nazi system of occupation? Cooperation with the SS was crucial in occupied Europe, and since SS or SA officers held key leadership posts in the OT, how much influence did Nazi paramilitaries wield? Was commitment to Nazi ideology most important to management and staff, or professionalism and technical excellence? What were the values of core OT personnel, and what sort of individual was attracted to the organisation? To help answer these questions, the professional qualifications of hundreds of senior OT staff are analysed and some measure of the ideological indoctrination of OT staff is made. Senior personnel at the organisation's headquarters are examined first, followed by SS and SA officers in the OT and finally staff working on site across Europe.

Todt and the OT's deputy leader, Dorsch, were high-ranking officers in the SA. Todt's successor, Speer, also joined the SA, as well as the SS. Other members of Nazi paramilitary groups in the OT's leadership were based at OT headquarters in Berlin and held organisation-wide responsibilities. These OT managers included SS-Obersturmbannführer Fritz Schmelter and SS-Sturmbannführer Alois Poschmann. Schmelter, who used the academic title 'Dr', became the OT's manpower administrator from mid-1942, having passed his civil service exams in 1933 and worked in labour administration in Berlin and Frankfurt am Main.[115] Dr Poschmann was put in overall charge of health at the OT in 1941, having qualified in medicine and received his licence to practise in 1937. He was also on the Fighter Staff, with responsibility for social welfare.[116]

The SS and SA were thus strongly represented among the OT's leaders and significant numbers of SS officers worked throughout the organisation. SS officers with important positions in the OT had one thing in common, however, apart from their membership of an organisation with a reputation for brutality and political orthodoxy in the Nazi era: they were well educated and qualified as engineers, physicians, architects, civil servants, miners, mechanics, electricians or skilled workers in other trades and professions.

The need for sound engineering skills could reasonably be considered essential in a specialist construction agency like the OT. Managers overseeing the building of bridges, roads and railways required expert knowledge of the technical challenges that construction teams faced in often-forbidding climates and terrains. The only high-ranking SS officer among the original seven OT regional chiefs deployed in Nazi-occupied territory, SS-Standartenführer Willi Henne, was therefore a fully qualified civil engineer. Henne, the head of the OT's operations in Norway, which included road and rail construction in mountainous Arctic areas, gained his engineering diploma (Dipl. Ing.) after studying from 1926 to 1930.[117]

In the higher ranks of the OT, the superior level of academic and professional qualifications is remarkable. Analysis of around 1,400 senior staff shows that a high proportion either possessed titles in the regional state administration in fields including construction and management or were trained architects or engineers, with many specified as having the 'diploma of engineering' (Dipl. Ing.) or the higher academic title of 'doctor of engineering' (Dr Ing.). Others had graduated in other disciplines. Since OT responsibilities included healthcare, some staff were qualified physicians or dentists. Altogether, 40.7 per cent of senior OT staff possessed these levels of qualifications.[118]

Among SS officers at the OT's Berlin headquarters, Fritz Schmelter was an example of an OT manager carrying out a vital task which linked to other power centres in the Third Reich.[119] Control over labour deployment obviously had the most significant implications for the OT's use of slave labourers in occupied Europe. Fusion of responsibilities across the various sectors, as well as OT influence over decisions regarding labour deployment, is well illustrated by his functions. Schmelter not only held the brief of special trustee for labour (*Sondertreuhänder der Arbeit*) at OT headquarters, but was simultaneously responsible for labour deployment at the office of the GBBau. At the same time, he was represented on the specialist labour staff of Fritz Sauckel, the general plenipotentiary for labour mobilisation, and issued instructions to OT personnel about the need for coordination.[120] As illustrated by the series of decrees jointly issued in ensuing years by Sauckel's office and the GBBau, it was a simple matter for Schmelter to put into practice the GBBau's plans and match them to the available labour and resources of the OT. In the occupied territories, OT regional leaders, as representatives of the GBBau, organised the labour of prisoners of war, civilian forced or slave labourers and indigenous Jewish workers, who were compelled to undertake extreme hard labour on OT building sites with grossly inadequate rations, accommodation and medical care.[121] Hitler spoke to Todt and Sauckel in October 1941, a few months before the latter's appointment, about his vision for conquered Eastern territories following the invasion of the Soviet Union which had begun that summer. The Slav inhabitants, whom he described as '*Indianer*', were to be starved in the cities. Some were to be selected for work and Jews were to be exterminated.[122]

Schmelter had a passion for statistics, and his style of managing labour deployment for the OT had a parallel in the SS WVHA, where Obersturmbannführer Gerhard Maurer won the respect of his superiors by introducing a system of work deployment cards showing prisoners' professional skills. The idea was to gather such information centrally in order to deploy prisoners on work sites in a more targeted and efficient fashion, although in practice it proved of limited value.[123] At the OT, Schmelter issued directives on pay and benefits for German OT personnel, while his forms gathering statistics provided OT managers with a mass of information.[124] He was backed up by Dorsch, who called the figures detailing labour deployment 'indispensable'.[125] Schmelter issued meticulous instructions on how these forms were to be completed, but viewed some problems arising from the categorisation of prisoners as straightforward. In a note explaining how labour deployment was to be recorded for one particular group, Schmelter said simply: 'Jews always count as prisoners.'[126]

Noting the significant numbers of SS and SA personnel in OT ranks, British intelligence concluded in the closing stages of the war that a number of factors contributed to firm support for Nazi ideology among the OT leadership. Early Nazi Party stalwarts were traditionally offered the perk of a supervisory post in the OT because it was a safer option than combat duty. These *'Alte Kämpfer'* (old fighters) had served Hitler and the party in the 1920s. Another group given access to such OT jobs included well-connected party officials and older SS members.[127] This suggests that at least some SS and Nazi Party officials entered the OT because they had the right ideological credentials. There is strong evidence to show, though, that Nazi ideology and engineering prowess were by no means mutually exclusive, and went hand in hand in the OT. As underlined in this section, mid- to high-level OT staff who were also SS officers almost invariably had advanced professional qualifications.

Although many OT personnel forged their careers entirely in the organisation, some switched either to or from the SS. The role of Hermann Pister in setting up Hinzert camp for the OT before he went on to become Buchenwald commandant has already been mentioned. Another SS officer who developed his career first in the OT was Heinrich Courté. Like Pister, his subsequent employment with the SS was connected to Buchenwald. He joined the Nazi Party in 1933 and then the Allgemeine SS later that year. Having gained his engineering diploma in his home town of Aachen in 1936, he worked on Todt's motorway-building team until the war started and transferred to the OT at the end of 1939. He was deployed at first in the Western occupied territories, then in Romania and finally, after Hitler's invasion of Russia, in the Eastern conflict zone until October 1942. He returned to the Reich and joined the Waffen-SS and Oswald Pohl's SS WVHA. He was put in charge of construction of a railway, ordered by Himmler, running from Weimar to an armaments factory near Buchenwald concentration camp. Around 800 prisoners from Pister's Buchenwald camp were assigned to Courté's task force, whose SS Death's Head guards included Ukrainians. Courté later joined Hans Kammler's special staff, was promoted to *Obersturmführer*, and used slave labourers once more for work to transfer Germany's key armaments production facilities underground to protect them from Allied air raids. Kammler's elite team of SS engineers specialised in the same rapid construction projects as the OT, including tunnels in the Harz mountains for V2 rocket production using 60,000 prisoners as slave labour. After the war, Courté used the cover name Hendrik Jaspers and tried to avoid capture, but was arrested and questioned, giving a statement to interrogators in Nuremberg in January 1947.[128]

While Todt had recommended Pister to Himmler, he showed an interest in attracting what he viewed as promising young talent from the Reich's security services into the OT. In a letter written in April 1941 to Reinhard Heydrich, Himmler's faithful lieutenant and head of the Reich Security Head Office (RSHA), he explained how the Organisation Todt was expanding operations into newly occupied territory in northern France, Denmark, Norway and Eastern Europe. Reflecting the optimistic mood of the Nazi elite two months before the German invasion of the Soviet Union and following the Wehrmacht's initial victories in the West, he even sketched out plans to build up the OT's personnel to be able to undertake the extensive construction tasks he envisaged for his organisation 'after the war'. Todt told Heydrich he was paying particular attention to appointments to the OT leadership and to those responsible for the care of the agency's employees. He needed gifted young men, and one had caught his eye who was then working in the police force. Todt explained that the young man, named Zoepf, had displayed great skill the previous year at Plassenburg in caring for OT men who had been injured on the Westwall or at other sites near the battlefront. Zoepf's efforts over just a few days, working with batches of eighty to 100 OT men at a time, had restored their self-confidence so they had been able to return to serve in exemplary fashion in front-line zones. Todt said he wished to employ Zoepf in personnel management supervising OT leisure-time activities. He promised to promote Zoepf, who was relatively junior, to the position of *Regierungsrat* (senior civil servant) in around a year.[129]

SS officers helped supervise OT construction projects across Europe, and the SS ensured its representation in every section of the OT through liaison officers. OT cooperation with the SS involved working closely with Oswald Pohl's SS WVHA after its founding in February 1942. The WVHA had its own construction unit of civil engineers and architects, known as 'Office Group C'. It was headed by engineer Hans Kammler and contained the highest concentration of technically trained officers in Pohl's entire organisation. This tight-knit technical elite corps achieved success in wartime projects, but was 'horrific for its brutal efficiency'.[130] The WVHA took control of the concentration camps in March 1942 and oversaw all SS economic interests. It had a staff of up to 1,700 in five main departments.[131]

Compared to the OT and Kammler's corps, concentration-camp commandants had few managerial skills, whether technical or administrative, before Pohl's reorganisation in the summer of 1942. They excelled only at terror. When Pohl replaced nearly one-third of his camp commandants, he picked new ones for their administrative skills and soldierly capabilities.[132]

Foreign workers under the Organisation Todt

OT engineers dispatched throughout occupied Europe were set gigantic tasks to secure and develop Hitler's empire, but they could never have achieved them without huge numbers of foreign workers. Slave labourers toiling under OT overseers were a significant proportion of the tens of millions estimated to have performed forced or slave labour between 1939 and 1945 for the benefit of the Third Reich's war economy.[133] The OT cooperated with the SS, the Wehrmacht and industry in the exploitation of slave labour, although it was sometimes in sole charge of labour camps or ran construction projects itself. The armed forces controlled prisoners of war, who were an important source of labour, and army engineers either supervised OT personnel or worked jointly on projects. The SS controlled concentration camps and most subcamps, hiring out prisoners to the OT or industrial firms. Foreign civilians were normally the biggest source of slave labour in the occupied territories and in the Reich.

Out of the OT workforce of close to 1.5 million at the end of September 1944, just over 351,000 were Germans and nearly 1,080,000 were foreigners. These foreigners included nearly 165,000 prisoners of war and more than 140,000 other prisoners, including Jews.[134] The figures represent only a snapshot at that date, and numbers fluctuated throughout the war. The overall total of foreign workers compelled to work for the OT throughout the Second World War was far higher than the figure included in the September 1944 calculation. British intelligence estimated the total OT workforce at between 1.5 and 2 million.[135] Despite the hugely increased numbers of foreign slave labourers toiling for the OT at the time these figures were calculated in the last year of the war, the organisation's desire for even more was often left unsatisfied.

OT efforts to maintain the numbers of its own core personnel to oversee the slave-labour force faced similar problems. The maximum level of German OT staff reached around 350,000, but at its lowest point the number may have dropped to below 75,000.[136] Successive drafts into the military drained young professionals from the OT. At the start of the Second World War the OT lost almost two-thirds of its employees, despite Hitler's order that work should continue on the Westwall and that the organisation's wartime tasks were fortifications and road building. OT workers were either conscripted into the Wehrmacht or broke their contracts to return home, resulting in the Westwall labour force dwindling from around 340,000 to 80,000.[137] The effect of waves of military drafts from 1942 meant the average age of OT staff rose to over fifty. Appreciable numbers of wounded and incapacitated Germans were sidelined into administrative posts in the OT. German personnel became vastly outnumbered by their foreign slave labourers, and the ratio of German to foreign OT personnel fell particularly low in occupied Soviet territory and the Balkans. By November 1944 Speer expected the OT general labour force within Germany alone to be increased by about 250,000, mostly Hungarian Jews, to reach more than 1 million. Foreigners also grew to represent a significant proportion of supervisors employed by the OT to manage forced or slave labourers. In the OT region encompassing France, Belgium and the Netherlands, for example, routine supervision of manual labour was placed as far as possible in German hands until manpower shortages in the latter stages of the war forced a shift to more reliance on Western foreigners. This meant Dutch, Belgian and French workers assumed low-level supervisory roles, such as assistant foremen, and by 1944 assistant camp supervisors. Those vilified under the Nazi racist code, such as Jews and Slavs, including Soviet civilians and prisoners of war, were excluded from any such positions.[138]

The trend towards hiring more foreigners into OT ranks also affected healthcare for the organisation's employees (as opposed to the vastly inferior, or virtually non-existent, care available to labour-camp inmates). Greater numbers of foreign OT doctors were appointed as the war progressed in occupied Western Europe, and they outnumbered German doctors by 1944. In the OT administrative area (*Oberbauleitung*) of Cherbourg (occupied France), which employed about 15,000 men, the OT had three German and seven foreign doctors, who were as a rule given very low OT ranks. The OT had its own hospitals and dispensaries.[139]

Incentives were offered to attract *Volksdeutsche* and 'people of German descent' (*Deutschstämmige*) into the OT, promising German nationality and equal status with citizens in the Reich. *Volksdeutsche*, as opposed to *Reichsdeutsche*, referred to ethnic Germans locked outside the new borders of the Reich after the redrawing of European frontiers under the Versailles Treaty after the First World War; *Reichsdeutsche* were those within the new borders. Hitler's decree of 19 May 1943 offered German nationality to foreigners having at least two German grandparents who joined the Wehrmacht, Waffen-SS, German police or the OT.[140] Dr Schmelter at OT headquarters issued detailed instructions on categories of OT staff, including how *Volksdeutsche* with the required official papers could be classified under the 'German' column in his forms for compiling labour statistics.[141] OT staff were recruited or joined up from nations allied to Germany, such as Hungary, Romania and Bulgaria.[142] Italian firms also provided personnel incorporated into the OT, although after Italy's armistice with the Allies in September 1943 large numbers of Italian soldiers designated as military internees were forced to work in the Reich.[143] About 500 French firms, along with some Belgian and Dutch companies, worked for the OT in France, where at least 500 German firms were employed by the organisation.[144] Foreigners from Western and Northern Europe, such as employees of French, Dutch, Belgian and Danish firms, joined the OT in various ways. Foreign firms could put their entire workforce and equipment at the OT's disposal and work for the organisation under contract, individuals could sign up or foreign firms or individuals could be conscripted into the OT.[145]

The engineer and the Organisation Todt

While the OT operated for most of its existence in foreign territory and massively exploited foreign labourers, it acted as a standard-bearer abroad for German qualities much prized under the Third Reich: modern technology, professionalism and advanced engineering. Todt championed his vision of the engineer under National Socialism in ways already described, while technology for Speer was one means of nurturing the myth that superior weaponry could still deliver a German victory. Speer persisted, almost to the end, in making exaggerated claims about armaments production and 'wonder weapons'. He deployed the OT in various armaments programmes, including V1 and V2 rockets and Me-262 jet fighters. His guiding principle was to maximise the war effort rather than pursuing the particular brand of ideology adopted by his predecessor to indoctrinate Germany's engineers. The two men's differing approaches feed into a complex post-war debate among historians on how engineers and technology fitted into Nazi ideology and whether Hitler's regime 'modernised' Germany.[146] One conclusion in this debate was that technocrats from Speer's Armaments Ministry and other main Nazi power blocs had gained such sway that 'by the end of the war and the "Thousand Year Reich", technocracy – and with it science and engineering – was emerging as one of the most powerful and last pillars of the National Socialist state'.[147] This and other research suggests that ideology for Nazi engineers changed relatively little during the Third Reich. However, the contrast between Todt and Speer, as just outlined, lends weight to the view that 'the Nazi ideological approach to technology was neither uniform nor continuous through the Third Reich. Rather it depended on the vision and political power of the individual charged with overseeing German engineers ... and on the willingness of the regime to actively foster that vision in the context of changing historical events.'[148]

Engineers belonged to a profession that gained social esteem in the Third Reich, unlike the lawyers and teachers so disliked by Hitler. Speer expressed high praise for his own staff, declaring in the spring of 1944: 'Due to the high priority of OT tasks in the occupied territories, the best managers and skilled workers of the German construction administration and industry have been continuously supplied in the last few years to this organisation.'[149] The most able engineers 'had been attracted by the more rewarding task with the OT in the occupied territories'.[150]

Perhaps unsurprisingly, because incompetence on the part of a construction engineer was visible and dangerous, employers valued technical expertise highly.[151] Engineers were relatively unscathed by manpower shortages caused by pre-war purges of Jews from the professions, and the quality of new recruits also held up better than those entering law or teaching.[152] Amid the country's rearmament boom, engineers were everywhere in demand, but in wartime Speer took urgent steps to fill gaps in OT ranks, such as enlisting engineers from academic staff. A letter from the Education Ministry to Hans Lammers, head of the Reich Chancellery, on 1 March 1943 said more than 300 urgently needed engineers would be made available to the OT and the Armaments Ministry by releasing teaching staff through the planned temporary closure of little-used construction, engineering and textile educational institutions. The Armaments Ministry sought rapid approval of a decree to this effect, since Speer and the OT were pressing for the staff.[153]

Organisation Todt transitions

Studying the themes of empire and architecture under the Third Reich reveals how closely the fates of Fritz Todt, Albert Speer and OT engineers became woven into Hitler's designs and the murderous slave-labour system used to put sections of them into practice. Todt worked on the *Autobahnen* and energetically began the OT's exploitation of foreign workers. Speer transferred his skilled Germania labour force into the OT shortly after his appointment and used foreign slave labourers with equal ruthlessness. Both men headed an organisation that expanded into every corner of conquered territory, building defence installations and transport networks to secure and supply the newly won land. The OT was formed and operated as a vital unit to help gain and preserve Hitler's empire.

Germany's imperial ambitions dominated the country's approach to both world wars, but whereas Kaiser Wilhelm II stood at the head of an already considerable empire in 1914, one of Hitler's goals in 1939 was to regain one. At the start of the twentieth century, Germany and the USA were the world's two greatest industrial nations, and the Second Reich's colonial possessions included German Southwest Africa. A revolt in the African territory in 1904 was savagely crushed by colonial forces, resulting in at least 60 per cent of the Herero and Nama peoples being wiped out.[154] Although historians have been tempted to see parallels between the horrors of German imperial warfare and later Nazi genocide, Wilhelmine Germany was not the same as Hitler's Third Reich, and violent campaigns by other colonial powers of the period did not differ significantly from German actions in Africa. Germany's decision to go to war in 1914 was motivated by internal perceptions that it remained territorially incomplete and constantly threatened by European rivals. Defeat in 1918 meant the loss of 13 per cent of its territory, and Germany was stripped of all its overseas colonies under the Versailles Treaty. Exploiting the resentment provoked by peace terms which included heavy reparations payments, Hitler set out his ideas for conquering land for the German *Volk* in the East in *Mein Kampf*. Appointed chancellor on 30 January 1933, he imposed dictatorship and launched an accelerated programme of rearmament to prepare for war.

For Hitler, recreating an empire after he started the Second World War meant seizing *Lebensraum* in the East, genocide of Jews and deliberate starvation of millions of people, especially Slavs in the Soviet Union. It also entailed crippling exploitation of the economies, raw materials and labour of German-occupied and dependent countries.[155] Under one of several settlement plans linked to Germany's invasion of the Soviet Union in mid-1941, 31 million people plus all the Jews were to be displaced to the East in Poland, the Baltic area, Belarus and northwest Ukraine; they were to be replaced over thirty years by 4.5 million Germans.[156] Hitler spoke shortly after the invasion of creating a 'Garden of Eden' out of the newly won eastern regions.[157] Actual settlement by Germans or ethnic Germans was limited and bore little relation to the plans. Hitler's estimate of the number of people in German-occupied lands from whom a labour force could be drawn was far more realistic. He declared in November 1941 that 'the area that works for us now includes more than 250 million people'. Since German experts reckoned 40 per cent of a population could be deemed employable, this meant a labour force of 100 million.[158]

Institutions like the Organisation Todt oversaw foreign labourers brought under the Third Reich's yoke. The picture that emerges of the OT is of an organisation with an SS- or SA-dominated centralised leadership and a highly qualified top to mid-ranking team of engineers in the field. It was run in contrasting styles by its two successive leaders, who were among Hitler's most powerful and trusted ministers. Fritz Todt, resolutely loyal to Hitler and the Nazi cause, sought to politicise engineers and formulated his own Nazi technical ideology; he excelled at improvisation, laying the groundwork for what Speer claimed as his 'armaments miracle'. Albert Speer, self-centred and ambitious, was a skilled politician with a flair for management and putting together young, gifted teams, focusing on their competence; he rose to be seen as Hitler's 'heir apparent' and sacrificed support for any specific technical ideology to focus on the war effort. Reflecting the transition between Todt and Speer, the OT publication *Der Frontarbeiter* marked Hitler's fifty-third birthday, fewer than three months after Todt's death, with articles praising the organisation's founder and citing the Führer as saying: 'The Organisation Todt, created by Dr Todt, overcame everything; for the man himself, the word "impossible" did not exist.'[159] On Hitler's next birthday, the front cover of *Der Frontarbeiter* showed Speer walking in OT uniform at the dictator's right-hand side in front of German military top brass – an image meant to portray him as the Führer's eventual successor.[160]

The OT underwent huge changes, and none was greater than in wartime. In Speer, especially, Hitler saw an architect who could design the impressive buildings he craved to bejewel his 'Thousand Year Reich'. These plans to refashion cities in Germany's core and throughout its imperial lands essentially looked ahead to the peace following imagined German victory. Speer shared his ideas on founding new cities 'in the East' with Alfred Rosenberg in early 1942. Outlining to the minister for the East how such cities should be planned and built, Speer pointed to the success of the Westwall, which showed how construction projects were best carried out by a well-integrated force of skilled labourers used to working with one another. The OT's high performance proved the worth of this model, Speer said, suggesting similar practices in the development in the East of cities twinned with German towns.[161] Hitler approved Speer's proposals regarding the new Eastern cities later that year.[162]

Apart from such architectural plans, both Todt and Speer were entrusted with key projects considered vital to winning the war. As for the quality of OT staff compared to rivals, Hitler, Todt and Speer frequently sang their praises. This was in spite of delays and mismanagement inevitable in handling huge projects over vast areas and often exceptionally harsh climates and rugged terrain. While successive drafts into the armed forces drained young staff from the OT, Hitler and the organisation's leaders remained convinced of the professionalism and performance of the core personnel of technical experts and engineers. The OT was perceived to possess speed and adaptability surpassing the engineers of the Wehrmacht; the OT's links to industry generally helped the organisation outmatch the ideologically hidebound SS in carrying out construction projects efficiently and economically; and the OT's links through Todt and Speer to Hitler provided unrivalled political clout which even the captains of German industry could not afford to ignore.

SS staff working for the OT appeared well integrated into the organisation and contributed significantly to its output as an independent organisation under the Third Reich, pursuing its own goals. SS officers in senior OT posts were well educated and highly qualified in their fields as engineers, physicians, architects and civil servants. Wider analysis of the level of professional training gained by OT engineers and other skilled personnel reveals a highly qualified workforce where Nazi ideology could combine easily, in many cases in the same person, with professional competence and efficiency.

The OT flourished under both Todt and Speer. It amassed most power in the final year of the war, having by then withdrawn partly into the Reich. Before that time, OT regional chiefs enjoyed considerable autonomy directing construction operations across occupied Europe. It was the range of projects they tackled and the numbers of slave labourers they were able to command which made them indispensable. The tasks undertaken by the OT are analysed next to show how the organisation helped strip occupied Europe of its resources in both raw materials and manpower for the benefit of the Third Reich.

2

Plunder in Europe

Rearmament was one of Hitler's top priorities from the earliest stages of his dictatorship. This was the real objective behind measures to tackle Germany's economic problems and reduce the number of unemployed, of whom 6 million were registered in early 1933. A showpiece motorway network and fast growth in car production contributed to a German recovery which Nazi propaganda portrayed as Hitler's 'economic miracle', but which in fact owed much to job creation and other schemes inherited by the Nazi government from its predecessors, as well as a worldwide economic upturn. When Hitler took office, Germany had virtually no air force and no capital warships, and its army was limited to 100,000 under the Versailles Treaty following defeat in the First World War. Between 1933 and 1935, however, the share of military spending in German national income rose from less than 1 per cent to close to 10 per cent, an extraordinary reallocation of total national production in a capitalist state in peacetime. On the eve of the next global conflict, Germany's rearmament programme had produced dramatic results, most significantly in aircraft production, while the army had nearly 750,000 men on active service and more than 1 million in reserve. As the war progressed and Speer replaced Todt as armaments minister in February 1942, Germany's growing military crisis meant that conscription (to replace soldiers who had fallen on the Eastern front) robbed the armaments industry of at least 200,000 workers in the first half of that year. The country's labour force needed to be replenished urgently, and the solution seemed clear: the best way to find the millions of workers needed for armaments production, construction and other vital industry sectors was to procure them from the occupied territories in the East.[1]

Funds provided from abroad totalled about one-quarter to one-third of Germany's war costs, with foreign forced or slave labourers making a huge contribution to the Third Reich's war economy.[2] The critical issue of the fate of these foreign labourers, in particular the hundreds of thousands who suffered or died under the OT, is at the heart of this book. Their accounts of their experiences, as well as violence in the camps and death rates among the prisoners, are fully examined in a later chapter.[3] The purpose here is to establish the significance of the OT's role in projects across occupied Europe and in the Greater Reich, and ask whether the organisation's goals were achieved. The way in which the OT helped to project German imperial power into conquered territory is described in the book's opening chapter; the nature of OT operations in occupied Europe, the organisation's exploitation of foreign workers, and the details and purpose of its various large-scale building projects are now fully explored.

To determine how the OT achieved its massive exploitation of resources and foreign labourers, its wartime management of labour must be examined. How did the OT acquire such huge numbers of foreign workers, and what policies were devised to exploit them? Sauckel's appointment as Hitler's labour supremo has already been mentioned, but how did the OT cooperate with him? After dealing with these questions, an investigation is conducted into the OT's vast projects for which the labour was required. OT operations are divided into two geographical zones: the first is occupied Europe, and the second is the Greater Reich. This separation into two regions covers different time periods. The first extends throughout the war, while the second predominantly involves its final year. The importance of OT projects to Germany's war effort in both geographical zones is assessed to determine whether they met or exceeded OT targets. The increasing number of those that failed in the final year of the war is analysed, together with Hitler's attitude towards the OT in relation to its performance, both good and bad.

The business of slave labour under the Organisation Todt

OT documents recording the running of the organisation's vast projects exploiting slave labour used language typical of international corporations. Performance targets and deadlines had to be met; a bonus system was required to motivate the workforce; labourers, both skilled and unskilled, needed to be recruited and retained; OT staff were instructed to set an example, show leadership and encourage teamwork. The differences compared to most West European businesses before or since the Second World War were that performance was determined according to a racist scale measured against a German worker; bonuses were small amounts of food supplementing what remained grossly inadequate rations; recruiting labour meant roundups executed by force; worker retention meant tighter security to prevent escapes; and OT leadership meant modelling an exemplary 'superior' race using routine violence.

This harsh business model evolved during the Second World War to govern OT management of its slave-labour programme. Both Todt and Speer strove constantly to improve the OT's performance to ensure efficiency and expansion. Soon after taking office in 1942, Speer issued decrees demanding better productivity from the OT's German and foreign workers, including prisoners. By the end of 1943 he was recommending a system that gave a sinister new meaning to incentives for workers: performance feeding.[4] The principle was to withhold a proportion of prisoners' already dangerously meagre rations and share the reserved food between labourers deemed to have deserved it under a work performance rating system.[5] Hitler issued a decree on performance feeding in February 1944.

In the drive to improve efficiency, OT administrators gathered statistics on a range of indicators to assess the output and strength of the workforce. Speer issued a decree in autumn 1942 to all OT regional chiefs, calling for better performance and skilful management of labour. He pointed out that foreigners, prisoners of war and detainees were in short supply, and ordered all OT regions to send him reports to show how productively they used their labourers. His action came at a time of setbacks in the Wehrmacht's campaign in Russia. Big projects being undertaken by the OT meant that the effects of a generally worsening labour shortage across Europe were being felt ever more keenly.

> The work force should only be used according to their capabilities and experience. It is forbidden to assign skilled workers, especially German skilled workers, to work which could be carried out just as well by trained or even unskilled labourers. If a German carpenter is employed as a navvy, or to supervise a few foreign manual labourers, this use of such a valuable skilled worker is absurd.[6]

Speer also ordered that only performance-based contracts should be made with firms, except where this was impossible for mobile OT units in occupied Soviet territory. The emphasis was on productivity, and the mark of a good construction-site manager was to achieve the highest output with the fewest workers. 'The performance of every labourer deployed by the OT must be increased by every possible means. Basically the same work output is to be demanded from foreigners as from a German worker.' He declared further: 'Only appropriate, economical and profitable deployment of human labour resources will enable the OT to fulfil its allotted tasks.'

Such decrees by Speer reflected the level of detail he went into to ensure the OT functioned as he wished, as well as the importance he attached to this. In 1944, Willi Henne's OT Wiking group was implementing the 'performance feeding' programme endorsed by Speer and which had already been introduced in German industry.[7] With thousands more Soviet prisoners of war due to arrive in Norway, the army and the OT were pursuing the policy and the measure was viewed as having consistently shown its worth by boosting work output.[8] Statistics were gathered on the work performance of foreigners and prisoners of war compared to German workers.[9] Because improving the quality of rations was not an option, food could only be increased in volume. Prisoners' ratings were entered in their work books, and performance of labour units was gauged against the output of an equivalent German work detail.

Although some sections of German industry were sceptical about performance feeding as an effective method to boost worker output, the OT manager in charge of the top-priority Valentin and Hornisse submarine projects in Bremen was enthusiastic. Marineoberbaurat Edo Meiners gave his foremen complete discretion on implementation of the policy for all prisoners of war. 'It [is] hereby ordered that foremen, pit shaft overseers, supervisors etc. of the various firms should be responsible for whether a prisoner of war receives food or not. All sentimentality should be set aside in such judgements, since in this case only severity can bring results.'[10]

These examples of OT managers ruthlessly pursuing efficiency arose when Speer was in charge. When German troops and armour swept into Poland in September 1939, while Todt was still at the helm, OT units came in their wake to shore up the country's transport network and infrastructure at the start of what would become a massive exploitation of foreign labour during the Second World War. Hitler's subsequent military thrusts westwards and into other parts of Europe, before turning eastwards again and pushing deep into Soviet territory, opened up further opportunities to bring millions of civilians and prisoners of war under the Nazi yoke. They were forced to work in their home countries, transported to Germany or deported to third countries in occupied Europe, and represented a human resource which the Third Reich's war economy proved unable to do without. What that meant for subjugated peoples in the various regions, as already explained, ranged between extremes of voluntary paid work to slave-labour torment and death. The many different sets of conditions that they experienced in between are fully investigated in the course of this book.

The scramble for manpower

Thousands of mostly German OT personnel worked in Poland in December 1939 on the country's transport network.[11] By early 1940, 25,000 Polish prisoners of war classified as Jews had died of hunger, cold or maltreatment after being put to work by German forces in the first months of a brutal and murderous occupation.[12] Requests from Germany for Polish workers met with the response in June 1940 that all recruitment in the Warsaw area had been suspended for six weeks because 4,000 Polish workers had to be put at the disposal of the OT.[13] Millions of citizens supported the German war effort as civilian workers, ghetto inmates or prisoners in labour camps. Göring decreed in January 1940 that the part of Poland known as the General Government was to be used as a labour pool and 1 million Poles were to be recruited to work in the Reich, where Nazi racist rules required them to wear the letter 'P' on their clothing. Of these, 750,000 were reserved for agriculture, half of them women.[14]

As Germany's military victories continued and its invasion of the Soviet Union began, seemingly limitless sources of foreign labour opened up. These included prisoners of war and also civilians, who were the largest category of foreign labourers working for the OT. Jews and Slavic civilians in East Europe (*Ostarbeiter*) were brutally persecuted as slave labourers, but West European voluntary workers and forced labourers initially experienced a much milder regime. In France, working for the OT could seem attractive for the young unemployed early in the war. The OT advertised for workers on billboards and in newspapers, offering wages significantly above the average in the sector up to late 1941. A secure source of food, amid inflation and shortages, was another bonus, as well as protection in principle from deportation to work in the Reich, although this last benefit often proved illusory. While the OT found it easy to recruit skilled labour in the initial period, it had to resort to economic, legal or violent methods later on to secure the workers it needed. Even foreign workers receiving a reasonable wage considered themselves to be forced labourers.[15] From January 1941, workers rendered unemployed by the closure of local construction sites were told by regional labour offices to apply for jobs with the OT. If they refused, they were threatened with loss of unemployment benefit or ration cards. By the end of 1942 most foreign workers were forced labourers and armed units, including police and German soldiers, were rounding them up either by threatening or using violence. At times, armed OT *Schutzkommando* guard units were involved.[16] The Atlantic Wall was the OT's biggest task in France, and by spring 1942 445,000 French workers were labouring on construction and other tasks for the OT and the Wehrmacht, with a further 400,000 working in the armaments industry for the German war effort. Around 1.58 million prisoners of war were sent to the Reich and more than a million worked there, as did 1.05 million French civilian labourers.[17]

In Norway the OT was involved in huge defence, transport and industrial projects, and around 60,000 Norwegian workers were employed by June 1941. The first big transports of Soviet prisoners of war arrived from August/September 1941 in transfers that would bring more than 100,000 Soviet, Polish and Yugoslav prisoners to Norway by the end of the conflict.[18] About a year before the end of the war, in April 1944, roughly half the total OT labour force of more than 79,000 in Norway and Denmark worked on fortifications, with the next biggest share going to railway building, which required more than 19,600 workers. The ratio of foreign workers to German personnel was more than thirteen to one for the railway programme, higher than in any other sector.[19] Out of more than 50,000 Norwegians working on German building sites in 1944, just over 11,800 were under the OT and more than 4,000 were assigned to the huge aluminium operation based in the country proposed by Heinrich Koppenberg, head of the Junkers aircraft firm.[20] In addition, OT records show that foreign workers from Denmark, France and Poland and other labourers from occupied Eastern Europe all worked for Nordische Aluminium AG (Nordag), the company created by the Reich Air Ministry to carry out the scheme.[21] More than 1,000 Danish workers were employed by Nordag by January 1944 out of over 10,300 who had gone to work in Norway.[22] In 1940 the Danish building contractor Christiani & Nielsen went to Norway to help build an aluminium plant with the OT and Luftwaffe in Aardal/Tyin.[23]

In Denmark itself, at least 74,000 Danes worked under the OT on anti-invasion defence works, while 80,000 worked in the Reich.[24] In the Netherlands, 450,000–500,000 Dutch labourers went to work in the Reich; at least 11,000 more were in German-occupied territories at the end of the war, especially on OT construction sites in Belgium and France. In Belgium, out of the 350,000–400,000 who went to work in the Reich, half were voluntary workers. On the territory of the former Czechoslovakia, thousands died in abysmal conditions in labour camps, including Flossenbürg subcamps such as Leitmeritz (Litoměřice), where predominantly Polish concentration-camp prisoners worked in an underground factory to produce engines and aircraft parts.[25] Elsewhere, in what became the protectorate of Bohemia and Moravia, residents were drafted into OT labour gangs digging trenches and constructing fortifications. Some civilians contacted by labour offices managed to avoid the summons. Czechoslovak-born Jaroslav S. was one of four men in a village about 100 kilometres southeast of Prague who were summoned by the local labour office in late 1944 to dig anti-tank ditches for the OT on the Austria–Hungary frontier. Unluckily for him, he was the only one who had to go, as the families of the other three pulled strings to avoid conscription. One had the support of the Catholic Church, another ran a large farm and the third used political contacts.[26]

Nazi grab for Soviet riches

Following Germany's invasion of the Soviet Union, labour was shifted from the Reich by the end of 1941 to vital projects identified by Hitler in the East. In the last months of Todt's life, major OT deployments were ordered into Soviet territory after an initial German OT force of just 20,000 in specialist motorised units followed the Wehrmacht into Russia. This extra manpower was for road building and other work, and the total OT force in the region in 1941-2 rose to 500,000, three-quarters of them Russian.[27] Dorsch estimated the workforce under the OT in occupied Soviet territory reached 800,000 for brief periods;[28] its average strength there was about half that number. In the first months of Operation Barbarossa, however, huge numbers of Soviet prisoners of war died as a result of shootings or murderous neglect in Wehrmacht compounds. As Todt strove to coordinate OT operations to improve transport links to aid German troops advancing into Soviet territory, it was Dorsch who highlighted the plight of these prisoners. Dorsch reported on the appalling conditions at a camp in Minsk some three weeks after the start of the German invasion. He described how 100,000 Soviet POWs and 40,000 civilians were packed so tightly into the camp that they were forced to relieve themselves where they stood. Guards shot prisoners, and some POWs went six to eight days without food. Civilian prisoners depended on getting something to eat from relatives, who waited in long queues to deliver provisions.[29] In line with Nazi racist principles branding Slavs as 'subhuman', as well as the ill-founded belief that the Eastern campaign would be another 'Blitzkrieg' victory, Soviet prisoners of war were considered dispensable. However, in October 1941 Hitler made a decisive intervention regarding slave labour which recognised that the Eastern front had turned into a war of attrition. The German dictator ordered Soviet prisoners of war to be deployed to work in the Reich for Germany's war effort. Even before then, the first shipments of Soviet POWs had arrived in Norway to work on major OT projects there.[30]

As the war continued, the sheer scale of the Third Reich's labour needs often proved impossible to meet. Because German labour was scarcely to be found as a result of repeated military drafts, the OT's manpower administrator Fritz Schmelter focused on foreigners. However, promises of their availability frequently proved empty. He requested 100,000 Italians be sent to Germany in 1944, but since this unrealistically high figure could not be provided by Sauckel, the requirement was lowered to 50,000. Despite Sauckel's promises of quick action, it was not until mid-June of that year that Schmelter announced the arrival of just 300 Italian military internees. Schmelter also sought large numbers of Soviet labourers, but once again Sauckel could not provide the requested workers. When Hungarian Jews were set to be exploited in the Third Reich's constant search for foreign labour, Himmler said in May 1944 he would transfer 200,000 Jews into concentration camps 'to deploy them on major construction sites of the OT and other tasks important for the war'.[31] Despite such statements by Himmler and directives by Hitler, the numbers of Hungarian Jews deported to the Reich remained well below those desired by industry and Speer's ministry. Addressing the Fighter Staff (Jägerstab) in late May, both Speer and Schmelter complained about this situation. Speer expressed scepticism about Dorsch's requirement for 220,000 labourers, including 100,000 Jews from Hungary, and commented that 'we have often made such calculations, but the people never came'. Schmelter, for his part, protested at the lack of younger male workers. 'Till now, two transports have arrived at the SS camp Auschwitz. For fighter construction were offered only children, women and old men with whom very little can be done ... Unless the next transports bring men of an age fit for work the whole action will not have much success.'[32] In the following month, even though Himmler had spoken of 200,000 Jews, Schmelter announced to aircraft industry representatives that just 20,000 Jewish women from Hungary and a further 20,000 women from concentration camps were available as labourers.[33]

During labour shortages, OT managers operating deep in occupied Soviet territory became desperate, as this note shows.

> Awaiting urgent reply when I can expect further supply of Polish labourers. Lack of workers approaching catastrophe. I beg you, do not leave me in the lurch.
> OT-Task Force Kertsch
> Signed: Dr. Ertl[34]

The appeal came from the OT engineer in charge of completing a bridge Hitler ordered in March 1943 to be built over the Kerch Strait from Crimea to the mainland. His message to Dr Schmelter in July 1943 followed a letter he had sent the previous month to OT headquarters in Berlin pleading for hundreds more Polish labourers. Out of 2,000 promised, only 369 had been sent and about one-third of those had escaped. Dr Ertl declared he could no longer work under such circumstances and project deadlines could not be met. Machines were constantly breaking down, and Polish labourers actually on site mostly did not possess the skills they were supposed to. All Dr Ertl's pleas were, in the event, for nothing. The bridge, being constructed beside a cable railway the OT completed that year, was only one-third finished when retreating German forces blew it up in October 1943.[35]

The Third Reich's wartime switch to heavy dependence on foreign labour in its economy was mirrored to the extreme in the OT workforce. From a virtually all-German pre-war strength of 340,000 for the Westwall, its labour force became predominantly foreign after the conflict started. Guidance issued by OT headquarters in April 1943 said tests had been carried out in south Russia to see whether 'Bolshevism' had extinguished good traits in the local population, but it had been established that 'prisoners of war are a valuable work force'.[36] After Hitler's decision in 1941 on Soviet prisoners of war, Sauckel's appointment as labour supremo heralded new levels of violence to procure foreign slave labourers for the Third Reich. He initiated brutal round-ups resulting in 2.8 million new foreign workers being sent to Germany between January 1942 and June 1943.[37] Over the same period, the SS was using prisoners in its concentration camps as a slave-labour pool to build up its armaments production inside the camps, rather than in Germany's existing armaments factories. In September 1942, however, Speer won Hitler's backing to break SS insistence on this practice and instead allow prisoners to work outside the camps and be deployed in the factories. This led to an explosion of satellite camps close to factories and construction sites, accelerated by a serious labour shortage in autumn 1943, when industry scrambled to acquire concentration-camp prisoners to keep their plants running. Many of the new subcamps were for the aircraft industry, which absorbed more than one-third of all working concentration-camp prisoners. As a result of intensive Allied bombing, which severely damaged the German aircraft industry in early 1944 and reduced production by up to two-thirds, massive programmes began to relocate armaments factories and fuel refineries underground. Under these schemes, foreign slave labourers toiled in hellish subterranean conditions under SS and OT supervision.[38] During the summer of 1944 the number of foreign civilian workers and prisoners of war employed in the Reich reached 7.6 million. The number of concentration-camp prisoners contributing to the German war effort at the end of that year was around 500,000, of whom 140,000 were labouring on SS engineer Hans Kammler's underground operations, 130,000 worked for the OT and 230,000 were employed by private industry.[39]

While manpower was a crucial resource for Germany as it expanded its empire, it was also eager to plunder newly acquired territory for raw materials. Having examined OT management of its forced- and slave-labour system, the enormous projects that could never have been undertaken without foreign workers are examined, first in occupied Europe and then in the Reich.

The Organisation Todt in Nazi-occupied Europe

Raw materials for armaments, as well as food, coal, oil and millions of foreign workers, represented what Germany saw as vital resources to be ruthlessly exploited in countries it occupied across Europe. Germany's shortage of fuel was its Achilles heel in the Second World War, and it sought to make up for its comparative lack of oil and other raw materials by both expanding its empire and producing synthetic replacements. Whereas the Anglo-American alliance was energy-rich, Germany lagged behind even after the Wehrmacht's stunning victories in Western Europe in 1939–40 captured vast new resources for the Third Reich. Hitler's invasion of the Soviet Union in June 1941 was, in part, to redress the balance and solve at a stroke what Germany saw as its excessive dependence on Soviet oil, food and other imports. Conquering the Eastern *Lebensraum*, while gaining complete control of those assets when German military power appeared invincible, looked like a gamble well worth taking.[40]

The Caucasus oilfields were a major (although ultimately unattainable) objective; other valuable commodities sought from the Soviet Union's vast reserves included phosphates, asbestos, chrome ore, manganese and nickel. But the Soviet Union, while offering vast potential riches, was not the only source of raw materials for Nazi Germany. The Third Reich also needed iron ore from Sweden, which in turn depended on German coal, and copper from the huge Bor mine in the Balkans. The OT was deeply involved in securing all these urgently needed raw materials to produce aircraft, tanks and munitions. Part of its task was to build road and rail links to transport the commodities. A major highway through occupied Soviet territory was the roughly 2,000-kilometres Transit Road IV, leading through Ukraine towards the Caucasus oilfields.[41] Another huge OT programme was to provide secure all-year-round road and rail links through Norway for Swedish iron ore to guard against a feared British blockade of sea routes.[42] Scandinavian ore was high grade, and securing it was one of the top priorities Hitler listed in 1936 when he set out his Four-Year Plan under Hermann Göring. The dictator declared that substitutes for other vital commodities Germany had to import, like petrol and rubber, should be developed so that the country's economy would be ready for war within the plan's timescale.[43] The state-run Hermann Göring Works was formed, despite strong opposition from private firms in heavy industry, to help attain Hitler's goals. It became a vast industrial conglomerate reaping the spoils of Europe. By 1940 Todt believed that its very size helped make economy measures more effective when introduced to preserve crucial raw materials like copper.[44] But when Speer took over in 1942, Hitler deliberately reduced the role of the Göring apparatus, as well as that of the armed forces, to minimise bureaucracy and assist rationalisation in armaments production and the war economy. The Hermann Göring Works was broken up and important sections of it brought under Speer's ministry in an efficiency drive.[45] Nazi Germany developed extensive programmes to reduce dependence on energy and commodity imports and boost self-sufficiency. The project to extract oil from shale in Estonia was launched, with German industry heavily involved and firms coming under IG Farben chief executive Carl Krauch as chemical industry supremo.[46] IG Farben also aimed to run a synthetic rubber plant at Auschwitz-Monowitz.[47]

Armaments and the Arctic railway

Since aircraft production took such a sizeable share of the Third Reich's war economy, the search for raw materials in occupied Europe to make aluminium serves as an example of how the OT played its part. The metal had been universally used in the aircraft industry since before the Second World War because of its lightness and strength when alloyed with materials such as copper. Following the Wehrmacht's invasion of Norway in April 1940, the Nordic country became the centre of a gigantic German programme to increase aluminium production. This was largely because Norway's vast potential for hydroelectric power could satisfy the high energy requirements of the aluminium manufacturing process. Koppenberg proposed the German aluminium venture and Göring gave his approval in November 1940. Under the scheme, Norway carried out the smelting and the raw aluminium was shipped south for processing at plants in central Germany.[48]

A key raw material in the production of aluminium is bauxite. This was sent to Norway from countries such as France, Croatia and Greece. The OT managed to quadruple output at the bauxite mine at Brignoles in southern France in 1943 through a combination of improving road and rail links with its 15,000-strong on-site workforce and supplying extra mining equipment. It also helped in bauxite mining in Mostar in Yugoslavia and on the shores of Lake Baloton in Hungary.[49] Copper needed for aluminium alloys in aircraft production, as well as for many other uses in the armaments industry and the war economy, was supplied by Sweden, which was Germany's most important source of the metal. The Third Reich's second biggest source of copper was the Bor mine in German-occupied Yugoslavia, where the OT mounted its largest operation in the region to exploit the metal and transport it back to Germany. The OT had an average of about 60,000 labourers at Bor, of whom only 3,000 were German.[50] The OT opened up a new mine, supplied equipment and built extensive new road and rail links to and from Bor, situated south of Belgrade. Apart from constructing administration buildings and accommodation for the work force, OT teams built a 75-kilometre railway from Bor to the Danube. The OT also constructed 150 kilometres of roads and a new port on the Danube at Kostolac.[51]

Koppenberg's scheme in Norway sucked in tens of thousands of workers, as well as large amounts of raw materials and funds. It was designed to counter American plans to increase its aluminium production to 450,000 tons per year by 1942. However, the vast cost, transport problems and shortfalls in raw materials and labour meant Koppenberg's own aluminium production forecasts proved wildly optimistic. He planned in late 1940, when German aluminium output was a world-leading 300,000 tons, to quadruple Norwegian annual production to at least 200,000 tons by 1944.[52] Speer revised the Norwegian aluminium project on becoming armaments minister in 1942, and the head of the OT in Norway, Willi Henne, undermined the scheme by suspending some of its operations and poaching labourers to work instead on major road and rail systems ordered by Hitler in Norway.[53]

This extraordinarily ambitious transport scheme in Norway was primarily designed to safeguard Scandinavian raw materials for Germany; but like the aluminium project, the plan ultimately fell well short of its promised goals. The road and rail system was to provide a secure land route for Swedish iron ore, which represented 83 per cent of German imports of the commodity in 1940. Germany had to import more than half its iron ore.[54] Apart from neutral Sweden, Norway was also a source of this key raw material. Norway's biggest reserves were in the far northeast and it exported 95 per cent of its ore, two-thirds of which went to Germany.[55] The iron ore was shipped via the Norwegian port of Narvik in the winter months, but Hitler feared the port could be seized by the British, thus blocking a vital commodity and strangling German armaments production. The planned road and rail links, stretching hundreds of kilometres along Norway's jagged coastline through mountainous Arctic areas, were therefore to provide an alternative route for the precious cargo. The road link was called Reichsstrasse 50 and was intended to be kept snow-free and passable for heavy trucks all year round travelling between Oslo and Kirkenes in the far north, a distance of around 2,500 kilometres. The OT took over the task from army engineers and the RAD in July 1941.[56]

Both Reichsstrasse 50 and the railway were examples of slave-labour projects in occupied Europe showing a complex interaction between the OT, the civilian administration, the SS and the Wehrmacht. Political intrigue, rivalry and also cooperation through mutual benefit manifested themselves at different times between different parties. Rivalry between Hitler's top representative in Norway, Reichskommissar Josef Terboven, and the Wehrmacht affected how slave labourers were controlled in labour camps set up for the Reichsstrasse 50, where the OT generally supervised SS-guarded labourers on work sites. Since the Wehrmacht was responsible for prisoners of war, Terboven was beholden to the military whenever he wanted to use Soviet or Polish POWs for his own construction projects. But he saw his chance of escaping this dependency with the arrival of 2,600 Yugoslav prisoners, whom German authorities designated as members of illegal 'gangs' rather than prisoners of war. In this way, automatic responsibility derived not to the Wehrmacht but to Terboven to accommodate, guard and deploy them for work. Since construction of the Reichsstrasse 50 came under the Main Technical Department in Terboven's administration and the Scandinavian branch of the OT, deploying the Yugoslavs on this project was operationally simple: Willi Henne was in charge of both. Terboven contrived to cooperate with the SS, rather than the military, in finding guards for the Yugoslavs and this was organised by Wilhelm Rediess, the higher SS and police leader (Höhere SS und Polizeiführer – HSSPF) in Norway. Former Dachau concentration-camp commandant Hans Loritz was appointed under Rediess in November 1942 and put in charge of labour camps set up for the Yugoslavs. Murderous conditions in the camps were reported in the foreign press. As a result, Terboven came under pressure and agreed to the remaining Yugoslav prisoners being transferred to Wehrmacht control in March 1943.[57]

As for the railway, this enormously costly and challenging task might never have been undertaken were it not one of Hitler's favourite projects in Norway. It illustrated how powerful individuals close to Hitler kept alive an unrealistic and ultimately doomed project which was in the end entirely run by the OT and resulted in misery or death for thousands of slave labourers. For very good reason, considering the geographical challenges and comparatively cheap alternative of sea transport, Norway possessed one of the least developed railway systems in Europe before the German invasion. Fritz Todt concluded on the basis of an aerial survey over northern Finland that construction of a railway in the region was not feasible. He informed Hitler of this in late 1941 and so the idea was buried, according to the German military commander in Norway, Nikolaus von Falkenhorst. But Terboven managed to revive it. He proposed a different route for the railway, and persuaded Hitler that the scheme was, after all, viable. While the original 1,200-kilometres railway had been planned to run from near Mo i Rana to Kirkenes, Terboven suggested its length be reduced by nearly one-third by cutting out the section between Narvik and Nordreisa. On this stretch, islands offered some protection for coastal shipping against enemy attack. He promised Hitler the railway would be completed within two years – an unrealistic pledge for such a technically demanding engineering feat in harsh terrain. It was early 1942 before Hitler gave his approval, and Todt was killed in February. Hitler therefore told Speer that, as well as shouldering all Todt's other responsibilities, the job of building the Arctic rail link fell to him.[58]

Even this did not finally launch the ill-fated railway from the planning stage into full-scale construction, although teams of engineers conducted surveys and huge volumes of material for the project were transported to sites along its planned route. In a last-minute twist, military setbacks for the Wehrmacht meant that von Falkenhorst persuaded Hitler to scrap the Arctic railway's most northerly section to Kirkenes. Hitler's change of heart on this aspect of the plan came shortly after Germany's momentous military defeat at Stalingrad in early 1943. He held steadfastly, though, to the southern section of railway reaching as far north as Narvik. After all the prevarications in the planning, in mid-1943 the OT took over the building of the railway entirely from army engineers, who had to be switched to the Eastern front. Progress constantly failed to match expectations. Further German military losses meant troops were forced to retreat southwards in autumn 1944, rendering the railway superfluous. A message to this effect was sent to Hitler, but blocked by the blindly loyal Keitel, head of the military High Command, who refused to disobey an order from the Führer to build the railway. Supplies sorely needed at home therefore continued to be shipped from Germany to Norway, where they were literally put on ice. By the end of the war only a fraction of the railway's original target length was built and the line was largely completed only up to Fauske, fewer than 200 kilometres north of Mo i Rana.[59]

The relentless search for raw materials for Germany's armaments industry extended across Europe. Having invaded Norway to ensure the flow of Swedish iron ore, Hitler took action elsewhere in Scandinavia, aiming to expand nickel production at Petsamo in Finland. The OT began work in the country in autumn 1941, and by mid-1943 its highest priority was to keep up nickel supplies from Finland, which provided about 90 per cent of Germany's needs. Roads had to be maintained to transport the nickel, partly in OT vehicles, while a 3.5-metre-thick reinforced-concrete shelter for the hydroelectric plant supplying the nickel works was built to protect it from Allied air attack.[60]

Aluminium was also used as a soft coating for tank rounds to prevent them deflecting off armour and to allow the hard core to penetrate. Tungsten was used for the armour-piercing core of the round, and the OT was involved in the mining of tungsten in France, including a site at Montbelleux near Fougères in the north.⁶¹ By agreement with the OT in mid-1942, the German firm Krupp exploited the Montbelleux mine and 50 tons of tungsten ore concentrates were sent to the Reich.⁶² In March 1943 Hitler approved a request for 1,000 more German workers to speed supplies of copper, chromium, molybdenum, antimony and lead from the Balkans. Chromium ore came chiefly in 1943–4 from Macedonian territory given to Bulgaria, as well as from Greece, Albania and Serbia.⁶³ The OT was heavily involved in exploiting chromium ore around Skopje and modernising operations at mountainside sites where pack animals had been used until 1941 to carry some of the ore down into the valley. Cable and narrow-gauge railways, roads and crushing plants were built. Elsewhere in the Balkans the OT built a cable railway and set up equipment and plants for an asbestos mine at Raška in Serbia.⁶⁴ Almost a quarter of the total supply of antimony, used as a metallic alloy in building submarines and tanks, came from Serbia. Molybdenum, used in refining steel, came chiefly from the Balkans and south Norway.⁶⁵ The OT also took part in expanding operations to extract manganese at Iacobeni mine in Romania.⁶⁶ In October 1943 manganese was desperately needed for use as a deoxidiser in crude-steel production, and 90 per cent of Germany's supplies came from the threatened Ukrainian Nikopol region. If Nikopol was lost, Speer estimated manganese stocks would only last for eleven or twelve months. A German bridgehead at the Dnieper River near Nikopol finally had to be abandoned in mid-February 1944.⁶⁷

The Organisation Todt in the east

In occupied Soviet territory, transport links to the Caucasus were given the highest priority. This was both to guarantee supplies to German troops on the Eastern front and to provide access to Soviet oilfields, which had figured prominently in Hitler's strategic calculations but in fact proved tantalisingly beyond his grasp. Extending the road network had added urgency because much of the Soviet railway system had been destroyed. The OT was given the task of developing 25,000 kilometres of roads in occupied Soviet territory, ranging from the most primitive to main highways stretching straight across the country into the east, known as transit roads.⁶⁸ The most northerly of these transit roads was numbered XII and the most southerly was IV, each with an OT engineer specifically responsible for it. OT maintenance depots were built every 50 kilometres on the transit roads. Factories to produce construction materials for these depots and OT bases were repaired and restarted.⁶⁹ Transit Road IV led to the Caucasus, connecting the part of Nazi-occupied Poland known as the General Government with Ukraine, and continuing southeast. The OT had the job of overseeing the development of this highway in cooperation with the SS. About 50,000 Ukrainian civilian slave labourers, as many prisoners of war and around 10,000 Jews were deployed along Transit Road IV in 1942.[70] It went via Rostov using a bridge built by the OT over the Don, which was frequently targeted in Russian air attacks. If this route was cut, an alternative way of supplying the troops was over the Kerch Strait from the Crimea to the Taman Peninsula.

Although Transit Road IV and supply lines towards the Caucasus remained vital as long as Germany continued to wage war in the East, Soviet forces were already driving German troops back from the oilfields they sought to capture in 1942. This prompted a desperate search for alternative sources of oil, resulting in the highest priority being given to an energy project in German-occupied Estonia. Total reserves of Estonian oil shale were then estimated at about 5 billion tonnes. Since contemporary methods allowed for 20 per cent extraction of oil from excavated shale, that represented a potential source of 1 billion tonnes of oil. Even before the launch of Operation Barbarossa into Russia in mid-1941, Germany's capture of France had prompted the new German state oil holding, Kontinentale Öl AG, to investigate how to exploit oil assets in territory mandated to France in the Middle East. Coupled with Polish and Russian oil under Kontinentale's control, the Nazi regime believed it could now overcome the problem of powering its planes, tanks and submarines. A sister company to Kontinentale, Baltöl, had been set up for the exploitation of Estonian oil shale in 1941. The OT was in charge of the technical side of the necessary construction work. After German military setbacks in the East culminated in defeat at Stalingrad, increasing the urgency of finding resources for Germany's war effort, the SS set up Vaivara concentration camp in autumn 1943, centred on the shale-oil works. Vaivara existed for about a year.[71] By February/March 1944 evacuations were under way as the Red Army advanced, and 12,500 prisoners of war were among those pulled out of Kiviöli, the site of a Vaivara subcamp and the centre of German industrial activity in Estonia, by the end of August 1944.[72]

During Germany's occupation of Estonia, the SS, the OT and Baltöl conducted the shale-oil operation. All three organisations exploited Jewish slave labour held in Vaivara, which contained about 9,000 prisoners in November 1943, but the shale-oil project had a very varied labour force. Baltöl relied at first on Soviet prisoners of war, many of whom were miners, for the bulk of its workforce. When the Wehrmacht, which was responsible for prisoners of war, switched these workers to military defence tasks, Baltöl turned to Jewish concentration-camp prisoners, although they still represented below one-sixth of its labourers. Other workers included civilian forced or slave labourers from numerous countries. The OT used Jewish prisoners, Soviet prisoners of war and civilian workers and forced or slave labourers from various countries, including Western Europe. Foremen on work sites were usually OT staff, and OT personnel sometimes acted as armed guards.[73]

Other major OT operations in occupied Soviet territory included vehicle and tank repair works at Pleskau, Riga, Minsk, Smolensk, Dnjepopetrowsk and elsewhere; construction of large-scale industrial plants and open-cast mines; construction of naval buildings in Reval, Odessa, Sebastopol and elsewhere; repair and restarting of plants producing construction materials and securing water supplies; and construction of accommodation for German troops close to the combat zone and in rearward occupied areas. One particularly challenging task for the OT was restarting Russia's then-biggest hydroelectric plant in Saporosje, on the Dnieper River. Despite considerable success, German engineers were compelled to blow up their own work as German forces were driven back. The OT also carried out rail improvements throughout Russia.[74]

Defence lines

As well as plundering Europe, the OT undertook massive tasks to fortify and protect the conquered territories whose assets were being stripped. This was to ensure the supply of raw materials and other resources continued. The OT built gigantic defence lines, the biggest of which was the Atlantic Wall. The remains of many of its bunkers, towers and gun emplacements, such as at 'Battery Todt' sites in northern France and coastal defences in Ørland in Norway, can still be seen today. The long series of Atlantic Wall fortifications were conceived to prevent an Allied invasion, which they spectacularly failed to do in 1944 when Allied troops landed in Normandy before thrusting eastwards to defeat Hitler. Before D-Day, Hitler had agreed to award the *Ritterkreuz* (Knight's Cross) to the OT regional chief in charge of the Atlantic Wall, Karl Weiß. Speer presented it to Weiß, but German embarrassment prevented a press notice being issued following the Allied assault in June.[75]

Plans for the Atlantic Wall gained special urgency in German military planning following setbacks on the Eastern front and with Hitler's declaration of war on the United States in December 1941. Hitler issued a directive on 23 March 1942 for the building of what was to become the cornerstone of his 'Fortress Europe'. The OT and army engineers cooperated in the task, although rivalry dating back to Hitler's intervention over the Westwall still simmered. As work on the Atlantic Wall progressed, Hitler himself was indignant at an army officer failing to acknowledge the work of the OT sufficiently in a Berlin newspaper in March 1943 and ordered that a counterbalancing article appear to praise the OT for its achievements, including the Westwall, and describe the role played by army engineers as secondary.[76] Coastal batteries and thousands of bunkers were constructed for the Atlantic Wall. In Norway alone, 400 batteries, including big guns near Harstad with a range of more than 40 kilometres, were installed by the end of 1944. They proved to be of questionable military value, and surviving records indicate never a shot was fired from any of the coastal batteries to defend German shipping.[77] In France similar defences were constructed that included super-heavy guns of the Battery Todt type. OT construction teams assigned to the Atlantic Wall built six submarine pens on the French coast at Brest, Lorient, St Nazaire, La Pallice, Bordeaux and Marseille. The Channel Islands off the French mainland attracted considerable attention from Hitler, who wanted them turned into fortresses to prevent any British attack. They had prestige value, being the only British soil conquered by Nazi Germany, and their fortification was to absorb one-twelfth of the resources needed for the entire Atlantic Wall.[78] Hitler worried about how to improve Atlantic Wall defences even in late 1943, when most positions defending key sites were largely finished.[79]

For the Atlantic Wall in Western Europe, the OT used a labour force of around 200,000. Of these, 16,000 were German labourers and a further 8,000 were members of the OT's own staff overseeing the construction work or OT personnel coopted from firms, with the rest of the workforce made up of foreign labourers.[80] Building the Atlantic Wall involved exceptionally hard labour – this was the case for all military defence installations sited along the coastline, whether they were heavy coastal batteries, submarine pens or launch sites in northern France for the 'wonder weapons' aimed at London.

After Germany's defeat at Stalingrad, Hitler ordered the OT in spring 1943 to present plans for an 'East Wall' defensive line to block a Red Army advance. Speer asked Hitler to designate separate construction sections for the OT and army engineers, to avoid conflicts over areas of responsibility. The dictator hoped the East Wall could be built within the period of Russia's seven frost-free months. He ordered in October that the northern section of the wall as far down as Minsk be tackled, and the OT's Russia-North group under Professor Giesler be held ready to undertake the task. Taking account of the shale-oil deposits in Estonia being exploited by the OT and Baltöl, he directed that the northern section of the East Wall take advantage of natural defences in the region, so it ran west of the Narva River, down alongside Lake Peipus and on to Pleskau. Work was begun in autumn 1943 on the development of a defence line 15 kilometres wide and 400 kilometres long between Lake Peipus and the Gulf of Finland, the so-called 'Panther Position'. By late autumn, however, advancing Red Army troops were already holding bridgeheads on the west bank of the Dnieper River.[81]

Wonder weapons

As the military situation worsened, German hopes were pinned increasingly on the country's engineers and 'wonder weapons' to reverse the tide of war. These included the A-4 rocket, later known as the V2. The rocket was the brainchild of Dr Wernher von Braun, a young SS engineer who was recruited by the United States after the war and became the father of the American NASA (National Aeronautics and Space Administration) space programme. A British air raid in August 1943 on the village of Peenemünde on the Baltic coast, site of the central German military testing facility for missiles, prompted a scramble to relocate A-4 rocket production to 'bomb-proof' facilities underground. The SS WVHA set up the satellite camp of Dora, in the Harz Mountains in central Germany, during the autumn in an existing tunnel system, where slave labourers worked in infernal conditions building facilities for rocket production. Hans Kammler, the SS engineer heading the WVHA's construction corps, was put in charge.[82] Before that, in the early stages of the rocket programme in spring 1943, the OT developed its plans for giant bunkers in northern France to act as launch sites for rockets aimed at England. The project for the large V2 rocket launch sites near Watten was codenamed 'Northwestern Power Station' (*Kraftwerk Nordwest*), but the installations were bombed before work could be completed.[83] The army's V2 rockets weighed 14 tons, including a 1-ton warhead, while the air force's V1 'Doodlebug' rocket was much smaller and had a shorter range. OT work crews began construction of ninety-six V1 launch sites in October 1943, but bombing destroyed most of them by December in that year.[84]

The OT was also heavily involved in building a launch site on the northern French coast for another weapon designed to target London: a high-pressure pump gun known as the 'Centipede' (*Tausendfüßler*), sited near Calais. Hitler closely followed its development.[85] The OT had around 5,000 workers excavating the site for the 'super-gun' in late 1943. The weapon consisted of a system of 150-millimetre super-guns with barrels more than 120 metres long placed in shafts embedded largely underground. The barrels of the gun were fitted at intervals with angled side chambers along their length to allow propelling charges to be fired automatically in succession to keep increasing the speed of the projectile before it left the gun. An underground railway, lifts and ammunition galleries enabled gunners to load and fire the weapon. Technical problems meant the weapon failed to reach its intended range. In August 1944 British air raids caused heavy damage to the site at Mimoyecques.[86]

The Organisation Todt in the Greater Reich

Having examined the ways in which the OT played a big part in helping to plunder occupied Europe's resources, it is necessary to investigate the role it played in exploiting them. The OT was a major player in the business of constructing armaments plants which needed the raw materials being delivered from abroad. Giant underground projects dominated OT operations in the final year of the war after the organisation partially withdrew from occupied Europe into the Greater Reich. The object of these vast subterranean construction programmes was to try to protect Germany's vital industries from devastating Allied bombing. Two major initiatives in the first half of 1944 led to fateful decisions condemning tens of thousands of slave labourers to toil in abysmal conditions: the creation of Speer's Fighter Staff (Jägerstab) on 1 March, and the launch in early summer of the Geilenberg programme, named after an official in Speer's armaments ministry.[87] The first was designed to boost fighter production, and the second to repair or relocate fuel refineries. A further subterranean project under OT management was the aptly named 'Riese' (Giant) network in Lower Silesia, incorporating a headquarters for Hitler and military facilities. Prisoners working under the OT in its underground projects suffered appallingly high death rates. Many of the victims came from a new source of foreign labour mercilessly exploited under the Third Reich in the final year of the war: Hungary's Jews. Germany occupied Hungary in March 1944 to prevent the country switching sides, as Italy had done some months previously, and to harness it more effectively to the German war effort. Out of some 765,000 Hungarian Jews who thus fell into German hands, about 458,000 were deported to Auschwitz, where around 350,000 were gassed. The remaining 108,000 who were deemed fit were sent to work in the Reich.[88]

As Allied armies forced the Wehrmacht to retreat further in 1944, the OT withdrew part of its labour force into the Greater Reich and acquired more powers than ever, gaining control of all military construction. The changes included unprecedented OT control over some of the Third Reich's biggest projects, spiralling death tolls among its foreign workers, an even larger deployment into the Greater Reich and the restructuring of the organisation there into eight administrative regions. These developments represented a watershed for the OT, and the horrors of the last year of the Second World War formed a distinct phase in the development of the organisation, much as it did for the SS-run concentration camps before the 'death marches' as camps were evacuated.[89]

Jet fighters

Hitler ordered the OT to carry out two Fighter Staff schemes centred on Dachau subcamp complexes, one at Kaufering and the other at Mühldorf am Inn, to mass produce Me-262 Messerschmitt jet fighters.[90] Kaufering was Dachau's largest subcamp network and, like Mühldorf, came under the OT's Task Group VI, headed by Hermann Giesler. Six semi-underground bunkers were originally to be built under plans presented to Hitler by Dorsch, protected by concrete up to 5 metres thick and containing factories to manufacture the jet fighters. In fact just four bunkers were started and two were abandoned, so that only Kaufering and Mühldorf remained. The Kaufering installation was 300 metres long, 90 metres wide and had six storeys.[91] The bunkers used a technique in which prefabricated concrete tunnel sections were made with railway tracks running through them. Gravel was thickly heaped on top of the sections, and then came layers of reinforced concrete. Once this concrete had set, the gravel was extracted through trapdoors in the tunnel and poured into railway wagons to be reused. The 'bomb-proof' roof could be extended section by section and the bunker's interior deepened and fitted out after extraction of all the gravel.

Both Kaufering and Mühldorf were only two-thirds completed. The prisoners' hard labour mostly involved construction, building sections of railway, and loading and unloading cement and other supplies. The OT was in charge of building the extremely primitive camps, where accommodation included shelters sunk into the ground with only a pitched roof remaining visible. The OT was also responsible for the prisoners' inadequate food and medical care. Mühldorf's SS commandant from late 1944 until the end of the war was Sturmbannführer Walter Adolf Langleist, who moved there after being in charge of Kaufering. Commandants of the Kaufering complex included SS-Hauptsturmführer Hans Aumeier, who was in charge from December 1944 to January 1945.[92]

During the final year of the war, the OT's own total labour force had reached around 1.5 million (end of September 1944), of whom nearly 838,000 were working in the Reich rather than in occupied Europe. Within the Reich, an influx of Hungarian Jews and slave labourers brought back with retreating German forces helped boost the OT's workforce in some of its new administrative regions where it controlled its highest-priority projects. In Deutschland VI, for instance, where Kaufering and Mühldorf were sited, the OT workforce increased to more than 112,000. In the northwest, its labour force in the Hansa region that included top-priority projects like the Valentin and Hornisse submarine-building works in Bremen reached nearly 89,000. Outside the Reich in parts of Europe still occupied by Germany, numbers were tumbling, but the OT's labour force in its Scandinavian region covering Norway increased sharply. The enlistment of more foreign workers and Norwegians meant the total rose to nearly 137,500, a surge of nearly 35 per cent by the end of September 1944 compared to August.[93] By the end of the war in Norway the OT's huge railway-building programme alone had a workforce of 30,000, mainly Soviet prisoners of war and civilian forced or slave labourers.[94]

While Norway's boost in labour totals bucked the trend in occupied Europe, OT worker totals climbed in the Reich. To acquire prisoners to work in Kaufering, Speer's Fighter Staff issued its requirements for labour and Jewish men and women were supplied from Auschwitz. From mid-1944, survivors of Polish and Lithuanian ghettos such as Litzmannstadt, Kauen, Kowno and Schaulen, as well as Hungarian Jews and small numbers of Jews from countries including the Netherlands, France, Italy and Czechoslovakia, were sent to Kaufering. The bigger camps in the complex contained 3,000–4,000 prisoners at times, while the smaller ones held a few hundred. According to lists drawn up by prisoner number 50272, a Luxembourg priest named Jules Jost, 28,838 Jewish prisoners arrived in Kaufering between 18 June 1944 and 9 March 1945. Because more transports arrived after that date, it can be estimated that between mid-June 1944 and the end of April 1945 around 30,000 prisoners went through Kaufering. Some 850 children and 4,200 women, mostly Hungarian Jews, were among these inmates. In the Mühldorf camp complex most of the slave labourers were Hungarian Jews. Four subcamps were set up near Mühldorf, of which two had 2,000–3,000 inmates and two were smaller. From 24 July 1944 the Mühldorf camp complex held 8,300 prisoners, of whom 7,500 were men and about 800 women.[95]

Apart from Kaufering and Mühldorf, the OT partly supervised a number of other Dachau subcamps. One was München-Riem, which was set up to hold hundreds of prisoners working to repair heavy damage caused by repeated Allied bombing of the airport there.[96] Another Dachau subcamp was Karlsfeld OT, set up around mid-1944, where OT staff supervised work sites. A former SS officer who was briefly camp leader said after the war that an average of 750 prisoners, predominantly Jews from Romania and Hungary, were held there. Most of the prisoners worked to repair bomb damage at Karlsfeld rail station, while others undertook bunker construction.[97]

The Dachau subcamp of Eching was founded in the final weeks of the war, but work by 500 prisoners to build an airfield runway under the SS and OT was abandoned just two weeks later.[98] The OT also used prisoners from the Dachau subcamp of Landshut, which existed from around September 1944 until the end of April 1945, to build a supply depot for the Wehrmacht. About 500 mostly Jewish prisoners, who were held under SS guard in a separate camp, worked under the OT levelling the area and constructing roads, a railway siding and buildings.[99]

Fuel, rockets and Hitler's headquarters

Huge resources were devoted to the operations under the Geilenberg programme and SS engineer Hans Kammler, yet the schemes were far from complete by the end of the war. Some project leaders and participating firms believed in the myth of success to the very end. As pressures and problems mounted, historian Jens-Christian Wagner concluded that OT and SS construction experts responsible for the implementation of projects on site often acted irrationally. Building plans were constantly changed, only to be replaced with still more ambitious schemes when they could not be maintained. 'The victims of this flight from reality were the forced labourers of the SS and OT deployed on the construction sites,' he wrote.[100] In the last year of the war, tens of thousands of concentration-camp prisoners died as a result of slave labour during the attempted relocation underground of the German armaments industry.

Up to 350,000 labourers worked overall on Geilenberg operations to repair or relocate fuel refineries underground. Mostly foreign civilian workers and prisoners of war were involved, but also tens of thousands of concentration-camp prisoners. Because the OT had many more skilled workers than were available to Kammler's staff and also had experience in overseeing prisoners on the Kaufering and Mühldorf projects, the organisation was used for many of the Geilenberg projects. Prisoners were always guarded by the SS, even in OT areas, but while cooperation was close between the two organisations, competition over labour resources caused friction between them. Attitudes of the SS and OT towards their workers, though, appeared similar. 'In the end, the OT Bauleiter (Construction Leaders), like the SS, showed scarcely any interest in keeping up the working strength of their forced labourers from the concentration camps,' Wagner wrote.[101]

In camps in the region of Kammler's underground network, prisoners worked under the OT on three projects outside the SS engineer's direct control. The Dachs IV project for an underground oil refinery near Osterode in the Harz Mountains was part of the Geilenberg programme. A workforce was assembled of German civilian employees, several thousand foreign civilian workers and prisoners of war, and several hundred German and Czech 'half-Jews' and *'jüdisch Versippte'* (Aryan partners married to Jews). Hundreds of concentration-camp prisoners from Buchenwald and Dora were also enlisted. Although it was clear the work could not be completed in time, the OT drove workers right to the end. When the SS withdrew its concentration-camp prisoners, the OT persisted with plans to deploy a further 2,600 miners and skilled workers. The two other projects run by the OT were called Turmalin and Porphyr, and were sited near Blankenburg on the northern edge of the Harz Mountains. Turmalin produced instruments which may have been for A-4 rockets, but the project was never finished. Construction work at the start of February 1945 was performed by around 400 mostly Jewish concentration-camp prisoners held at a subcamp near the work site and 300 foreign workers, including 200 Italian convicts for some of the time. Labour shortages at Turmalin could only really be explained by rivalry between the OT and Kammler's staff. Porphyr also suffered labour shortages; the project's purpose may have been the relocation underground of facilities to produce aircraft and tank parts, but it was never completed. Its subcamp held about 500 mostly Belgian inmates, while 400 German and foreign civilian workers, as well as some Jewish labourers, were also assigned to Porphyr.[102]

The Geilenberg programme included a complex of subcamps known as 'Wüste' (Desert) to extract oil from shale in Württemberg. Some of the prisoners, as well as the guards who tormented them, came from the Vaivara concentration camp in Estonia, where they had also laboured on a shale-oil project. These prisoners and guards were transferred following the evacuation of all Vaivara camps by autumn 1944 before the Red Army overran them. Just as the OT had been heavily involved in SS-run Vaivara, so was it deeply integrated into the Wüste shale-oil project on the fringes of the Swabian Alps. Seven subcamps of Natzweiler concentration camp came under the scheme. Dautmergen was the largest of a network that also included Bisingen. But whereas the Estonian shale oil was of very high quality, the deposits in Württemberg were mediocre. While shale-oil production in Estonia reached 3,585 tonnes in May 1944, output from the Wüste camps in Württemberg was never significant despite the deaths and misery suffered by the prisoners.[103] SS WVHA chief Oswald Pohl, who visited the Wüste camps in late 1944 and established that no early flow of oil could be expected, blamed the OT for the failure.[104]

As already mentioned, outside the Geilenberg scheme the OT ran a major subterranean complex called 'Riese' (Giant) in the Owl Mountains in Lower Silesia. It involved a 'bomb-proof' headquarters for Hitler and living quarters for 20,000 government personnel, military and SS. It was begun in November 1943, but was transferred from the original building company to the OT in April 1944 because of the slow pace of work.[105] After the OT took over, it ran the complex of up to 12 subcamps under Oberbauleitung Riese, based in Jedlina Zdrój (Bad Charlottenbrunn). The camp commandant was SS-Hauptsturmführer Albert Lütkemeyer, and Riese had a total of 853 SS guards. Building works covered an area of around 35 square kilometres, involving seven tunnel complexes. The construction complexes had between three and six tunnel entrances, and were from 500 metres to 3 kilometres long. The OT assigned various building firms to carry out the project, including Sager & Woerner. Speer told post-war interrogators how he had argued against big underground projects like Riese, telling Hitler: 'Bombers cannot be fought with concrete, only with fighter planes.'[106] Because of the advancing front, construction of Riese was halted in January/February 1945 and a number of tunnels were blown up.[107]

Construction of Riese had originally been started using exclusively prisoners of war and forced or slave labourers in four labour camps. When the OT took over, however, most of the 13,300 Jewish workers on the project were prisoners supplied by the SS from Gross-Rosen concentration camp. Between May and October 1944 the SS sent regular transports of Jewish prisoners from Auschwitz to Riese. About 70 per cent came from Hungary and the Hungarian region of Transylvania, and 25 per cent were Polish Jews from the Łódź ghetto and Krakau-Plaszów concentration camp. Smaller prisoner groups came from Greece, Czechoslovakia, Germany, Austria, Yugoslavia, Italy, France, Belgium, Luxembourg and the Netherlands. The OT was responsible for the workers' deployment, rations, accommodation and clothing.[108]

Navy projects

After Speer succeeded in acquiring the resources of the construction departments of both the navy and the air force in May–June 1944, two of Germany's most prestigious large-scale naval projects came under OT control:[109] the Valentin and Hornisse bunkers in which submarines were built. They serve as examples of how the OT gained responsibility for programmes of the highest priority in this manner, whose urgency Speer was at pains to emphasise. Speer declared as late as February 1945 in the final stages of the war that 'the soon to be completed submarine building works *Valentin* and *Hornisse* must be speeded up by all means'.[110] His appeal would have applied still more pressure on the Bremen shipyard construction teams under Marinenoberbaurat Edo Meiners, who had run the Valentin project for the navy and remained in charge after the OT takeover. Meiners became head of the OT Oberbauleitung Unterweser and had responsibility for both Valentin and Hornisse. Up to 10,000 labourers worked daily at the huge Valentin site, including prisoners of war, civilian forced or slave labourers and concentration-camp prisoners. The last category comprised around 2,000 prisoners from the Neuengamme subcamp of Bremen-Farge.[111] Just after the OT took control, the organisation's records showed in July 1944 that a workforce of 6,462 from a variety of OT and other camps laboured under the 'OT-Oberbauleitung Unterweser, Bremen-Farge'.[112]

Last-ditch defences

As the Red Army advanced westwards in 1944, the OT oversaw construction of major defence installations such as bunkers and anti-tank ditches on Germany's Eastern front. These included some major camp complexes along the Vistula River, in former Polish territory conquered by Germany in 1939, as well as in areas further west. They had one remarkable thing in common for tasks conducted by a specialist construction agency such as the OT and involving hard physical labour: the prisoners were Jewish women. In the early years of the war, improvement works along the Vistula River requiring tens of thousands of slave labourers had been a vital component of German settlement plans in the region to promote agriculture and transport for ethnic German settlers on land from which the Polish population was to be largely removed. The scheme prompted Hans Frank, head of the part of occupied Poland known as the General Government, to declare in May 1940:

> Every question that is posed here in the East regarding reconstruction has to address the problem of regulating the Vistula. If the Vistula is not developed, only a quarter of these areas will be accessible altogether. But if it is developed from source to mouth, in a grandiose and modern fashion, it will have an immense colonizing significance for the Germanness of the East.[113]

In 1944, however, the task was to bolster defences against the Russian advance in an area which Speer was urging as late as March 1945 should be defended to the last man. Although he opposed the wanton destruction of German industry in a 'scorched-earth' policy, Speer proposed to Hitler a robust defence of the region between the Rhein and the Vistula, where the Red Army was halted at that stage. He believed 'a dogged defence of the current front line for a few weeks may yet demand respect from the enemy and may yet be able to influence the end of the war in a positive direction'.[114] Some six months before Speer wrote these words, thousands of Jewish women were labouring under the OT to shore up German defence positions in the region. Two of the biggest subcamps of Stutthof concentration camp held the female Jewish prisoners in two OT construction detachments working on defence installations in the region of the Vistula River. One of the OT construction units was called 'Ostland', based in Elbing, the other 'Weichsel' (Vistula), based in Thorn (Toruń). The OT Elbing complex, which was guarded by the SS, was formed in August 1944 as part of the Stutthof concentration-camp network. In response to a request from the OT, the Thorn complex was formed on 24 August 1944 under the overall supervision of the OT.[115] The SS in Stutthof concentration camp sent 10,000 Jewish women in August 1944 to be divided equally between Ostland and Weichsel, which in total received about 30,000 prisoners from Stutthof.[116]

Another OT project exploiting female Jewish labour to fortify the eastern border of the Reich with anti-tank ditches, trenches and defensive walls was known as 'Unternehmen Bartold' (Operation Bartold). Conditions were harsh in the camps accommodating these women, which were set up in Silesia from October 1944 as subcamps of Gross-Rosen concentration camp. They included Hochweiler, Kurzbach, Birnbäumel and Schlesiersee I and II. Five thousand Jewish women were sent from Auschwitz and divided between the camps.[117]

Hitler and the Organisation Todt

This examination of OT operations demonstrates the breathtaking extent of the organisation's plunder of Nazi-occupied Europe's raw materials and exploitation of foreign workers for the benefit of the Third Reich's war economy. Regarding foreign slave labourers, Hitler made three significant policy changes that had dramatic repercussions for the OT. The first was the dictator's announcement in October 1941 that Soviet prisoners of war should be deployed to work for Germany's war effort. The two other major changes were the appointment of Fritz Sauckel in March 1942, which led to the round-up of millions of Soviet civilians deemed imperative for Germany's labour needs, and the order in early 1944 that Jews should return as labourers to the Reich, which had previously been declared 'Jew-free'. This last measure had a particular impact on the OT, which had previously operated almost exclusively in German-occupied Europe, as it partially retreated with the Wehrmacht into the Greater Reich in the final year of the war. Hitler explained his change of heart to a meeting of NSDAP Reichsleiter and Gauleiter, saying that Hungarian Jews were 'to supply useful work for our war aims'.[118] The OT played a significant role in 1944–5 in the brutal and murderous treatment of tens of thousands of Hungarian Jews exploited as slave labourers. The men, women and children, among more than 400,000 deported from Hungary within eight weeks in the largest such operation in the Nazi persecution of the Jews, toiled on huge subterranean projects such as Riese and the jet-fighter factories, as well as on fortifications requiring extreme hard labour.[119]

Analysis of OT operations shows how Hitler repeatedly chose the OT to carry out projects he considered of the utmost priority. At the same time, it reveals that while the dictator often pointed to the OT's early success with the Westwall, he continued to rely on the organisation late in the war when it suffered disastrous failures. Nazi Germany's hopes were pinned on OT engineers to help deliver 'wonder weapons', subterranean plants to produce jet fighters and desperately needed fuel to turn the tide of war. However, Germany headed instead to defeat, and the programmes to relocate German industry underground proved less able to produce high-tech aircraft and rockets than to create hellish places of death for slave labourers.

Catastrophic conditions in the Dachau subcamps for the OT's underground plane factories caused huge loss of life among the prisoners. When viewed purely in terms of delivering what their designers intended, Kaufering and Mühldorf also represented significant failures for the OT. They were not the only examples of the OT disappointing Hitler, and this raises the question of why he kept faith in the organisation. Among other major projects principally managed by the OT, the Atlantic Wall proved ineffective as a bulwark against the D-Day Allied landings. It could be argued in this case that the OT successfully completed what turned out to be a critically flawed military concept. But a string of other projects existed where the OT fell far short: Dorsch broke his promise to Hitler to finish the jet-fighter factories in six months, and they were still not ready by the end of the war; in Norway, the Arctic railway on which Hitler set so much store progressed at a snail's pace and never came anywhere near completion; and the Wüste shale-oil scheme in the Reich never produced any significant amount of fuel.

So why did Hitler persist in turning to the OT to carry out what he considered to be programmes vital to the war? It was true that OT 'failures' (in terms of measuring up to the regime's requirements) multiplied in the later stages of the war, when resources and time were short. As Allied victory neared, Hitler's options narrowed. Increasingly unrealistic hopes were placed on the shoulders of the nation's scientists and OT engineers to snatch victory from the jaws of defeat with the power of technology. Failures had to be balanced against what appeared to Nazi leaders as the tantalising promise of a military turnaround. In the OT's favour, it had earned a considerable store of credit with its Nazi paymasters through past successes. It had benefited, too, from being led for most of the war by the dictator's most favoured ministers. Hitler trusted Todt, while Speer was considered the Führer's 'heir apparent' before relations became more volatile in the final months of the conflict. The OT's achievements were considerable and Hitler had repeatedly praised the organisation to the detriment of the Wehrmacht, notably when comparing OT and army engineers' efforts in building the Westwall and Atlantic Wall. He congratulated OT workers for their swift repair of strategic Ruhr dams blasted in the British Dambuster raid in May 1943.[120] He praised them for building transport links in 1943 over the Kerch Strait, supplying troops heading to the Caucasus.[121] Putting Dorsch in charge of building underground factories for fighter planes in 1944, he said the OT's performance as a construction agency was unsurpassed.[122]

Viewed as a whole, the OT's balance sheet remained positive in Hitler's eyes for most of the war and only tipped seriously into the red in the final stages of the conflict. At this stage, military setbacks and diminishing resources enforced the need for compromise. Hitler entrusted the OT with his most cherished projects virtually to the end.

On all its projects the OT mostly worked in close cooperation with the SS, the Wehrmacht or industry, and sometimes with all three. The interaction between these key players in the exploitation of foreign slave labourers under the Third Reich, as well as between the OT and the Nazi Party, is the subject of the next chapter. How did they share responsibilities, what goals were they each pursuing and what determined their share of control over individual programmes? Intense rivalries between the partners were inevitable. The extent to which the OT succeeded in furthering its objectives beyond those of its competitors would determine its future.

3

The Organisation Todt in the Nazi system

After a trip to the Arctic with a violinist and a conjuror to boost the morale of OT units over Christmas 1943 and celebrate the New Year at the start of 1944, Speer fell ill and became easy prey to intrigues swirling in Berlin while he lay confined to his hospital bed. Speer's power had reached a peak in mid-1943, when he was widely seen as having become Hitler's heir apparent. Moves to undermine Speer by Bormann and Göring, once Hitler's unchallenged deputy, led to one of Nazi Germany's most dramatic wartime political crises, in which the armaments minister and effective controller of the Third Reich's economy threatened to resign. The drama revolved around the OT and Speer's deputy in the organisation, Xaver Dorsch. It was symptomatic of the shifting alliances and rivalries between the various power centres of the Third Reich, on this occasion chiefly involving Speer as head of a vital ministry and leader of the OT, Bormann as head of the Nazi Party Chancery and Hitler's secretary, and Göring as leader of the Lutfwaffe. Göring was also head of the Four-Year Plan, but his hold on the economy had been wrested away by Speer's successful manoeuvring. The Organisation Todt was central to the plot because first Bormann, then Göring, used Dorsch to try to achieve their own ends. The result was that Hitler commissioned Dorsch directly to build six underground factories for jet-fighter planes, including those later undertaken at Kaufering and Mühldorf, enraging the incapacitated Speer and nearly bringing about his downfall.[1]

The crisis was important because it illustrated once again how much faith the dictator placed in the capabilities of the OT and how powerful the organisation became, especially in the final year of the war. It also showed how Speer, formidable armaments minister that he was, could ill afford to drop his guard in matters regarding the OT. Both Göring and Bormann had become jealous that Speer had so obviously won Hitler's favour, with the former smarting not only from Speer's political victories over him but also from a more general loss of prestige due to a devastating Allied bombing campaign his Luftwaffe had failed to prevent. Both Speer's rivals seized their opportunity when his illness physically removed him from the political action, hoping to exploit the weaknesses of a minister who possessed no power base of his own and depended so heavily on Hitler's patronage. Bormann had gathered information on Speer's long-standing collaborators, filing away details on their 'anti-Party' attitudes that could be used to discredit the armaments minister. This 'evidence' of political heterodoxy among Speer's closest confidants was fed to Bormann repeatedly by a very well-placed informant: Xaver Dorsch. Speer managed to have the documents containing this information extracted from a sealed filing cabinet by unscrewing the back panel, and sent to him in Hohenlychen hospital.[2] When he discovered that Dorsch, at Bormann's instigation, had spoken to Hitler of 'worries' Speer's ministry was causing him and the OT, Speer wrote a rambling, agitated note to the Führer, telling him about the machinations of a 'camarilla' around him and Dorsch's 'breach of trust'. Reflecting the depth of his anger and perhaps his own isolation and insecurity in hospital, Speer wrote that he thought it necessary to discipline one official in his ministry by sending him to a concentration camp, and that Dorsch should be sacked.[3]

Hitler delayed any response and Speer's health deteriorated. Although initially in hospital because of a knee injury, there were complications. His doctor was Himmler's favourite SS physician, Professor Karl Gebhardt, who carried out experiments on inmates of Ravensbrück concentration camp and was executed in 1948 after being sentenced to death in Nuremberg. Speer claimed after the war, when he was anxious to distance himself from the SS, that he narrowly escaped being murdered in Hohenlychen because Himmler wanted him out of the way.[4] Given the close cooperation between Himmler and Speer before and after the armaments minister's stay in Hohenlychen, as well as the ease with which Gebhardt could have dispatched his patient in a 'natural' death if Himmler had really desired it, this is highly implausible.[5] Speer did recover, and was moved to a castle near Merano to convalesce.[6]

While Speer was still recuperating, Göring used Dorsch in his plot to undermine the armaments minister, inviting the deputy head of the OT to accompany him to conferences with Hitler as an engineering expert. At such a conference in mid-April 1944, Hitler showed enthusiasm for Dorsch's plan to construct 'bomb-proof' underground bunkers to manufacture fighter planes, and was assured by the OT engineer that it would be feasible to build them within six months. Hitler told Dorsch only the OT could build such installations, and he would direct that it should carry out large-scale building projects in the Reich in future. This was despite Speer's known views that plans for such large bunkers for plane factories would drain resources from other high-priority arms programmes. Hitler declared the output of the OT 'far outdid the achievements of the Panama Canal'. He pointed to attainments even before the OT's official formation, namely the *Autobahnen*, as well as subsequent construction of the Westwall and Atlantic Wall. As a result of this discussion, Hitler placed Dorsch directly under him and ordered the OT engineer to construct six underground bunkers, handing a major victory to Göring.[7]

Speer responded with a letter proposing a reorganisation to avoid friction between the OT and his ministry's construction department. Dorsch's responsibility would be restricted to the occupied territories, while two of Speer's closest collaborators, Willi Henne and Walter Brugmann, would respectively be in charge of the underground bunkers and in overall control of construction. If Hitler found this unacceptable, Speer would resign. Hitler reacted with fury, rejecting Speer's proposals and calling his resignation threat 'impertinent'. Reluctantly, though, he later sent a message via Erhard Milch of the Reich Air Ministry, who accordingly assured Speer that the Führer 'holds you dear'.[8] Speer's initial reaction was to hold firm to his original demands, but after several hours he relented. He insisted that Dorsch be placed under his authority, however, and drafted a letter ordering Dorsch to build the six 'mushroom bunkers'. Hitler signed it the next day. When Speer flew to see Hitler in person, the reconciliation appeared complete. Speer officially presented Dorsch to the dictator as the new head of the building sector under Speer's authority. Göring did not conceal his fury, while Bormann assured Speer of his steadfast comradeship.[9]

Speer's reimposition of control did not hide the fact that he had been weakened and forced to grant Dorsch greater authority. All the same, he soon managed to notch up another success against his rival Göring. The Luftwaffe chief's steepening fall from grace because of Germany's ineffective fighter response rendered him vulnerable. Hitler agreed in June to Speer's proposal that aerial armaments be absorbed into his ministry, thus capturing a sector that had previously escaped his economic empire. Since a bridgehead had been established with Hitler's order for the OT to build the six huge underground bunkers for fighter-plane production, expanding control to the rest of the sector seemed a logical step. As part of the agreement for the bunkers, construction in the Reich was reorganised to create Amt Bau-OT, which meant merging OT operations with those of all construction in the Reich under Speer's ministry.[10] Speer was in overall control, and took credit when fighter-plane production more than doubled as a result of wider efforts to increase Germany's output. Dorsch, whose failure to complete the underground bunkers in the promised six months rapidly diminished him in Hitler's eyes, headed the new structure.[11]

The plotters who manipulated Dorsch against Speer provoked a crisis demonstrating the effects of the Nazi polycratic system.[12] The OT, which was at the centre of events, became ensnared in a conspiracy involving key figures from competing power centres. The OT collaborated constantly in its normal operations with these major players, but in this instance representatives of the military and the Nazi Party (respectively Göring and Bormann) conspired to bring the OT leader down. The fact that the OT was so central to the plot underlines how essential it is to revise early understanding of Nazi power centres and include the organisation among them. A landmark study by the German-American social scientist Franz Neumann in 1942 restricted the cartel of Nazi power blocs chiefly to the army, big business, the civil service and the NSDAP.[13] Since then, researchers have begun to accept that the OT should take its place among the principal Nazi power centres.[14] We have seen how Hitler used the OT to help project Germany's imperial might to the world, and how the organisation reaped the spoils of Europe for the Third Reich. Its relations with other Nazi power blocs must now be investigated to see how far the OT was able to hold its own against its rivals, or surpass them.

To analyse the fiercely competitive environment in which the OT found itself, the organisation's dealings with the SS, industry, the Wehrmacht and the Nazi Party are examined in turn. The first three were the OT's main partners in exploiting slave labour, while the Nazi Party was the other powerful entity with which it dealt. The question must be asked as to why each or any of them needed the OT. What were the OT's strengths and weaknesses, and what qualities did it seek in the other organisations to help achieve its goals? How important was Hitler's influence in the OT's relationship with its partners? Could slave labour have successfully driven the Third Reich's economy without the OT? All these questions are addressed in this chapter, and a summary of conclusions is presented at the end.

The Organisation Todt and the SS

The SS and the OT cooperated extensively in exploiting foreign slave labour, but competed for ever-diminishing resources as Himmler strove to develop an economic empire, build settlement outposts in conquered Eastern territory and control a share of arms production. Before the war, Himmler and Speer had discovered a way in which they could work together while the future armaments minister was still primarily occupied with plans to rebuild Berlin. Himmler and

Speer reached a deal in 1938 under which concentration-camp prisoners were used to produce granite and bricks for new buildings for the German capital. Speer provided the funds from his Berlin reconstruction budget to enable the SS to develop and build its own quarries and factories to supply these materials. Previous SS forays into industry had been for more ideological than economic purposes, including a porcelain manufacturer whose products reflected Himmler's artistic tastes and included statuettes of members of the Hitler Youth. This new move, however, was far more significant, and Himmler looked to Oswald Pohl, whom he had appointed head of SS administration, to maximise its economic potential. The creation and expansion of a major SS enterprise, the German Earth and Stone Works (Deutsche Erd- und Steinwerke GmbH – DESt), was central to the scheme. Himmler's accord with Speer enabled him to solve a number of problems, including constant criticism about the size of his concentration camps and wastage of manpower at a time of acute labour shortage. Under the agreement with Speer, these protests could readily be silenced since the prisoners were producing supplies for a prestigious project. Another concern of Himmler's was to retain control of prisoners being sent out to work, but that was solved if the businesses in which they laboured belonged to the SS.[15]

These schemes failed dismally, but they proved to be a milestone in the history of the concentration-camp system. An SS brickworks at Oranienburg was a disaster, having to be rebuilt using a different production method. As for the SS supply of granite, Speer obtained a poor return from his bargain because the product was not of a high enough quality for buildings in Germany's planned imperial capital. All the same, this did not stop Speer from further collaboration with the SS in other projects. The SS established concerns in annexed or occupied territories, where the OT almost exclusively worked for most of the war. These included Poland and France, where the DESt set up a quarry near Natzweiler concentration camp in late 1940. Speer had noticed a remarkable red granite there on an inspection tour, and prisoners were used as slave labour to exploit it.[16]

Many SS concerns suffered from a lack of technical know-how and commercial expertise, but there were economic successes, such as the Texled firm supplying clothes for SS armed units. Crucial factors in this success were that the company was run by a businessman and a tailor, while women prisoners in Ravensbrück concentration camp were employed using modern sewing machines. Texled's profits appeared to prove, in the words of historian Michael Thad Allen, that 'there is no inherent contradiction between modern business organization, slavery, and barbaric ideology'.[17] While the DESt granite and brick ventures were totally mismanaged, they had set a template for further cooperation. The

Himmler–Speer deal could therefore be seen as having helped to persuade Nazi decision-makers that sending people to concentration camps could be justified economically. This paved the way for expansion of the slave-labour system and an explosive increase in the camps and their satellites.

The OT came to depend heavily on concentration-camp prisoners supplied by the SS to help satisfy its labour needs, but the two organisations competed to exploit other categories of foreign workers. This was especially true in German-occupied Eastern territory, where Himmler, in his capacity as Reich commissioner for the strengthening of the German people, sought labourers, including prisoners of war and civilians, to build settlement outposts. The SS competed largely in vain with the Wehrmacht and the OT for the huge numbers of foreign workers required to achieve its goal. The Wehrmacht's tasks in this region, such as defence installations and securing supply routes for the German armies, were all carried out within the framework of its cooperation with the OT. There was thus limited remaining leeway for the SS to acquire the workers it needed to build police outposts and SS bases required for settlements. SS plans to prepare the eastern *Lebensraum* for large-scale German settlement received a further blow when the OT took over all technical operations in the East, significantly boosting its profile in an area of supreme ideological importance for Nazi racist expansion. This takeover wrested control from civilian administrations in a vital sector in areas like the Baltics, Ukraine and other Soviet regions, while further reducing SS chances of obtaining the labour it needed. The measure in favour of the OT represented one of the biggest shake-ups involving the organisation in the occupied East, and occurred shortly after Speer took office. A decree by Hitler in June 1942 laid down that Speer would take over all matters in the occupied East regarding armaments, construction, energy, road building, waterways, ports and the water industry.[18] This had most impact in southern areas, where the OT greatly increased its operations in Ukraine in food production and coal mining. Other big areas of expansion included river transport, irrigation and the repair of the huge hydroelectric plant at Saporosje, on the Dnieper River.[19] These OT operations, as well as others carried out in cooperation with the Wehrmacht, undermined SS plans to exploit Soviet workers for its own ends. Himmler's plans to obtain sufficient labour for building settlement outposts using concentration-camp inmates, Soviet prisoners of war and Jews all ultimately foundered, in part because so many of these prisoners died.

As a result the SS had to look elsewhere, and the OT became its model for exploiting one further resource: private firms with skilled workers and specialist equipment, interlinked under so-called SS front-worker enterprises (SS

Frontarbeiterunternehmen). The SS disposed of private firms in the occupied territories in the same manner as the OT, which grouped together individual firms operating under contract to the OT but remaining formally independent. The name SS *Frontarbeiter* echoed the one given to core personnel in the OT, known as OT *Frontarbeiter*, working in units providing close support to German front-line troops and typically tasked with repairing bridges and communications. The way in which the SS copied OT practices was so close that, just as OT *Frontarbeiter* were accorded the status of Wehrmacht auxiliaries, so SS *Frontarbeiter* were designated 'Wehrmacht auxiliaries of the Waffen-SS', coming under the SS disciplinary code. In addition, what was possibly the first SS front-worker enterprise actually worked for the OT. However, even this latest SS attempt to marshal scarce labour resources went awry, and cooperation with private construction firms was anything but harmonious. Since the Dutch were considered 'Germanic', Pohl's WVHA tried in 1942 to engage Dutch firms to build bases on occupied Soviet territory. The following year the director of the Dutch firm Nederlandsche Oost Bouw NV (N.O.B.) complained that Dutch workers were not treated as members of a '*Brudervolk*', but like prisoners of war or slaves who had to go around in rags, and he blamed the SS for their misery. In a devastating criticism of cooperation between N.O.B and the WVHA, his report stated: 'With the OT, everything is much better organised.'[20]

The SS *Frontarbeiterunternehmen* never even came close to solving the labour problem for the construction of bases for Eastern settlements, and the SS plans for developing its own armaments plants also failed to be realised fully. The SS had little success in its efforts to cooperate with industry from 1940 to 1942 because firms shrank from using concentration-camp prisoners while alternatives were available. The SS also had little interest at that time in hiring out prisoners.[21] However, Fritz Todt's death in February 1942 and the advent of Hitler's favourite, Speer, brought about a decisive change in the organisation of the armaments production industry.[22] This was coupled with radical change in the management of the supply of labour with the appointment of the 'strong man', Fritz Sauckel. This transformation led Himmler to fear he would lose control of the concentration camps and their prisoners because of these major shifts affecting the armaments industry and labour needs, so he hurriedly integrated the Inspektion der Konzentrationslager (IKL, the SS Inspectorate of Concentration Camps) into Pohl's WVHA on 16 March 1942, just five days before Sauckel was installed. This absorption of the concentration camps into the WVHA prompted Pohl to declare that his initial aim was to boost armaments production and drive prisoners until they dropped.[23]

Time and again, Speer managed to press his advantage as the SS strove to expand its business interests and armaments production. In April 1943 Speer complained to Himmler that the SS was wasting its resources. Himmler's own efforts to cooperate with the arms industry always remained of little significance, and SS efforts to gain control of production in concentration-camp factories were also largely in vain. Speer, who backed business in this tussle, explained to Himmler that industrialists were 'not keen to build up the SS as competition'.[24] Despite these humiliations, the SS continued to pursue its goals in armaments production. Its biggest operation was an underground factory for V2 rockets in the Harz Mountains, which was built by prisoners from the Buchenwald subcamp Dora from August 1943 under Hans Kammler. This followed the British air raid on the German missile testing facility at Peenemünde, prompting Hitler to insist that armaments production and vital German industry be protected underground from Allied bombs. In February 1944, when Sauckel was failing to round up enough foreign workers for the armaments industry, Speer wrote to Himmler and asked him 'to help armaments to an even greater extent than before with the deployment of concentration camp prisoners in places where I view this as particularly urgent'.[25] The WVHA therefore made every effort to increase prisoner numbers in the concentration camps, which spread their tentacles throughout Germany by means of satellite camps to put prisoners close to factory sites. By mid-1944, however, Speer had succeeded in persuading Hitler that he should have at his disposal all the labour force available for armaments production, so his Armaments Ministry not only controlled foreign workers rounded up by Sauckel but also determined where concentration-camp prisoners should be deployed. Speer's appointment of Kammler to the Fighter Staff greatly raised the profile of the SS in the armaments sector, and Kammler's SS construction department became one of the biggest building concerns in Germany. In terms of operations to build subterranean factories, it was second only to the OT. Speer, however, gained the upper hand by placing all construction operations in the Reich under the OT in June 1944.[26] The SS construction enterprise was drawn organisationally ever more under Speer's Armaments Ministry and the OT, which became known as the OT Construction Office (Amt Bau-OT) and also came to control army, navy and air force building operations.[27]

In the Third Reich's last, desperate year of the war, Amt Bau-OT thus ran all construction for the war effort, including a large part of the two massive schemes to relocate armaments and fuel production underground. Despite the inevitable frictions, SS and OT cooperation remained extensive. To head off conflicts and ensure the SS could wield as much influence as possible in its dealings with the OT and other agencies, the SS leadership appointed officers to powerful posts enabling them to take wide-ranging decisions to protect SS interests. Martin Weiss, a former SS commandant of Neuengamme and Dachau, simultaneously represented the interests of the WVHA's Office Group D in dealings with the OT, ministries and Kammler's staff concerning vital armaments projects. These included the top-priority Kaufering and Mühldorf projects within the Fighter Staff programme. Both these subcamp networks outstripped their main camp of Dachau in size, numbers of prisoners and economic importance, so Weiss focused his attention on them. When he arrived in Mühldorf in October 1944, he viewed his task as being the technical SS link man with the OT Construction Office. Unusually for an SS officer in the concentration-camp system, he had excellent professional credentials, being a qualified machinist and electrical engineer. He was arrested in Mühldorf in May 1945, sentenced to death in the Dachau war crimes trial the same year and hanged in May 1946.[28]

Although schemes like Kaufering and Mühldorf ultimately proved fruitless and a disastrous waste of diminishing resources, this did not stop appallingly high death rates and suffering among the slave labourers forced to work on them. The SS jealously guarded its control of concentration-camp prisoners, and any transfer of labourers by OT staff could bring a sharp rebuke. Because of the wide powers granted to both the Fighter Staff and Geilenberg, senior figures in Himmler's concentration-camp empire saw their authority trimmed. An OT instruction to reassign prisoners prompted a reminder by the camp commander of Auschwitz III (Monowitz) in August 1944 that this was the prerogative of the WVHA:

> There has been a case recently in a sub-camp of a concentration camp where the head of an OT office ... wanted on his own initiative to make the camp leader transfer some hundred prisoners from this reserve to another labour camp within the domain of a different concentration camp. This OT leader thus attempted to assume powers to which he is not entitled.[29]

Another example of a clash between OT and SS officers over the control of slave labourers was on Alderney in the Channel Islands. OT Bauleiter Leo Ackermann strove to improve performance and extend his control over prisoners for the benefit of OT operations there. Ackermann took charge on Alderney in late 1943, when death rates in OT camps on the island had reduced from a peak nearly a year previously. He worked closely with the SS, which had arrived in spring that year with concentration-camp prisoners in SS Building

Brigade-I. Former camp inmates told Allied interrogators after the war that Ackermann inspected work sites with SS and Wehrmacht officers and did not intervene to prevent severe beatings of prisoners.[30] Testimony by survivors and witnesses showed conditions remained pitiful for prisoners in OT camps under Ackermann's leadership until foreign workers finally left in 1944. Yet to impose his authority as senior engineer controlling prisoners on technical matters at work sites, Ackermann clashed with the head of the SS Building Brigade, SS-Hauptsturmführer Maximilian List, in a way that backfired on him dangerously. Ackermann raised objections that SS guards were beating up prisoners from the SS-run Sylt camp on 'his' work sites 'so that their capacity for work might be adversely affected'.[31] It turned out, however, that one of the beaten prisoners had been a Jew, who for the first time had been included in an SS building brigade.[32] So Ackermann faced a counterclaim by the SS that he was soft on Jews – an accusation that could have had exceptionally serious repercussions for him if the matter had not been dropped following intervention by the senior OT administration in Cherbourg.[33]

A further point of conflict between the OT and SS involved Transit Road IV. OT and SS cooperation on a western section of the route appeared to have been successful, whereas discord flared further east in Ukraine. In the west, the SS and OT organised Jewish and other labourers in Silesia. Himmler had appointed SS-Brigadeführer Albrecht Schmelt as a special commissioner in the region and his organisation began building its own camps throughout Silesia. Tens of thousands of men were recruited from Jewish districts in eastern Upper Silesia, but it is unlikely that the labour camps were established and operated by the SS alone. A significant number of the Jewish camps built after autumn 1940 belonged to the OT and the *Autobahn* authorities.[34] However, further to the east in Ukraine matters did not proceed smoothly. The SS were heavily involved in marshalling and guarding slave labourers needed to work on Transit Road IV and the HSSPF of Ukraine and southern Russia, Hans-Adolf Prützmann, was in charge of this. Prützmann, who later reported to Himmler in December 1942 that 363,211 Jews had been killed in his area, complained about the resulting drain on SS resources.[35] The situation led to conflicts because of overlapping responsibilities, which had to be resolved with a compromise, apparently resulting in the SS being accorded overall control but with the OT in charge of technical supervision of work sites.[36]

This example concerning Transit Road IV reflects the mixture of mutual advantage and rivalry which typically marked relations between the SS and OT. The OT depended very heavily on the SS for concentration-camp labourers, yet the SS could not do without OT technical expertise. Keen to press ahead with settlement building in the East, the SS even went so far as to copy OT formations in its efforts to achieve its purpose in an area so vital to its ideological aims. The result of all these conflicting currents in their relationship was that in matters involving the OT's specialist field of construction, neither organisation could entirely escape dependency on the other.

The Organisation Todt and industry

German industry was an indispensable partner to the OT, which oversaw slave labourers in cooperation with some of the Third Reich's industrial giants in concentration camps from Auschwitz to Vaivara. The OT also joined forces with mining, engineering, construction and other specialist firms to exploit the natural and labour resources of occupied countries across Europe. Companies from across the Reich, including IG Farben, which made explosives and synthetic rubber and fuel, took part with the OT in major projects.[37] Krupp did the same as it expanded its share of the armaments business. The Munich construction firm Sager & Woerner, which had employed both Todt and Dorsch, also frequently teamed up with the OT, as we have already seen. Hermann Giesler was another example of a prominent OT figure associated with particular firms chosen for a number of OT projects exploiting slave labour. The construction firm of Polensky & Zöllner was contracted to work in Giesler's Russia-North sector before being picked later for the Mühldorf project in the OT region in Bavaria he subsequently headed. Leonhard Moll AG participated in tearing down the main synagogue in Munich in 1938, the year when Hitler put Giesler in charge of rebuilding work in the city. Space was thus cleared for Giesler to further Munich's architectural plans, and Moll was later signed up to undertake operations in Kaufering, also in Giesler's Bavarian OT district.[38]

IG Farben's chief executive, Carl Krauch, was central to the German war effort and the search for German self-sufficiency in finding synthetic substitutes for key imported commodities. His first priority was aviation fuel, and his second was rubber. The OT was deeply involved in Krauch's projects, using slave labour from Auschwitz and other concentration camps. Krauch was among IG Farben executives who appeared before the Nuremberg War Crimes Tribunal in 1947–8 on charges including plunder, slavery and mass murder. Like the other defendants, he received a relatively mild sentence and was imprisoned for six years.[39] The judgment was based on evidence of Krauch's activities stemming from his wide wartime powers to oversee programmes using slave labour for the production of explosives, chemical warfare agents, synthetic oil, synthetic rubber and light metals. The harshest penalty of eight years' imprisonment was handed to Otto Ambros, who managed IG Farben's Auschwitz operations and other plants.

Fritz Todt took steps as early as August 1939 to supply 13,000 workers for 100 construction projects for what was called the 'Krauch Plan'.[40] By March 1942, just after Speer succeeded Todt, the OT was planning its own building administration in Auschwitz in parallel with IG Farben management, cooperating with the firm on labour allocation and quotas for the supply of materials. The OT was to be assigned construction jobs, including the works' railway station, waterworks and parts of a Reich-owned armaments plant at Auschwitz.[41] In an illustration of how closely the OT was integrated into operations at Auschwitz, documents used in evidence at the IG Farben trial revealed how much importance Ambros placed on the need to maintain contact with the OT to ensure the supply of foreign workers.[42] By July 1943 IG Farben managers needed 3,500 more workers, and Speer, in an initial response, promised 200 Czechs. The OT was integrated into the administrative and accounting system with IG Farben, whose eight compounds on its Auschwitz site included the Monowitz concentration camp. Monowitz was initially designed to produce synthetic rubber, but by October 1943 was producing methanol, vital for aircraft fuel and in the manufacture of explosives.[43] Around 25,000 of all the 35,000 concentration-camp prisoners sent to Monowitz died.[44]

Apart from Auschwitz, the OT played an important role in two slave-labour projects to extract oil from shale that were also linked to Krauch. The first was in Estonia, and the second was the Wüste (Desert) programme within the Reich in Württemberg. The OT took up some roles in Vaivara that were usually the preserve of the SS, such as subcamp commander. OT personnel also regularly carried out duties as armed guards in camps.[45] Hitler considered the Baltic shale-oil project so important that he ignored the dangers of the advancing Red Army and blocked the evacuation of 450 Jews and other workers from Estonia in August 1944. A ship with the Jews aboard had been ready to depart from the port of Reval, which in fact did not fall to Soviet troops until later the following month.[46] Since the dictator regarded the Estonian scheme as having such high priority, it was natural that the Wüste programme was pursued with similar urgency. Krauch was key to the development of Wüste, having been pressed by a senior figure in the Armaments Ministry, SS-Brigadeführer Walther Schieber, to do more to capitalise on Germany's own shale-oil resources. Schieber was the ministry's foremost representative for the deployment of concentration-camp slave labour. The biggest camps of Wüste, which was incorporated into the

Geilenberg programme, were built in 1944 after Allied bombing threatened to choke off fuel supplies for German tanks and warplanes.[47]

Just as IG Farben's cooperation with Todt switched smoothly into the Speer era, Krupp fostered close ties with both armaments ministers. Todt named Krupp's chief weapons designer, Erich Müller, widely known as 'Kanonen-Müller' (Cannon Müller), as head of a national committee overseeing guns and artillery.[48] After Speer took over from Todt in 1942, his ministry asked Müller whether Krupp could build a camp for skilled foreign Jewish labourers. Plans for Krupp to make anti-aircraft gun parts at Auschwitz were dropped, and although the firm began using concentration-camp labour there in mid-1943, it decided to move its machinery westwards to its Bertha plant near Breslau.[49] The OT had 3,000 construction workers among the 15,000-strong workforce at the Bertha works in October 1944.[50] Müller showed his appreciation for the OT's use of Jewish slave labour at Bertha, noting in correspondence in 1942 that because mostly Jews were working there on OT-supervised construction, 'valuable German manpower' did not have to be tapped. The OT also took part in work at Krupp's fuel plant at Gelsenberg, erecting a primitive tent camp for 2,000 Jewish women forced to clear debris after a heavy air attack in 1944.[51]

Another high-profile German firm to work on a big project involving the OT was Volkswagen, which by summer 1941 was becoming almost exclusively an armaments concern. It sought Jewish slave labourers in 1944 for the task of relocating underground some production of the Fi 103, better known as the V1 flying bomb. Erhard Milch of the Reich Air Ministry had picked the small aircraft firm of Fieseler to design the missile, and Volkswagen was chosen to take on orders for the manufacture of the Fi 103, making the larger company's relocation underground more pressing.[52] Its new 'bomb-proof' subterranean site was in the Tiercelet iron-ore mine. The OT developed and carried out construction at the mine, situated near Thil in the part of Lorraine retained by France. In mid-March 1944 transports of slave labourers from Russia, Ukraine and Belarus joined French and Serbian prisoners of war there, overseen by German OT personnel. The OT also took care of guarding the prisoners, employing Flemish and Danish guards armed with carbines and batons. Conditions for the prisoners were especially poor regarding food and clothing. In May Volkswagen sent an engineer, Arthur Schmiele, as its representative to Auschwitz to recruit Hungarian Jews as additional labour. Schmiele chose two groups of concentration-camp prisoners. The first group of 300 included metalworkers and around 40 engineers and technicians, who were all sent to Volkswagen's main plant for instruction in manufacturing the Fi 103. A second group of 500 metalworkers were transferred directly to Tiercelet, where the first group joined them about a month later. SS and Luftwaffe guards were assigned to the concentration-camp prisoners who, because of the site where they were deployed, came under Natzweiler concentration camp. Despite being recruited as skilled workers, the prisoners were made to perform routine tasks like transporting quarried stone and laying cables and cement. In August 1944 the Tiercelet workforce numbered around 2,000, including 800 concentration-camp prisoners. However, due to chaotic planning Tiercelet was evacuated to focus underground production of the Fi 103 in Mittelbau-Dora instead. Concentration-camp prisoners were sent from Tiercelet via Dernau to Mittelbau-Dora in various transports by around the end of 1944.[53]

A bizarre feature of OT cooperation with Volkswagen in 1941 involved Armaments Minister Fritz Todt urgently requesting what became known as 'OT stoves' from the firm to provide heating for troops on the Eastern front suffering from the extreme cold of the Soviet winter. As Volkswagen tried to adapt its output to wartime, it often took on jobs which other firms thought less attractive, such as the production of anti-tank mines and OT stoves. Despite the absurdity of the high-tech Volkswagen plant churning out such simple products, Todt's order proved to be highly profitable for the firm. The very large number of OT bunker heaters required meant that revenue from them more or less kept the company afloat in the winter of 1941–2. Volkswagen's main plant had produced 221,505 heaters by the end of 1942.[54]

Industry's place was at the heart of the OT from the very beginning, with firms combining their resources to build Fritz Todt's motorway network and many making the transition with their staff to the Westwall in 1938. Big business was in many respects an active partner in Hitler's national revolution, and Fritz Todt, Ferdinand Porsche, Willy Messerschmitt and Ernst Heinkel were all awarded the German National Prize, Germany's equivalent of the Nobel Prize, in October 1938.[55] Todt's own experience at Sager & Woerner and his connections to the business world helped frame the way the OT functioned and formed the basis for its success. Individual firms contracted to the OT could be seen as equivalent to units or soldiers in the Wehrmacht.[56] Firms either signed up voluntarily to work under contract as OT entities, or were conscripted. Industry took advantage of favourable contracts with the OT while Todt was in charge, and it was not until Speer took over that reforms brought the introduction of fixed-price contracts. Companies could keep any savings below the agreed price, in a system designed to reward efficiency. Speer's reforms also brought more centralised control.[57]

Profit was a principal motive for industry's cooperation with the OT, even in the final, desperate stages of the war. Private firms increasingly also looked to protect their core staff and machinery, and to prepare for peacetime operations as defeat for Germany loomed.[58] Renegotiation of contracts was frequent as problems with supplies and labour mounted. Oddly, this even led to big firms criticising slave labour, which they themselves massively exploited: the objective was to secure more lucrative terms under their contracts with the OT. The big firms, which employed large numbers of skilled German workers, argued that they should be rewarded more highly than smaller firms, whose more limited resources obliged them to resort to foreign slave labourers with lower productivity and relevant skills. The OT initially rejected the argument of the big firms and favoured smaller enterprises for a deal in August 1944 on payment for workers on one of the Mühldorf sites, Weingut I. Just two months later, however, the OT decided to adopt a standard contract favouring the big firms, under which their many skilled German workers were factored into the contractual profit-sharing calculation. This followed negotiations with firms carrying out work under the OT at the Valentin submarine-building works in Bremen-Farge and at a fighter-plane factory in Bedburg, which was similar to the one at Mühldorf. The swift reversal in OT policy reflected how much it depended on the big firms to press ahead with major armaments projects, whose urgency only heightened in the final stages of the war.[59]

The Organisation Todt and the Wehrmacht

The OT changed dramatically from 1938 to 1945, being transformed from a virtually all-German civilian labour force to a Wehrmacht auxiliary whose core German staff were vastly outnumbered by foreign slave labourers. In wartime the OT followed closely behind German troops to build transport links and defence installations across occupied Europe. The effectiveness of both Todt and Speer in championing their organisation derived from their status as close confidants of Hitler: they could help the OT compete for limited resources against rival claims for supplies and labour from the heads of the army, navy and air force. As successive armaments ministers, they had no serious opposition from the pliant head of the High Command of the Armed Forces, General Wilhelm Keitel, whom Hitler appointed when he named himself commander-in-chief of the armed forces in 1938. Being head of state, the dictator already held the office of supreme commander of the armed forces. Of the other military figures,

Göring was the most powerful. He displayed his ability to challenge Speer, as already described, through his plotting and manipulation of Dorsch, although the failures of the Luftwaffe and the collapse of Hitler's faith in him undermined his authority.

Relations between the army and the OT had a rocky pre-war start when an impatient Hitler wrested the job of building the Westwall from army engineers in 1938 and gave it to the OT. The same friction between the OT and the Wehrmacht spilled over into their next mammoth fortification task, the Atlantic Wall. Speer intervened in support of OT units, for example in 1943. He succeeded in obtaining Hitler's support to block what he perceived as an attempt by Field Marshal Gerd von Rundstedt, the commander-in-chief in the West, to exceed the bounds of the military's authority. Speer believed von Rundstedt had been seeking to undermine the right of OT construction teams to take their own decisions concerning building equipment and work sites.[60] All the same, there was no question the OT and Wehrmacht depended heavily on one another. During the rapid German advance in the Western campaign, OT mobile units relied on the army for protection and took operational orders from army engineers, and this strong bond between the OT and the military was again displayed in 1941. Before the German invasion of the Soviet Union, a 20,000-strong OT force of mobile units, made up mostly of road- and bridge-building specialists, stood ready to follow German troops as they advanced eastwards.[61] The OT earned the respect of the Wehrmacht during the Russia campaign more than in any other sector, with operational decisions often having to be taken locally because centralised control was exceptionally hard over such vast areas. OT and army administrative personnel were often quartered together for reasons of military security, and an especially close interdependence existed in the early days in Russia between the OT and the Wehrmacht.[62] However, disruption to OT operations resulting from the remoteness of some army officers and their perceived failure to grasp front-line realities caused frustration among senior transport staff, such as NSKK Obergruppenführer Willi Nagel. Interrogated by Allied officers after the war, he blamed the failure to complete Transit Road IV on such behaviour:

> Firm roads were as good as non-existent. If the need to create them was occasionally grasped and somebody, for example the O.T., tackled it, these works would nevertheless soon be halted. Some army officer, who understood nothing of the importance of supplies and was himself on an official flight, or travelling in good weather in a field vehicle, had suddenly a far 'more important' use for the construction troop and it was withdrawn.[63]

Tensions with the armed forces also affected the OT's operations with the SS at the infamous Klooga subcamp of Vaivara concentration camp in Estonia. The OT and a special navy unit produced cement-clad mines at Klooga, and other operations at the subcamp included construction projects. The OT's Oberbauleiter Wein oversaw 1,800 Jews among a 2,000-strong workforce. The navy protested strongly over a proposal to hand over land at Klooga for use as an SS training ground, saying in a letter on 8 August 1944 that the OT was producing vital equipment for the military and output should not be jeopardised. Wein himself said his operation, built up over two years, had involved an 'exceptionally large' investment in equipment and labour. Workers produced vital supplies for the army and navy, operating a cement works, sawmill, shoe factory and a big carpentry workshop.[64]

In the north of occupied Soviet territory, the High Command of Army Group North investigated complaints about OT supervisors and trainers maltreating Russian civilian workers and prisoners of war in the summer of 1943. OT staff were said to have beaten prisoners and forced them to work excessively long hours. The Russian labourers were also given inadequate rations, clothing and shelter. One military report to the High Command said the protests originated largely from civilian labourers working eleven-hour days who were given less food than prisoners of war. Their plight as members of a road-building squad was worsened because they were given mouldy bread and were switched to sites in more remote areas, denying them the extra food they were able to procure closer to their homes. Regarding the labourers' accommodation, the report said the complaints would only have been justified the preceding winter, when Russian civilians were rounded up en masse at short notice to work on road building. However, another military report said workers' accommodation failed to meet basic needs and criticised the quality of work foremen, noting that where Poles performed this function 'they often get carried away by their hatred of Russians to maltreat people'. Such failings only increased the number of escapes by prisoners of war and civilian slave labourers. The OT's Russia-North sector replied to the High Command, saying Russian escapees from OT work sites often justified their flight by claiming they had been badly treated. All the same, the OT acknowledged that 'construction work on roads and railways is very hard' and that the working day of up to eleven hours was longer than the eight-hour day performed by Russian labourers elsewhere with the military. Promises made to the labourers when recruited could not be kept, and clothes and shoes issued by the OT 'are often pretty poor'. Additionally 'the prescribed food rations are below the present standard of living of the Russian small farmer. After having finished his work the worker is unable to procure anything from irregular sources and is compelled to make his living on what is prescribed by our authorities.'65

In Norway, boosting the performance of Soviet prisoners of war and juggling manpower resources required close OT cooperation with the Wehrmacht. Henne, the OT chief in the country, wrote in late 1942 to the appropriate regional army officer to clarify how responsibilities should be shared when providing for POWs as a foreign labour force. Henne summarised what he said had been agreed with the area commander for prisoners of war regarding clothing, blankets and medical care, all of which the army would take care of. The OT would provide accommodation for the prisoners, complete with cooking equipment, lighting, heating and beds with straw mattresses. Henne said these rules would apply to prisoners supplied to the OT as labourers via the area commander, but the OT would take full responsibility for all other German or foreign prisoners, who would be guarded by the police or the OT itself.[66] This was important, because it meant that thousands of Yugoslav prisoners, who were not initially classified as prisoners of war, were among slave labourers in this category. Under Henne's guidelines, the prisoners' care was entirely the responsibility of the OT, although the SS guarded the camps. Other examples of this class of prisoner were inmates of the SGL Nord complex in Norway, who were mostly German convicts overseen by Justice Ministry officials and the OT. An additional way in which the OT shared responsibilities with its slave-labour partners involved POW labour battalions. For such battalions specifically assigned to it, the OT decided independently of the army how the prisoners were deployed.[67]

Army officers belonging to various Nazi Party groupings within the military raised complaints about the OT late in the war. Such party-affiliated bodies were formed in every institution within German society under the Third Reich, and the OT was accustomed to criticism from its rival, the German Labour Front (Deutsche Arbeitsfront), which was a labour organisation controlled by Robert Ley and entirely subservient to the Nazi Party. Reacting to the army officers, Speer responded formally in October 1944 to their strong protests about OT practices raised at a meeting of National Socialist military officers (*NS-Führungsoffiziere*) that autumn. He promised, in cooperation with Ley, to implement measures to educate political attitudes within the OT, although it was clear there would be little practical result from such a move at that late stage in the war.[68] Goebbels, appointed general plenipotentiary for the mobilisation of total war after the 20 July 1944 assassination attempt against Hitler, wanted to participate in an investigation into the OT following widespread complaints about the state of the organisation.[69]

Despite such frictions, the OT was tightly bound to the Wehrmacht, since it undertook top-priority projects for every arm of the military. The OT also depended on the Wehrmacht for one of its most important sources of slave labour, namely prisoners of war, who were generally the responsibility of the military. In the extreme environment of the war in Russia, though, the usual rules often did not apply when the OT or army engineers were in need of labour. Allied intelligence observed that manpower was obtained simply by stopping convoys of Russian prisoners of war on their way to the rear and putting them to work until they were relieved by the next convoy of prisoners. Hundreds of thousands of prisoners of war and civilians were press-ganged in this way and compelled to work by firms often contracted to the OT.[70]

One important common experience forming a bond between many members of the OT was their time spent in the military. A significant number of OT personnel appointed to senior positions, including OT engineer Wilhelm Griesinger, who supervised slave labourers in the Mühldorf complex, were recruited from among construction managers in the Luftwaffe.[71] Todt himself served in the air force in the First World War and was made a *Generalmajor* in the Luftwaffe in 1939.[72] Giesler also worked around the start of the Second World War in the Luftwaffe construction programme. This link to the Luftwaffe among OT personnel had a striking parallel with the construction corps of the SS-WVHA under Hans Kammler, himself a doctor of engineering from the Luftwaffe construction arm.[73]

The Organisation Todt and the Nazi party

The contrasts between the characters of the OT's two leaders meant that its relations with the Nazi Party underwent a marked change on Todt's death and Speer's takeover. Todt, ever the party stalwart, ensured that frictions with the NSDAP were kept to a minimum; Speer, on the other hand, came into conflict with powerful Nazi Party figures such as Bormann. The most high-profile clash between the two came during the political crisis dealt with in this chapter, which revolved around Dorsch and the OT and prompted Speer's threat to resign.

Even under Todt, however, dealings between the NSDAP and the OT were by no means always smooth. The OT clashed with the Nazi Party before the war over its uniform, which included a swastika armband even though it was not a party organ. The armband was worn to ensure that OT staff could not be confused with French soldiers in their khaki uniforms. The OT had been given

Czechoslovak military uniforms that had fallen into German hands in 1939 and whose colour was similar to the brown of the Nazi Party. Bormann, in his capacity as head of the Nazi Party Chancery, objected to the use of the swastika armband by the OT on the grounds that wearing the NSDAP symbol was the exclusive right of members of Nazi Party organisations.[74] Hitler later intervened to insist on OT staff wearing the swastika, which with the sharp increase of foreigners in OT ranks prompted alarm that non-Germanic personnel were sullying the Nazi Party's symbol by wearing it. Strict orders were issued in one region of the Reich in 1944 that the OT swastika armband was only to be worn by *Reichsdeutsche,* Germanic people like Danes, Dutch and Norwegians, and *Volksdeutsche* or members of the OT defence corps who had sworn an oath to the Führer.[75] Both Speer, who led by example in wearing the OT uniform himself, and Todt made efforts to regularise OT uniforms and eradicate frequent improvisations that did not conform to official guidelines. The two successive leaders of the OT held contrary views, however, on what SS officers serving in the OT should wear. As we have seen, Todt argued in favour of SS officers in the OT senior ranks wearing field-grey uniforms, worn by the Waffen-SS, to show the OT leadership had 'developed strongly from party structures'.[76] Speer insisted on his OT staff wearing the OT uniform, rather than that of the Nazi Party's paramilitary offshoots, even if they happened also to be SS officers.[77]

When Speer took office, it was his ambition and determination to pursue his goals that caused his sparring with Bormann. The head of the Nazi Party Chancery scored a significant victory when Hitler rejected Speer's nomination of Karl Hanke, *Gauleiter* of Lower Silesia, as general plenipotentiary for labour mobilisation in 1942. This was a vital area for the OT, which depended so heavily on slave labour, but Bormann's favourite, Fritz Sauckel, was chosen instead.[78] Then, in October 1943, Speer clashed again with the top echelons of the Nazi Party, including Bormann: he incensed *Gauleiter* at an armaments conference in Posen by calling for curbs on consumer goods, so that resources could be diverted to armaments production. Delivering an open challenge, Speer threatened the *Gauleiter* that he would close down civilian industry and deal accordingly with offenders if useless consumer production was maintained. The *Gauleiter* saw this as not only a thinly veiled threat against them personally, but also an attack on favoured businesses in their regions. Their complaints to Hitler and Bormann damaged Speer and his relationship with the Führer distinctly cooled. When Speer addressed *Gauleiter* in Essen in June the following year, just after the crisis involving Dorsch, Hitler demanded to see the text of Speer's speech to ensure no repeat of Posen.[79]

Just the following month, OT foreign labourers carrying out major works at Rastenburg initially came under suspicion after the 20 July 1944 assassination attempt against Hitler, with potential implications for Speer.[80] More seriously, it transpired that the plotters, including Claus von Stauffenberg who placed the bomb at Hitler's headquarters in East Prussia, had put Speer on a list of 'ministers' for their planned government. Fortunately for Speer, though, a question mark was placed against his name with a note saying 'to be won over'. In fact, Speer played no part in the conspiracy, despite insinuating in his post-war writings that he sympathised with the plotters.[81]

While Speer all too often clashed head-on with Bormann and the *Gauleiter*, the OT project to build Me-262 planes in underground factories in Bavaria provided an example of a powerful *Gauleiter* proving a highly important contact for the OT. The regional head of the OT whose area included the factories was Hermann Giesler. His contacts with Hitler as an architect already placed him among the dictator's favourites, but he also had a powerful sibling: Paul Giesler was the Nazi Party *Gauleiter* for Upper Bavaria, whose district happened to overlap with the OT's Deutschland VI sector headed by his younger brother. This connection with the party's top regional chief considerably strengthened Hermann Giesler's position and added to his authority in conducting OT operations in the area.

Apart from such personal bonds between the NSDAP and the OT, the two organisations cooperated before the war in the important area of transport. As we have seen, this cooperation involved the NSKK providing fleets of vehicles to ferry supplies to OT construction teams working on the Westwall. The NSKK was also used by Speer to provide construction materials for the programme Hitler appointed him to carry out to rebuild Berlin. Cooperation between the OT and the NSKK expanded, and the Nazi Party transport group delivered supplies for the OT in occupied Europe. Construction projects in the Reich and occupied Europe depended on a vast road, rail and shipping network to ensure adequate supplies. The NSKK and the OT became so interlinked that Speer decided to break the NSKK's ties with the Nazi Party altogether. After Speer took over from Todt in 1942, two entities called the NSKK-Transportgruppe Todt and the Legion Speer were set up, comprising around 70,000 men and almost 50,000 vehicles, under the leadership of Brigadeführer Willi Nagel. This split was needed because a party organisation like the NSKK could only employ Germans. The Legion Speer, by contrast, was made up of foreigners, largely Russian prisoners of war, with Germans commanding them. By early 1944, however, the overall chief of the NSKK, Reichsleiter Kraus, was convinced the OT was manoeuvring to swallow up his organisation and thus tear it from its party roots. His fears were justified, for Speer, Dorsch and Nagel were indeed determined to cut links with the NSKK and hive off what by then had been renamed the Transportgruppe Todt. In an attempt to forestall this, Kraus wrote to Speer signalling his intention to remove Nagel from his post over accusations of drunkenness and other failings. Speer replied with a robust defence of Nagel and copied his letter to Bormann. Speer explained that the Transportgruppe Todt, just like the Organisation Todt itself, 'cannot be a party-related formation, since it must start from quite different fundamental principles, namely the current conditions for labour deployment'. Kraus lost the battle, and a new formation called the Transportkorps Speer was formed and transferred under the Wehrmacht, with no links to the NSKK.[82]

Although rivalries involving the OT so far described were largely confined to the core of the Reich, similar tensions erupted in German administrations across occupied Europe. Leaders of OT operations in the various countries had to cooperate with powerful Nazi Party figures who had been *Gauleiter* in regions of the Reich. Examples included Erich Koch and Hinrich Lohse, respectively Reich commissars of Ukraine and the 'Eastern lands' of the Baltic states; another was Josef Terboven, Reich commissar of occupied Norwegian territories. These regimes of German occupation frequently cooperated to help run OT projects by providing administrative support.[83] The OT's takeover of all technical tasks in the East in 1942, however, significantly encroached upon these civilian administrations' areas of responsibility. The measure meant that the OT took over technical and engineering works in southern areas from the civilian administration in Ukraine. The civilian administration of Reichskommissariat Ostland, meanwhile, surrendered technical matters in White Ruthenia to the OT's central Russia region, while handing over to the OT's Russia-North region in the rest of its territory.[84]

Powers given to OT regional chiefs in countries across Europe meant they were significant players within the occupying administrations. Types of government under occupation varied, but the OT regional chief often worked with senior Nazi Party figures acting as Hitler's chief representatives in occupied states and cooperated with them in the allocation of foreign workers on OT projects. This was the case in Norway, where Hitler appointed Terboven as *Reichskommissar* in April 1940, giving him virtually unlimited power in the country, and Henne was put in charge of the OT's Wiking group from 1942. Hitler's 1940 decree left unclear the exact division of responsibilities between Terboven and the Wehrmacht, so struggles between these two centres of power lasted throughout the occupation. Terboven used his close link to Hitler to resolve such tussles and ensure that he almost invariably ended up the victor. He also used industry contacts, established while he had been *Gauleiter* in Essen before being assigned to Norway, to guarantee that big firms such as IG Farben and Krupp had representatives appointed to his administration.[85] Against this political backdrop, the OT's Henne established control of construction projects in Norway, depending on Terboven to help force through his demands for resources. Henne relied on the Wehrmacht for the supply of 100,000 Soviet prisoners of war as slave labourers. Henne's powers rested partly on an agreement between Fritz Todt and Terboven to widen the OT's role in Norway and on an order by Hitler in May 1941 providing the basis for Wiking's central role under Henne in construction there. Henne amassed an impressive array of titles and his powers, including that of plenipotentiary for construction, meant he took all major decisions regarding construction in the country. His goal was above all to press ahead with Hitler's pet project of the Arctic rail link at the expense of other economic sectors. Although only a fraction of this planned 1,200-kilometre rail link was built by the end of the war, Henne's ruthless pursuit of what had already become an unrealisable project meant that out of more than 85,000 prisoners of war and forced or slave labourers in Norway at the time of the German surrender, 30,000 mostly Russian slave labourers were toiling in abysmal conditions on the OT rail project alone.[86]

Key players in slave labour

Rivalries and squabbles over sharing out workers often soured relations, but the OT, SS, Wehrmacht and industry cooperated in the slave-labour economy because they each possessed resources and skills the others valued. As for the Nazi Party, whose powerful representatives led civilian administrations in many areas of German-occupied Europe, its interaction with the OT was a similar mixture of tense competition interspersed with active support. Such political manoeuvring and shifting alliances were typical of the Nazi polycratic state, in which the various power centres competed with one another to expand their influence in a system where areas of responsibility frequently overlapped or were left intentionally vague. Although vying with formidable competitors, the OT was able to withstand them through a combination of strengths: its skilled core workforce of engineers and construction experts, its flexibility and its strong ties to German industry. The OT had a further trump card: Hitler's enduring support. The dictator expressed admiration for Todt and his organisation from the outset, subsequently choosing the OT above its rivals to carry out a series of vast construction projects he saw as vital to the war effort. With Todt and Speer enjoying unlimited access to Hitler, the OT was at least as well placed as its slave labour partners to gain the dictator's support to achieve its aims.

The OT was also most successful in cooperating with all its other partners simultaneously because slave labour became increasingly vital to the huge building projects which justified its very existence. By contrast, its other partners had quite different primary functions: the SS were the 'political soldiers' of the regime, the Wehrmacht was a fighting force, German industry was in business to make a profit and the NSDAP was a political party. The OT was therefore free to concentrate on its main purpose, acting as a facilitator to combine the resources of its partners to obtain and manage slave labourers to carry out its tasks. The OT looked to the SS for its supply of slave labour in the form of concentration camp prisoners, as well as SS personnel to administer and guard labour camps; it sought prisoners of war as slave labourers from the Wehrmacht, while its staff worked together with army engineers; its collaboration with German industry provided a vital source of skilled labour and equipment, as did foreign firms; and the OT also benefited from the support of Nazi Party officials in powerful positions across Europe.

In return, the OT offered various advantages and services to its partners. The SS generally relied on OT technical expertise to oversee labourers at work sites; the Wehrmacht benefited from the OT's role as an armed forces auxiliary, working closely with the military, securing road and rail communications and assisting army engineers behind the front line; German industry viewed the OT largely as a source of lucrative contracts to carry out gargantuan construction projects across occupied Europe; and Nazi Party officials facilitated the OT's operations involving infrastructure and other projects useful to their administrations in occupied Europe or in the Greater Reich.

Clearly, though, OT–Nazi Party relations did not always run smoothly. While the OT and its slave-labour partners had good reasons to cooperate for their mutual benefit, Nazi Party figures like Bormann proved a powerful adversary for Speer, who often appealed to Hitler to resolve clashes. For much of the time Speer could count on this tactic, but Bormann still managed to outmanoeuvre the armaments minister and OT chief. Perhaps the most striking example was when he plotted with Göring to engineer the crisis in 1944 leading to Speer's resignation threat.

Having examined how the Third Reich's powerful organisations competed or collaborated in the exploitation of slave labourers in the Second World War, the next chapter is largely devoted to the camp inmates. They describe their experiences in hellish conditions in the labour camps, where so many victims overseen by OT personnel were beaten or worked to death.

4

Slave labourers under the Organisation Todt

Arie P. feared he would be rejected as too small for the labour transport from Auschwitz. He tried to look older than his thirteen years. Arie thought that if he was not chosen to go with his elder brother, standing in the row in front, then that would be the end of him. Organisation Todt people in khaki uniforms had come to Auschwitz to select workers to take away with them. Arie's brother, Itzhak, was chosen and went forward to have his name recorded. Arie was forlorn, anxious. But his brother, so admired by his younger sibling as a 'survivor', managed in the confusion of so many prisoners to present himself again for selection. No one recognised the Jew from Oradea whose name had already been listed for the transport. This time, though, Itzhak gave his younger brother's name, and they were both scheduled for the transport. Prisoners were dismissed and those chosen had to come forward later, at the appointed time, when their names were called. The brothers feared discovery at any moment. When prisoners duly assembled once more, the brothers stepped forward when ordered to do so. First came Itzhak and then Arie, who went on tiptoe, trying to appear taller. All went to plan. They obeyed orders, as preparations went ahead for the coming journey, to go for disinfection, wash and receive new clothes. They were given food. They boarded a train with the other prisoners deemed fit to work and left Auschwitz. Arie did not know how long they travelled before, in that summer of 1944, they reached Kaufering.[1]

The Kaufering camp complex where Arie and his brother toiled until the end of the war held slave labourers building subterranean aircraft factories designed to be safe from Allied bombs. This ill-conceived plan was never completed. The reality for the 30,000 mostly Jewish slave labourers who passed through the Kaufering camps was extreme hard labour and misery; for about half of them, it meant death.[2] Arie's story is important because it describes conditions in one of the most brutal camps where the OT exercised a high degree of control. It helps illustrate how the OT operated in the final throes of the war.

The Kaufering complex was part of the Dachau concentration-camp system and consisted of eleven subcamps. In the last months of the war it held about 10,000 prisoners.[3] Violence in the camps by SS guards, OT overseers and employees of construction firms was a daily routine, and some executions were also carried out. In Kaufering Camp I six prisoners were hanged in November 1944 for 'sabotage', because they had taken scraps of material to wrap round their feet for protection.[4] Apart from lethal force, survivors typically attributed high death tolls to malnutrition, sickness and abysmal conditions in the camps.[5]

Kaufering was situated west of its infamous parent camp of Dachau, near the Bavarian city of Munich and just to the north of Landsberg am Lech, where Hitler was imprisoned in 1924 and dictated *Mein Kampf* following his failed putsch the previous year. But the choice of Kaufering had less to do with the Führer's political roots than with the availability of gravel and other resources to construct a subterranean factory, where so many slave labourers would perish. When Arie, the fourth of nine children in his Orthodox Jewish family, first arrived from Auschwitz-Birkenau, he was allocated to Kaufering Camp VII, in a wood about 1 kilometre from Landsberg. Barrack huts, each taking about thirty prisoners, were sunk into the ground with only the roof showing above the surface. For two or three weeks Arie carried bricks, sand and cement sacks, which normally weighed 50 kilograms, for construction work at an airfield, before being picked again by the OT to help harvest the potato crop. Soviet prisoners of war worked alongside Jews like Arie, taking charge of horse-drawn, plough-like farm implements that unearthed the potatoes for collection before they froze in the ground as winter closed in. Their 100-strong labour detail was guarded by just two or three army soldiers – these were older men 'who were not so strict with us'.[6]

Camp guards beat prisoners with rubber-coated metal batons, and Arie received blows to the head on one occasion, knocking him over and making him feel as if his skull was cracked. He did not identify the guard, but the beating left him with long-term deafness in one ear and affected his sight in one eye. Despite his injuries, he still went to work the very next day. Such beatings were also delivered by Kapos, but Arie said some acted humanely. During his time on the construction site, a Hungarian Jewish doctor named Winkler was an example. Arie said he was a 'nice man' who would shout and curse prisoners loudly so as to be heard by German guards, but would rarely beat camp inmates, only making a show of doing so.

After some weeks in Camp VII, Arie was told to join a line-up for selection and take his shirt off. He was picked to go to Landsberg Camp 1, also known as Kaufering I. He received the Dachau concentration-camp number 112273 and worked for a firm contracted by the OT, Leonhard Moll AG. He learnt to say the number as quickly as he could in German to avoid a blow with a rifle butt from a guard. Arie's fourteenth birthday came on 2 December 1944. Work was hard and they unloaded equipment from railcars in the snow and bitter wind, their clothes often sodden. Arie had to learn techniques to stave off exhaustion.

> Sometimes I played tricks because I already had no strength left. I took an empty [cement] sack, filled it with other sacks and put it on my back and went along like that several times to give myself a rest. I pretended to be lugging a sack because the guards were not too close to us. They were about 100 metres or so away from us. That was in winter. Snow. He had a camp fire and watched from there, or didn't watch. In brief, it worked. And so I could still preserve my last remaining strength. But not always. Every ten or fifteen sacks, I went round twice with it, so that everyone saw that. It became dangerous because everyone tried to do it too. And we had to deliver cement there. Also, there were, no, not SS people, but people from the Organisation Todt and they were harsher than the SS people. They dealt fatal blows. They were Hitler's faithful, but right to the end. Volunteers, older men. So the cement had to arrive.[7]

Arie's description clearly explains the rules of survival. OT overseers drove prisoners mercilessly, even in the final phase of the war. Other work he was required to do was just as demanding. Because an existing railway line stopped 3–4 kilometres from the underground factory, an extension was needed. Prisoners had to carry railway tracks, about a dozen of them being required to bear the heavy weight of each one, and Arie tried to stand tall for his shoulder to reach the metal at least, so as not to arouse the suspicions of guards sitting round fires to keep warm. German prisoners – skilled workers, with some privileges – then took the tracks, positioning and securing them under supervision of older OT professionals.

> We worked like this for about a month. It was hard. It was already about the beginning of March. We didn't wash ourselves, we didn't change our clothes. On Sundays, whenever there was a chance, when it was sunny, but also when it snowed, our occupation was to sit outside, in order to be able to see well when we took our shirts off, to kill lice. Lice were everywhere. Like apes, we checked each other for lice. The lice devoured us and troubled us greatly.[8]

Having toiled and survived like this, Arie and other remaining prisoners were eventually forced on a death march from Landsberg to Dachau, which was liberated on 29 April 1945 by American troops.

After the liberation came the painstakingly slow task of identifying the victims of Kaufering. More than four years after the end of the war, the names of only six of them had been officially determined: four Lithuanian Jews, one Frenchman and a woman of unknown nationality. SS destruction of virtually all files relating to Kaufering made the task especially hard, but H. Cleve-Olsen of the International Tracing Service (ITS) was clear about some details of the camp complex in November 1949. 'There were about 1,500 guardsmen, most of whom (70 per cent) were SS men and the others from the Wehrmacht. The guardsmen have guarded the camps and brought the prisoners to the working-places and back. At the work the prisoners have been guarded and supervised by the OT men.'[9]

Hard labour under the Organisation Todt

The stories of camp survivors like Arie P. and what they suffered, specifically under the Organisation Todt, are the focus of this chapter. Their voices have scarcely been heard. The accounts of these former prisoners tell us about the circumstances surrounding violence and deaths in the camps. They also help to reveal the individuals and organisations responsible. SS guards carried out mass shootings of prisoners, but OT staff also practised mass killing by shooting, beating and working prisoners to death, or 'selecting' sick camp inmates to be sent to extermination camps such as Auschwitz-Birkenau to be murdered.[10]

OT personnel routinely practised direct physical violence on prisoners, and the organisation's nature as a specialist construction agency meant that camp inmates usually endured the worst possible conditions, undertaking extreme hard labour in the open in all weathers. It was the OT that generally set the pace on work sites, since it was predominantly responsible for all technical matters. OT staff therefore drove labourers to perform tasks with widespread acts of direct violence, including beatings. The OT was also mainly responsible for providing prisoners with food, and the almost invariably inadequate rations caused a large proportion of the deaths among prisoners.

OT staff inflicted all these forms of direct violence on camp inmates, but another important type of violence was rife in the labour camps: 'structural violence', which was committed indirectly. The term was coined by Norwegian political scientist Johan Galtung in 1969, and the concept has filtered into historical research on concentration camps to describe the denial of basic needs as acts of violence in themselves.[11] It is a useful expression in examining OT treatment of slave labourers in camps, since it covers areas for which the organisation was responsible. OT staff were not only in charge of supervising prisoners on work sites and supplying food to them, but also providing shelter, clothing and medical care that were either inadequate or entirely lacking. All these OT abuses translated into prisoners' deaths through exhaustion, hunger, exposure and disease. It was these afflictions which were the biggest killers in satellite and labour camps, rather than physical violence by guards.[12]

To assess how much responsibility the OT bore for all types of violence, the degree of control it exercised in the camps must be established as far as possible. The OT mostly operated in close cooperation with the SS, the Wehrmacht and industry in exploiting slave labour, so it is necessary to identify how duties were shared. The OT amassed considerable powers in the Greater Reich in the final year of the war, when it was in overall charge of many major projects. It was also in sole charge of some camps in German-occupied territories in Europe. Where it was not in complete control, it had specific duties relating to care of prisoners. Assessing OT responsibility where it was in sole charge, or its duties were clearly defined, is relatively straightforward. When tasks were shared, identifying each partner's exact level of responsibility for the foreign workers' maltreatment and deaths was often problematic. The overall picture was complex and anomalies were frequent. In general, though, the SS carried out most mass shootings of prisoners that occurred. The OT was typically responsible for beating or working individuals to death, providing pitifully inadequate rations, 'selections' of the sick or 'structural violence' against labour-camp inmates under its control.

The OT's widespread failure to provide adequate basic care for prisoners had catastrophic consequences. Deaths resulted from this denial of basic needs. As the survivors' accounts show, physical and other forms of violence spilled over into one another. This phenomenon has been scarcely recognised in analyses of camp violence so far. Prisoners crazed by hunger were killed by SS bullets as they tried to grab food;[13] SS guards murdered camp inmates in mass shootings to prevent epidemics caused by lack of medical care;[14] and prisoners beaten by OT overseers to make them work harder subsequently died of exhaustion.[15] In the inhumane environment of the camps, the distinctions between different types of violence tended to blur.

To provide a framework for survivors' accounts, the first of four sections in this chapter investigates how much control the OT exercised over camps. The greater the degree of OT control, the more opportunity the organisation had to curb or increase violence, and vice versa if it exercised less control. The stories of former camp inmates are analysed and placed in the context of additional evidence to determine how levels of violence varied. The second group of survivor accounts concentrates on the ethnic origin of inmates and the effects of the Nazi racial hierarchy on prisoners' fates; the third assesses types of labour performed; and the fourth examines differences between the treatment of male and female prisoners.

Survivor accounts are analysed as they are presented, but a summary of conclusions comes at the end of the chapter. The camp inmates' accounts complement evidence from other sources of OT abuse of foreign workers presented in this book. They allow the labourers to describe their experiences themselves. Evidence from post-war Allied and German investigations is included whenever it illustrates conditions in the labour camps. Statements offering similar insights by OT and SS personnel are also used where a critical review of the context and sources indicates they had no compelling reason to lie.

Organisation Todt control over camps

The OT took charge of several major military projects in the Greater Reich in the final year of the war, exercising more control than ever over slave labourers in a crescendo of violence. OT personnel committed acts of lethal violence against prisoners working on all major projects in which their organisation had a principal stake at this time, including the Dachau subcamp complexes of Kaufering and Mühldorf, the Riese (Giant) network and the Wüste (Desert) programme. Kaufering and Mühldorf were examples of projects not only run by the OT but where the organisation was responsible for the prisoners to an unprecedented extent within the Third Reich's concentration-camp system. The satellite camps in these complexes represented a new type operating in Germany's core in which the SS, while still performing guard duties, largely withdrew from administration. The OT was thus substantially in charge of networks of subcamps where thousands of prisoners died.[16] It even took part in 'selections' of exhausted or sick prisoners for transport to death camps. This integral part of Nazi terror, normally performed by the SS, was frequently carried out in Mühldorf by an OT physician, Dr Erika Flocken. While this degree of OT responsibility in concentration-camp subcamps represented a significant change in the core of the Reich, the OT had long imposed a lethal regime of its own in labour camps in German-occupied Europe.

The high level of control exercised by the OT in the Greater Reich in this period of the war coincided with especially high death tolls in the camps it oversaw. In all the projects just listed, the OT either had effective control of running the camps or was responsible for providing all or most of the inmates' needs in terms of food, shelter and medical care. Accounts of survivors of these camps are analysed first, before turning to examples of more equally shared control with the SS, the Wehrmacht and industry in the occupied territories. How did the OT adapt, and how were levels of violence affected by the changing circumstances? Survivors' descriptions of camps in occupied East, North and Southeast Europe, where conditions were generally far harsher than in West Europe, are analysed to try to answer these questions. Finally, smaller camps in Norway and on the Channel Island of Alderney, off France's Brittany coast, are examined, where for specific periods the OT was in sole command.

Greater Reich

Among camp complexes within the Reich, the horrors of Kaufering were graphically depicted in Arie P.'s account of life there at the beginning of this chapter. While physical and other forms of violence caused the high death toll, it is significant that murders by SS guards were not uppermost in every survivor's mind. For Abram Grünstein, hunger, exhaustion and illness took the heaviest toll. Grünstein arrived in Kaufering Camp XI from Auschwitz in autumn 1944 and was forced to do construction work under OT supervision. He recalled the bodies of prisoners who had died overnight being found in the morning.

> I don't remember murders being committed in Kaufering Camp XI. But I know that many prisoners died in the camp. We lived in inhuman conditions, many of the prisoners had already experienced several camps and were completely run down. We received scarcely anything to eat and we had to perform very hard labour. The prisoners died of malnutrition, cold and there were also very many who became ill from potato peelings (dysentery) and were not medically treated. We lived in bunkers and when I woke early in the morning I saw a few times that prisoners had died during the night. The corpses remained in our bedroom when we went to roll-call and when we came back from work in the evening we found they were no longer there. I suppose that those prisoners who stayed in the camp for cleaning work must have cleared away the bodies.[17]

Abraham Katz, a prisoner in Kaufering X, witnessed no killings through physical violence either, but described how inmates died of sickness and the effects of appalling camp conditions.

> We buried 4–5 of my fellow sufferers outside the camp. But they died as a result of inhuman conditions, sickness etc. It was winter when we all had to hand in all our clothes for de-lousing. We had to stand completely naked for some hours

until we got our clothes back from the disinfection. One of my fellow sufferers, who came from Lithuania, I don't remember his name any more, fell sick as a result of the freezing weather and died after one or two days.[18]

Kaufering IV, the camp hospital, was known as the death camp because of its high daily death rates. Kaufering VII was normally reserved for those too weak to work, and was where thirteen-year-old Arie P. was held before being transferred to Kaufering I.[19] Arie recalled a daily routine of toil in the open, exposed to bitter winter weather without sufficiently warm clothing. His description of lice infestation among the prisoners reflected pitifully unhygienic camp conditions. He described how he and other ravenous prisoners ate raw potatoes while working in the fields. Workers shod only in wooden clogs used cement sacks to protect their feet in winter. The sacks were also used to wrap around themselves and to cover planks on which they slept, to provide a little extra insulation and warmth.[20]

Reflecting the level of sickness and abuse of prisoners in Kaufering in December 1944, an OT overseer, Stabsfrontführer Gerhard Buschmann, stated: 'The prisoners have been subjected to such abuse over the past period that today 17,600 prisoners are being fed, but of these only 8,319 are fit to work. Those prisoners only capable of light work are even supposed to be included in this total.' He said almost every OT staff member on the Moll firm's sites carried sticks to beat prisoners and so 'train' them to work better, yet some of the main reasons for labourers' poor productivity were lice infestation and poor management by OT staff themselves. He supported using force to cure prisoners' 'lethargy', but believed beatings should not replace proper leadership.[21] Buschmann's criticism of OT behaviour was motivated by a desire to raise productivity rather than concern for prisoners' welfare, and the OT could act ruthlessly to achieve its goals. Firms would complain to the OT about having to pay for a given number of prisoners, even though they failed to turn up for work or were unable to work if they did. As a result, the OT had told the SS in the main Dachau camp as early as the autumn of 1944 to take away prisoners representing a 'burden' for Kaufering and Mühldorf. A total of 1,322 were selected as incapable of work in September–October 1944 and sent from Kaufering to Auschwitz, where they were murdered.[22]

Apart from physical degradation due to work and camp conditions, guards and supervisors constantly employed brute force in the Kaufering complex. Arie P. was a victim, even though he did not clearly identify who struck him to the ground with a baton, causing lifelong impairments to his sight and hearing. Like virtually all prisoners, he also suffered the more routine blows from rifle butts, shovels or other implements which SS guards and OT and Wehrmacht overseers dealt out to camp inmates. He described OT personnel, specifically, as harsher than the SS, while army soldiers who guarded his potato-harvesting detail were less strict.[23] Elsewhere in the Kaufering complex, Hungarian Ervin Deutsch saw OT staff hit two inmates of Camp III with a spade or shovel in separate incidents, killing both victims.[24]

Conditions in the Mühldorf complex were similarly catastrophic. A German survivor, Elois Eisenhändler, described a site where prefabricated concrete tunnels, used in the construction of Mühldorf's underground factory to produce fighter planes, were built in the locality of Ampfing.

> As medical orderly for this building site, I can say here, in particular, that a string of young prisoners – it involved 14- to 16-year-old Hungarian Jews – died while working on the building site. As the entire population of Ampfing can confirm, we returned in the winter months daily to the camp with several dead, and often up to 20 utterly exhausted prisoners, who were incapable of walking on their own.[25]

Near-starvation racked prisoners in the Mühldorf camp complex. Zoltan B. said fellow inmates were so driven by hunger they would risk death for just a few wheat grains scavenged from the rubble of a ruined mill. As the column marched by on the way to work, some would dash to scoop a handful of debris from the site in the hope of finding something edible. The SS guard would shoot at them every time, not always with fatal results.

> On occasion, it was just a handful of rubble, but at other times a few grains were there and for that they ran the risk, for life had no worth. And we had to take the dead with us to the work site and bring them back afterwards, because the tally had to be right at the entrance. However many had gone out had to return.[26]

Zoltan's story illustrates how interconnected the various types of violence became in the camps: the extreme inadequacy of rations supplied by the OT caused severely malnourished prisoners to brave SS bullets in their desperate search for food. Similarly, exhaustion and lack of adequate medical care and shelter led to prisoners falling sick and being 'selected' to be murdered in Auschwitz. Hunger and death, whether through hard labour, disease or homicide, were so widespread that any distinction between various types of violence as definitive causes of death in every case appeared arbitrary. In both Kaufering and Mühldorf the OT held wide responsibilities for the prisoners. Court documents from the Mühldorf trial in 1947 showed that beyond overseeing the extreme hard labour performed by inmates at work sites, the 'OT was contractually responsible for housing, food, medical supplies and medical treatment for all workers, including inmates, engaged in any aspect of the project'.[27] The situation in the Kaufering camps was the same.[28]

Like many prisoners, Zoltan was compelled to work at a number of different camps, including Mühldorf and Kaufering. An electrician from a Jewish family in Romania, he described prisoners' extreme hunger in Kaufering and how they were forced to eat leaves, acorns and beech nuts. His weight dropped by almost half, from 60 kg to 32 kg, from the time he went there to the time of his liberation.[29] He had earlier been in one of the camps in the Riese (Giant) complex, whose parent concentration camp was Gross-Rosen. At this network of subcamps in Lower Silesia, the OT was responsible for overseeing prisoners at work and providing them with rations, accommodation and clothing.[30] Describing the constantly mounting death toll at a Riese camp called Fürstenstein, Zoltan said one prisoner died every day in small huts where workers slept closely packed on the ground. Corpses were stacked in the washroom, and a dead inmate's place would be taken almost at once by another fit enough to work. In such desperate conditions, Zoltan said survival depended on being able to work to be given food, since those judged unfit received less and risked 'selection' for transport to a death camp. Sheer luck saved him from this fate. Zoltan had been 'selected' because he became too weak, but a work-site foreman rescued him because he needed an electrician. 'It was chance. If he hadn't come, if no electrician had been needed at that moment, I would have been transported the next morning to the gas chamber and to the crematorium and it would have been over.'[31]

Selections of pitifully weak workers such as Zoltan in satellite camps usually signified a death sentence and transportation either back to the main concentration camp, to a specially designated camp for the sick within a big complex, or to an extermination camp. Seeking maximum worker output with minimum outlay for their care, the concentration-camp SS followed no set pattern, conducting both mass and individual selections to maintain what they saw as the required work rate.[32] Zoltan's physical condition stemmed from OT abuses causing hunger and exhaustion for many of his fellow inmates also in danger of 'selection'. However, instead of being listed for immediate transportation to Auschwitz, prisoners unable to work were sent to designated camps for the sick in large networks such as Riese. Dutchman Hartog P., a Jewish slave labourer in the Riese complex, told how he was earmarked to be sent to Dörnhau subcamp after contracting typhus. He described how he at first hid under a pile of potato peelings to avoid being sent to the camp, but then changed his mind, fearing that prisoners would be counted and he would be missed. He ran after his fellow prisoners and joined them just in time.

> And then we had to line up and then they counted and two men were missing. They went into the camp with dogs. Two men were hiding in the toilet, down below, so that they stood that high in filth, and then they had to come out. They came running towards us and they were beaten as they ran until they reached the station. There, they were beaten for so long that they died.[33]

Hartog survived Dörnhau, but the very existence of such camps reflected not only the fear of all camp staff of succumbing to typhus epidemics themselves, but also the ruthlessness with which they weeded out those unable to work. In the Wüste (Desert) complex, for instance, where an estimated 2,000–3,000 OT personnel worked on the project to extract oil from shale, the SS commandant for its two biggest camps, Hauptsturmführer Franz Hofmann, explained simply that he 'just wanted to get rid of the sick prisoners from Bisingen and Dautmergen'.[34] One survivor, Jacek Z., described desperate conditions in a block specially designated for the sick in Dautmergen camp, the largest in Wüste.

> People stayed there who couldn't even go to work. They were the convalescents, some after a stay in the so-called hospital. In the middle, there was a stove. A big, cast iron stove for heating. The people came down from the pallet-beds and gathered around the stove. They were convinced that it would get warmer round the stove. That it was not producing heat was unimportant. They didn't have the strength to search for lice after taking their shirts off. They just took them off and shook out the bugs. The big things fell down there, believe me, I was there and I saw them. The floor was moving. The floor was really moving. Such conditions reigned there.[35]

Jacek was a Polish former inmate of both Auschwitz and Dautmergen, where he described having to go barefoot until he was able to acquire wooden clogs from an inmate who had died. Inmates working in winter possessed nothing more than summer clothes. He rated Dautmergen worse than Auschwitz after being sent there aged 18. He said he made the comparison 'in terms of the extent of evil', but acknowledged he had 'a hell of a lot of luck'. Jacek described life for the vast majority in Dautmergen as 'unadulterated horror'. But he said that after arriving there from Auschwitz in August 1944 he managed to get a job under a Polish prisoner doctor in the camp sick bay, where conditions were better. When an SS officer put him back on hard-labour duties, he once more gained access to privileges through being chosen to work in the SS quarters, where he said a middle-aged *SS-Oberscharführer* gave him extra food.

The main tasks for OT staff working in Dautmergen and other camps in the Wüste complex included building the prisoners' accommodation, cooperating with the SS on site and organising firms and labour to do the work. In Bisingen the OT provided the inmates' meagre rations, which were further reduced by the SS siphoning off food for their own use. The OT were also responsible for the prisoners' pitifully inadequate accommodation. As for physical violence, beatings of prisoners were a daily routine at the hands of the SS, OT, firm employees and 'Kapo' prisoner functionaries. One OT member named Kabus was sentenced to death and executed by a French court for severely mistreating Bisingen inmates.[36] But for all the brutality displayed by OT and SS personnel, production of shale oil was insignificant at Bisingen, and it had to be extracted in a process far more laborious than was needed in German-occupied Estonia, where the oil content in shale deposits was much higher. The oil produced in the Wüste programme was in any case useless for aircraft engines without further refining. Bisingen survivor Alfred Korn told how thousands of prisoners under OT and SS overseers were driven mercilessly to the bitter end. He described how a pipe from the shale oil plant to a cistern at the station would deliver just one drop of oil about every five minutes, underlining the pointlessness of the entire Wüste project in terms of its contribution to the German war effort.

> ... In any case, thousands of prisoners had worked so that every five minutes a drop dripped, and then nothing for five minutes and then again, drip. The drop went into the cistern and that was the extent of production of the shale oil plant in Bisingen.[37]

East Europe

Having examined big camp complexes in Greater Germany where the OT exercised very high degrees of control, the next step is to investigate how the organisation adapted to sharing the management of camps in a more balanced fashion with its partners in the exploitation of foreign forced and slave labour. In German-occupied Soviet territory, the Third Reich's concentration-camp system extended into the Baltics, where the OT was heavily involved in supervising Jewish inmates of the SS-run Vaivara complex. This concentration camp became infamous for mass shootings carried out by the SS. While the SS ran Vaivara, the OT was one of the main employers, alongside Baltöl, in the major project to extract oil from shale. Ways in which OT personnel contributed to violence against inmates in the Vaivara complex included direct physical assaults and providing the pitifully inadequate rations for prisoners. Newly established Vaivara subcamps were also sometimes initially run by OT personnel, and a small camp remained under OT command during Vaivara's year-long existence.

These elements, with varying levels of OT control and responsibility for rations and work-site supervision, contributed to the miserable conditions in Vaivara subcamps. OT staff acted as commandants in a few camps, but this was mostly for short periods and the OT exercised lower levels of control overall than in camp complexes like Kaufering and Mühldorf in the Reich. Vaivara's Jõhvi subcamp was exceptional in that it was controlled throughout by an OT commandant, but it was relatively small. Jõhvi was an important centre for OT and Baltöl operations, and was not incorporated into the Vaivara complex when the first 201 prisoners arrived there in October 1943. While the OT provided guards and Jõhvi never had an SS officer in charge, a brutal SS medical orderly, Erich Scharfetter, was active there. The OT briefly controlled Auvere and the subcamps of Vaivara and Vivikonna, as well as Ereda, whose first commandant was an OT member.[38] A prisoner sent to Ereda in September 1943, Bernard Zalkindson, stated: 'The camp leader was a Todt man who stole a lot while the Jews were starving. He divided a loaf of bread among six persons, i.e. 20 decagrams. Later he raised it to 30 decagrams. A tiny bit of fat and marmalade. All of them were very hungry.'[39] Ereda was divided into an upper section and a marshy lower section and a former inmate of the latter, Sholem Shub, said:

> Here, in Lower Ereda, worked for Todt in jobs like: 25 km from Ereda, digging bunkers; women, 12 km [away] in Kohtla-Järve in an oil shale factory; a small group 1.5 km [away] worked loading parts of the shale factory and oil shales that were shipped to Hamburg. Mortality in Lower Ereda was high, about 1–2 persons a day.[40]

Eta Weismann, a Wilna-born survivor of the lower camp in Ereda, said the work was very hard, there was little food and many prisoners died in severe conditions, sleeping in tents in winter. 'During the night our hair froze on to the walls ... I remember that the sick and weak who were unable to march out in the morning to work were no longer there in the evening. I suppose they had been killed.'[41]

Although the name of the whole concentration-camp complex was Vaivara, there was also a subcamp of the same name. Former inmate Zelik Gurwicz recalls that when he arrived there in summer 1943, the commandant was a member of the OT, 'a fat man who wore a leather jacket'. Shortly afterwards the SS took over and Helmut Schnabel became commandant, with a deputy called Kurt Pannicke. Gurwicz's comments about an incident concerning Pannicke clearly show his fear not just of the SS, but also of the OT.

> I had to steal leather for Pannicke from the O.T. and make boots for his girlfriends and three pairs of boots for him. When I refused the task of stealing

leather from the O.T. because I was afraid I would be shot, Pannicke said: 'That doesn't matter. Whether the O.T. shoots you now, or whether I shoot you later is of no importance.'[42]

Franz Leichter, who worked for the OT with a German firm in Ereda camp, said a uniformed OT staff member who was a 'staunch National Socialist' was in charge of where they were quartered, in a camp separated from the Jewish labour camp by barbed wire. He described the prisoners' enclosure at Ereda before its evacuation: 'The conditions in the camp were atrocious. There was neither clothing nor means of heating; the accommodation was also extraordinarily primitive; there were not even blankets. The clothes consisted merely of rags. Nevertheless, whether man or woman, the people were woken every day at 4 a.m. and sent to work no matter what the weather.' Leichter said camp inmates laboured mainly either doing woodwork or in sawmills, with the OT and with staff of his mining firm, Dailmann. Severe punishment beatings by SS officers on the roll-call square were frequent. Two or three deaths from various causes occurred daily. 'The food consisted basically of watery soups and was without doubt completely insufficient.'[43]

Physical violence by OT personnel also took its toll on Vaivara prisoners. Philipp Alwin, who was deported from Wilna ghetto to Ereda camp with his two sons, said:

> During our work, we were often beaten by a member of the Org. Todt, called Zimmermann, with his belt, planks of wood or clubs. Since he had treated us well before, I asked him one day why he now beat us. Upon which he answered me that he himself was pained by it, but he was following an order of [SS camp commandant Helmut] Schnabel's.[44]

The OT supervised prisoners performing extreme hard labour at work sites, contributing to the number of deaths of exhausted prisoners weakened by hunger. The SS, meanwhile, regularly carried out selections of the sick to be sent from Vaivara for extermination, and resorted to mass killings of the able-bodied in the final evacuation phase. Atrocities included shootings at Klooga and Ereda subcamps. Deaths from causes other than SS mass shootings were high, with 1,506 deaths overall between October 1943 and June 1944, meaning more than one-sixth of inmates died of illness, individual maltreatment and targeted killing of the sick.[45]

The OT's assumption of roles usually filled by the SS, such as guard duties, reflected how tightly their operations were interwoven. SS barbarities therefore played out before OT staff at close quarters. Leichter saw SS men carrying out a mass killing of Jews in July 1944 before Ereda camp was closed. His firm's main task at the camp had been to build shafts to mine the oil shale, and he described what he and his colleagues witnessed:

> From the shaft tower we now saw from a distance of about 40–50 metres that the Jews were led up to the pits in groups, about 100–150 at a time. They thus stood in rows behind one another and the Jews finding themselves at the earth ridge had to kneel down and were killed by three SS people firing pistol shots to the neck, and pushed into the flames in the pit ...[46]

The close relationship between the OT and SS, working side by side in Vaivara, was illustrated by a sex scandal involving an SS commandant at Ereda. Heinz Drohsin asked OT personnel to help him escape when he became embroiled in a scandal over his love affair with a Jewish woman among a group of Germans and Czechs transferred to the camp. Leichter said the woman's name was Inge, and their relationship came to the attention of Drohsin's SS superiors. Drohsin was helped by OT staff to flee, but in the end committed suicide with his girlfriend.[47]

In another illustration of the OT and SS sharing tasks, OT staff member Otto Schmid said he was supplied with a weapon whenever he was detailed to guard a camp for Jewish labourers at Palemonas, near the city of Kaunas in the Baltic state of Lithuania. He also worked under the OT for the Trucksäss company in Vaivara in summer 1943, and described OT duties as guards for slave labourers:

> We had to build a large barracks camp there, near an oil shale works named Kiviöli. We were billeted in the camp for Jews in Vaivara, near the station. We of the OT were only assigned to guard the Jewish camp in Vaivara. The camp for Jews guarded by us in Vaivara held about 250 Jews. We had brought these Jews every day to the oil shale works at Kiviöli.

He said the distance from Vaivara to Kiviöli was 3 kilometres, and the Jews were marked with a star of David. 'The guarding of the Jews during the transport, or march, from Vaivara to Kiviöli was only done by OT men, as well as the supervision at the work site. As soon as we had brought the Jews back to the camp, Estonian soldiers, who wore field-grey uniforms, took over custody.' Schmid was also assigned to Jewe (Jõhvi) camp, where OT personnel guarded a camp for Jews and Russians, whom they took to and from the work site and oversaw during construction of a big military hospital.[48] Otto Hefele said he worked as a head guard when he was sent by the OT in early 1942 to Palemonas. There were about 300 Jewish men and women in the work force and 'many ... used to run away from work'. Like Schmid, he then acted as a guard at Jewe.[49]

When not on guard duty, OT personnel cooperated with the SS in their more usual role of work-site overseers of male and female Jewish workers at Vaivara. Paul Hanke was sent as an OT staff member to Vaivara's main oil-shale mining camp of Kiviöli in winter 1942. His quarters were in an OT camp across the road from a large camp for Jewish prisoners where men, women and children were all held together. 'I had a work detail of Jews. This "Kommando" consisted of 400 men and 200 women. During the work period they were led to work by 10 OT foremen. They were guarded at work by 20 Estonian policemen, who were under the SS. The work detail was again also employed cutting wood.'[50]

This arrangement of the OT collecting prisoners from camps and supervising them at work sites while the SS stood guard was also in place at Palemonas camp, where Hanke had been posted earlier. The OT oversaw Jewish and Lithuanian civilian workers there and his Berlin engineering firm, Heinrich Köhler, had been contracted by the OT to carry out work in Lithuania. Hanke mostly oversaw Jewish and civilian workers felling trees and producing railway sleepers. The camp was under SS guard, so OT staff fetched Jews daily from the camp and took them to work. When Hanke switched from Köhler to the firm of Trucksäss, he supervised 200 Jewish women working under the OT in a gravel pit near Wilna (Vilnius).[51]

Roma were also among the OT's slave-labour workforce scattered across Europe. Konstantins C., the youngest of ten children in a Roma family from Latvia, was just sixteen years old when he was sent to Jõhvi, and remembers a life of hunger, cold and bare survival that led him to the point of planning to commit suicide by crushing himself between railway wagons. But a friend pulled him back. 'I just cried, he pulled me away from there, otherwise … I would have killed myself.'[52]

In the rest of the occupied Soviet Union, hundreds of slave-labour camps were set up for Jews and the OT exploited prisoners on a massive scale. This included conscripting slave labour to carry out road building over vast distances. Transit Road IV was of high strategic importance, since it led to the Caucasus oilfields.[53] As with all such roads, a senior OT engineer was put in charge. OT personnel ran some of the camps where slave labourers were held in wretched conditions on the route of Transit Road IV. Landesbaurat Arnold Adam, in his capacity as OT Linienchef DG IV, was responsible for technical oversight of the work, in which various German construction companies were also involved. About twenty primitive camps lay on the Ukrainian section of the road, run by the SS, police or OT. Newly arrived prisoners in all camps were subject to 'selections' of the sick, elderly or those otherwise deemed unfit to work, to be sent off for extermination. Food was totally insufficient in the camps, which often lacked running water, and prisoners were invariably infested with lice so that epidemics of diseases, especially typhus, were frequent. Most Jews either worked directly on the road, broke stones in nearby quarries or laboured in gravel pits. Several hundred Jews, men, women and children, were typically held in existing buildings that were commandeered and surrounded by barbed wire. Prisoners were frequently packed into barns or cattle sheds alongside farm animals. In Michailowka, for instance, about 12 kilometres from Gaisin, 500 Ukrainian and Romanian Jews were held until November 1942 in stables in which horses were kept at the same time.[54] During an inspection trip in 1942, OT press and propaganda chief Rudolf Wolters noted in his diary the 'exceedingly wretched' appearance of Jews working on the road under OT supervision and made clear they understood the grim fate they faced. He said he had been told some of the Jews 'work voluntarily for two successive shifts. They know what's at stake now.'[55] Around 20,000 Jewish slave labourers died on just one 265-kilometre section of the road eastwards from Przemysl.[56]

OT records give details of hundreds of Jews, prisoners of war and civilian slave labourers working on Transit Road IV in the Gaisin area in Ukraine from 1942 to 1944. The reports, while an incomplete mixture of weekly and monthly tallies, show daily figures of workforce strengths provided by the German *Arbeitsgemeinschaft* (working combine) August Dohrmann, which was a syndicate of smaller firms contracted to the OT for the construction of the roughly 50-kilometres stretch of road between Gaisin and Krasnopolka. They reveal that the labourers worked a seven-day week, although numbers were much reduced on Sundays. A directive from OT headquarters in Berlin in January 1943 instructed firms to fill in forms each month to report worker strengths under column headings, including German foremen and skilled workers, company employees and *Ostarbeiter*. Another column is shared between prisoners of war, to be entered on the left, and Jews, to be entered on the right. Jews and prisoners of war generally figured in greater numbers on these labour reports, but on some days *Ostarbeiter* equalled or considerably outnumbered them. The highest daily total of 714 Jews was recorded in early January 1943.[57]

Prisoners were also exposed to Soviet air raids. At the 'gateway to the Caucasus' further to the southeast, an OT unit built a road bridge over the River Don, near Rostov, in just over six weeks as winter closed in in 1942. The workforce comprised 1,100 prisoners of war and more than 660 Soviet civilian labourers, plus about half that combined total of OT personnel, or 'front workers'. Two bombs fell on the OT POW camp for the bridge-building operation, killing or wounding around 100 prisoners of war and causing the deaths of two OT staff in an air attack on the night of 24–25 September 1942.[58]

North Europe

Outside the Soviet Union, a big OT operation in North Europe exploited Soviet labour in Norway to build coastal defences, as well as road and rail links up into the Arctic Circle. Levels of OT control differed to some extent from inside the Reich, where the organisation was put in overall charge of big projects like Kaufering, Mühldorf and Riese. OT responsibility for violence and deaths among prisoners in Norway derived from complete or shared control of individual labour camps or networks, supervision of hard labour and provision of profoundly inadequate rations, medical care, clothing and shelter. The large number of foreign workers deported to Norway made this operation stand out among the many gargantuan construction tasks relying on slave labour across Nazi-occupied territory. The vast majority of the foreign labourers were Slavs. The 110,000 Soviet prisoners of war and civilians, as well as 6,600 Yugoslavs and Poles, suffered every type of violence at the hands of OT, SS and Wehrmacht guards, and more than 18,400 died.[59] The OT, led in Norway by SS-Standartenführer Willi Henne, became a dominant player in the country's construction sector.

One Russian prisoner, aged thirty-one, writing in his diary on the fifth birthday of one of his daughters, Tamotseka, in February 1943, described life in Camp 3 near the Norwegian port of Trondheim, where he complained of being 'half-starved' but nevertheless received care when he was ill for three weeks in the camp ward.

> If you only knew what hardships your father must endure in damp, foggy and rough Norway. There cannot be anything worse than such a life. More correctly termed it is no life, at any rate not the life of a human being, but that of a beast ... When they laugh at you and have the right to spit in your face, to strike you without having to answer for it and being punished for it, that is the condition of a slave, what can be worse and more shameful?[60]

When he and 200 fellow prisoners were transferred by ship to a more northerly camp in the Arctic Circle later that month, he writes:

> We have arrived in the new place, an island. In Harstad we were taken ashore. The camp is situated 3 to 4 kilometres from the town and is much worse than the one we left. There are summer barracks, which look like stables and are dirty, damp and cold ... even now it is clear to me that we have been brought here to perish. Of the old 600 PW [prisoners of war] who arrived here 4 months ago, there are only 274 left, the rest are dead.[61]

This anonymous Russian prisoner's diary, which ended abruptly on 25 April 1943, was found at Trondenes camp, where the OT used Soviet POWs to build coastal batteries. These included four 406 mm guns in the Atlantic Wall defending approaches to the port of Narvik. More than 1,000 of the prisoners died.[62] Hitler fretted in August 1942 about delays in construction of batteries at Trondenes and in the Narvik region, complaining about shortcomings in the navy's planning and authorising the OT to report to Speer if work failed to meet Westwall standards.[63] Accounts by former Soviet prisoners of camp life in Norway provide only fragments of the overall picture,[64] although British war-crimes investigators interviewed Russian survivors when mass graves were discovered near Skibotn, Mallnitz and other Arctic camps, around 175 kilometres to the northeast of Trondenes. Dr Klementi Gogia, aged thirty-four and a camp survivor, helped to care for around 560 fellow Russian former prisoners at Øvergaard hospital in the immediate aftermath of the war. Many of the Russian survivors of Mallnitz and the other camps, where they worked under German army supervision, including a POW labour battalion assigned to the OT,[65] were severely emaciated and suffering from tuberculosis or gangrene. Investigators found evidence of cannibalism on some bodies in the mass graves. Dr Gogia, a navy captain in the Caspian fleet who was captured at Stalingrad and deported to Norway, said he thought many of his patients would die in Øvergaard hospital or on the journey back home.[66] Apart from such accounts by Dr Gogia and the anonymous diarist, detailed evidence of the German occupiers' murderous treatment of Soviet prisoners is contained in war-crimes investigations.[67] The names of thousands of Russian survivors shipped back to the Soviet Union via Murmansk in summer 1945 were listed in OT records.[68] The thousands more Russian prisoners who perished were buried in Norwegian soil.[69]

British and West German post-war investigations found that the OT was responsible for 'inhuman' living and working conditions for slave labourers in Norway. The German investigation focused on SS-run camps for Yugoslav prisoners at Karasjok, Beisfjord, Osen, Korgen, Rognan, Botn and OT-administered Ørlandet. Living and working conditions in the camps were harsh in the extreme. Many died of illness, exhaustion and cold. Many were killed by SS guards, overwhelmingly before the Wehrmacht took over all the camps in March 1943. Of a total of about 4,000–5,000 Yugoslav prisoners transported to Norway during the war, 1,622 were still alive at the end. At all camps, the works carried out by prisoners were under the leadership and supervision of the OT.[70] Out of 400 prisoners originally sent to Karasjok camp in Norway's northern Arctic region, where inmates mainly worked on the north–south highway known as Reichsstrasse 50, guards shot about 130 of them and roughly the same number died for other reasons. Of the latter group, 'most of the prisoners died as a result of insufficient food and clothing, of malnourishment, exhaustion and infectious diseases, especially as medical care, for which an OT doctor was responsible, was similarly inadequate'.[71] At all the camps, numerous prisoners were deliberately killed and many died of exhaustion or illness. Beisfjord and its subcamps had the highest death toll, with around 900 Serb prisoners transported there when the camp was set up in July 1942 and estimates of only eighty to 150 survivors when the camp was closed in October the same year. These survivors were moved to Osen or Korgen camps. 'The rest of the prisoners either fell victim to the hard work and living conditions or were killed'.[72]

Stjepan Pištignjat, then eighteen and from a Yugoslav ethnic Serb family, witnessed a mass killing of prisoners in Beisfjord camp on the night of 17–18 July 1942.[73] The commandant of Beisfjord, SS-Obersturmbannführer Wilhelm Goecke, had 287 sick prisoners shot dead that night by guards with machine guns, and then reported their loss in a typhus epidemic to his superiors in Oslo.[74]

> At night, but it wasn't proper nighttime, the night is as light as day there … They divided us up. They asked whoever … didn't feel well, not well enough to work, to go over into the huts over there, where they would get better food and recover, and once they had recovered they should go back to work again. And many did respond. Those who were sick went forward … and went over there behind the huts. And when they had gone over there, the German … soldiers stood there with wire and fence wire. They separated them from us. They forbade us to go up to the wire and they forbade them to do that too. And then the shooting began in the course of the day, as soon as someone went out from the huts there, where they had isolated them, he was shot immediately. They [the Germans] reported that typhus had broken out in the camp. And with that they then covered up the fact that they had killed the people there. It was scarcely credible, there was no typhus at all. In this way they murdered around 200–300 people between 17 and 18 July '42.[75]

Terzic Hilmo, another Yugoslav inmate of Beisfjord, also described the mass shooting and agreed that the murdered prisoners did not have typhus, only a 'slight fever'.[76]

Typhus epidemics were common in the camps, as senior OT and SS personnel were well aware. The mass killing at Beisfjord was another example of how direct and indirect types of violence became so interconnected that they appeared to merge. Whether or not typhus cases were among those shot, fear of disease among OT and SS personnel was very real, and measures to avoid infection of their own ranks were vigorous and frequently extreme. Abysmal camp conditions and hard labour in Beisfjord caused weakened prisoners to fall sick, and Goecke's order for the mass shooting was to wipe out 'typhus'. The OT was also integrally involved in labour-camp systems under which the sick were isolated in specific camps and OT medical staff, including Dr Erika Flocken at Mühldorf, selected sick prisoners for 'liquidation'.

The extent to which OT personnel were involved in denying basic needs to prisoners within SS-run camps in Norway was revealed in some detail by a remarkable report by SS-Sturmbannführer Dr Bauer, who was sent by HSSPF Nord Wilhelm Rediess to inspect camps in Norway in July–August 1942. He described serious failings and health dangers to both prisoners and German troops in his report, criticising the OT especially for providing insufficient food. Because of inadequate rations given out by the OT at Osen camp, whose commandant was SS-Sturmbannführer Hermann Dolp, 'the work output of the prisoners on this diet would very soon drop'. The OT's Baurat Schmidt had already informed his superiors of the situation at Osen and received promises of extra prisoner rations, but up to that point only on paper.[77] Rations were deficient in vitamins, and some prisoners had died of food poisoning after eating fish remains scavenged from a waste bin.[78] In Rognan, where the camp commandant was SS-Hauptsturmführer Fritz Kiefer, Dr Bauer noted that there were only a few cases of exhaustion caused by insufficient food.

Describing Jernvatn, where Goecke had built an overflow camp because of typhus in Beisfjord, Dr Bauer said the OT building officer in charge of the sector had refused point blank to rectify the camp's failings, including inadequate rations and shelter for the prisoners and guards.

> There can be no talk of a camp here of any description, neither regarding accommodation for the prisoners nor that of the guard detail. Describing any of the accommodation as a camp is laughable … Weather conditions provoked the most serious illnesses among the prisoners and also coughs and colds among the guards. Greater losses by the day were therefore unavoidable. Some of the prisoners were half-naked and could not be put to work. They lay in snow and rain, completely drenched, without means of warming themselves in the open air. Food was provided by the OT in insufficient quantity, both for the prisoners and for personnel. It was anyway impossible, since the access roads were completely unusable for vehicles and 3 of the 4 OT trucks were out of action. Baurat Köhling in Narvik, who is responsible for this camp sector, explained to me regarding my ideas, in response to repeated questioning on many occasions in front of witnesses: 'He was not in a position to offer any remedy.'[79]

At Nordreisa, further north, Dr Bauer was astonished that a camp supposed to accommodate 800 prisoners and their guards had scarcely been started, with only the bare structures of four huts for 120 men on site. Bauer insisted on a written confirmation from the OT leader there of this state of affairs. Prisoners were said to be already on their way to Nordreisa, on the route of the Arctic railway ordered by Hitler. Despite such delays, as well as the sheer scale of the task, the dictator brushed aside attempts by Speer to explain the practical difficulties of the project to him.[80] The railway was never completed.

At Karasjok, to the east of Nordreisa in Norway's far north, Dr Bauer once again appealed in vain to army officers and a regional OT chief to take steps to tackle the health risks to German troops and prisoners alike from lice-infested straw bedding in the makeshift camp lacking basic medical facilities. 'Lice infestation of the prisoners poses a very great danger of epidemics, especially also for the troop barracks directly next to the prisoners' camp,' he wrote, saying that OT engineer Dr Walter Beck declined to help. Beck, interviewed during a post-war West German investigation, spoke of 'bad food, bad equipment and the unfavourable weather conditions' hampering his road-building task in Karasjok using Serb labourers. He suspected SS personnel running the camp, who had lavish meals, of claiming for themselves some of the camp rations destined for prisoners.[81]

After his time in Beisfjord, Stjepan Pištignjat was sent on to other camps heavily criticised by Dr Bauer, including Osen and Korgen, where prisoners carried out road-building work under the OT.[82] Brutality by guards was not as extreme as at Beisfjord, but shootings and torture occurred. Extraordinarily, Pištignjat said the notoriously violent Osen camp commandant, Sturmbannführer Dolp, intervened to save his life when his leg was crushed by a rock so he could no longer work. 'I certainly expected him … to say: "Throw him in the pit" … and then one shot and finished!' Instead he called over a Yugoslav doctor among the prisoners, who examined Pištignjat and said the leg could be successfully treated. Dolp ordered this be done, and Pištignjat was allowed to stay in camp for some months until his leg healed.[83]

Cakic Avdo, another Yugoslav prisoner in Osen, described the brutal side of Dolp for which he was better known among the prisoners. He said Dolp used to visit the hut for the sick every morning to find out how many prisoners had died during the night. If he saw that some were very ill, he ordered they be buried alive. Avdo said he and fellow Yugoslav Terzic Hilmo, who had also been transferred to Osen, had to bury a still-living prisoner, Jurisic Josip, in December 1942. Hilmo told a guard that Josip was still breathing, but was threatened with being shot himself if he did not keep quiet and obey instructions.[84]

After the mass shooting in Beisfjord, Pištignjat and Hilmo both said they were taken with up to 500 other prisoners from Beisfjord to Bjørnfjell for road construction work. Many died in Bjørnfjell, and those who fell sick were shot. 'Every day about 10 people were buried and thrown into this common grave that we had dug when we arrived,' said Pištignjat. They had to sleep in the open for three weeks before they were told to build huts.[85]

In OT operations across Norway the organisation's personnel carried out technical supervision at work sites. Labour battalions were often formed of 1,000 or more prisoners, providing slave labour for major road and rail projects, airports, fortifications, timber felling for fuel, quarrying and snow clearing.[86] Exposure in the country's Arctic north caused many deaths. Amputations due to frostbite maimed more than 100 workers in just one camp in the winter of 1944–5. War-crimes investigators concluded that starvation probably contributed more than anything else to the death toll of prisoners. The already-insufficient rations were reduced still further by German personnel siphoning them off for their own use.[87]

Southeast and Central Europe

In the Balkans, Russian prisoners of war formed part of the slave-labour force at the important Bor copper mine. OT duties at the mine included acting as armed guards to escort labourers from camps to work sites.[88] Jewish labour became increasingly in demand, and in February 1943 the OT put out an urgent request for 10,000 more labourers at the Bor mine, for which Hungarian Jews were sought. While oil was a top priority for the Nazi war economy, the regime was also keen to exploit raw materials in occupied Europe for its armaments industry. The large copper mine at Bor, in Serbia, was a valuable prize. Although pre-war production levels were never reached, Bor provided almost a quarter of Germany's copper needs between spring 1942 and September 1944. Serbs were mobilised to work in the mine, and the OT was responsible for recruiting workers. In October 1942 figures for the number of workers at the Bor mine ranged between 18,000 and 30,000, but then dropped sharply, so the OT issued a report flagging up the shortfall of 10,000 labourers in February the following year. A letter to the Foreign Ministry in Berlin said 10,000 Jews were sought from Hungary for this purpose.[89] Up to September 1944, a total of 6,200 Jews worked in the Bor mine and on a railway between Bor and Žagubica. Few survived. Nándor H., a Jew born in what was then the kingdom of Hungary, recalled tunnelling in the Bor mine as 'extremely hard labour'. After blasting with dynamite, workers were sometimes killed by falling rocks.[90] Around 80,000 workers were deployed in Bor in the summer of 1944.

Milan Pantoviç, a Yugoslav then in his early twenties, recalled poor food and lice-infested blankets when he worked as a slave labourer in Bor, and described the plight of Italian military internees there. Apart from mining copper, labourers were required to work on railway lines between Bor, Žagubica and Požarevac. Pantoviç worked on a Žagubica tunnel and described how the Italian military detainees in the slave-labour workforce were treated so harshly that many were driven to trade some of the few clothes they possessed for extra food.[91]

On the Austria–Hungary border, Czechoslovak-born Jaroslav S. worked among forced or slave labourers under OT supervisors who were assisted by pro-Nazi Czech personnel. This limited sharing of control with local sympathisers contrasted with the OT's usual practice of cooperating with the SS or Wehrmacht. While German OT staff were in charge of overseeing the work, the pro-Hitler Czechs, who wore white linen uniforms and a belt with a swastika, helped organise the labour force under the direction of the OT. Jaroslav said the Czech assistant supervisors belonged to an institution in Prague called the Curatorship for Youth Education. His group was among 2,000–3,000 Czech labourers in the town of Mönchhof, all from the Protectorate of Bohemia and Moravia. Jaroslav was compelled to dig anti-tank ditches in severe winter conditions in 1944–5. The ground was frozen, blunting the workers' pickaxes. Jaroslav and fellow workers slept in a barn with a damaged roof and would sometimes wake up to find their thin blankets covered in snow.

> The German Organisation Todt supervised our work, a German organisation. They were veteran German soldiers from the front, predominantly the wounded, some of them invalids who were no longer fit for frontline service ... so they oversaw us in these uniforms, khaki uniforms with a swastika on the sleeve, they had machine-pistols and ... we had to keep moving, yes? ... we weren't allowed to stay still.[92]

The ditches had to be 7 metres wide and 5 metres deep, sloping diagonally inwards and downwards from the sides. The OT supervisors checked workers' daily performance and, although they swore and shouted if they deemed work insufficient, Jaroslav said he saw no shootings or punishment beatings. He said two young prisoners committed suicide, though, because 'their nerves simply couldn't bear it any more'. One drowned himself in a well and Jaroslav helped pull out his body, while the other hanged himself. Prisoners had to assemble at 5.00 a.m., when they were given black 'coffee', butter substitute and about 200 grams of bread, which had to last until after work stopped at 5.00 or 6.00 p.m. The evening meal was soup made with root vegetables and no meat. When Jaroslav suffered frostbite in his toes, he and a couple of friends persuaded the farmer's wife to let them sleep in the animal stall, which reeked of dung but was warmer and 'like paradise'.

Sole Organisation Todt control

Working in the vastness of the occupied Soviet territories and across Europe, the OT needed to cooperate with other German forces to complete its tasks. Share of control between the OT, the SS, the Wehrmacht and industry was the norm in labour camps. Every degree of OT control has been examined so far through the eyes of former prisoners, except for when the OT was in sole command. Two examples of such OT-controlled complexes in German-occupied Europe were at Ørlandet, in Norway, and on Alderney, one of the German-occupied Channel Islands which Hitler ordered in October 1941 to be turned into an 'impregnable fortress'.[93] These camps are particularly significant not because of their size, which was much smaller than the big complexes so far dealt with in this section, but because the OT alone was responsible for the prisoners in the camps over a specific period. It is therefore possible to draw conclusions about whether levels of violence were higher or lower when the OT operated by itself or when it worked together with forces such as the SS or the Wehrmacht. This helps answer the question of whether OT personnel practised violence on their own initiative, or only when influenced by the brutality of the SS. In the case of Ørlandet, direct comparison can be made with Wehrmacht command of the camp from March 1943, following about six months of sole OT control; in the case of Alderney, comparison can be made to death tolls before and after the arrival of the SS, also in March 1943.

Uroš Majstorović, the Ørlandet survivor whose description of the camp formed the start of this book, recalled that three prisoners were hanged for trying to escape. Camp inmates were then forced to march past the bodies.

> That was during the time of the Organisation Todt. When the Wehrmacht came, there were no more hangings. It only happened while we were still under the Organisation Todt.[94]

Majstorović had arrived at the camp in November 1942, following an initial transport of 156 Yugoslavs to Ørlandet in September. By March 1943, when the Wehrmacht took over, sixty-four prisoners had died, including the three hanged and two who had been shot.⁹⁵ Majstorović described how there had been no running water, no power and no heating in the prisoners' huts when he arrived. At this point the camp held about 300 prisoners, with fifty men in each hut and buckets provided because there were no latrines.⁹⁶ Subsequent transports brought the camp's prisoner total to as high as 500. During Majstorović's stay of more than two years there, constant beatings with rifle butts, clubs, spades, fists or boots took their toll on prisoners weakened by hunger due to the meagre rations provided.⁹⁷ Majstorović was forced at times to work overnight, and was treated harshly at Ørlandet while working under the OT to build coastal fortifications. When the army took over the camp, conditions became 'a little better, more bearable'. Before then the situation was desperate. 'The Organisation Todt, they were worse than the Wehrmacht … and the question was, if the Wehrmacht hadn't taken us over, who would then have survived at all?'⁹⁸

The death toll at Ørlandet during the time the OT was in sole command of the camp provides evidence the organisation did not require direct influence from partners like the SS to encourage its staff to practise violence. The Stuttgart firm Müller-Altvatter, which Majstorović remembered and which operated for the OT at Ørlandet-Austrät, produced accounts for the OT from early October 1942 to March 1943 showing that mostly Serb prisoners, along with Russian prisoners of war, had worked for the firm. An average of 150 prisoners worked on shifts of eight to eleven hours every day, with odd exceptions like Christmas and New Year's Day, on tasks including Ørlandet fortifications and construction of barracks.⁹⁹ Describing the type of work at Ørlandet, an OT engineer told West German prosecutors after the war that he had been employed by Müller-Altvatter and his task had been to supervise labourers installing a triple-turret (28 cm) gun from the former battleship *Gneisenau* as a coastal battery, along with accompanying accommodation and ammunition stores.¹⁰⁰

Before Ørlandet, Majstorović was sent following his arrival in Norway to another camp in the Trondheim area, Steinvikholmen, where he stayed for two months among about 200 inmates.¹⁰¹ Describing physical violence by OT staff, he recalled a particularly brutal *OT Meister* whom they nicknamed Saint Ilya, apparently a darkly humorous reference to the Orthodox seventeenth-century saint renowned for his strength.

> He was probably a sadist … Not a single camp inmate he hadn't beaten at least once. And he took delight in it, that was terrible … We came early in the morning to wash. People took their shirts off to wash and he came and beat them all on their backs! Terrible.¹⁰²

Conditions improved in SS- and OT-run camps from spring 1943, when the Wehrmacht took over all camps where mainly Yugoslavs like Majstorović were held. However, this did not mean that members of the Wehrmacht were always more moderate. The death toll at Ørlandet, for example, more than doubled by the end of the war, although the period of Wehrmacht control was around three times longer than that of the OT.[103] Elsewhere in Norway, too, abuses and resulting deaths continued under the Wehrmacht. In a notorious camp called Rognan-Botn, beatings, torture and persecution persisted until the camp commander, Captain Karl Weustenfeld, was court-martialled and dismissed because of a permanent order for punishment beatings.[104] Some Wehrmacht officers resisted orders to commit war crimes, but the general commanding Luftgau Norway 'personally ordered the shooting of 20 prisoners of war as a reprisal for the murder of two Germans'. One commander of a battalion guarding the 'notorious extermination camp at Mallnitz' ordered beatings and shootings. These facts revealed that the popular belief that the Wehrmacht's behaviour was generally good was 'completely erroneous ... for in number the Wehrmacht crimes exceeded those of the Gestapo and in some instances equalled them in intensity'.[105]

While the pitiful conditions at Ørlandet were typical of many camps for foreign labourers in Norway, the high death toll at OT camps on Alderney was exceptional compared to labour camps elsewhere in West Europe, especially early in the war. Foreign workers told of routine violence by OT staff in camps on the island which, although not French territory, came under the OT's administrative structure in occupied France. One Jewish former inmate of an OT-run labour camp on Alderney recalled his arrival by ship with other prisoners:

> We arrived at night and disembarked on 15 August 1943 at three o'clock in the morning. In the darkness we were forced to run the two kilometres to [the camp], while the German guards continuously stabbed into our backs with their bayonets while also kicking us all the time. There were many men among us over seventy years of age but nobody was spared. Work, hard physical work for twelve and fourteen hours a day, every day, building the fortifications. Every day there were beatings and people's bones were broken, their arms or their legs. People died from overwork. We were starved and worked to death, so many died from total exhaustion.[106]

Albert Eblagon was held in Norderney camp, one of four main camps run by the OT on Alderney. The others were Helgoland, Borkum and Sylt, which the OT handed over to an SS building brigade in March 1943.[107] The SS-Baubrigade 1 had been sent to help the OT fortify Alderney, which was the only one of the Channel Islands on which both the SS and the OT operated. Death rates in OT camps before the arrival of the SS on Alderney were proportionately around as high as in the SS-run Sylt camp.[108] Just as Ørlandet provided a direct comparison with Wehrmacht treatment of prisoners, camps run solely by the OT on Alderney can be contrasted with the SS-run camp set up later on the island. The OT used similar levels of violence as the SS without the notoriously brutal SS even being present on Alderney.

There were 4,000 foreign labourers on Alderney in May 1943, many of them Russians, Ukrainians and Poles. The daily regime was twelve hours or more of hard labour on construction sites, seven days a week, with a half-day off one Sunday a month. Survivor accounts of bodies being buried near work sites or dumped at sea provide evidence of the death toll being above the 437 identifiable graves. The estimated overall death toll for the Alderney camps varies from 437 to 1,000 or more, but a definitive figure may remain elusive since many of the records were destroyed.[109] One Russian former camp inmate, Kirill Nevrov, recalled how bodies found in the huts of Norderney camp were collected and tipped from trucks into pits on the seashore.

> In the morning, many people were found dead in their beds, and the naked corpses were loaded into trucks. A truck would tip the corpses at low tide into pits dug in the beach fifty to a hundred metres off the shore. There would be about twelve people in each pit ... I saw the bodies being buried with my own eyes, because I was working about fifty metres away on a concrete wall.[110]

Former Norderney camp inmate Norbert Beernaert described the brutality of two of the OT staff. 'The big boss was [OT Haupttruppführer Adam] Adler, who was drunk from morning to night, and all the time he played with his gun. [OT Meister] Heinrich Evers, the deputy camp commandant in Norderney, was a small man and a sadist; I saw him beat people to death many times.'[111] Prisoners were also obliged to undertake construction work on the neighbouring Channel Islands of Jersey and Guernsey. Between 1,000 and 3,000 forced or slave labourers are estimated to have died on the Channel Islands, including those travelling to and from them.[112]

This examination of levels of OT control in labour camps shows that whether operating in the Reich or in occupied Europe, the organisation practised its most extreme violence when it had most authority, irrespective of SS influence. The fact that OT staff were generally engineers and construction experts, rather than exclusively members of the notoriously violent SS, did not improve prisoners' survival chances in camps like Kaufering and Mühldorf. In other major projects in the final year of the war, the OT failed to initiate significant measures to improve conditions for prisoners or dramatically reduce death rates. The heightened urgency of vital projects in 1944–5 helped to cause catastrophic camp conditions.[113] Top priority given to underground projects to produce armaments and fuel increased pressure on overseers of slave labourers, including the OT, to drive workers harder. This led to harsher conditions and higher death rates, whether in the Greater Reich or in occupied countries like Norway as Germany's military suffered mounting losses and the OT raced to complete tasks. However, timing was not always a critical factor. Death rates were particularly high in the two camp complexes of Alderney and Ørlandet, where the OT had sole control, much earlier in the war. Elsewhere in occupied territory, Soviet civilians, prisoners of war and Jews suffered dire conditions and high death rates working on Transit Road IV, whose labour camps were run by the SS, police or OT. In Vaivara subcamps the OT sometimes took jobs normally reserved for the SS, such as camp commanders and armed guards. As in Kaufering and Mühldorf, OT control therefore extended to some degree into the structure of concentration-camp administration in occupied territory, as well as in the Reich.

Nazi racial hierarchies

This chapter has so far concentrated on analysing the impact on prisoners of high levels of OT control in labour camps, as well as the effect of responsibilities being more equally distributed between the OT and its SS, Wehrmacht and industry partners. This section concentrates on whether the ethnic origin of foreign labourers was always paramount in determining the survival chances of labour-camp prisoners supervised by the OT in German-occupied Europe. Some historians have argued that Nazi racist ideology remained pure and uncompromised at the heart of the system to the end.[114] Within this framework, survival rates for prisoners in the concentration-camp system were determined according to a rigid racial hierarchy throughout the war.[115] More recent research, however, has revealed a more complex picture in which SS racist notions were sidelined by economic and other pressures as the war progressed.[116] Factors like the type and urgency of forced- or slave-labour projects, as well as the prisoners' age, gender and ability to work, came into play.[117] As an illustration of how apparently unshakeable Nazi beliefs could be modified at the very highest level, Hitler himself could show considerable ideological flexibility. He approved the deportation of female *Ostarbeiter* to Germany in September 1942, so that Slavic Russian women, vilified under the Nazi racial code, could work in German households.[118] More generally, German use of Jews and Slavs among the more than 7.6 million foreign civilian labourers and prisoners of war working within the Reich in mid-1944 made a mockery of the Nazi ideal of a fatherland for a pure German race.[119]

Racism was integral to the practices of the OT, like other big Nazi institutions, and profoundly anti-Semitic views were held by senior engineers.[120] Treatment of prisoners generally reflected this orthodox Nazi racist thinking, but accounts by labourers under the OT lend weight to research showing that racist ideology was pushed aside late in the war. Jews and Slavs typically suffered the harshest persecution, representing the lowest ranks for slave labourers in the Nazi racial hierarchy.[121] As survivor accounts show, both these groups suffered catastrophic conditions under their German overseers in complexes in the Reich, such as Kaufering, Mühldorf and Wüste (Desert). They laboured under similarly murderous conditions in the occupied East, such as in Vaivara and camps attached to Transit Road IV. In stark contrast, non-Jewish and non-Slavic foreign workers experienced immeasurably better treatment in West Europe under the OT, especially in the first two years of the war. This reflected their high ranking on the Nazi racial scale, although other issues need to be considered as well. Abundant foreign labour was still available at that time, and German occupiers did not need to resort to force to secure workers. In addition, a high rank in the racial hierarchy did not always protect workers late in the war. As accounts in this section show, orthodox policy was often jettisoned at that stage, and West European prisoners suffered as a result.

At the bottom of the Nazi racial hierarchy, prisoner accounts show how Jews and Slavs suffered separately under the OT in certain camps and regions. Examples are the almost exclusively Jewish prisoner population of Kaufering, and the Slavic prisoners in Norway, who were mainly Soviet prisoners of war. In other cases, Jews and Slavs laboured side by side although held in different camps. This was the situation in Estonia, where Jewish prisoners from Vaivara laboured on work sites beside Soviet prisoners of war, who were detained outside the administration of the SS-run concentration camp. Although only Jews belonged to the Vaivara system, Jewish and Slavic inmates were often held in barrack huts of different camps separated only by barbed-wire fences. Philipp Alwin, a survivor of Vaivara's Ereda subcamp, described how Soviet prisoners were murdered in a blazing camp near Ereda, before Jewish inmates were evacuated to Stutthof in autumn 1944. 'Before the departure, petrol was poured around a prison camp near Ereda and it was burned down. The Russian prisoners staying there were prevented by machinegun fire from leaving the burning camp to reach safety. The next day, prisoners from Ereda, including myself, were directed to bury the dead.'¹²²

The victims of Vaivara concentration camp itself were Jews, but camp survivors told of beatings and atrocities for slave labourers who were not inmates of Vaivara but worked shoulder to shoulder with them – all Soviet prisoners of war and civilian workers. Jewish concentration-camp prisoners in Vaivara represented only about one-sixth of the workforce for Baltöl, which with the OT managed the project to extract oil from shale. Apart from the Soviet POWs and civilians, forced labourers were deployed there from many countries whose nationals typically received better treatment under the Nazi racial system, including France, Spain and the Netherlands.¹²³ Jews and Slavs, however, were targeted mercilessly. Baruch Goldstein, a Warsaw-born prisoner working in Jöhvi to build a military hospital, said he was overseen by uniformed *OT Meister*, mostly from Austria, who beat both Jews and Slavs. 'One of the Hauptmeister was of small stature, crooked, rather hunchbacked figure. Some of them treated us fairly well. Most, however, beat the prisoners while they worked. They were brutal people and it must be emphasised here, too, that they not only hit [Jewish] prisoners but also Russian prisoners of war who worked together with us.' Goldstein said the OT engineer in charge was a 'reasonable' man. 'The "hunchback", on the other hand, was a very bad man.'¹²⁴

While Jews and Slavs suffered together in these instances in Estonia, forced or slave labourers from other ethnic groups experienced vastly different conditions depending on where they came from in the German-occupied territories. Another important determinant for their conditions of labour and their survival chances could in certain circumstances be timing. Early in the war, levels of violence in West Europe were comparatively low and non-Jewish and non-Slavic foreigners worked voluntarily and were as a rule paid. The reasons for this included the high standing on the Nazi racial scale of French, Dutch and other workers, but additional elements also influenced prisoners' fates. In France, 1942 was a rough transition point between mostly voluntary, paid employment for foreign workers and an ever-more-violent switch to mostly forced labour. In the early phase, other factors were at least as important as ethnic origin in determining how non-Jewish, non-Slavic prisoners were treated in countries like France. These included the fact that the OT had no need to use force to recruit labour because unemployment was so high. Initially workers came voluntarily, attracted by relatively high pay, sufficient food and protection in principle from being deported to the Reich, although this promise was often breached. Later, workers who were originally voluntary lost the right to quit their job and the OT placed workers who did not live locally in large, guarded labour camps. This trend was broadly similar in German-occupied Italy from September 1943, although the picture was more complicated, with sharp differences by region. Workers suffered far higher levels of violence in front-line areas than in the north of Italy. There was also a mixture of compulsion and voluntary work from the start.[125]

Foreign workers spoke of relatively good conditions in France on the Atlantic Wall in the first two years of the war.[126] Policy regarding international conventions and human rights under the Third Reich was broadly to respect provisions for West European workers. This was not the case for East Europeans.[127] Reflecting German policy towards West European workers in France, therefore, labourers in the Bordeaux area reported that the work was acceptable, they suffered no punishment and they were paid. Spanish labourer Enric Casañas said he worked under the OT from the start in 1940 and 'it was not labour as punishment, no, no, they really did pay us'. He described himself, though, as a forced labourer, and said this was the worst of working for the OT.

> The fact that I had to work for a system I did not want to support. That, in itself, was already very bad for me. For, in fact, forced labour did not mean being beaten or having to carry heavy loads or something like that, you see? Because, no, the work was basically quite normal, like any other ... It was normal work, but it just was enforced.[128]

This paints a far milder picture than any portrayal of the brutality of slave labour under the Nazi yoke in Eastern Europe, or for ruthlessly persecuted ethnic groups like Jews and Slavs wherever they were made to work. In France the OT mostly carried out military construction tasks, contracting German firms and deploying foreign workers en masse. In the spring of 1943 the OT had a workforce of nearly 200,000 in the country, overwhelmingly French civilians, whereas just before the June 1944 Allied landings the total was around 290,000, mostly foreigners from third countries. After the D-Day assault about 200,000 civilians were enlisted for trench-digging and clearance jobs.[129]

The experiences of foreign labourers in West and East Europe were extremely different, but working for the German occupiers became harsher in West Europe as the war continued. Spaniard Joaquín Gálvez was sent to work under the OT in northwest France in 1941–2 to help construct and camouflage airfields in Gael and Dinard. He described construction work in Gael: 'At any rate, your hands go to pieces and are full of cuts, blood and cement. The only remedy consisted of pulling out the "flute" in the evening and urinating over your hands. That helped. So in the evening, at dinner time, it was called "Operation Flute".'[130]

Elie P., a Frenchman living under Marshal Pétain's Vichy regime, was sent to Germany in 1943 to work for the OT in the Ruhr region repairing damage caused by the British Dambuster raid. He said he was paid a salary and placed under the OT in Hagen.

> What was really bad was that with the OT we got soup only once a day. One litre of soup with a small ration of bread. There we suffered enormously, most of all from hunger. I suffered also from the work being so hard, from the more or less bad treatment by OT leaders, who were pretty hard people, pretty rough ... On December 2nd our camp was completely destroyed [by bombs]. When we came out of our shelter ... We put out the fire. Some comrades burned to death. There were seventeen dead.[131]

Civilian labourers

Other foreign civilians rated relatively high on the Nazi racial scale, such as Italians (before the September 1943 armistice with the Allies) and Danes, complained to their German employers about working conditions. Having a 'voice' to protest about their treatment in a way that Jews or Soviet prisoners of war did not, their disapproval of conditions in such harsh environments as the Arctic regions of Norway surfaced in OT records of operations in the area in 1942.[132] Italians working for the German firm Paul Stephan under the OT's regional administration in Kirkenes complained about 'bad treatment, that they had to work together with Russian prisoners of war [and] they were basically not treated any better'. In reply, the Stuttgart construction company denied this was true and accused one Italian worker, Giovanni Ponzi, of being a 'shirker' who was 'the first to eat and the last to work'. The argument was resolved by Ponzi and two other Italians involved in the complaint being returned to Germany. After Italy's armistice, Speer issued a directive in October 1943 regarding the deployment of large numbers of Italian military internees. OT headquarters wrote to the task force in Norway and others throughout Europe emphasising that Italians should be held separately from Soviet prisoners of war 'to avoid acts of sabotage'. This was despite the urgency of exploiting this large Italian labour force to help the OT attain its goals.[133]

As for complaints by Danish civilians about working conditions in Norway, written protests described delays in salary payment and pest infestations in their accommodation. Regarding the Danes' complaints to their employer about payments, Sager & Woerner said salaries of 250 Reichsmarks (RM) were promptly paid, although delays could occur if employees filled in Deutsche Bank questionnaires incorrectly. The firm requested further details and promised to follow up the complaints. Regarding the pest infestation, two Danish drivers, Gunlaug Larsen and Otto Lindhardtsen, had complained of inedible food and being badly bitten by bedbugs. In response to the protest, NSKK-Hauptsturmführer Rieckmann in Ørlandet wrote that staff had taken energetic steps to improve catering standards, although they 'cannot yet be described as good'. All drivers had been deloused and their barracks rendered pest-free.[134]

The OT was keen to resolve disputes involving foreign civilian skilled workers, including those from the Protectorate of Bohemia and Moravia employed in Norway's Arctic region. Engineer Franz Duben, together with twelve others from the protectorate, complained they had worked for fourteen months for the OT without being permitted to take holiday, whereas German colleagues also working with the organisation in Narvik were allowed leave every six to eight months. OT headquarters in Berlin, which sent on the complaint to the OT task force in Oslo, requested that the matter should be dealt with 'conscientiously and swiftly'. Within three months the senior OT manager in the region declared the dispute resolved: arrangements were made for foreigners to take leave who had been waiting for more than a year to do so, including Dipl. Ing. Duben and others working under the OT with the firm Laule-Kirchenbauer.[135]

These examples illustrate how OT staff generally made every effort to investigate and put right problems highlighted by civilian foreign workers such as Danes. They were sensitive to complaints from this quarter because, as OT correspondence reveals, the organisation was struggling to recruit workers in Denmark in early 1944. Concerning Italians, the examples show that OT staff acted with a certain tolerance towards them, even those deemed malingerers, before the country's armistice with the Allies, but showed great determination to exploit the labour of Italian military detainees thereafter. As for the dispute involving Duben and twelve others from the Protectorate of Bohemia and Moravia, the OT acted relatively swiftly to ensure retention of skilled workers, even when they came from a Slavic population not ranked highly on the Nazi racial scale, although above Poles and *Ostarbeiter*.

While the OT's non-Jewish, non-Slavic foreign workers experienced relatively good conditions in West Europe until 1943, economic and other pressures frequently pushed aside Nazi racist ideology. In the desperate last stages of the conflict, West European labourers in OT operations close to advancing enemy forces in territory still occupied by German forces could lose advantages they experienced in their home countries under the Nazi racial system earlier on.[136] OT workers ranking higher in the 'racial hierarchy' now suffered pitiful conditions.

Frenchman Maurice V. was an example. Maurice toiled under the OT in what was then the German city of Breslau (Wroclaw) in Silesia, digging defensive positions in bitterly cold weather in December 1944. Before that, he had done arduous overnight work in a metal foundry in the city. When the foundry was closed, he was among 300–500 French workers held in a labour camp set up in an abandoned factory. They were guarded by army soldiers, although their labour was supervised by the OT. Out of a total of 1,680 French trapped in Breslau, only about 400 survived, Maurice said. He recalled they used to work furiously at the beginning of a shift to ensure the trench they dug was deep enough to enable them to shelter in it from the frequent Russian air raids, slacking off their pace once this goal had been reached. In the days before Breslau was taken by the Red Army in early May 1945, bombs had landed to left and right at their work site in the central administrative quarter, but their trenches saved them. He recalled that they were then overseen at work by hard Hitler Youth supervisors, who were tougher on them than the middle-aged soldiers who otherwise guarded them.[137]

Like Maurice, Frenchman Paul R. undertook hard labour building defensive lines, having been arrested and sent to the Reich following German reprisals against the French Resistance in mid-1944. Paul dug anti-tank trenches under OT supervision near the village of Wolkow, close to Danzig, having arrived there in early 1945 just before his twentieth birthday. He described the OT as being 'as bad as could be'. The OT oversaw countless jobs across Europe involving comparatively small military defence tasks. Paul was among fifty or sixty slave labourers, including other Frenchmen and Spaniards. They slept on straw in a school in the village.

> But there, we had it bad because it was the Todt concern ... they were the yellow dogs, we called them that because they had overalls, they had a black and yellow cap. We called them the yellow dogs. They were sort of SS ... In the morning, they came to gather us together, to count us ... Then they sent us there, out into the fields, to make trenches. Then, afterwards, there was too much snow. So they made us clear the roads to let the army pass. And the railway track, too.[138]

Paul explained how he and his fellow prisoners twisted up rags to protect their hands because their skin stuck to the shovels in the bitterly cold weather. They called them 'Russian socks', and also wrapped rags round their shoes to help insulate their feet. He said the Germans forced local Polish civilians, including teenagers and the elderly, to work for them too.

As the advancing Russian army approached, one of his tasks under the OT was to clear the roads of snow so that retreating German forces could take with them mostly French civilian forced labourers from farms in East Prussia, as well as other prisoners. Describing catastrophic scenes in which German forces shot dead those too ill or sick to walk, Paul said refugees in covered wagons, 'like the Americans, the cowboys', passed by among columns of slave labourers and concentration-camp prisoners.

> So there were lines of, I don't know, 300 to 400 women sometimes, from camps for women, from camps for men. So, they passed by … in the snow. Well, we were the ones who cleared the snow. These poor, thin people were being made to pass through. Those who couldn't walk, Bang! There was one, they killed him, like from here to that chair over there, and my shovel, my shovel in my hand. He couldn't go any further. They lifted him up, Bang! And afterwards it was us, the deportees, who picked them up, we put them on a sledge, they were taken, I don't know where. That was sad.[139]

With the Red Army about to overwhelm the German positions, Paul and his fellow prisoners suddenly found themselves without OT guards: 'the next morning, the yellow dogs, they had made themselves scarce'. Although the abandoned prisoners hid as best they could, they were discovered by German soldiers still in the area, who, after listening to their story of the OT leaving them to their fate, somewhat bizarrely gave them the job of looking after 500–600 cows. Having fed and milked the animals for about three weeks, Paul and the others escaped and made their way to Danzig, which Russian troops reached in early April.[140]

Stefan K. described desperate scenes in East Prussia in similar terms to Paul R., but had worked for more than two years as a forced farm labourer in the region before being switched to trench digging under the OT. Like so many other Poles persecuted under the Nazi racist code, Stefan had been compelled to work in agriculture after being deported to the farm of Germans Paul and Maria Klim in 1942, when he was nineteen years old. Although he was beaten by a local policeman when the farmer's wife reported him for 'disobedience', Stefan said food was plentiful and the work, while involving unremittingly long hours, consisted of routine tasks. He had to use a horse-drawn plough, look after farm animals, clear out stables and perform other maintenance jobs. It was not until August 1944 that he was ordered by local authorities to dig trenches at various locations, including under the OT at Ragnit, near the Lithuanian border. His spell of hard labour on such defensive work ended in October and he was soon caught up in the westward flight ahead of advancing Soviet troops, in his case in a horse-drawn cart carrying members of another German family who briefly employed him.[141]

Racism was deeply ingrained in the institutions of the Third Reich, including the OT, but the Nazi racial hierarchy could be overturned. German officials and OT supervisors were capable of unleashing extremes of brutality, even against fellow 'Aryans' or citizens of a former European ally, namely Italy. In the first case, this brutality was directed against German convicts or soldiers found guilty of desertion or similar offences; in the second, it was aimed at captured Italian soldiers, whose country Nazi Germany branded a 'traitor' for switching sides in the war. Following Italy's armistice with the Allies in September 1943, more than 600,000 Italian soldiers were designated as military internees and transferred to work in the Reich and occupied Europe to alleviate acute labour shortages. Within months, the health of many of these men, who ranked below Anglo-Saxons but above Slavs or Jews on the Nazi racial scale, had been wrecked by appalling living and working conditions.[142] Brutality against these 'traitors' was widespread and included, for example, severe punishment beatings by OT supervisors.[143] The military internees suffered some of the harshest treatment of any slave labourers, typical for those among the lowest in the Third Reich's racist political hierarchy. Conditions for them were worst in mining, construction, some sectors of heavy industry and under the OT.[144] Around 50,000 of the Italian military internees died.[145]

Lino Monchieri described in his diary how residents showed contempt for him and other Italian military internees on arrival in the bomb-shattered central German city of Hannover in 1943 to carry out clearance work for the OT.

> We alight at Hannover's bomb- and fire-destroyed main station. The time is 14:30. We have to march in rank and file through the city streets. The people pay us no compliments, but curse and swear at us, calling us traitors and Badoglios … An old woman bares her teeth at the window and sticks her tongue out. Some youths spit at us. The children mock us.[146]

Another Italian military internee, Giovanni Bonotto, was sent to various labour camps and forced to work during the harsh winter of 1944–5, at one point digging military defensive positions under the OT near the Vistula River.[147] Before that he had been in a coalmine near Dortmund, where he said they always worked under close German supervision because their overseers feared sabotage in the mine, where a flame or spark could cause an explosion, killing miners and shutting down production. German miners had protective leather helmets and masks, Bonotto said, whereas 'we had nothing'.

In Italy itself, the Wehrmacht carried out what it called 'slave hunts' (*Sklavenjagden*) in September 1943 and some 50,000 Italians were thus rounded up to work for the OT digging trenches and constructing defence lines. These sweeps were conducted in villages in southern and central Italy as German troops were forced to withdraw northwards. Many Italians, including partisans, volunteered for work with the OT to try to avoid deportation to the Reich.[148] By autumn 1944 between 120,000 and 130,000 labourers were working on defensive lines and military bases in Italy. By the end of March 1945 around 240,000 men and women were working in northern Italy on fortification projects under the OT and Wehrmacht.[149]

German prisoners

OT brutality against fellow Germans, members of the 'master race' according to Nazi ideology, occurred in the infamous camp network in Norway known as SGL Nord. This camp complex was exceptional because the majority of prisoners were German citizens. These prisoners were treated violently because most were German criminals and soldiers found guilty of such crimes as desertion. The OT worked closely with the German Justice Ministry in supervising the camps' inmates, consisting of German convicts from Emsland prison camp and some prisoners from occupied Europe. The OT, which set the pace for labourers at work sites, was responsible for providing food, accommodation, clothing and medical care, while the Justice Ministry supplied the guards. The camp network was run with particular brutality, resulting in high prisoner death rates. In a letter dated the month after the camp began operating in August 1942, the SGL Nord commandant gave totals of 1,998 prisoners, ninety-seven Justice Ministry officials and originally fifty-three OT staff.[150] The overall death toll among SGL Nord's originally 2,000-strong workforce is hard to determine, with sick prisoners being shipped out and some replacements arriving, but just over 1,000 survivors were recorded at the end of 1944 before final evacuation shipments back to Germany began.[151] The OT's role in extracting maximum output from its slave labourers undoubtedly contributed to this death toll. Both the OT and the German Justice Ministry considered the prisoners expendable.[152] A similar camp complex to SGL Nord, known as Prison Camp West or Commando X, was set up in France. By the end of March 1944 it held 2,474 prisoners, mostly sentenced by German military courts, who worked on projects in northern France supervised by the OT.[153]

Although most SGL Nord prisoners suffering extreme violence were Germans deemed to be at the top of the Nazi racial scale, the brutality extended to ethnic groups at the bottom of the scale. Members of the Slav minority in the camp suffered intense persecution. One inmate who died at the hands of his overseers was a Polish-speaking labourer, Johann Sierpinski, born of a German mother and Polish father near Kelheim, Bavaria, and described in SGL Nord's camp records as stateless. Before his arrival in SGL Nord, Sierpinski had been detained in Berlin's infamous Plötzensee prison and sentenced to five years' penitentiary for theft. He was sent to Norway on 29 June 1943.[154] While Martin Bauer, SGL Nord's last commandant, was in charge (from January 1944 until the evacuation), Sierpinski escaped, but was recaptured and executed by firing squad at around 10.30 a.m. on 9 May 1945.[155] The fact that Sierpinski's execution occurred after Germany's official surrender took effect at one minute past midnight that morning illustrated the level of violence in the camp, as well as the extent to which camp officials acted at will. What happened to Sierpinski was described in some detail by witnesses questioned by British war-crimes investigators. According to witness statements, he was interrogated and beaten by Martin Bauer's number two in the camp's Justice Ministry administration, Inspector Otto Bauer. Sierpinski was forced to sign a confession to an escape bid and executed, even though the witness statements described how the Polish-speaking Sierpinski mostly understood neither his interrogator nor the document he was signing. It seems he was just scavenging for food, but paid with his life.[156]

Many Poles, duped by OT recruitment propaganda, volunteered for work and were sent to Norway, while Polish prisoners of war were also shipped there. Little is recorded about the experiences of Polish prisoners persecuted by German occupiers in the Nordic country, but OT documents throw some light. They show the names of two Poles who suffered a cruel fate in May 1944. Tomasz Staniak, then aged forty-three, and his son Janusz, aged sixteen, were listed on a work detail for a firm under the OT's Arctic Fauske building administration.[157] They had left Warsaw on 26 April and arrived on 16 May in Norway, where they started work on 25 May. Janusz was shot dead by German forces that month, and his entry in OT records states simply that he ended work on 31 May and that he was 'shot'.[158] The OT records do not identify who killed him, but Janusz was one of eight Poles shot after escaping from a camp in the Sørfold region. His father, who played dead and so survived the shooting incident and the war, had to watch his son die beside him.[159]

Some Polish Jews faced racism from their own compatriots in camps such as the Flossenbürg subcamp of Leitmeritz. The OT shared responsibility with the SS for construction there. Zecharja S., a Polish Jew who was sent to Leitmeritz in March 1945, said he suffered anti-Semitism from other Polish prisoners. He and fellow Jews were pushed to the end of food queues and forced to sleep on the floor rather than in bunks.¹⁶⁰ Hunger drove prisoners to extreme lengths at the camp: they would eat flowers or gnaw on lumps of soft brown coal in their desperation.¹⁶¹ More than 17,000 prisoners worked in terrible conditions in Leitmeritz, and about 4,500 died between March 1944 and May 1945.¹⁶²

Just as prisoners suffered racist abuse from fellow camp inmates, a Jewish slave labourer witnessed how OT personnel denigrated their Romanian allies as 'gypsies'. The OT used Jews to help build a bridge over the Dnjestr River, now on the Ukraine–Moldova border. Liviu B., having recovered from typhus, worked on the bridge as a teenager in Moghilev (Mohyliv) and noticed that two Germans in the OT spoke derisively about Romanian policemen acting as guards, even though Romania was allied to Germany.¹⁶³

> Romanian police were responsible for guard duty and two Germans were also on site from the construction organisation called Todt. The Organisation Todt … I remember that these two Germans were extremely dissatisfied. We could understand what they said … As soon as we paused briefly, the policemen hit us with rifle butts. That was their work … But the Germans also spoke extraordinarily scornfully about the Romanian policemen. I understood what they said. They spoke the whole time about 'these gypsies'. That is what they thought of their allies, who unfortunately behaved terribly cruelly for as long as I worked there. They delivered a beating immediately, as soon as they saw that anyone was not shovelling busily.¹⁶⁴

He also worked in a joinery when a Jewish carpenter asked one of their overseers if Liviu could be transferred as an assistant. Liviu spoke of the despair among the community there.

> Very many died who had lost hope, who had in their own minds given up the fight … They died above all from the cold and typhus. We were crawling with lice, there were no washing facilities, the conditions … the level of hygiene was abysmal. The only chance of having a wash was to walk to the Dnjestr … All these factors led to a high death rate, above all death through hunger edema, which was typical for the camps.¹⁶⁵

In 1943 the number of Jews sent as slave labourers to construction sites in Transnistria increased. In August that year the Romanians put 100 Jews at the disposal of German construction teams building the railway bridge where Liviu had worked at Mohyliv-Otači.¹⁶⁶

Half-Jews were included in another category in the Nazi racial hierarchy, and one thus identified, Peter Demetz, described being a slave labourer under the OT in 1944–5.¹⁶⁷ The category of *Mischlinge* was for individuals with a Jewish parent or grandparent. Demetz's Catholic father had worked as a drama adviser at the German theatre in Prague and his Jewish mother designed costumes for the actors. Born in Prague, Demetz himself went to a German school in Brno and then to a German high school, before switching to a Czech school. Such a background was common among half-Jews, whose classification proved problematic for Nazi racial lawmakers. The OT played an important role in implementing a decision to use half-Jews as forced labourers. In October 1944 an operation initiated by Himmler to transfer all *Mischlinge* to OT construction work and manual labour led to a sharp increase in their use as forced labourers. Although *Mischlinge* were classed as 'free' workers, they were in effect forced labourers, guarded at all times and prohibited from leaving the camps.[168]

Demetz was clear about how he viewed the work he was compelled to do after the Labour Office shipped him off to Germany as unemployed. 'That's where the slave labour starts,' he said. Demetz described work under the sole supervision of the OT in the Breslau area as chaotically disorganised. He worked in two different camps run by the OT for half-Jews, one helping to construct an airfield near Breslau and one at Kálek in the *Erzgebirge* (ore mountains). About 200–300 half-Jews were put on a train to be transported to the first camp, where he said organisation was non-existent. 'Organisation: zilch. The train arrived in an open field. We were unloaded and somebody, I don't know, probably from Organisation Todt, a technical organisation running these camps, explaining that we had to build the camp. And they gave us the materials, the wood, nails and the hammers, and we built sort of very primitive barracks, prefabricated walls.' On the way to the camp, Demetz and the others had been afraid they were being transported to Auschwitz. When their fears proved unfounded on arrival at the site near Breslau, Demetz judged it reasonable that what he called the 'unofficial' camp leadership, mostly composed of engineers, advised caution. 'They said, I believe wisely: "It's better to survive here than organise a revolt and end in Auschwitz."'[169]

The half-Jewish labourers broke stones in a quarry for ballast for a nearby airfield. Soviet Kyrgyz *Hilfswillige*, so-called *HiWi* employed by the Germans, worked with them, living in nomad tents with their families and looking after their sheep. Demetz, then aged twenty-two, saw no SS or Wehrmacht guards.

> We were fed with a soup. In the morning we were fed bread and some kind of coffee and in the evening, a kind of potato soup. And the important thing was ... not to line up too early because when you take the soup, the early portions are really watery, because the potatoes have a tendency to sink to the bottom, and when you come late, you have a chance to get ... the stiff parts of the soup. That I learned the third day.

Demetz was arrested after a short time working there and taken to Prague in late 1944 for interrogation by the Gestapo about an organisation supposedly printing communist material. He was released and sent in early 1945 to the second camp run by the OT, where he cut timber with other half-Jewish labourers. The site of the camp in mostly flat, snow-covered landscape was so remote that escape seemed impossible and work was carried out with minimal supervision. In March 1945 OT personnel ordered Demetz and the rest of the labour force to line up, because police were investigating an allegation of rape by a local woman. After the woman, accompanied by a police officer, went down the line-up without identifying a perpetrator, the labourers were dismissed. The following month, when Demetz and his fellow workers heard that OT camp overseers had abruptly left, he began an arduous journey back to Prague. After the war he settled in the United States and became professor of German and Comparative Literature at Yale University.[170]

The OT supervised *Mischlinge* and *jüdisch Versippte* (Aryan partners married to Jews) from early October 1944 at Holzen, in the core of the Reich. By the end of 1944 a total of 532 inmates were held in Camp Lenne at Holzen, among them 334 Jews, half-Jews and *jüdisch Versippte* from all over the Reich. The others included inmates 'of German blood', French, Italians, Flemish and Lithuanians, mostly men, as well as *Ostarbeiter*. The camp leader was OT Obertruppführer August Biel.[171] Those held in Camp Lenne were aged between fourteen and seventy-five.[172] The camp, which came under the *OT Oberbauleitung* in nearby Eschershausen, was set up following the same order issued by Himmler which resulted in Demetz being pressed into forced labour. Camp Lenne documents include an unusually explicit reference to cooperation between the OT and SS to get rid of the long-term sick. OT staff were told to alert the SS about inmates who were chronically sick, so they could be returned to where they were transported from. This could amount to a death sentence if they were sent to an extermination camp like Auschwitz. A note by the *OT Oberfrontführer* at Eschershausen, entitled 'Exclusion of Jews, *Mischlinge, Versippte* unfit to work', said the OT should alert the senior SS officer, Obersturmbannführer Busch, who would arrange for inmates to be examined by a police doctor. The OT would then organise a return transport for sick inmates as necessary.[173] Camp Lenne inmates included Jews in so-called 'privileged mixed marriages', half-Jews and *jüdisch Versippte*, but such distinctions of Nazi racist classification were sometimes ignored. In February 1945 a Gestapo report said that 'the Jews' in Camp Lenne had been transported to Theresienstadt on the nineteenth of that month. Five of the Camp Lenne inmates escaped during preparations for the transfer and two were recaptured.[174]

These examples of foreign workers' experiences under the OT across Europe broadly reflect trends revealed by recent research into slave labourers generally under the Third Reich, showing that the Nazi racial hierarchy was not always the prime determinant of prisoners' survival chances. Even when the fate of foreign workers did conform to orthodox Nazi racial ideology, for instance in West Europe before 1943, other factors were in play. The relatively good conditions experienced by OT workers in France occurred when unemployment was high and there was no need to compel labourers to work. In times of labour shortage, however, foreign workers were brutally rounded up and even those towards the top of the racial scale suffered harsh conditions, especially later in the war.

Types of labour

Most OT projects involved heavy construction and extreme hard labour for prisoners. Conditions are graphically illustrated in the preceding sections on Kaufering, Mühldorf and other vast projects in the Greater Reich. Further evidence regarding this kind of labour is presented in accounts by former slave labourers in Norway, East Europe and elsewhere. Research into the survival chances of slave labourers under Nazism has traditionally concentrated on the distinction between work on construction sites and production in factories. Conditions and death rates were generally found to be significantly worse in the former than the latter.[175] However, since the OT specialised in construction, no such comparison can easily be made. The salient point to mention instead is that the vast majority of foreign workers labouring in construction for the OT worked in a sector where conditions were typically the worst possible. Inmates of huge complexes administered by the OT, such as Riese (Giant), Wüste (Desert), Kaufering and Mühldorf, suffered some of the highest death rates of prisoners compelled to work under the organisation. This combination of extreme hard labour and abysmal camp conditions represented the most pitiful fate for inmates which the OT had to offer.

Slave labourers under the OT, both men and women, toiled largely in the open in all weathers. Their tasks typically included carrying 50-kilogram cement sacks or railway tracks and digging trenches with primitive pickaxes in frozen or flooded ground. Work was also carried out underground, when tunnel blasting, drilling and rubble clearing were deafening, filthy, choking and potentially deadly because of falling rocks. Adequate equipment and protective clothing were often lacking, increasing the risk of injury and illness, which in turn heightened the likelihood of prisoners being 'selected' for transport to an extermination camp. Road building, such as on Transit Road IV, involved collecting and carrying sand, gravel and stones, which had to be broken up by hand or with rudimentary tools. Labourers had to build embankments, dig drainage ditches, shovel snow, hack ice or construct protective walls against snowdrifts.[176] The same exhausting stone breaking and unloading of heavy materials and equipment was required for all construction, whether building airport hangars and runways, factories, hydroelectric plants, bridges, cable railways or dams. Other tasks performed by prisoners included forestry and agriculture.

OT staff also oversaw slave labourers clearing debris and repairing damage after Allied air raids on German cities. Unexploded bombs and unstable buildings put prisoners' lives in peril, and they were also locked in barracks whenever the warning sirens sounded while their overseers sought the safety of air-raid shelters.[177] Lino Monchieri, an Italian officer cadet forced to clear bomb damage in Hannover as a military internee in October 1943, recorded in his diary that he was woken at 5.30 a.m. on the first Sunday of that month and allocated to OT supervisors with some of his fellow countrymen. 'Kilometre after kilometre by foot through the terribly destroyed city. My section, like many others, is assigned to clearing the rubble. The last bombing was two days ago but the ruins are still smoking.' Five days later, he writes that 'our hangman's helpers don't let us out of their sight for a second; if you pause, punches and kicks hail down, if you work, they drive you on so that you slave yourself to death'.[178]

Slave labourers were confronted with a seemingly endless list of dangerous, exhausting tasks, but there were some jobs under the OT that did not require extreme physical exertion outdoors. Acquiring such jobs could dramatically improve survival chances. Skilled labour for the OT within the broad category of construction could also offer improved conditions for prisoners. This is illustrated by the case of Zoltan B., who earlier in this chapter relates how he was rescued from deportation to Auschwitz by a work foreman who wanted an electrician. Avoiding the Auschwitz transport was a stroke of chance, but possessing a skill could mean survival against the odds. Jacek K. also relates in this chapter how finding a job under a Polish prisoner doctor in Dautmergen improved his lot.[179]

As for Martin K., working for the OT saved him from a worse fate in the large Dachau subcamp of München-Allach, where the OT supervised construction to protect the Allach BMW works from Allied air raids. Martin, a Jew from Transylvanian territory handed to Hungary during the war, was seventeen when he was sent to Auschwitz and then a month later to Allach in mid-1943. At first, as a German-speaking youth, he was chosen to clean the Kommandant's rooms, avoiding being sent to the BMW machine works like most of Allach's more than 4,700 inmates.[180] Then, having 'won' a potato-peeling contest, he was sent with nine others to work in the camp kitchen, where his task was to serve food to members of the OT.[181]

> And my life was really good, for in the kitchen I worked as a sort of piccolo [apprentice]. I prepared food for the Germans. Did I know at all how to do that? But as it turned out, I did know. And what was really interesting, for example … I don't understand this, even today, whenever I cooked soup, there were bones and the Germans didn't eat the bone marrow … and I ate that and that gave me quite a bit of strength.[182]

Martin's access to the kitchen enabled him to obtain extra food for both himself and his father, with whom he was sent to Allach. Reflecting after the war about a trip he made with his granddaughter to Poland, where his mother and sister were presumed to have died in Hochweiler, a subcamp of Gross-Rosen concentration camp, Martin was struck by how his own fate had turned out.

> And only there did I grasp the extent of the catastrophe which the Nazis brought upon the Jews. For actually, it could have been worse in the camp, apart from them having killed my family – I say, apart from that. I, personally, had no problems. I was young, I worked, I had no … I actually only suffered from hunger in Auschwitz. Later not. I had something to eat and somehow coped.

Andrej K. was another example of an OT forced labourer who benefited from learning a skill. Andrej, who lived in the Ukrainian village of Korotich, was just sixteen when he began working on road repairs under OT supervisors. He worked throughout the winter of 1941 on the Charkiv–Kiev road, forced into manual labour like most other local youths following the German invasion that summer. He managed to be classified as a skilled worker by learning road-surfacing techniques by the time the road could be fully repaired in the following spring. He worked under the OT repairing roads until 1943. They received thin soup at midday and 200 grams of bread. He was paid some money as a skilled worker in German marks. Andrej said he was told while he was employed by the OT that as long as he did this work, he would not be deported to the Reich.[183]

His work involved relatively small groups of labourers toiling under very few OT staff in remote areas of occupied Europe. Communications with regional administrative centres, let alone Berlin, were poor. The concept of an effective centralised OT leadership in these situations was therefore at its most tenuous. The prisoners' fates depended entirely on individual OT personnel, whom they perceived to be either 'good' or 'bad' overseers. Andrej judged his boss to be a good man, while an assistant who beat them repeatedly was 'evil'.

> And under ... the Organisation Todt, we had a commandant – Willi Gras. A very good, clever man ... he's no longer alive, may he rest in peace. He was an engineer himself, an educated man, and he took pity on us, honestly. He stuck up for us. But there was his assistant ... August Rosche[r] – he was a genuine fascist. He had this golden, this badge ... This Hitler badge ... He was so evil. Still, he was a bit afraid of his boss ...[184]

In Andrej's case, though, even the 'evil' OT overseer was capable of showing some humanity towards his prisoners. Andrej recalled that while they were in Hungary, Gras, his OT chief, protected a couple of Ukrainian labourers in their group who were caught stealing from a local miller's house. August Roscher also intervened, refusing to hand them over to Hungarian police and insisting they would be delivered to German headquarters for punishment. Gras then simply had them detained for two weeks in their makeshift camp in a local synagogue before ordering them back to work. Regarding the normally 'evil' Roscher, Andrej had some praise.

> So he did well, he didn't hand them over, otherwise the Hungarians would have shot them. Theft was punished very severely in their country. And this August was, it's true, a vicious man, but he had pity on them ... He beat you straight away if you did anything. But we deserved it. Mostly it was because we pilfered something from somewhere. Sometimes vegetables, sometimes fruit. Well, we just wanted some of it. And the owner came out and complained. So he beat us with a stick. And then that was the whole punishment.[185]

The example illustrates how OT workers like Andrej depended entirely on the whims of one or two individual OT overseers when engaged in this sort of itinerant labour across Europe. In Andrej's case, the relatively benevolent nature of his OT boss, who Andrej believed commanded the respect and obedience of his violent deputy, rendered his ordeal more bearable. In addition, even Roscher appeared to possess a measure of humanity. Andrej said Gras gave them working clothes, including wooden-soled shoes with leather upper coverings, and they were treated better than wretched-looking prisoners with 'OST' (*Ostarbeiter*) on their backs, whom they saw being marched along in groups.

Andrej's case illustrates both the advantages gained by being a skilled labourer under the OT and the violence prisoners could face in this type of prolonged itinerant labour. In addition to the positive actions of his OT boss, Andrej described humane behaviour by SS personnel during his travels: two young members of an SS Death's Head armoured division, whom he got to know because they were billeted with a neighbour, protected him when he hid in a chest to avoid being rounded up in a German operation to deport young locals to the Reich. He described Erich and Willi as 'good lads, even though they were SS soldiers'.

Andrej worked in the Kiev area, in Jassy in Romania from early 1944, then shortly afterwards in Kovin, Yugoslavia, where he was among a 1,000-strong labour force taken there to help build a big air base. A larger number of Italian military internees were already working there. As Russian troops approached, Andrej's group was sent to Debrecen, in Hungary, and then to the eastern Alps in Austria. He was liberated by American troops in Linz on 7 May 1945.

The importance of the type of labour performed by individual workers is illustrated once again by the story of Dutchman Ellis H., a Jewish bacteriologist. Ellis's qualification as a scientist enabled him to work in clinics and laboratories in various camps, avoiding hard labour in all but one of them. Although he was forced to build bunkers in a Sachsenhausen subcamp, Ellis survived Westerbork, Theresienstadt, Auschwitz and Dachau, working in either clinics or laboratories.[186] It was thanks to OT incompetence that he managed to escape. Sloppiness by OT staff guarding the labourers allowed the Dutchman and fellow prisoners to give their overseers the slip and eventually reach the protection of American troops. When Ellis was transported south from Dachau in January 1945, the train made an overnight stop in the south Bavarian village of Mittenwald. Shooting broke out and, in the confusion, German troops accompanying the prisoners disappeared.

> Then we went off to sleep overnight in a pile of hay, we were rounded up again in the morning, but where were we headed? Then we were formed into columns, and the military who had to assemble us, they were not professionals, they came from the Organisation Todt ... They didn't walk along beside the column but behind the columns, and if you then come into woods, you can get away really quickly, and we did just that, the four of us, two Czechs and two Dutch, Ludwig Geels and I.[187]

Another example of the type of work affecting a survivor's fate is recounted by Leszek Z., a Warsaw-born prisoner aged twenty when he was sent to Leitmeritz in February 1945. He said he had the 'luck' to be ordered to do building work above ground, rather than in the underground factory, although Allied air raids meant he feared being killed by bombs.[188] The OT, plus an SS team under Hans Kammler, was responsible for the construction of Leitmeritz, about 70 kilometres north of Prague, on the border between the Sudetengau and the Protectorate of Bohemia and Moravia.

These accounts by foreign workers under the OT exemplify the distinction between types of labour that could decide a prisoner's survival chances. At one extreme, inmates of large complexes like Kaufering and Mühldorf suffered horrific conditions and high death rates; at the other, skilled workers could have comparatively better survival chances or prisoners might be given jobs not involving hard labour. These were the contrasting experiences of slave labourers under the OT, whereas the opposite poles of construction and factory work were typical elsewhere in the slave-labour economy.

Women under the Organisation Todt

The Organisation Todt was a major exploiter of women as slave labourers under the Third Reich. Thousands of women worked under the OT in many of the big camp complexes so far described in the accounts by survivors. About 4,200 women and 850 children were held in Kaufering camps, out of a total of around 30,000 inmates.[189] In the Mühldorf complex about 800 of the 8,300 inmates were women.[190] Women prisoners were forced into hard labour in Vaivara, where OT staff oversaw women in their labour force, and in the Gross-Rosen subcamp network known as the Bartold Operation (Unternehmen Bartold), set up to build defences including anti-tank trenches in Lower Silesia. Jewish women also laboured on Transit Road IV in occupied Soviet territory and at sites including the Bor copper mine.

As the first transports of Hungarian Jews arrived in 1944, Oswald Pohl, the head of the WVHA, asked Himmler for advice when about half those fit to work were women. Pohl sought approval for them to be used as labourers on OT construction projects, since the OT was ready to take them. Himmler's reply in May 1944 stated: 'Of course Jewish women are to be put to work.'[191] Research into the fate of concentration-camp prisoners in satellite camps in the wider slave-labour economy under the Third Reich has shown that women generally had greater survival chances than men.[192] There is evidence that the same was true for women working under the OT. Available figures for five SS-guarded women's subcamps of Gross-Rosen concentration camp, whose prisoners performed hard labour under the OT's Bartold Operation, appear to be in line with this overall trend and show fewer deaths among women than men.

All the same, there is a perhaps more remarkable point to be drawn from the comparative figures among the Gross-Rosen subcamps. Women working under the OT, whose staff forced them to undertake extreme hard labour, suffered generally higher death rates than other women's subcamps of Gross-Rosen. Death rates among female prisoners under the OT were well above Gross-Rosen women's average of under 1 per cent.[193] This indicated that the punishing physical toll of working for a specialist construction agency like the OT contributed to the higher number of deaths. Relevant figures from another concentration camp, Stutthof, provided stronger evidence for this conclusion. Death rates among Jewish female prisoners in two major OT-managed subcamp complexes were exceptionally high.[194] The complexes of SS-guarded subcamps were at Thorn (Toruń) on the Vistula River and OT Elbing to the northeast, near the Baltic coast.

Taking the example of the satellite camps of Gross-Rosen first, about 5,000 Jewish women were held in five SS-run subcamps providing labour for the OT's Bartold Operation. In one of the camps, Schlesiersee I, female Jewish prisoners worked in all weathers with primitive shovels to dig 4-metre-deep trenches, overseen by OT staff who would beat them mercilessly. Punishments included latrine cleaning. The women's accommodation included a barn and animal stalls, and their food and winter clothing were grossly inadequate. Death rates before evacuation from Schlesiersee I and other camps in the Bartold Operation were up to four times higher than the average of under 1 per cent among Gross-Rosen's forty-five women's subcamps. As already noted, a probable cause was the type of work they were forced to do under the OT, demanding great physical exertion. Extreme hard labour for construction and similar tasks has consistently been shown to have been a significant factor in causing high death rates among slave labourers compared to production jobs in factories.

Death rates among women in the OT's Bartold Operation camps were therefore higher than in other camps for female prisoners in the Gross-Rosen network. However, they were still much lower than in the men's camps: the death rate for male prisoners doing hard labour in the 13 Riese subcamps of Gross-Rosen was more than 27 per cent.[195] The reason for this big disparity was partly because all women in Gross-Rosen subcamps dug trenches for no more than three months, between October 1944 and January 1945. Male prisoners in the Riese complex did longer stretches of extreme hard labour between May 1944 and May 1945.[196] The fact that women worked for a much shorter period than the men accounted for much of the difference in this case. However, research into similar contrasts in survival rates of men and women in other concentration-camp complexes has shown that further determinants may have been in play. Studies have found that the gender of prisoners, even more than their position in the Nazi racial hierarchy, could significantly affect survival chances.[197] In subcamps of Neuengamme, for instance, principal reasons for lower death rates among women than men included dramatically higher levels of violence in male subcamps, more SS guards in men's than in women's camps, greater collaboration among women prisoners and a lower average age among women.[198]

Turning to Stutthof, the second concentration camp in this study of death rates in women's subcamps involved in OT-supervised work, thousands of Jewish women were forced to perform hard labour constructing fortifications in Thorn and OT Elbing. In the latter, the prisoners' employer was the OT and female prisoners from countries including Hungary, Lithuania and Poland worked under OT personnel and were held in the SS-guarded camp complex. OT Elbing was formed in August 1944 as part of the Stutthof concentration-camp network.[199] Prisoners dug ditches and built bunkers and other military fortifications. In early October 1944 the camp population was 6,440 women, and by 24 January 1945 it had dropped to 5,036. One of the harshest labour detachments was at Gutowo. The first group of 1,000–1,200 women there lived in makeshift tents, and were later moved to unheated barracks. They performed hard labour from dawn to dusk in all weathers, which increased sickness and death rates. The Gutowo camp was closed on 17 January 1945. After the Red Army reached Gutowo, a report stated:

> We have discovered a female camp. One hundred sixty-three women in a state of ultimate devastation, with frostbitten legs, some of them had wounds, 140 had phlegmon and ulcers on their arms from injections of some sort of toxic fluids intended to kill them ... Besides that, we also discovered a mass of female bodies in the camp, in canvas tents or nearby, varying in age from twelve to fifty-five. We managed to count 120 corpses upon a rough count.[200]

Thousands of Jewish women were also held in an SS-guarded Stutthof subcamp complex centred in Thorn (Toruń), which was under the overall supervision of the OT. The women did exhausting work like digging anti-tank ditches, and laboured five-and-a-half days a week, being woken as early as 3 a.m. and working until dusk. Around 40,000 forced or slave labourers and prisoners of war also worked on the Vistula River scheme. Conditions at all camps in the Jewish women's Thorn (OT) complex were extraordinarily harsh, and hundreds died due to hard labour, inadequate clothing, shelter and food, and sickness. Violent SS guards also killed prisoners.[201] Ludwig Denzler, head of the construction section for military defences in the River Drewenz (Drwęca) and Thorn areas, said conditions defied description in two of three Stutthof subcamps for Jewish women that he visited.[202]

> The medical care ... was not enough, because under those conditions the number of the sick was a large one. Besides I noticed that in the stable where about 50 inmates tried to peel potatoes with spoon handles there were, at a distance of about 15 meters from them three sparingly clothed Jewesses lying on the floor who had died the day before ... About the numbers of deaths I can state only the following: According to the stories I heard, 6 to 10 died every 3 or 4 days. They were buried together. This was an extremely higher percentage than that at the other camps at the Drewenz fortifications.[203]

Death rates among the Jewish women forced to work under the OT in Thorn and OT Elbing were therefore exceptionally high compared to others along the defence line. For female inmates of other Stutthof subcamps, OT brutality continued even as the camp network disintegrated before Germany's final defeat. OT staff were among 150 guards and escorts, including about thirty SS men, overseeing mostly female Jewish prisoners being evacuated from a group of Stutthof subcamps in the Königsberg area of east Prussia in late January 1945. The guards' desire to save themselves and avoid being captured by the advancing Red Army led to the largest massacre of prisoners during this period of camp evacuations and 'death marches'. The guards and OT personnel, with the head of the local branch of the Nazi Party, reached an agreement which sealed the fate of those in their charge. The prisoners were told on the night of the main mass killing on 31 January–1 February that they were being taken to the Baltic coast where boats would evacuate them. After 3,000 prisoners were herded from the town of Palmnicken and lined up on the shore, guards opened fire on them with machine guns. Few survived. A further 1,500 prisoners died on a forced march from Königsberg to Palmnicken.[204]

Describing slave labour in the heart of the Reich, one Jewish woman compelled to work on both construction and production provided a graphic account of her experiences. Judith A. described cruelly unusual twists of fate that do not fit easily into the normal categories of Nazi terror. Judith was forced to perform both hard labour building bunkers and roads and factory work producing munitions. She spoke favourably of the OT compared to the SS, and worked at Gelsenkirchen-Horst, a subcamp of Buchenwald.

> But in addition to the SS men there was the 'Organ. Todt' ... And, they were not the worst to us. They treated us like humans sometimes. They made some very vulgar remarks and ... vulgar words to the girls, but ... they didn't beat us ... The SS would, if you did something wrong, they would beat us. But not the Organ. Todt. They had a yellow uniform. And we worked very hard ... At night, when we came to the camp, we had our own dish, we got a spoon, we got ... a

potato, a bowl of soup and sometimes everyday a slice of bread and sometimes every other day, a slice of bread. But enough ... not to die of hunger. Hungry by all means, at all times. So when we walked to work, if we found a little cabbage on the floor, or potato peels, we picked it up and we ate it because we were still very hungry but not enough to die of the hunger. But very hard work. We worked only day shift in Gelsenkirchen, but the bombs were coming down and one night the camp was bombed and many of our girls from my group were killed and many of them lost legs and arms and it was terrible ... One girl, only one girl remained alive ... she lost her leg. The rest of them died.[205]

Judith said none of the women wounded in the air raid at Gelsenkirchen-Horst were treated for their injuries. In a labour camp where such lethal neglect was shown to bomb casualties, she recalled some small kindnesses. She said that, occasionally, a member of the OT 'would throw us a little piece of bread ... They had pity on us.'

Judith later worked in a Krupp factory, within the OT's Task Group III region known as Hansa, where her survival chances could be expected to be comparatively high. She was a prisoner at a satellite camp in Essen, where inmates were sent to work at the factory producing munitions and tank parts. Although this task was far less demanding physically than construction work, any sickness or serious injury could still be an effective death sentence: a prisoner who could no longer work was liable to be sent to an extermination camp. Judith, the youngest of six children in a Jewish family from Czechoslovakia, suffered an injury resulting in her being listed for deportation to Auschwitz. A piece of iron had fallen and broken her wrist. Help came from an unexpected quarter, however, when a female SS officer took her to hospital. The SS woman, Erika, drove Judith to be treated in Essen, where a cast was put on the broken wrist, and then arranged for Judith to work back at the factory as a translator. This saved Judith's life, but lice crawled in and ate her skin under the cast, so when it was taken off after six weeks the wound was open and raw to the bone. Nevertheless, she survived the war.[206]

In Vaivara concentration camp many women worked on manual tasks connected to the principal goal of extracting oil from shale. Nora Lewin, a Jewish woman prisoner in Ereda camp, said: 'I myself was detailed to do hard labour – always outside the camp – while I was in Ereda camp. My work group of about 100 men and women were hustled every morning to the work site.' She described prisoners' clothing as 'completely inadequate' for winter, adding that workers who collapsed through exhaustion or hunger were shot by the SS.[207]

Eta Weismann, another Jewish prisoner in Ereda, described how an OT member had been involved in a 'selection' of children there. Weismann, who told in an earlier section how she and other inmates had to sleep in a swampy area in the lower camp at Ereda, said: 'I ... remember a selection in the upper camp. This involved a selection of children. These children were loaded onto railway wagons and taken away. A German named Schneider accompanied this transport. He belonged to the Organisation Todt and his hand had been amputated. He wore a black glove over his hand.' Although Weismann was clear an OT member had participated, she was not sure the man had been called Schneider and could not be certain whether the child transport had been in Ereda or Vivikonna, another camp in the Vaivara complex where she had been held immediately before Ereda.[208] Former Ereda inmate Philipp Alwin told post-war investigators, in connection with a murder case against camp commandant Helmut Schnabel, that his then eleven-year-old younger son 'was taken away from me by force in 1944 and brought from Ereda to Auschwitz with 80 other children. Schnabel was not present on this occasion.'[209]

Molly Ingster, another survivor of Ereda, recalled a selection there in which her daughter was picked to go to Auschwitz. Ingster escaped with her four-and-a-half-year-old daughter after they first arrived by train in Estonia from Wilna ghetto in the summer of 1943. Hungry and thirsty after three days hiding in woods, she slipped into the ranks of an OT-guarded column of labourers, her daughter concealed under a coat, as they marched back to camp in the dark and thus entered Vivikonna subcamp. Having both survived a typhus epidemic that winter, she and her daughter were taken in January 1944 to Ereda, where 200 children were selected to go to Auschwitz-Birkenau. Ingster's daughter died in the gas chamber. Ingster herself, who was also deported to Auschwitz-Birkenau, survived a year there before being taken to Bergen-Belsen, where she was liberated.[210]

Such descriptions by women prisoners in satellite camps where OT staff were heavily involved in overseeing work sites illustrate the harsh conditions they suffered. A specialist construction agency, the OT exploited women to the full in forcing them to perform extreme hard labour. Records of death rates were often incomplete or unavailable for OT-managed subcamp complexes for women, but some estimates did show they were above average or very high compared to other women's subcamps. The women were forced to perform typical OT tasks involving extreme hard labour, and this took a punishing physical toll. At the same time, the figures for Gross-Rosen seemed in line with research into the wider slave labour economy showing that fewer women prisoners died overall than men.

Violence in the camps

Survivor accounts in this chapter show that the Organisation Todt practised its most extreme violence against slave labourers when it had most control over them. OT personnel took no effective action to reduce violence when they possessed most authority to do so; on the contrary, all types of violence became exceptionally intense, causing high death rates among prisoners. OT personnel beat or worked prisoners to death, or 'selected' hundreds of sick camp inmates for extermination, in circumstances in which the influence of brutal SS practices was reduced or absent.[211] The accounts also illustrate how exhaustion, hunger, sickness and exposure, rather than physical violence, took so many lives. At the same time, they reveal the interconnected nature of physical and other forms of violence – a phenomenon that has attracted too little attention in historical studies. SS guards in Norway, for example, carried out a mass shooting of prisoners suffering from 'typhus' caused by catastrophic camp conditions; prisoners in Mühldorf, mad with hunger, risked death by an SS bullet for the chance of a handful of grains; OT personnel beat prisoners on work sites to force the pace of their extreme hard labour, causing death by exhaustion. Although research has shown that more labour-camp prisoners died from types of violence other than shootings and lethal assaults by guards, insufficient analysis has until now been devoted to the reasons behind this and who was responsible.

When the OT did not have complete control, it shared tasks usually performed by the SS, such as guard duties and the role of subcamp commandants in SS-run concentration camps. Its staff, who were thus integrated into the SS system, participated in selections of sick prisoners, either explicitly in the case of the OT's Dr Flocken in Mühldorf or more indirectly by alerting the SS to pick out certain prisoners. OT guards also worked closely with the SS during the evacuations of concentration-camp networks in the war's final stages and herded prisoners during 'death marches'.

OT staff physically assaulted prisoners and had complete, or overriding, responsibility for inadequate food and the denial of other basic needs to prisoners. Camp survivors describe these abuses in the first section of this chapter, devoted to projects where OT control was highest. The extent of OT responsibilities in the succeeding sections, when it shared duties with the SS and other partners, is also broadly identifiable. The accounts by former prisoners describe every element of their living and working conditions, especially hunger and extreme hard labour. Grossly inadequate shelter was virtually universal for labourers working in such harsh conditions as in the Arctic and deep in occupied Soviet territory. Labourers compelled to work in bitter winter conditions often possessed only the clothes they had been wearing when rounded up the previous summer and deported.[212] Sickness and disease, such as typhus, was widespread, especially in the major camp complexes in the Reich described in the first section, in the occupied East and in Norway. The OT also brutally exploited women, forcing them to perform extreme hard labour in all weathers in camps such as Kaufering, Mühldorf and SS-run Vaivara, as well as subcamps of the Riese complex, Bartold Operation and the Gutowo and Thorn subcamps in the Vistula River project.

Although camp inmates mostly regarded SS guards as more physically violent, they generally viewed OT staff as harsher than army soldiers. Shootings and other types of lethal violence against labour-camp inmates were carried out by members of all three organisations.[213] OT staff carried weapons on guard duty in occupied Europe and had their own armed unit. They also beat or worked prisoners to death, and were involved in killings during camp evacuations and 'death marches'.

No consistent policy governed the use of foreign workers in German-occupied Europe, and this produced stark contrasts between the regions.[214] Extreme violence and high death rates in labour camps were most evident in German-occupied East and North Europe, whereas non-Slavic and non-Jewish foreign civilian workers experienced far better conditions in West Europe early in the war. Workers took jobs voluntarily and were paid relatively highly. Many French and Danish civilian workers, for example, enjoyed such conditions. Thousands of Danish civilians were recruited to work in Norway, where any complaints they lodged with the OT about working conditions were generally investigated and rectified. In times of labour shortage late in the war, violent round-ups to ensure sufficient foreign workers for Germany's war economy became routine. From around the end of 1942 at the latest, foreign workers 'high' on the Nazi racial scale generally suffered pitiful conditions under the OT as their treatment became ever harsher and structural pressures overrode ideology. Conversely, ideology could be overridden to retain skilled civilian workers among ethnic groups ranked relatively low on the scale.

Out of about 8,300 inmates of the Mühldorf camps, around half died. Similarly, roughly half the 30,000 prisoners died who were sent to the Kaufering complex.[215] In the Riese camp complex in Lower Silesia, conditions were similarly catastrophic and all types of violence were endemic. After the OT took over, there were 13,300 Jewish inmates. Around 5,000 prisoners died.[216] In the camps of the Wüste shale-oil project in Württemberg the pattern regarding use of violence was similar. While 1,716 out of 4,714 inmates in Dautmergen died in the camp itself, about 1,200 died in Bisingen out of a total of 4,163 by the end of the war.[217] Many Bisingen inmates were shipped back to the Reich from the Baltic concentration camp of Vaivara, where they had also worked on a shale-oil energy project. They often endured abuse from the same guards who had travelled back from Estonia with them.

Accounts of the camps in Norway, from both former inmates and German and British investigations into war crimes, paint a particularly consistent picture of violence across the spectrum by OT personnel, who were for a time in sole control of Uroš Majstorović's Ørlandet camp. This emerges from the many statements by former prisoners, but also from the report by SS-Sturmbannführer Dr Bauer on the various camps. Out of 110,000 Soviet workers deported to Norway, about 15,400 prisoners of war died of hunger, sickness or harsh working conditions, or all three; many more were killed by their guards and the possibility of undiscovered graves means the overall death toll of foreign workers in the country could be higher. Death rates among more than 5,000 Yugoslav prisoners shipped to Norway were especially high and 2,900 perished. Of 1,600 Polish prisoners sent to the Nordic country, 165 died.[218]

In the occupied East, all types of violence were practised by the OT in camps in the Vaivara concentration-camp complex, as well as by the SS. Survivor accounts testify to routine use of physical violence by OT personnel. For Transit Road IV in the southern Soviet Union, the OT oversaw camps where workers were kept in the utmost squalor and thousands of slave labourers died overall during the construction of the highway. OT records show hundreds of Jews and local civilian workers laboured on Transit Road IV in the Gaisin area. Several accounts referring to air raids highlight the dangers for foreign labourers working with no access to bomb shelters, or on defence installations or transport links close to front lines.

Following this examination of the fate of foreign workers overseen by the OT, to a large extent by presenting their own accounts, the next chapter looks at OT personnel. Evidence from war-crimes trials, as well as post-war German investigations into perpetrators and suspects, is analysed to try to establish what drove OT staff to act as they did.

5

Engineers as slave drivers

When the alarm was raised in February 1943 that twelve Jews assigned to a wood-cutting squad had escaped, armed OT staff in Radoskowice, a town in German-occupied Soviet territory, were ordered to surround the ghetto. Shots were fired. The object was to corral the remaining 200–300 Jews in the ghetto and prevent any further escapes. It took some time before SD-led security troops from a nearby German base arrived. When they did, Jews from the ghetto were rounded up and herded into a barn, where they were told to lie down on the ground. Members of the execution squad then shot the men, women and children systematically in the backs of their heads. The bodies were doused with petrol and set alight, so the barn was quickly ablaze.[1]

The head of the local OT operation where these events took place in Radoskowice, near Minsk, was Winand Schneider. Post-war accounts by other OT staff of his actions on the day of this mass killing differ, although one witness said Schneider alerted the SD about the escape of Jewish workers, prompting the murderous reprisal. Schneider was also alleged to have shot dead a young Jewish man weeks later. This testimony led post-war German investigators to take urgent steps in 1960 to ensure that an imminent statute of limitations deadline applying to the charge of abetting murder did not stop further inquiries into the Schneider case. A letter to Cologne prosecutors urged that witnesses be interviewed in time, using the appropriate judicial procedure, to suspend the running of the statute. It proposed questions to be put to them, and set out the context of the Schneider case in the region where he was posted northwest of Minsk. It referred to the mass shootings of Jews and other potential opponents after Germany's invasion of the Soviet Union in all larger towns like Radoskowice, in the German wartime administrative region of White Ruthenia. If victims were not shot, they were put in ghettos, which as a rule in 1942 were decimated by shootings and in 1943 totally emptied. Einsatzkommandos 7a, 7b, 8 and 9 had all been active in White Ruthenia and later, briefly, Einsatzkommando 1b. Witnesses were to be questioned specifically on whether Schneider had been on home leave at the time of the mass shooting in February 1943. This was necessary because 'the excuse that they were on leave is often given by the accused in order to create an alibi for the time of the crime'.[2]

After this, more statements were taken in the investigation of the Schneider case, some giving further details of the mass killing in Radoskowice in 1943 and some describing an even bigger mass shooting in the area about a year previously. Versions of what occurred at this earlier mass slaughter of Jews in February or March 1942 were given by a number of OT staff, some of whom mentioned Schneider as having been present but without implicating him in the shooting. One statement was taken from a young German woman about yet another incident involving Schneider in the marketplace in Radoskowice in April 1942. Elisabeth Gareis, then a salary accountant aged twenty-one who had arrived about ten days previously, had been walking beside Schneider in the street behind a Jewish boy, aged about thirteen.

> Schneider always carried a loaded pistol in the pocket of his leather coat or in a pocket of his uniform. On this day, Schneider drew his pistol for no apparent reason and shot at the Jewish boy, hitting him in the back. The boy fell at once to the ground.[3]

Gareis explained that she was so deeply shocked that she ran straight back to her office and did not know if the boy was killed outright or wounded. When she challenged Schneider later over his action, he made out that it was a trifling matter.

> He made light of the incident. He dismissed everything with a wave of his hand. I can't remember whether he said on this day that the Jews were no great loss. It could be, though I'm not sure, that he said on firing the shot: 'Get out of the way, you Jewish lout!' Schneider used that sort of language constantly, although I just don't know whether he said it this time as well. I am firmly convinced that Schneider shot the boy intending to kill. He considered the Jews fair game.

Schneider himself gave his version of the various events.[4] In a statement on 6 February 1961, he said he was on home leave at the time of the first mass shooting in 1942. At the time of the second in 1943, he took no part in the shootings, carried out by Latvian and German SD, and only assembled Jews who had escaped the ghetto and hidden in a nearby OT building. After the initial alarm, the police or members of his staff in the OT office had alerted the SD, not him. Regarding the shooting weeks later of the young Jewish man, who was an escapee, he said this was not carried out by him but by a German lieutenant after the youth had been judged to be a partisan. Schneider made no mention of the shooting of the Jewish boy in the marketplace in his post-war statements. However, an OT member called Peter Schmitz, who had been in Radoskowice and whom investigators viewed as a possible suspect himself, said Schneider's accuser, Elisabeth Gareis, had not been in the town at the relevant time.[5] In 1967 the murder investigation was closed following Schneider's death.[6]

Regardless of what the outcome might have been of any trial if Schneider had lived, the documents collected by state prosecutors in North Rhine-Westphalia contain exceptional insights into OT methods in the German-occupied former Soviet Union. Schneider's case provides a window into OT operations in a vast territory where German treatment of slave labourers was notoriously brutal. It shows how an OT construction leader could act in his particular fiefdom with virtual impunity. The case is worth examining in considerable detail to shine a light on the OT's slave-labour operations in the occupied East, where research of this kind has so far been limited.

The wider purpose of this chapter is to attempt to answer important questions regarding OT perpetrators. Did OT war criminals or suspects possess a typical profile? How do OT perpetrators fit into the wider debate about the nature of those responsible for atrocities in the Hitler era? Then there is the complex issue of why OT personnel accused of war crimes acted as they did. What motivated them to beat or work prisoners to death? Was racism the critical determinant? How crucial was ideology? Were structural factors more important, such as economic pressures, supply shortages or battlefield events? Were OT engineers driven to murderous abuse of prisoners by professional zeal and construction deadlines? All these questions are examined, but Schneider's case is first fully presented as an example of an OT operation in occupied Soviet territory.

The Organisation Todt in Radoskowice

OT Haupttruppführer Schneider operated in White Ruthenia, situated to the southeast of the Baltic territories, in a region known in its entirety to the occupiers as Reichskommissariat Ostland. He had been employed as a surveyor by a Cologne road-building firm called Rom, whose workers were drafted into the OT and deployed behind German lines after the invasion of the Soviet Union in 1941. Former colleagues from the firm who worked with Schneider in Radoskowice portrayed him as a fanatical anti-Semite and an overbearing man who liked to show he was in charge, acting more or less as he chose. He shouted abuse at Jews, kicking them in the street, and carried a heavy whip with which he beat Jews in the ghetto. Violence and racism were in his nature, they said, just as they were among the SD officers whose company he so often sought out. The principal accusations against Schneider are set out in detail below, but first it is important to analyse the wider implications of facts emerging from the investigation into his case.

The most important of these was the high degree of coordination between the OT and SD squads carrying out mass shootings of Jews and other victims. The reason for this level of cooperation went to the heart of what might appear a puzzling contradiction between two Nazi goals: mass murder according to racist ideology on the one hand and, on the other, the use of Jews, Slavs and other 'inferior races' as slave labourers to increase Germany's war effort. To the hard-line Nazi there was no contradiction; it made no difference to a racist advocating genocide whether a Jew was worked to death or murdered in an extermination camp.[7] We have seen how the OT cooperated with the SS in the concentration-camp system, both in the occupied East and in the Greater Reich, to decide whether Jewish and other prisoners should live or die according to whether they were considered fit to work. This happened either directly through OT staff selecting sick inmates to be sent to extermination camps or indirectly by relaying firms' complaints of prisoner sickness to the SS, which would then send those camp inmates to the gas chambers. The Schneider case reveals how the OT also collaborated with paramilitary killing squads to control the numbers and efficiency of the slave-labour force. But this time they picked out skilled labourers for OT projects, rather than selected sick and exhausted prisoners for extermination. The OT, in what was in 1942–3 common practice in occupied Eastern areas, filtered out skilled Jewish and other workers for slave-labour tasks before mass shootings by SD killing squads. After that, if the craftsmen were not worked to death, they risked being shot as soon as their labour was no longer needed.

At the time of the 'death marches' in the final stages of the war, the OT again collaborated with SS killing squads. A pattern of OT staff ordering prisoners to dig graves before SS troops murdered sick or exhausted inmates occurred at two Auschwitz subcamps, Blechhammer and Tschechowitz-Vacuum, in late January 1945. On the day of the evacuation of Blechhammer, survivors told how an armed OT unit arrived and ordered prisoners to dig a pit to burn corpses of camp inmates. The OT personnel also shot several prisoners whom they caught red-handed with equipment or food. A few days later, SS troops murdered weak prisoners left behind after the Blechhammer evacuation and the bodies were thrown into the pit and burned. At Tschechowitz-Vacuum a ten-member OT unit ordered prisoners to dig a burial pit and SS men then murdered about 100 sick prisoners left in the subcamp following the evacuation of inmates who had been judged fit enough to leave.[8]

The OT in Radoskowice cooperated with paramilitary killing squads in the two mass shootings in 1942 and 1943, detailed descriptions of which were presented by witnesses in the Schneider case. This collaboration ensured skilled Jewish workers were picked out beforehand so they could be retained for slave-labour tasks. The Jewish ghetto in Radoskowice was a significant source of slave labour. Schneider's OT subordinates described him as having close contacts with officers of the SS security service, the SD, from whose ranks the *Einsatzgruppen* killing squads were formed. Schneider himself told investigators he had been in frequent touch with an *SD-Führer* named Grave, who was based in Wilejka (Vileyka) but often made trips to the ghetto in Radoskowice with Latvian SS men.[9]

OT staff all agree that Latvian or Lithuanian squads, commanded by German officers, shot around 1,000 Jews in the first mass killing near Radoskowice in February or March 1942 and 200–300 in the second killing in February 1943.[10] Victims were herded into barns on both occasions, after which the buildings were set alight. Jokob Abenstein, an OT foreman working under Schneider for the Rom firm, was in Radoskowice on the days of both mass shootings. Jewish men, women and children were rounded up and assembled in a gorge in the Radoskowice area between 10 March and 20 March 1942.

> I estimated at least 1,000 Jews had been rounded up. About 50 metres from the gorge was a barn. From a distance of about 100 metres, I could observe how four Jews at a time were led from the gorge into the barn, or they had to run in there. I couldn't see into the barn itself, but shortly afterwards shots were heard. By 11 or 12 o'clock, all the Jews had been shot dead.[11]

After the shootings the barn was doused with petrol and set alight. Abenstein said Winand Schneider had picked out Jewish craftsmen from those assembled in the gorge because he wanted to keep them as workers on OT sites. Such selection of skilled workers, including Jews, was common before mass killings in occupied Eastern territories like White Ruthenia (post-war Belarus) during this period.[12] Describing the scene, Abenstein said:

> Before the shooting, the Jewish craftsmen were selected out, with their families. Winand Schneider was particularly interested in keeping the craftsmen. During the sorting of the craftsmen, which happened in the gorge shortly before the shooting, Winand Schneider was there. As I recall, about 100 Jews were picked out and not shot on that day.[13]

The second mass killing a year later, in February 1943, was prompted by Jews in a wood-cutting detail escaping from a road-maintenance depot about 500 metres from the ghetto. Heinrich Frantzen, another OT foreman for the Rom firm, described how he, Abenstein and other armed OT staff surrounded the ghetto for some ninety minutes before an SS squad arrived, about thirty strong. Frantzen was certain Schneider had tipped them off, although he could not say exactly how. 'Schneider was at that time the leading man in Radoskowice. His alarm, which he triggered because of the 12 escaped Jews, brought about the execution of the Jews.' Before the killings, the Jews had their valuables taken from them and were made to run the gauntlet between rows of SS men, who beat them with rods. The Jews were then made to enter the barn and lie face down on the ground before being shot in the back of the head. A German major headed the execution squad. As Frantzen recalled:

> In this way, about 300 Jews – first the men, then the women and children – were killed on this Sunday between about 11.30 and 16.00. By the end, the victims lay heaped in the barn up to about a man's height. The whole pile of bodies moved slightly up and down. One had the impression through this that not all the victims were quite dead. The heaped pile of bodies was doused with petrol and set alight immediately after the killings by the militia and the Lithuanian SS. In an instant, the whole barn was aflame. The neighbouring buildings were endangered by sparks flying. So Schneider deployed a fire-fighting detail with which [OT cook Karl] Ross and I helped, or were made to help ... I saw everything that happened from close up. Ross and I were directed by the German major who led the Lithuanian SS to stand right by the barn where the shootings were carried out ... This act of victimisation can only have originated from Winand Schneider, who must have told the major accordingly ... The whole shooting action was observed from start to finish by Winand Schneider and the German major from a distance of about 10 metres. Winand Schneider sat right next to the German major on a bench.[14]

Another OT employee working under Schneider, Hermann Körtgen, said about thirty Jewish workers, 'essentially craftsmen', were selected as labourers before the 1943 mass shooting.[15] This picking out of Jewish craftsmen, kept back to carry out tasks for the OT requiring trained labourers, was mentioned in testimony by several OT staff in Radoskowice regarding the mass executions there.[16] The Radoskowice ghetto provided an average of 500–600 Jews for the OT's almost exclusive use, but this resource was constantly depleted, not least by the two mass killings already described. The objective of keeping back Jewish workers before executions was always to fulfil immediate labour needs for the OT or the Wehrmacht, or for other purposes. Abenstein stated that Jewish skilled workers spared at the time of the 1942 mass shooting near Radoskowice were shot during the mass killing in the town the following year.

This was the norm in occupied Eastern areas, including the administrative region of White Ruthenia. The OT was one of the biggest employers in what became known after the war as Belarus, together with the German paper industry, the railways and the Wehrmacht. Prisoners of war and Jews were compelled to work, and hunger was a strong motivation for local civilians to register at labour offices since ration cards were only issued to labourers.[17] The German occupiers' need for labour was so acute in Belarus that, unlike in other areas, the murder campaigns all but ceased around the turn of the year from 1941 to 1942. The most likely explanation was that the civilian administration wanted to preserve specialist workers who were urgently needed. However, mass executions resumed in the spring of 1942 in Vileyka district, including the towns of Vileyka and Radoskowice (Radoszyce).[18] 'Almost all the murders of White Russian Jews followed a particular pattern up to autumn 1942. There was scarcely a massacre not preceded by a selection of the required labour force,' historian Christian Gerlach concluded.[19] As the evidence presented here shows, the OT was deeply implicated in this process of selecting workers before massacres in the area.

Apart from the exploitative and murderous practices employed by the OT to control the numbers and efficiency of its slave labourers, the Schneider case paints a much more detailed picture of OT operations in the East in other ways. For instance, it is clear that OT staff were required to be armed and open fire on prisoners to prevent escapes from the Jewish ghetto at times of crisis. This applied to OT personnel in general, not just specifically designated OT Schutzkommando armed units. The practice was described by Körtgen, who took part in the operation by OT staff from the Rom firm to surround the ghetto in 1943 after the alarm was sounded at about 6 a.m.

> Because of the alarm, we all went out, with carbines in fact. We saw Jews fleeing, as well. All the people from the Rom firm opened fire. I shot, too, although intentionally into the air. Most of us did that also. You had to take part in some form or other, otherwise you attracted unwelcome attention.[20]

Heinrich Frantzen said about twenty-five Rom employees who had joined the OT to go to Radoskowice witnessed the shootings. While weapons were routinely issued to OT staff working in areas where enemy partisans were active, their purpose was generally self-defence. As described in Chapter 4, OT staff also acted as armed guards in German-occupied Eastern areas to control prisoners from concentration camps such as Vaivara.

Schneider took several steps to ensure his subordinates became involved in armed paramilitary operations. Shortage of labour and attacks by partisans seriously affected OT operations across the region. Schneider's close contacts with the SD at their Vileyka base drew not only him but members of his OT unit into the activities of the paramilitaries who carried out the mass killings. Schneider himself took part in 'hunts' by armoured units, so-called *Jagdkommandos*, for Jewish and other local workers for OT jobs, or on actions against partisans.[21] It was an attack by partisans which prompted Schneider to join the armoured patrol that caught the young Jewish man he was alleged to have shot. This close cooperation between the OT and SD in Radoskowice was no doubt influenced by Schneider's character and choice of companions; but he was not the only OT member to take part in these raids.

OT member Johannes Horn said he was sent to Radoskowice in late 1941, and during his six-months stay there he was ordered to join an armed unit sent during the night to a place where five OT staff had been killed by partisans. He believed Schneider had instructed the SD in Vileyka to take him with them. About twenty or thirty people were in the truck sent to the small locality of Bolbow, including members of the SD and volunteer East Europeans known as *Hilfswillige*, who worked for the Germans. Horn described the situation.

> I remember very well that three people had been badly injured, including one who had had a swastika cut into his forehead with a knife. The *Hilfswillige*, or the SD members from the base in Wileyka, rounded up all the residents of the small locality and later drove them in front of a truck to Radowskowicze. There were about 50–70 people, women, men and children. They were then put in a cellar underneath the quarters of the *Hilfswillige*.[22]

When the families were later taken to Wileyka, Horn was told to accompany them, because he had the papers of the dead OT members and was required to act as a witness. He described meeting Schneider's SD contact, named Grave, in the SS security service's regional headquarters.

> When we were led into a room by Herr Grave ... I could see into a neighbouring room. I saw a woman standing there naked and a Latvian was beating her. We were also in a garage, Russian men were standing there with hands raised. Their faces were smeared with blood and looked like mere lumps of flesh. Obviously, it was a matter of the interrogation methods of the time.

Horn said that before he returned to Radoskowice he heard shots, and was certain most of the prisoners were killed.

Horn's conviction that it was Schneider who had contacted the SD to ensure he was included in the reprisal sortie has echoes elsewhere in witness testimony.

It seemed Schneider had a habit of putting his men close to the action, perhaps to involve them in the violence against Jews and the local population in which he chose to participate. This was reflected in accounts given by Abenstein, Frantzen and Gareis; the latter said she was very well aware that OT staff joined retaliatory raids against the local population after attacks by partisans.

Schneider's actions went far beyond the remit of an OT construction chief overseeing Jewish and other slave labourers requiring technical supervision. But although his behaviour attracted the attention of his superiors, he seems to have been able to continue to act with virtual impunity. They apparently took no effective action to stop him. Elisabeth Gareis, the OT salary accountant, stated that a senior OT manager in Minsk felt Schneider was acting well beyond the boundaries of his job. Gareis said Oberbaurat Hartwig told her he opposed the actions being taken against Jews and the local population. 'Hartwig told me at the time that our people, meaning Schneider above all, should confine themselves to our task of building roads. He couldn't stand it whenever OT people took part in the pursuit of partisans.'

In addition to Hartwig's reported concerns about Schneider's tendency to stray outside his duties as an OT construction chief, the head of the Rom firm seemed to have similar worries. Josef Peter Rom said he clashed with Schneider on many occasions over this issue, apparently to no avail. 'Of Wienand [sic.] Schneider, I can only say that I often had arguments over his behaviour and his dealings, above all, with the Sicherheitsdienst [SD].'[23] Rom explained his inability to control Schneider by saying that because he only visited his firm's various sites across Europe for a few days now and then, he had limited time to influence the OT *Hauptruppführer*.

Schneider's eagerness to take part in military sorties is analysed later in a deeper investigation into what drove his violent behaviour. All his actions clearly affected his team and conformed to some of the prevailing practices regarding the use of slave labour by German occupation forces in occupied Eastern areas. Details about the manner of OT operations in the region emerged as part of the post-war West German prosecutors' investigation, which was most concerned with specific allegations against Schneider related to abetting murder. Other evidence emerged in allegations by witnesses that Schneider personally shot two Jews. One involved the shooting of a Jewish boy, as described by Gareis. The other was the shooting of a young Jew recaptured after the escape of a dozen labourers on a wood-cutting detail in the Radoskowice area. Körtgen, whose account was backed up in similar terms by Frantzen, described the alleged shooting by Schneider two to three weeks after the original escapes by the Jewish workers.

One day, I saw that a young man, aged about 21, had been tied to a tree, Indian-style, just by the construction site. The young man was a Jew. I knew him, he had worked previously in my detail. After some hours, the man was led away by Schneider in the direction of the edge of the wood. After some time, Schneider returned without the young man … On the same day, I was told by a work colleague … that Winand Schneider had killed the young man with a shot in the neck … The grave was said to have been prepared beforehand. The man who told me that at the time was also in the Rom firm. He had been working alone in the wood, according to his account at the time, and observed from close by how Winand Schneider shot the boy.[24]

An Organisation Todt chief in the East

Schneider was born on 2 October 1905 in Euskirchen, about 30 kilometres southwest of Cologne. After finishing his education he worked in banking and the commercial sector until 1934, when he switched to train as a surveyor. He was employed by various state concerns, including Germany's motorway and railway networks. Schneider joined the Nazi Party in 1933 and became a member of the SS in February of that year. He rose to the rank of *Unterscharführer*, but was expelled from the SS on 18 October 1938 for embezzlement. He was also expelled from the Nazi Party.[25] In 1940 he started with the Cologne firm Günther and Rom as a land surveyor and construction supervisor. In November that year he was among twenty-five Rom employees who were kitted out with uniforms at the OT headquarters in Berlin. He received the rank of *OT-Haupttruppführer* before beginning the assignment in occupied Soviet territory in Radoskowice. An OT unit led by OT-Haupttruppführer Ruminski was already operating in the town, and after two months Schneider took over from him. His direct OT superior was Baurat Kleinecke, and his own deputy was called Bungart. Schneider stayed for the most part in Radoskowice until the end of 1943, when he was deployed to southern France. After the war ended he spent five months being interrogated in the custody of the Americans before returning to Cologne.[26]

What is remarkable about Schneider's curriculum vitae compared to other OT staff of his rank is his expulsion from the Nazi Party and SS. Also noteworthy is his criminal record, which he extended after the war. He was convicted on several occasions between 1952 and 1954 for fraud and embezzlement – a fact he denied before West German investigators challenged him. Similarly, most of his colleagues said the extreme violence and brutality rooted in Schneider's racism set him apart. Other OT staff, both above and below his rank, singled him out as more radical than them in his anti-Semitism and resulting violence, which they alleged went as far as murder. So was Schneider's case exceptional and unrepresentative of the OT? Certainly the witnesses against Schneider, whose responses must be seen in the context of a war-crimes investigation in which their own actions came under scrutiny, accused him of deeds stemming from racist beliefs for which he was notorious. Only one of Schneider's subordinates, truck driver Peter Schmitz, gave evidence in his defence.

All these facts about Schneider paint a picture of a man holding extreme views that his OT colleagues said were not typical of the rest of them. Nonetheless, considerable evidence exists in OT files of staff committing acts of violence against prisoners vilified as 'subhuman' across Nazi-occupied Europe, so it is impossible to dismiss Schneider as completely unrepresentative of his peers. Much evidence has already been set out in this study and more is given later in this chapter on mid- to senior-ranking OT personnel causing significant death rates among slave labourers. Their behaviour could be interpreted as less physically violent than Schneider's, while at the same time causing high numbers of fatalities.

As for whether Schneider can be described as an 'ordinary man', in the sense used by some historians about Nazi perpetrators, we may only examine details about him *before* his deployment in Radoskowice. This was a region of Eastern Europe where the brutality of Nazi occupiers was notorious; once there, his actions might stem partly from the extraordinary situation in which he found himself. Any perpetrator may be 'ordinary', for example, up to the time of being assigned (perhaps as a police reservist previously in civilian life) to a killing squad and taking part in the first mass shooting. In Schneider's case, therefore, possible reasons for excluding him from 'ordinariness' might be his prior conviction for embezzlement and expulsion from the SS. One colleague who knew him in the Rom firm before his deployment, Peter Rollmann, testified after the war that Schneider had been a 'show-off'.[27] On the plus side, Schneider held jobs in business and as a surveyor for about fifteen years before being picked to head the OT construction unit in Radoskowice.

In sum, Schneider's case, based on the evidence of his actions presented in the post-war investigation, is valid for inclusion in an examination of Nazi perpetrators in the OT. Violence and anti-Semitism were endemic to the organisation. His case must be seen in the wider context of the OT, not just measured against the way most of his colleagues portrayed him under questioning by post-war investigators. Numerous examples of OT staff causing high death rates among camp inmates have already been presented in this study;

more cases follow. Most importantly, Schneider's actions before and after his arrival in Radoskowice should be assessed separately. Members of Reserve Police Battalion 101, for instance, whose mass shootings of Jews in Poland in 1942–3 have been well researched, had everyday civilian jobs in Hamburg before they became hardened killers.[28]

However we categorise Schneider, there is one exceptional element in his career as a *Haupttruppführer* in the OT: the fact that his activities resulted in him coming under investigation at all. To examine what motivated the small number of OT perpetrators and suspects who were tried or interrogated, a wider perspective is required. The first of four upcoming sections therefore presents the broader picture emerging out of research into Nazi perpetrators, and analyses how Schneider's case fits into it. The second looks at how the OT functioned, focusing on three main issues: the drive for efficiency, OT oversight of foreign labour and how far the OT can be viewed as an 'ordinary' organisation. The third section analyses OT perpetrators, while the fourth presents conclusions.

Nazi war criminals and the Organisation Todt

Nazi perpetrators were portrayed in the initial post-war period as 'monsters', but more recent historical studies have added to unsettling evidence that the extremes of Nazi-era violence did not spring simply from pathological personalities. Even in 1946, psychological examination of the major defendants at Nuremberg pointed to this conclusion. When Speer stood trial with Göring, Rudolf Hess and other major Nazi figures before the tribunal, the accused had undergone careful psychiatric observation and completed intelligence and other tests. One of these was the Rorschach test, requiring interpretation of a series of symmetrical inkblots varying in shape and colour. A psychiatrist appointed to the Nuremberg trials, Douglas Kelley, said he wanted to arrive at 'the clearest possible picture of these individuals, the greatest group of criminals the human race has ever known'. He suffered a remarkable setback when ten Rorschach experts, mindful of public expectations, failed to submit their evaluations of data collected from the Nazi defendants. It was left to Kelley to declare publicly what had actually been discovered about those accused at Nuremberg: 'From our findings we must conclude not only that such personalities are not unique or insane but also that they could be duplicated in any country of the world today.'[29]

The tendency to demonise the mass murderers of Hitler's regime in the post-war years changed in the 1960s after the Adolf Eichmann trial. Philosopher

Hannah Arendt, in her reflections on the proceedings, wrote of the 'banality of evil' to describe an amoral bureaucrat carrying out orders in a genocidal programme. Since then, historians have shifted their focus. Drawing on studies including data from the Stanley Milgram and Stanford Prison experiments, research pointed to a universal human readiness to inflict suffering and underlined the importance of social factors and situational power relationships.[30] In groundbreaking studies from the 1990s, historians moved away from the idea of individuals acting as automata to implement the commands of superiors. Instead, they revealed a broad spectrum of perpetrators who, far from unthinkingly carrying out orders, acted independently and were motivated by their own convictions.[31] As one research team pointed out: 'For this reason, the true horror of Eichmann and his ilk is not that they were unaware they were doing wrong. On the contrary, it is that they *really believed* that what they were doing was right.'[32]

The historian Michael Thad Allen argued in a separate study that this attitude was prevalent among administrators in the WVHA, who were performing similar tasks to OT managers across Europe in organising slave labour. 'WVHA officers were anything but technocratic automatons. Believing in their cause, the office's mid-level managers hoped to deploy their prison labor force in efficient industrial production,' Allen wrote.[33] He noted that SS officers invariably blamed the poor performance of working prisoners on 'poor human material', and there was no mention of the atrocious camp conditions.[34] The OT's administration covered all occupied Europe, plus the Reich in 1944–5, and the SS possessed a similar network. The central building directorates of the SS extended across Central Europe and its civil engineers were big fish, conscious of their own authority within their regions. 'Within their hierarchies, mid and lower-level administrators were accorded free room for independent action. They used this autonomy to act according to principles of what they, either as individuals or collectively, thought were right; what they interpreted as the appropriate purpose of their organization,' Allen concluded.[35]

OT regional managers throughout Europe also possessed considerable authority, as well as room for independent action within their spheres of operation. With the OT's partial withdrawal into the Reich in the final year of the war, the chiefs of the organisation's newly created administrative regions accrued still more powers. In the same way as the SS, these senior and lower-level managers were authorised to take significant decisions on their own initiative. There is much in OT documents to support the view that staff believed what they were doing was justified.

Among the OT's middle ranks, Haupttruppführer Schneider, as has been demonstrated, seems to have used to the full the extensive freedom of action he was afforded. Significantly, he fitted an important category used by researchers in the analysis of convicted or suspected perpetrators: generation. Schneider, born in 1905, belonged to a category of German youth seen as particularly susceptible to Nazism for a number of reasons. Too young to have served in the First World War, their passage into adulthood included the experiences of their nation's military defeat, rampant inflation and the mass unemployment of 1929–33. They were a 'lost' generation brought up in a culture of violence and subjected after Hitler took power in 1933, when Schneider was aged twenty-eight, to an ever-more-intensive barrage of racist propaganda by the government.[36]

Schneider's anti-Semitic views were extreme, but his enthusiasm for military adventure was another motive for his violent racist behaviour. As we have seen, he habitually carried a handgun and took part in missions in armoured vehicles to round up Jewish and other labourers. He acknowledged that, on one such mission, the Jew he was alleged to have murdered had been tied to a tree in the manner described by Körtgen. In descriptions of his other exploits, Schneider recounted how he 'by chance' managed to lead his OT men to escape from an attack by partisans that wiped out his German military escort of three 21-tonne tanks and four armoured cars. The armoured escort had been provided to protect Schneider's OT labour force, tasked with building bridges in the area. Schneider said his entire OT squad emerged safely from the attack. On another occasion he brought back the mutilated bodies of German soldiers whose infantry unit, which he could not fully identify, had been wiped out.[37]

Schneider's propensity for violence, drunkenness and bullying nature are reflected in descriptions of him by virtually all witnesses. These insights into his character form an essential part of this analysis of what motivated his behaviour. Frantzen states his OT superior's reputation was so bad that nothing could be put past him. He was a habitual drunkard and reputed to engage in heavy drinking sessions with SD officers. Körtgen viewed him as a braggart and a careerist. Since many of the OT staff interviewed in the post-war investigation came from the Rom firm, some knew each other before their deployment to occupied Soviet territory. Peter Rollmann, who worked for the company before the war, remembered Schneider as a boastful character.[38] Ferdinand Wolf, a foreman for Rom, said Schneider was 'very unpopular' while in Radoskowice, with 'a strange way of dealing with his people' and spending a great deal of time with the SD.[39] Erwin Jehlen, who did accounting work in the OT office, remembered Schneider as a 'very overbearing' man and a drunkard who was disliked by his staff.⁴⁰ Elisabeth Gareis considered Schneider had complete power over his staff. OT truck driver Josef Löhrer emphasised the way Schneider acted 'high and mighty'. 'Whenever Schneider had been drinking, he went into the ghetto and struck Jews with a heavy dog whip. Even though I was not there when he struck out, there should still be no doubt, because I heard the terrible cries and then saw Schneider come out of the ghetto with his whip. I myself witnessed this twice.'⁴¹ Peter Fröbus, a steamroller operator with Rom, was particularly pointed in his condemnation of Schneider, declaring him to be 'Satan in human form'. 'Schneider was a brutal man. He had no consideration for anyone. He was terribly heavy-handed and brutal with us and especially with the Jews. Whenever Jews had to approach, he kicked them. It didn't matter to him where he kicked. He simply kicked them in the stomach and other sensitive parts of the body.'⁴²

It is clear from these descriptions of Schneider that he did not fit the profile of a Nazi perpetrator who simply 'followed orders', the unfeeling automaton identified by Arendt. On the contrary, all the evidence pointed to him defying regulations and breaching the limitations of his brief as a local OT construction chief. He took part in armed operations to round up workers and against partisans, appearing to be able to act at will in the area where he commanded OT operations. Because he had been too young to fight in the First World War, he had been exposed to the jingoistic home-front propaganda portraying the trenches as a gallant, masculine adventure.⁴³ This might explain why he participated so enthusiastically in military exploits involving his SD contacts. He not only took part himself but included his OT subordinates in these activities, convincing some of them he was purposefully placing them at scenes of mass murder and acts of violence.

In seeking to discover other motives for Schneider's actions, it is useful to examine how his individual case fits into other categories chosen by researchers into Nazi perpetrators. One fact about Schneider was that he ranked far below the Nazi Party and SS elite who were most associated with war crimes of the Third Reich. We have already discussed whether Schneider can be described as an 'ordinary' man, but it is reasonable to argue that his profession, at least, would not exclude him from that classification. He was neither a soldier nor a policeman, but a surveyor. As noted, OT personnel were particularly well qualified to be categorised as 'ordinary men', and Schneider was a mid-ranking officer in the organisation.

What marked Schneider out, as already indicated, were his expulsions from the SS and the Nazi Party. In his statement to post-war prosecutors, he said these both occurred in 1938, but he only linked his 1938 conviction for embezzlement to his exclusion from the SS. He could not explain why a document concerning his expulsion from the Nazi Party was dated 30 January 1942, nor the nature of his offence prompting that punishment. If 1942 was the date of his exclusion from the NSDAP, this would have been during his OT assignment in Radoskowice.[44] Like so many SS men and some OT staff,[45] action against Schneider was taken under the Third Reich's legal system and charges against him were not linked to his maltreatment of slave labourers or alleged shooting of Jews. This skewed sense of morality and justice in Nazi institutions was exemplified by an arrogant young SS jurist named Konrad Morgen, who gained a reputation for tackling SS corruption and deviance as part of a campaign ordered by Himmler that resulted in the downfall of concentration-camp commandants such as Karl Otto Koch, who headed Buchenwald and Majdanek and was executed shortly before the war ended. Morgen attempted to portray himself as a supporter of law and order after the war by testifying against some former camp SS men, but was in fact a committed SS officer who obeyed Himmler's warped desire to erase blemishes from 'virtuous' SS killers.[46]

The fact that Schneider had been expelled in disgrace from the SS and the Nazi Party, yet was allowed such freedom to act more or less as he pleased in the Radoskowice area where he was in charge, says much about the way the OT was run in occupied Soviet territory. The dynamics and management of organisations such as the SS and OT, and the circumstances in which their personnel operated, have become key to the latest research into Nazi perpetrators. Recent historical studies on this subject have developed an 'interactionist' approach, according to which both the individuals and the situations in which they found themselves were transformed through their interplay.[47] To understand better the behaviour of OT personnel in complex situations, such as the German-occupied East, the manner in which the OT functioned as an institution needs to be examined in more detail. This provides the context in which individuals like Schneider took decisions and acted.

Managing the Organisation Todt

The drive for efficiency

Speer's campaign for efficiency had dramatic consequences for OT engineers in the field across Europe. They describe their experiences of working to deadlines, against seemingly impossible odds, in documents held in OT records and in the files of post-war investigations. A German civil engineer in Norway, Dr Ing. Walter Beck, spoke of having to build barrack huts in Karasjok on arrival with little equipment. 'We were very poorly equipped with tools. For example, the construction company only had a hammer and a saw. My geologist's hammer was for a time the OT people's only hammer.' Hundreds of Serb prisoners then gradually arrived to help build the Reichsstrasse 50 highway further into the Arctic Circle. 'Work output was relatively low. The reason was the bad food, bad equipment and unfavourable weather conditions.'[48]

The problems facing OT engineers attempting to fulfil Hitler's instruction to build hundreds of kilometres of railway in Norway's mountainous Arctic territory were illustrated in a detailed report by Regierungsbaurat Merkle. He was the OT engineer in charge of a central section, based in Fauske, and was among geologists and engineers who in May 1942 made an aerial survey of the entire route of more than 1,000 kilometres. Just one 80-kilometre section from Fauske towards Narvik involved construction of thirty-three tunnels, with a total length of 27 kilometres, and twenty bridges. Six hydroelectric and three steam power plants were to be built to help provide power for drilling and other equipment, as well as lighting for tunnel building and labour camps. Workers and equipment were in lamentably short supply, according to Merkle's report, written in March 1945, just two months before Germany's surrender. It appeared largely aimed at exonerating himself and his team, who had not only missed successive deadlines but also completed no more than a fraction of their allotted task.

> As in the field of equipment supply, the work force fell far short of fulfilling requirements. This fact is one of the main reasons for the failure from the very first day to keep to the construction programme. Available statistics show clearly that only half the necessary total work force was available at any one time.[49]

By May 1944 the labour force was 7,741 strong, comprising 795 Germans, 208 Norwegians, 402 foreign civilian workers and 6,336 Soviet and other prisoners of war. This compared with a forecast drawn up the previous year envisaging a total workforce of around 14,000.

> The majority of the work force were made up of Russian prisoners of war, whose average work output equalled about half that of a German worker. The German and foreign employees and workers were accommodated throughout in barrack huts, the prisoners of war predominantly in OT tents. Twenty big camps were set up in total.[50]

After the Soviet prisoners of war had spent their first Arctic winter in tents, having arrived in 1942, the first railway tunnels were begun in the spring and summer of 1943. Ships bringing equipment were unloaded day and night, seven days a week, to ensure rapid turnarounds and continuation of supplies by sea. During 1944 work picked up significantly.

> Since German or foreign miners were not, or scarcely, available, the prisoners of war had to be trained in the handling of equipment for tunnel construction, especially in the use and operation of hammer drills and serrated drills. Weeks and months often went by until the individual columns had worked themselves in sufficiently for satisfactory performances to be achieved.[51]

Employees of specialist firms could also train German workers in how to use explosives for tunnel blasting. Merkle praised the training of the Russians to deal with rubble in the tunnels, saying that skilful handling and schooling of these workers could produce similar results with manual labourers as with machines. Fuel shortages meant that use of machines had to be temporarily cut back in September 1944, and all construction work north of Torkeleng, about 25 kilometres northeast of Fauske, had to be abandoned. Equipment was to be transferred to another OT rail construction administration or prepared for shipment back to the Reich. However, in November the order was issued to return all machines and equipment destined for the Reich back to the construction sites and resume work to the full. Merkle declared that at the time of his report on 8 March 1945, 'The vast majority of the construction sites are today set up again and works are going ahead. The rest of the work sites should be completely started up by the end of March. Calculated all together, the suspension of construction caused delays to deadlines of 4–5 months.' Giving performance totals for 1944, according to which tunnel construction amounted to only 10 per cent of the target figure, Merkle commented that the results reflected the 'completely insufficient' supply of labour and equipment during the two-and-a-half years since the start of the project.[52]

Merkle's report provides a powerful insight into the way senior OT managers viewed their jobs. As they saw it, they did the best they could with the equipment and labour available. Skilled engineers like Merkle followed their superiors' directives to boost performance as far as possible. If that involved teaching Soviet prisoners of war to work in tunnels as efficiently as machines, it would be done. If work had to proceed at maximum pace in March 1945, with the Red Army advancing ever closer, on a project his report proved was doomed to fail, that target was met. Merkle's struggle to meet impossible deadlines was replicated elsewhere on the Arctic railway project, which was originally planned to reach Kirkenes in Norway's far north. Dr Ing. Renner, who headed the OT's Nordlandbahn rail construction operation based in Mo i Rana, told the OT's deputy chief, Xaver Dorsch, in March 1944 that more workers and equipment were desperately needed. Even his initial goal of turning the port of Rognan, south of Fauske, into a rail–ship transfer hub could not be achieved until the end of 1945 without reinforcements.[53] Overall, the OT's Wiking group foresaw the need for 38,000 more workers, including 17,500 convicts and prisoners of war, to reach a total target of 100,000 for its various projects in 1944.[54] Railway building alone, including the Nordlandbahn, was projected to require nearly 30,000 prisoners of war in that year.[55]

The determination of OT staff to achieve their organisation's goals was founded in large measure on their professionalism. As historian Peter Hayes wrote of IG Farben's top managers, that quality 'insulated them from their actions; more than that, it transmogrified in their eyes the ethics of their deeds'.[56] Another spur for OT staff was knowing that many of their projects had been accorded the highest priority. The Norway rail link had been ordered by Hitler himself and the Führer followed its progress closely, rejecting all opposition.

So was it professionalism and the urgency of their work that motivated other senior OT managers to drive on their prisoners with such merciless zeal? Willi Henne, Merkle's overall boss in Norway, conducted OT projects in his sphere of operations with ruthless determination, as we have seen. There were many other examples among mid- to high-level managers in the organisation, including Arnold Adam, who was in charge of the notorious Transit Road IV road leading to the Caucasus, on which Jews, *Ostarbeiter* and other slave labourers toiled in pitiful conditions. A further example of an OT manager whose operations caused high death rates among prisoners was Walter Brugmann, who headed the OT's Russia-South sector. This was an area deep in occupied Soviet territory where, as has been described, desperate operations in a combat zone resulted in brutal and lethal conditions for slave labourers under the OT. Yet another example was Hermann Giesler, whose case has also been described. He ran the OT's Russia-North sector before returning to the Reich to head Deutschland VI, where about half the more than 38,000 mostly Jewish slave labourers in the Mühldorf and Kaufering complexes died.

All these OT managers, as well as others examined earlier in this study, were encouraged in their actions by a sense of common purpose. They were engaged in a whole series of top-priority projects, often in the final year of the war, and made every effort to achieve what was required of them. Whether it was road and railway links in Norway, shale-oil works in Estonia and later in the Wüste (Desert) programme, or the vast underground armaments and fuel projects in the Reich, all the evidence points to the fact that OT personnel drove slave labourers right up to Germany's final defeat.

Foreign labour

Dependence on foreign slave labour had a huge impact on the way OT staff operated in German-occupied Europe. OT maltreatment of foreign workers stemmed from racism deeply ingrained among the organisation's employees, but there were other reasons for their actions. Working in often remote sites in foreign territory heightened a German OT man's sense of the 'alien' and 'otherness' of the enemy, but also his self-sufficiency and belief in the superior nature of German labour. Such convictions were clearly held by men such as Merkle, working to overcome huge obstacles blocking the Arctic railway project in Norway. For German workers, the concept of 'German quality work' was equated with Germanness and excluded foreigners. It was a belief in their own superior technical skills that could endure despite the harsh realities of operations on the ground, whose failures OT staff blamed on insufficient labour and equipment. Hardships merely fuelled a German worker's stubborn self-reliance (*Eigensinn*).[57] Just as German soldiers, in their letters home, came to regard exterminating 'others' as work,[58] so OT staff applied themselves to the task of exploiting foreign slave labour in murderous conditions.

Abundant evidence has already been presented of racism in OT ranks and persecution of the organisation's foreign workers. A particular example is worth examining in detail, since some of the events throw light on motives driving OT staff. Among the OT *Linimienchefs* managing the major transport routes in occupied Europe was an Austrian-born engineer, Professor Ernst von Gottstein. He was responsible for the Reichsstrasse 50 north–south highway in Norway. Just before the war, Todt praised him highly for his engineering skills in building motorways, as well as for being an 'exemplary National Socialist'.[59] Especially grim evidence emerged of the racist beliefs of von Gottstein when he was captured after the war. His virulently anti-Semitic views were revealed in a secret tape-recording made in November 1945 while he was at a British army-run detention centre. Reacting to a man who had been on guard detail at Auschwitz, who said he was unable to bear the screams of victims for too long and that the smell of the crematorium 'used to remain in your nostrils for days', von Gottstein replied: 'The only really good thing about the whole affair is that a few million Jews no longer exist.'[60]

Racism against Serbs prompted a murder involving an OT man under von Gottstein that resulted in a post-war court ruling on the defendant's motivation. The case of Diederich Scholz, who was convicted of attempted murder by the Munich court in 1962, was also significant because it showed in unusual detail how an OT man acted amid SS brutality in German-occupied Norway.[61] We have already seen how OT staff were capable of murdering prisoners without an SS presence in both Alderney and Ørlandet, but the legal judgment regarding Scholz is significant. Scholz was twenty-two years old when transferred in June 1942 to the SS-run Karasjok camp, in the far north of Norway, as part of an NSKK transport unit assigned to the OT. He took the job after being released from the army as unfit for service because of an eye condition. His unit's task was to transport OT supplies for mainly road- and bridge-building operations, as well as delivering food to a camp for Serb slave labourers. Its commandant was SS-Obersturmführer Franz de Martin, a 'brutal man, given to drink' who had personally shot many Serb prisoners for trifling reasons. Around 300 of these Serb labourers were engaged in building a section of a highway stretching the length of Norway, for which von Gottstein was responsible. One day in August 1942 Scholz heard shots fired from a barracks hut where he and de Martin were quartered, which he discovered had come from de Martin's gun and killed a Yugoslav prisoner outside. When he learned that another Yugoslav was to be 'executed', he asked the SS officer whether he 'couldn't also finish off a Serb'. De Martin replied that he didn't care who shot the man, so both went to the edge of a wood where two graves were dug, one already containing the first victim. When the second Yugoslav prisoner was led up, de Martin fired three shots at his head and he fell into the prepared grave. Scholz, who had obtained a colleague's pistol, then fired two shots, aiming for the man's heart. Scholz's superiors said he told them he had fired because the man was not yet dead. An OT letter to the 'NSKK-Transport Group Todt' in Berlin advised Scholz should be dismissed for 'insufficient aptitude' and because he had 'shown himself … as a sadist'.[62]

Scholz sought to explain his action in a pre-trial statement in 1961, saying that de Martin was present when his OT superiors interviewed him at the time about the incident and that 'he did not want to appear to the SS as a weakling and had therefore played the 100 per cent National Socialist, who was ready without further ado to liquidate a prisoner-of-war'. The court rejected this, finding Scholz's contemporaneous version of events more credible, and reasoning that any attempt to impress de Martin, who knew the facts, would have been futile. It emphasised that Scholz's actions 'could not be explained solely by an education under National Socialism and also cannot be mitigated by the fact that SS-Führer de Martin's bad example might have influenced his decision to act'. The court found he acted out of 'unnatural pleasure at the extinction of a human life'. Since de Martin's may have been the fatal bullets, Scholz was convicted of attempted murder.[63]

The ruling was therefore that it was Scholz's murderous intent, rather than the effects of de Martin's brutal SS practices and Nazi ideology, which drove him to fire his gun at the Serb prisoner. OT staff, however, generally showed a different kind of ruthlessness towards 'subhuman' prisoners than men like Scholz, who wanted the chance to 'finish off a Serb'. They routinely treated foreign slave labourers with lethal brutality without necessarily aiming bullets at their hearts. For them, what came first was the desire to finish a top-priority task at all costs. As a consequence, OT staff forced prisoners to perform extreme hard labour in abominable conditions, causing high death rates.

The Organisation Todt: an 'ordinary' organisation

The 'ordinary men' of the OT shot, beat or worked prisoners to death while employed by a state organisation authorising the use of force. At the Nuremberg trials the prosecution designated Nazi forces like the SS and Gestapo as criminal organisations, while the OT and most other German institutions fell outside that category.[64] Yet extensive research has shown that it was not just the 'illegal' organisations which carried out mass killings of Jews and other victims. State forces including the army and the police did so too. So in examining Nazi war crimes, is the idea of 'criminal' or 'abnormal' organisations as flawed as that of viewing all perpetrators as pathological monsters?[65]

Sociologist Stefan Kühl, in a comprehensive study of organisations in the context of the Holocaust, concluded:

> The organisations which specialise in torture and killing do not fundamentally function differently to organisations which care for the sick, advertise ice cream, teach schoolchildren or produce cars. The worrying discovery is that, not only are the members of organisations specialising in mass killing often completely normal people, but also the organisations by which the mass killings are planned and carried out display characteristics of perfectly normal organisations.[66]

Kühl conducted his analysis using as an illustration the German Reserve Police Battalion 101.[67] His purpose was not to present new facts about events, but to examine the example of Reserve Police Battalion 101 and draw general insights into the involvement of members of organisations in mass killings. Kühl finds that Hitler's regime could rely on organisations whose central structures, such as hiring, firing and redeploying personnel, developing programmes and creating communication channels, were perfectly normal. They could 'bring their members to do things which they would not do outside their organisation'.[68]

Among organisations classed as 'criminal' at Nuremberg, therefore, a lawyer in the Reich Security Head Office could be redeployed as the head of an execution squad, or a finance official at the WVHA could work in a death camp.[69] Among organisations not deemed illegal, soldiers in the army and reserve policemen could be 'redeployed' in the same way and their roles switched to take part in the Holocaust. As Kühl states: '[The regime] required – and that is one of the frightening lessons of the Holocaust – no completely novel programmes to carry out the killing operations, no new communication channels and no specially selected personnel.'

There is evidence that OT personnel participated in the mass shootings of Jews in German-occupied Eastern territories,[70] but OT staff belonged to a 'normal organisation' which mostly caused exceptionally high death rates among prisoners by different means. As in the case of members of the Order Police, who switched tasks to form killing squads to carry out mass murder of Jews, so the same personnel in the OT were assigned different programmes and roles. When Dr Erika Flocken practised as an OT doctor following the death of her husband (also an OT physician) in a plane crash in Soviet territory, she was deployed to Bavaria.[71] There, as described earlier, she carried out 'selections' of sick slave labourers in the Mühldorf camp complex so they could be sent to Auschwitz to be murdered. There are also examples of members of 'criminal' organisations, like the SS, who worked for the OT. One such officer (Willi Henne, who rose through SS ranks to *Standartenführer* in the Waffen-SS Reserve and never faced trial) supervised predominantly German labourers during pre-war building of the Westwall before Todt redeployed him to lead OT operations in Norway. There, as we have already seen, he worked until the end of the war, overseeing foreign slave labourers toiling in appalling Arctic conditions.

Another case mentioned earlier was Hermann Giesler, originally an architect, who became the ruthless OT task group leader in Russia-North and later for the region including Kaufering and Mühldorf. Yet another example in this chapter illustrates how the OT could assign skilled workers from German industry to projects in occupied Eastern Europe: Winand Schneider was transported from his job as a surveyor in a German road-building firm to command an OT unit overseeing Jews performing slave labour near Minsk, where he coordinated with SD-led execution squads to decide the prisoners' fate.

In this way, the OT managed its staff to ensure huge numbers of foreign slave labourers were exploited to the full. The organisation also sought to extract the best possible performance from its core, mostly German, skilled workforce. The OT had formal expectations about how its members should operate on joining up. It made efforts to motivate them by persuasion or punishment, but in the end cared only to a limited extent about the real motives of its personnel. As Kühl states: 'What counts for the organisation in the end is solely that the action it expects is carried out.'[72] To motivate staff and outline OT objectives, Speer issued a number of directives: using both carrot and stick, he not only strove to ensure the advancement of his favourites, but also issued dire warnings to anyone who stepped out of line. Addressing what he perceived to be failings among senior OT staff in 1943, Speer threatened to punish offenders severely, since failing to be a good role model for the rank and file in the OT undermined discipline. 'To be a Führer means first and foremost not to give orders, but to lead by example! … My responsibility for tasks vital to the war, as given to me as head of the OT by the Führer, compels me to intervene ruthlessly in future against offences … without regard to the identity and position of the person concerned.'[73]

Speer's warnings on discipline were drummed home at a more routine level by regular bulletins issued by OT headquarters.[74] The *Mitteilungsblatt der Organisation Todt-Zentrale*, which issued practical instructions, and *Der Frontarbeiter*, an illustrated publication with a high propaganda content, were both vehicles for the organisation's leadership to project its message and give direction to staff. Apart from these two publications, the OT employed other means to spread its message. The man in charge of culture, press and propaganda at OT headquarters was Rudolf Wolters, a Speer loyalist.[75] The OT arranged propaganda films and press coverage, and employed artists to record its achievements 'for posterity' in sketches or paintings.[76] All these activities informed its own members and the public at large.

Articles by 'OT war correspondents' in *Der Frontarbeiter* portrayed a career in the organisation as a tough but adventurous foray into far-flung regions of foreign territory, providing close support to German soldiers. Photographs of armed, well-equipped OT *Frontarbeiter* braving the challenge of working in Arctic conditions were designed to appeal to Germans who valued what they saw as manly virtues of physical fitness, resilience, military expertise and courage. Pictures of vast OT building sites suggested German technical prowess. Ten months after the Wehrmacht's invasion of the Soviet Union, *Der Frontarbeiter*'s March 1942 issue bore a cover photograph of two OT members in a snow-shrouded village in the occupied East. It contained an article entitled 'With shovel and gun' describing armed OT staff supporting the Wehrmacht in hostile territory. Members of the OT *Frontarbeiter* unit had been overseeing a column of local Ukrainian-led 'civilian workers' engaged in road clearing, but had to fight alongside German soldiers to repel a night-time Soviet assault. 'So the men in brown uniform, who bear the name of their brilliant and never-to-be-forgotten Dr Todt, are not only tirelessly working at their assigned tasks, but also constantly ready to take action, whenever necessary, and exchange the shovel with the gun.'77

Such articles created an image of the OT which the organisation wanted to project, emphasising that its engineers and other trained staff stood shoulder to shoulder with Germany's troops. Speer made frequent trips to raise the OT's profile and boost morale among its units posted around Europe. His visit to Seefeld in June 1943 included an award ceremony at which OT *Frontarbeiter* Josef Hinkerohe received the Knight's Cross with Swords for services clearly regarded as representing a model career in the organisation. Hinkerohe, in his early forties at the time, had worked on the Westwall from 1938 before supporting the Wehrmacht in 1940 in an OT unit closely following victorious German troops into Western Europe. A potted biography issued at the time of the award depicted Hinkerohe as an example of how OT front-line workers (*Frontarbeiter*) were now definitively taking their place beside front-line soldiers. Hinkerohe worked in France on oil depots and submarine bunkers before switching to Romania and then to Ukraine, building roads towards the Caucasus. He had set a 'stirring example' by keeping roads clear despite snowstorms and 'constant Soviet attacks', performing worthy labours on transport links in the Crimea area. Speer lauded him as a '*Frontarbeiter* with an exemplary readiness for sacrifice' and a standard-bearer for OT men across Europe.78

This portrait of a 'model' OT man depicted him criss-crossing the Third Reich's (at that time) vastly enlarged empire. He was an instrument of conquest and occupation. Speer wanted OT personnel to see themselves as being a vital part of forces battling to extend and secure those new frontiers against what the regime called the 'Jewish-Bolshevik' enemy. As well as ramping up Germany's colonial pretensions and extolling the OT's potential after imagined 'final victory', *Der Frontarbeiter* did not shrink from publishing articles on the 'Jewish question'. One stated in May 1943 that there existed 'clarity in the world that the decisive epoch had begun with this war which, as the Führer has already repeatedly said, will end with the destruction of Jewry. Precisely in the course of this war, the Jewish question has been demonstrated more and more to have become not solely one of race, but in the meantime also an eminent political question.'79 Such articles clearly represented the views of the OT leadership, and the organisation expected its members to support them.

The OT thus used various means to instruct, influence and inform members on many issues, including racist ideology. The organisation sharpened its own self-image by these means, and sought to guide and inspire its members. The clarion call to OT *Frontarbeiter* to go into battle alongside the Wehrmacht drew attention to their role as armed auxiliaries. The barrage of instructions to increase efficiency in top-priority tasks ordered, in many cases, by Hitler racked up pressure on OT personnel. This was a powerful factor in driving them to beat and work labour-camp inmates to death; the OT management's official publications also reinforced Nazi racism, telling staff their prisoners were subhuman and that Jews should be exterminated.

Having examined how the OT functioned as an organisation, and the loyalties and common professional goals that bound its members to one another, analysis is next conducted into OT perpetrators who came before Allied and other courts after the war. Their various backgrounds and the charges on which they were convicted are presented with additional reference to the operational pressures just explored.

Organisation Todt perpetrators

The most prominent war criminal in the OT was Speer. Barely more than a dozen other members of the organisation came to trial after the Second World War and they ranged in rank from senior level to among the lowest. Their backgrounds were varied, so no typical perpetrator profile can be extracted.

The details of the Nuremberg trials are well known, but it is worth noting that Speer's role as leader of the OT was weighed in evidence leading to his twenty-year sentence for war crimes and crimes against humanity. This was unusual among the judgments of Allied military tribunals and other post-war courts, which brought few OT members to trial in the first place. In its judgment of Speer, the military tribunal explicitly mentioned his role as head of the OT.

> Speer was also directly involved in the utilization of forced labor as Chief of the Organization Todt. The Organization Todt functioned principally in the occupied areas on such projects as the Atlantic Wall and the construction of military highways, and Speer has admitted that he relied on compulsory service to keep it adequately staffed. He also used concentration camp labour in the industries under his control.[80]

Out of a total of fourteen OT staff convicted of wartime crimes, three were executed and the rest served custodial sentences. Apart from Speer's Nuremberg trial, three OT personnel were sentenced in Dachau, three by French courts, five in Belgrade and one in East Berlin.[81] Only Scholz was tried by a West German court, being sentenced in Munich.

The Dachau trial involved the most high-profile OT case after Speer, Hermann Giesler. Born in the western region of Westphalia, Giesler volunteered to join the armed forces in the First World War and afterwards worked as a bricklayer, carpenter and metalworker before studying to become an architect. He was little known before being put in charge of rebuilding Munich in 1938.[82] Like Speer, Giesler's senior position in the OT and its use of slave labour were significant factors at his trial for crimes at the Mühldorf complex. Giesler's life sentence was reduced and he was released in 1952.

Two more members of the OT were convicted and sentenced at the Mühldorf trial in Dachau. Dr Erika Flocken was sentenced to death for her part in ill treatment of prisoners, including selection of sick or exhausted camp inmates to be sent to their deaths at Auschwitz. Dr Flocken, the youngest OT staff member to be convicted of crimes not involving direct physical violence, was thirty-four at the time of the Dachau trial in 1947 and belonged neither to the Nazi Party nor to the SS. She studied medicine in Cologne, Königsberg and Marburg and became an OT physician after her husband, Erich, died in an air crash in May 1944, having worked as an OT doctor in the organisation's Russia-South region.[83] The court found that the evidence:

> ... established that she knew that at least the great bulk of all sick inmates shipped to Auschwitz Concentration Camp were exterminated ... that she knew the sick inmates selected by her on the several occasions were in fact shipped to Auschwitz; that, under these circumstances and with full knowledge that some would die en route and at least the great bulk of them were to be shipped to their death, she selected additional hundreds for such shipments ...

Flocken's death sentence was commuted to life imprisonment, however, before being further reduced. The SS had for a long time had no doctor of its own in Mühldorf, unlike in Kaufering, and so entrusted Dr Flocken with selecting sick prisoners there. This SS practice of enlisting other organisations and institutions to be complicit in its bloody crimes had a parallel in its securing the Wehrmacht's support in operations in which the *Einsatzgruppen* carried out mass murder. A third OT staff member in the dock at the Mühldorf trial was the organisation's 'principal technical supervisor' at the camp's main construction site, Wilhelm Griesinger, who was sentenced to twenty years' imprisonment. 'The evidence established that the accused assumed an important role in the common design; that he had no regard for the health and lives of the inmates; and that he beat and ordered the beating of inmates.'[84] Employees of the Polensky and Zöllner firm contracted by the OT to work on the site were also indicted, and two were convicted and sentenced.[85]

Other OT personnel were sentenced after the war for maltreating slave labourers in Norway. Christian Schrade, an OT engineer working at Ørlandet, the labour camp holding Yugoslav prisoners mentioned at the start of this book, was sentenced in Belgrade in 1946 to ten years' hard labour. Schrade worked at the camp from July 1942 to March 1943.[86] Three other OT staff who worked at Ørlandet were sentenced in Belgrade, one of whom was condemned to death: OT Meister Oskar Lindner was executed. He was accused of beating around ten prisoners to death and ordering the torture or poisoning of others, resulting in the deaths of some. OT Meister Josef Starkens, who worked at Ørlandet from September 1942 until the end of the war, was sentenced to fifteen years' imprisonment with hard labour. He died in a Yugoslav prison on 29 December 1947. OT Meister Bruno Wendtland, based at Ørlandet from August 1942 until the end of the war, was sentenced to six years in prison with hard labour and released in October 1950.[87] A fifth defendant listed in the Belgrade court judgment, Max Leopold, described as a medical orderly based near Trondheim and holding an OT rank, was condemned to death and executed[88] for throttling a sick prisoner on a ship sailing to Norway.[89]

Another OT engineer posted to Norway was Fritz Autenrieth, who headed the OT administrative region including such infamous camps as Karasjok.[90] He was born in 1908 in the southern city of Ulm, and worked as a civil engineer before the war. After being assigned to work for the OT he was based in Pleskau, in occupied Soviet territory east of the Estonian border, before being sent to Alta in Norway's far north.[91] He said in a statement in 1977 to West German prosecutors investigating wartime events in Karasjok that he had been taken prisoner in 1945 and held by British forces before being handed over to Russian custody. In 1950 he was sentenced to fifteen years' imprisonment in East Berlin by a Russian military court for taking part in aggressive war against Russia.[92]

Regarding sentences for OT staff in post-war trials in communist East Europe, researchers have analysed prosecutions of this kind relating to the Second World War. No statistics are available on such trials in Yugoslavia, where the five OT members were convicted in Belgrade, capital of the post-war communist state under Tito. But in other communist states, such as the Soviet Union under Stalin, some data have been collected. Such states sought to show their own populations that fascist crimes, like those perpetrated in the Nazi era, were punished. Mass trials of thousands of German soldiers were conducted in the Soviet Union by military tribunals that were entirely lacking in any judicial rigour. Elsewhere, 5,400 Germans and 13,000 Polish citizens were convicted in Poland in post-war trials, including the Auschwitz war-crimes case. Although hatred of the occupier meant the accused were maltreated during interrogations, prosecutions were conducted in roughly similar fashion to those carried out by German lawyers in Western occupation zones.[93]

At a trial in 1949 in France concerning wartime events on the Channel Island of Alderney, OT Haupttruppführer Adam Adler, a former commander of Norderney camp, and OT Meister Heinrich Evers, his deputy, became the only two OT personnel to be convicted for war crimes there. They were accused of subjecting French Jews to 'superhuman work' and 'systematic ill-treatment'. Adler was sentenced to ten years and Evers to seven. In a judgment concerning wartime events in the Reich, a French military court sentenced to death a member of the OT named Kabus who worked at a forge on the building site in Bisingen. He was executed for severely maltreating prisoners.[94]

Some post-war investigations involving OT personnel in Norway did not end in convictions. Both a 1946 British war-crimes investigation and one drawn up in 1978 by West German prosecutors held the OT leadership in Norway to account. The British report spoke of the OT's 'inhuman use of slave labour', while the report by Nuremberg prosecutors on killings of Yugoslav prisoners in various camps also spoke of the OT leadership's large share of responsibility for the 'inhuman living and working conditions of the prisoners'. The West German prosecutors' closing investigations into the relevant camps found, however, that the OT leadership could not be directly blamed for premeditated killing. Their assessment was published a year after the death in 1977 in Wiesbaden of the OT's chief in Norway, Willi Henne.[95] They said their investigation into the SGL Nord camp network in Norway, run by the German Justice Ministry with the help of the OT, was halted either because suspects had died or could not be identified, or for lack of evidence. In one case, insufficient evidence was found for any charge of murder or abetting murder by Dr Karl Thurn, described in a Czechoslovak report as having been responsible for the camps' intolerable medical conditions because of his position as chief medical officer. Former Czechoslovak inmates of SGL Nord described catastrophic conditions in the camps in a report submitted to the United Nations War Crimes Commission.[96]

From this small number of convicted OT perpetrators, the main conclusion that can be drawn from analysis of their backgrounds and education is that they were remarkably varied. The number of crimes involving direct physical violence was relatively high, meaning that Speer was the most prominent figure who could be classified as a 'deskbound perpetrator'.[97] Speer's leadership of the OT and Giesler's senior job in the organisation were weighed in the evidence against them. Dr Flocken's original death sentence was based on her 'selection' of prisoners to be sent to death camps, while Autenrieth's conviction by a Russian court was for waging 'aggressive war' against Russia.

Flight from reality

OT personnel, clinging to their own belief in 'German quality work' but frustrated by the inadequacy of available resources, drove prisoners with ruthless intensity, resulting in high death rates. The fact that so many of the OT's mammoth projects in the final stages of the war were ill considered, unviable and ultimately futile did not slacken the pace of work. On the contrary, the organisation's engineers appeared intent on slamming their train powered by slave labour at full tilt into the buffers. Speer exhorted them to greater efficiency, and they responded to the very end. Their overwhelming complaint was not that slave labourers would be worked to death, but that there were never enough of them.

With hindsight, the question seems unavoidable as to why all available workers continued to build a railway in Norway when the project was hopelessly off course. Even the OT professionals building it at the time produced cogent reports proving this, yet the work and the unremitting misery and loss of life among the prisoners kept grinding on. If the railway had been an exception, it could be argued that it was an aberration. But other giant OT projects with similar fatal flaws were ruthlessly pursued by managers who appeared intent on taking the same flight from reality. Slave labourers died as a result in their tens of thousands. The underground factories for jet fighters in Bavaria were never completed. The shale-oil plants in the Württemberg subcamps of the Wüste scheme produced pitifully little low-grade oil in the final weeks of the war. Other OT-run projects in the Geilenberg programme to repair or relocate fuel refineries underground remained unfinished. The extensive Riese (Giant) subterranean network housing Hitler's headquarters and military facilities proved redundant, washed up like flotsam on the tide of war.

Where the OT worked alongside SS engineers similarly hell-bent on rocket and other military programmes, whatever the cost in prisoners' lives, their methods broadly coincided. At the Dora subterranean complex producing V2 missiles under SS engineer Hans Kammler, OT and SS staff displayed the same indifference to the fate of concentration-camp inmates and even competed to secure their labour.[98] Former OT engineers worked on Kammler's specialist staff, whose leader Speer judged to be a man of extraordinary talent.[99] Yet whatever the points of contact between the OT and Kammler's elite construction team in the SS WVHA, the fundamental purposes of Himmler's SS and the OT under Speer were entirely different. The 'worker soldiers' forged by Todt and inherited by Speer, while including significant numbers of SS or SA among their leaders and staff, were not Himmler's 'political soldiers'. So if elements of SS ideology were diluted, but still present, in the ranks of the OT, what other motives drove them to work and beat labourers to death, or select them for extermination in Auschwitz? Referring to Kaufering and Mühldorf, historian Edith Raim said the OT 'sacrificed (prisoners) to absurd armaments projects which were to have served to prolong the war'.[100] In the satellite camps within the Wüste programme, indifference towards prisoners and active abuse by OT staff and employees of construction and shale-oil research firms contributed to the misery in the camps and inmates' deaths. Using every possible means to maintain the pace of construction, these staff beat prisoners or caused them to be selected for the gas chambers.[101]

OT personnel were 'ordinary' men and women in the maelstrom of Nazi terror. More than seventy-five years after the Second World War, however, their full role in the Nazi slave-labour programme has until now been largely obscured. The phenomenon of Wehrmacht participation in mass murder of Jews in the German-occupied East has been well researched.[102] 'Ordinary men' in the German Order Police also carried out mass shootings of Jews in Poland.[103] It has been established, too, that the SS involved soldiers and policemen in genocide and thus made them partners in crime. These facts have been widely publicised. But the OT was also drawn into the concentration-camp system to perform duties that were normally the exclusive preserve of the SS. The OT ran entire operations within the networks of concentration camps, including Gross-Rosen, Dachau and Stutthof. OT engineers and construction teams treated slave labourers across Europe with brutality and murderous neglect, contributing to the deaths of tens of thousands of camp inmates through direct and indirect violence. The question of why they did so has scarcely been investigated. This book undertakes such an examination, and comparisons can be drawn with results of research into the actions of common soldiers and policemen. Like the soldiers and policemen, OT personnel had absorbed a barrage of propaganda advocating hatred of Jews and 'Bolsheviks' since Hitler took power. They differed, however, in that they worked for a construction agency, not for state organisations created to wield military might or powers of law and order. Neither was their institution founded as a force of 'political soldiers' like Himmler's SS. They were 'ordinary men' operating in the deadly currents of Nazi racist ideology. As they strove to perform German 'quality work', blaming poor-quality labour and resources for failures in practice, OT engineers and managers pursued their various projects late in the war, whatever the cost to camp inmates. They reacted to a multitude of forces, including urgent deadlines, directives on efficiency and wartime chaos. OT staff contributed, either through passive acceptance or active participation, to a murderous system delivering wretchedness and death to prisoners on their construction sites.

Conclusion

Throughout its existence, Hitler personally commissioned the OT to carry out vast construction projects he saw as vital to the Third Reich's war effort. His support and high regard for the organisation, led in turn by two armaments ministers, underpinned its central role in Germany's slave-labour programme. The dictator's faith in mammoth fortifications and underground industrial plants and factories caused deaths and misery among the slave labourers building them under OT supervision. The ultimate futility of these German programmes did not halt or slow their pace; on the contrary, death rates among the foreign workers toiling to complete them soared during the war, especially in the final year.

Of the five major themes explored in this study, analysis of how the OT became inextricably woven into Hitler's dreams of empire shows that the dictator used the organisation as an instrument of subjugation and occupation. This central purpose of the OT is highlighted by the fact that the organisation's initial, virtually exclusive, area of operation was in conquered territory. Members of the OT projected imperial power through technological and architectural feats, while helping to secure foreign lands won through war by constructing massive defence lines, military installations and communications. The jobs Hitler first gave to his two successive OT chiefs, the *Autobahnen* to Todt and the 'Germania' project to Speer, fitted the men he chose perfectly well. He created those posts to fulfil important goals in his own imperial designs. The dictator's passion for architecture undoubtedly drew him to an organisation which attracted so many gifted men in that field, including Speer, who quickly expanded OT operations in occupied Europe. Speer transferred his own considerable Germania workforce into the OT, and seized control for the OT of all technical operations in occupied East Europe. Mid- to high-level OT managers had considerable leeway to act on their own initiative throughout Hitler's empire, and a remarkably large proportion of the organisation's core personnel, including SS and SA members, were highly qualified as engineers, architects, surveyors, doctors or in other professions.

Regarding the second major theme of this book, the OT played a prominent role in the plunder of occupied Europe to boost Germany's war economy. A string of *Blitzkrieg* successes by the Wehrmacht resulted in the OT, industrial firms and other German forces systematically taking possession of the resources of defeated European nations for the benefit of the Third Reich. This stripping of the assets of conquered nations by OT task groups was hugely important to the Nazi regime. While Todt did much to pave the way, it was Speer who, in effect, gained control of the war economy through his role as the dominant member of Central Planning and his appointment in September 1943 as minister for armaments and war production. The OT, with its established network throughout German-occupied Europe, exploited its leader's powerful position to extend its operations. It played a key part in the Third Reich's slave-labour programme, and industrial giants, including IG Farben and Krupp, looked to the OT for lucrative contracts.

As for the third theme, the OT is clearly shown to be one of the major players in the Third Reich's system of competing powers, alongside the SS, the Nazi Party, the Wehrmacht and German industry. Both Todt and Speer cooperated closely with Himmler's SS, whose concentration-camp inmates formed such an important source of labour for the OT. Just as crucial to OT operations were prisoners of war, controlled by the Wehrmacht. Across occupied Europe the head of the OT and task group leaders cooperated with senior Nazi Party figures acting as Hitler's representatives in occupied countries. Last but not least, Germany's industrial giants were vital to the OT, possessing vast resources of highly skilled labour and machinery. All these power centres enmeshed so firmly in the OT's operations combined to form a highly volatile mix, generating political intrigues that threatened to cause Speer's downfall in 1944. Speer overcame this challenge and the OT played a central role, right to the end, in driving slave labourers to their deaths.

Regarding the fourth theme, evidence presented in this study shows that the extent of lethal violence practised by the OT was far greater than previous research indicates. The OT took no effective action to stop, or reduce, violence against prisoners even when it had most authority to do so. Instead the reverse was true: death rates were exceptionally high when the OT exercised complete or very high levels of control over projects and the influence of the notoriously brutal SS was reduced or absent.

The exact number of foreign slave labourers who died solely as a result of OT violence or neglect will probably never be determined, since the organisation did not generally operate alone. However, the number of deaths among foreign workers resulting from slave-labour projects carried out by the OT with the SS, the Wehrmacht or industry can be estimated at more than 185,000.[1]

Crucially, the OT bore a large part of the responsibility for this estimated death toll among slave labourers. OT staff killed prisoners outright with physical violence by shooting, hanging or beating them to death. They forced camp inmates to perform extreme hard labour in all weathers, working many of them to death. Foreign workers under the OT generally suffered the worst possible conditions because the agency specialised in construction. Over and above all this, the OT supplied its foreign labourers with pitifully insufficient food. Altogether, hunger, sickness, exposure and exhaustion generally caused more deaths among labour-camp inmates than physical violence by guards.

The OT was an integral part of the Nazi terror machine during the Second World War. The full significance of the organisation's role in the Nazi slave-labour programme had not been reflected in the historiography until now. Apart from the lethal violence already described, OT staff helped exterminate Jews and other victims by 'selecting' sick prisoners, either directly or indirectly, to be sent to the gas chambers of Auschwitz-Birkenau. They were also involved in 'death marches' at the time of concentration-camp evacuations, when death rates among prisoners were exceptionally high. Camp survivors have provided graphic accounts of their experiences undertaking extreme hard labour in often hellish conditions under the OT. Their evidence underlines the scope of OT operations throughout occupied Europe and the intensity of terror in labour- and concentration-camp networks in the Greater Reich in the last stages of the war. Extremely high death rates and violence in the camp networks of Kaufering, Mühldorf, Riese, Wüste and Transit Road IV and on OT transport and defence projects across Europe have been described through the eyes of the victims. Most of the numerous projects were dismal failures in terms of significant production for the German war effort, and provided murderously catastrophic conditions for slave labourers.

Evidence in this work shows that traditional distinctions between physical and other forms of violence could disintegrate in the extreme conditions of the camps. The OT's denial of the basic needs to prisoners, which itself claimed so many victims, led to further loss of life through physical violence. For instance, OT staff denied slave labourers adequate sanitation and medical care, then selected sick camp inmates for extermination in Auschwitz-Birkenau. Prisoners insane with hunger because of inadequate rations grabbed forbidden food, prompting guards to shoot them dead. SS officers, fearful of typhus epidemics, massacred inmates falling sick because of abysmal camp conditions. Prisoners physically assaulted by OT staff on construction sites died of exhaustion in extreme hard labour.

OT treatment of forced and slave labourers varied markedly, but generally became harsher as the war progressed. Non-Jewish and non-Slavic residents of

Nazi-occupied West Europe initially enjoyed relatively good conditions of labour under the OT. In Eastern Europe, by contrast, foreign workers toiled in infernal conditions virtually from the start. OT operations resulted in untold deaths in remote areas of the Soviet Union especially, where reliable figures are hard to find. In occupied Soviet territory OT construction chiefs could brutally mistreat slave labourers with virtual impunity in an area where massacres of Jews were carried out by the *Einsatzkommandos*. Inside the Greater Reich, meanwhile, where estimates of deaths are based on firmer data, the OT's enhanced powers in the last year of the war and domination of gargantuan construction projects in the desperate final stages of the conflict meant it bore heavy responsibility for high death rates among foreign slave labourers, as well as German Jews and German convicts.

Nazi racial hierarchies and their implications for forced and slave labourers under the OT are examined in considerable detail. Between the extremes of the 'Aryan' worker at one end and Soviet prisoners of war and Jews at the other, survival chances for foreign workers were broadly better towards the top and worse towards the bottom of the racial scale, but there were many exceptions. The plight of Jews, Soviet prisoners of war, concentration-camp prisoners and German convicts under the OT is examined extensively in this book. The fate of foreign civilians, who constituted the OT's largest foreign labour force and whose death rates were considerably lower than the four categories just mentioned, is also studied. The experiences of foreign civilian labourers higher on the racial scale (including Danes, Norwegians, Dutch, Flemish, French and Italians), as well as those lower down (*Ostarbeiter,* Poles, Serbs and Czechs) are all analysed. Survival chances for non-Jewish foreign civilians conformed to their position on the Nazi racial scale, so that Poles and *Ostarbeiter* were among those who suffered the worst. Still, there were exceptions. Andrej K., an *Ostarbeiter* due to his Ukrainian origin, benefited from pay and slightly better conditions because of his status as a skilled worker. He pitied the wretched labourers who marched by in columns with 'OST' on their backs. Frenchmen Maurice V. and Paul R., towards the top of the racial scale, toiled in arduous conditions in Breslau and near Danzig respectively in the final months of the war. Engineer Franz Duben, considered inferior by Nazi ideologues because he came from the Slavic region of the Protectorate of Bohemia and Moravia, was granted his right to a holiday from work in the Arctic after he protested that he and twelve compatriots were not treated on a par with German work colleagues.

Turning to the final theme of Nazi perpetrators, members of the OT fitted the category of 'ordinary men', so often used by researchers, more aptly than any other group so far investigated by historians. It is also clear that there were astonishingly few post-war prosecutions of suspected OT war criminals. Unlike for the OT's partners in the Third Reich's slave-labour programme, post-war trials have thus contributed very little to public understanding of the vast scope and brutal nature of OT activities. By contrast, prosecutions brought against members of the SS, captains of German industry and prominent Nazis are far more revealing. Overall, prosecutions of SS offenders in the aftermath of the Second World War were generally seen as having been pursued as successfully as possible in the circumstances, despite serious shortcomings caused by the chaos in occupied Germany and pressures such as the need for quick sentences. While it is accepted that the great majority of concentration-camp offenders went unpunished, the Allied courts nevertheless sentenced most surviving commandants of the camps and most top officials of the SS WVHA. German and Austrian courts also handed down some severe punishments, even if early post-war proceedings flashed warning signals, including superficial investigations and lenient sentences.[2]

The OT, by contrast, appears to have largely escaped the attention of war-crimes prosecutors. It is striking that the OT as an institution has not been the subject of any trial, unlike the way in which German industrial giants such as IG Farben and Krupp were called to account at Nuremberg. The firms' executives stood accused of crimes relating to the plunder of occupied countries and the Nazi slave-labour programme. The comparison is noteworthy because major OT operations, many ordered personally by Hitler, ranged across all occupied Europe and the Reich itself. The Nazi slave-labour programme meant misery or death for millions. An example of a leading OT engineer who avoided prosecution was Speer's deputy, Xaver Dorsch, who set up his own firm of consulting engineers in 1950.[3] The shock waves of Germany's surrender in 1945 had less impact on the country's engineers than on comparable professions.[4] The author of one study wrote that, as 'Victor of the Defeat', the German engineer 'could almost carry on life in his profession as if the 8th of May 1945 had never been'.[5]

With the most prominent exception of Speer, the majority of the convictions of OT staff were for direct physical violence. Legal notions of individual culpability fit more successfully with such cases, rather than deaths caused indirectly. Similar issues are encountered when assessing the roles of 'ordinary Nazis' in the German civil administration, who became Hitler's 'facilitators' in helping to pave the way to genocide. A civil servant who helped organise the ghettoisation of Jews, who were subsequently deported and exterminated, practised what one historian termed 'systemic violence'.[6] Such functionaries typically viewed themselves as 'mere administrators', and might be likened to engineers who saw their tasks as 'merely technical'. Speer, who took pains to present himself as an apolitical technocrat, was punished for his war crimes, but one contemporary German journalist, Sebastian Haffner, saw him as symbolising a type of single-minded organiser in an age of technicians who would endure. 'The Hitlers and Himmlers we may get rid of, but the Speers … will long be with us,' Haffner wrote in 1944 in *The Observer* newspaper.[7]

The Nuremberg trials formed part of judicial proceedings vigorously pursued by victorious powers, together with diplomacy, after the Second World War to try to prevent such a catastrophe ever being repeated. Similar efforts were made after the First World War, but it took only just over two decades for global conflict to return. Following the devastation of 1939–1945, the nagging question remains: could such terrible events as occurred under the Third Reich happen again? One Auschwitz survivor, Primo Levi, thought so. Presenting his own conclusion and speaking for other survivors, he wrote: 'It happened, therefore it can happen again: this is the core of what we have to say.'[8] Other former camp inmates who lived to tell their harrowing stories reinforced this view. David Rousset, the French writer and concentration-camp survivor, believed the crimes of the Nazi camps could be repeated 'in another form'.[9] Historians have been more circumspect, but leading researchers pose the question time after time.[10] While emphasising that history does not repeat itself, they point out the enduring relevance of the period of Hitler's rule: the Third Reich represents not only an extreme example of the dangers of racism and militarism, but also of the potential for hatred and destruction existing, however slightly, in all humanity.[11] This study of the OT analyses the actions of 'ordinary' people, in this case German engineers and construction experts serving under Hitler's regime, and concentrates on part of the sinister and fateful mosaic of the Nazi slave-labour system. Each interlocking institution assisted the others in making the horror of Nazi genocide and murderous slave labour possible, showing how evil can spread, insidiously and inexorably, among those living under a dictatorship.

Notes

Introduction

1. Kristian Ottosen, 'Arbeits- und Konzentrationslager in Norwegen 1940–1945', in Robert Bohn (ed.), *Neutralität und totalitäre Aggression. Nordeuropa und die Großmächte im Zweiten Weltkrieg* (Stuttgart, 1991), p. 359; see also Robert Bohn, 'Zwangsarbeiter und Zwangsarbeiterinnen im Reichskommissariat Norwegen; Fakten und Erinnerungen', in Dieter Pohl, Tanja Sebta (eds), *Zwangsarbeit in Hitlers Europa; Besatzung, Arbeit, Folgen* (Berlin, 2013), pp. 293–300; some other details on camps in Norway in this section are drawn from these works.
2. Uroš Majstorović, interview on 7 July 2005, translated into German from Croatian (Archiv-ID ZA 137), in 'Zwangsarbeit 1939–1945, Erinnerungen und Geschichte, ein digitales Archiv für Bildung und Wissenschaft', www.zwangsarbeit-archiv.de (accessed 8 December 2013)
3. OT records list the administrative name for construction in the district (*Bauleitung*) as Ørlandet, with a camp leader (*Lagerführer*) for Örlandet-Austraat (Ørlandet-Austrät); see RAFA 2188/1/G/G3/G3a/L0037/0001.
4. Albert Speer, *Erinnerungen* (Frankfurt am Main, 1974), p. 196.
5. Bohn, 'Zwangsarbeiter', p. 294.
6. TNA WO 331/13, Skibotn-Kvesmenes investigation, Appendix E(i)III.
7. TNA WO 208/3225, 'War Crimes in Norway', para. 123 (note 5).
8. Majstorović said the Organisation Todt ran Ørlandet alone before the Wehrmacht took it over in March 1943. A post-war West German investigation implied the same, stating that it was unknown whether Ørlandet 'was ever under SS leadership'. See BArchL B 162/9066, p. 371. See also Dirk Riedel, 'Norwegen,' in Wolfgang Benz, Barbara Distel, *Der Ort des Terrors; Geschichte der nationalsozialistischen Konzentrationslager*, Band 9 (Munich, 2009), p. 431 (note 36), in which Riedel cites details of a fourth ship transport of Yugoslavs held outside SS control in two OT camps, including (Ørlandet-)Austrät. There were three previous ship transports in June 1942 to Bergen, Trondheim and Narvik.
9. BArchL B 162/9066, p. 371. The document cites Yugoslav sources for the total.
10. TNA WO 208/3225, para. 82.
11. Majstorović (Archiv-ID ZA 137).
12. TNA WO 208/3225, para. 183.
13. Franz Seidler, *Die Organisation Todt: Bauen für Staat und Wehrmacht 1938–1945* (Koblenz, 1987); similarly, Hedwig Singer (ed.), *Quellen zur Geschichte der*

Organisation Todt (Osnabrück, 1987). Seidler also wrote a biography of Todt, *Fritz Todt: Baumeister des Dritten Reiches* (Munich, 1986). Seidler's *Die Organisation Todt* is now recognised as a whitewash; see Marc Buggeln, '"Menschenhandel" als Vorwurf im Nationalsozialismus. Der Streit um den Gewinn aus den militärischen Großbaustellen am Kriegsende (1944–1945),' in Andreas Heusler, Mark Spoerer, Helmuth Trischler (eds), *Rüstung, Kriegswirtschaft und Zwangsarbeit im 'Dritten Reich'* (Munich, 2010), p. 200; Christine Glauning, *Entgrenzung: Das Unternehmen 'Wüste' und das Konzentrationslager in Bisingen 1944/45* (Berlin, 2006), p. 201; Jens-Christian Wagner, *Produktion des Todes: Das KZ Mittelbau-Dora* (Göttingen, 2001), p. 111; Fabian Lemmes, 'Arbeiten für den Besatzer; Lockung und Zwang bei der Organisation Todt in Frankreich und Italien 1940–1945,' in Dieter Pohl, Tanja Sebta (eds), *Zwangsarbeit*, p. 84; Wolf Gruner, *Jewish Forced Labor Under the Nazis: Economic Needs and Racial Aims, 1938–1944* (Cambridge University Press, 2006), p. 98.

14 Examples are Edith Raim, *Die Dachauer KZ-Außenkommandos Kaufering und Mühldorf: Rüstungsbauten und Zwangsarbeit im letzten Kriegsjahr 1944/45* (Landsberg am Lech, 1992); Glauning, *Entgrenzung*; see also Edith Raim, *Überlebende von Kaufering: biografische Skizzen jüdischer ehemaliger Häftlinge, Materialien zum KZ-Aussenlagerkomplex Kaufering* (Berlin, 2008).

15 BArchB R 3/1808, Die Beschäftigten im Bereiche der OT Einsatzgruppen 30 September 1944. A British military intelligence report put the OT's total strength as high as 2 million; see TNA WO 208/5042, p. 3.

16 Willi Boelcke, *Deutschlands Rüstung im Zweiten Weltkrieg; Hitlers Konferenzen mit Albert Speer 1942–1945* (Frankfurt am Main, 1969), p. 352.

17 TNA WO 208/5042, p. 1.

18 Ulrich Herbert, 'Forced Laborers in the Third Reich: An Overview,' *International Labor and Working-Class History*, No. 58, (2000), p. 193; Mark Mazower, *Hitler's Empire: Nazi Rule in Occupied Europe* (London, 2008), p. 299.

19 European colonial powers among the Allies expanded their use of forced labour in overseas territories rich in raw materials, especially in Africa. Examples in wartime were the Belgian Congo and Nigeria, where Britain instituted forced-labour policies in 1942 to increase tin production; see Raymond Dumett, 'Africa's Strategic Minerals During the Second World War,' *Journal of African History*, Vol. 26 (1985), pp. 381–408.

20 Mark Spoerer, Jochen Fleischhacker, 'Forced Laborers in Nazi Germany; Categories, Numbers, and Survivors,' *Journal of Interdisciplinary History*, Vol. 33 (2002), pp. 169–71.

21 Van Waterford, *Prisoners of the Japanese in World War II: Statistical History, Personal Narratives and Memorials Concerning POWs in Camps and on Hellships, Civilian Internees, Asian Slave Laborers and Others Captured in the Pacific Theater* (Jefferson, NC, and London, 1994), pp. 144, 236–47; Felicia Yap, 'Prisoners of War and

Civilian Internees of the Japanese in British Asia: The Similarities and Contrasts of Experience,' *Journal of Contemporary History*, Vol. 47, No. 2 (2012), p. 320.
22 The term '*Ostarbeiter*' (Eastern workers) was used to describe Soviet civilian labourers. For estimates of the overall numbers of dead among foreign workers see Adam Tooze, *The Wages of Destruction: The Making and Breaking of the Nazi Economy* (London, 2006), pp. 519–23.
23 The vast majority of these foreign workers were forced or slave labourers.
24 Mark Spoerer, *Zwangsarbeit unter dem Hakenkreuz. Ausländische Zivilarbeiter, Kriegsgefangene und Häftlinge im Deutschen Reich und im besetzten Europa 1939–1945* (Munich, 2001), pp. 221–9.
25 Ulrich Herbert, *Hitler's Foreign Workers: Enforced Foreign Labor in Germany under the Third Reich* (Cambridge, 1997), pp. 1, 26.
26 Spoerer, *Zwangsarbeit*, pp. 9, 24.
27 Herbert, *Hitler's Foreign Workers*, pp. 1, 296–8.
28 *Arbeitsjuden* included Jewish slave labourers from ghettos and those held in labour camps.
29 The 'double counting' resulted from 885,000 POWs being switched to civilian status and 250,000 civilians switched to concentration camps. Spoerer, *Zwangsarbeit*, pp. 221–3.
30 Spoerer, *Zwangsarbeit*, pp. 224–9.
31 The term was used by historian Jens-Christian Wagner; see Wagner, *Produktion des Todes*, p. 578. The broader issues of how Nazi economic needs and racist ideology combined are also examined by Ian Kershaw, *The Nazi Dictatorship: Problems and Perspectives of Interpretation* (fourth edition) (London, 2010), pp. 47–68.
32 These themes are explored in depth in Chapter 4.
33 Trial of the Major War Criminals before the International Military Tribunal (IMT), Vol. 1, pp. 62, 73, 332.
34 Richard Overy, *Interrogations. The Nazi Elite in Allied Hands, 1945* (London, 2001), p. 475.
35 For background see Marc Buggeln, 'Were Concentration Camp Prisoners Slaves? The Possibilities and Limits of Comparative History and Global Historical Perspectives,' *International Review of Social History*, No. 53 (2008), pp. 101–129; Nikolaus Wachsmann, *KL: A History of the Nazi Concentration Camps* (London, 2015), pp. 410–11; for an example of a former labourer under the OT describing his work as 'slave labour' see Peter Demetz, interviewed in English on 16 December 2005, (Archiv-ID ZA573), in 'Zwangsarbeit 1939–1945, Erinnerungen und Geschichte, ein digitales Archiv für Bildung und Wissenschaft,' www.zwangsarbeit-archiv.de (accessed 9 December 2013); for analysis of the 'slave' debate and categories of forced labour see Ulrich Herbert, 'Zwangsarbeit im 20. Jahrhundert; Begriffe, Entwicklung, Definitionen,' in Pohl, Sebta, *Zwangsarbeit*, pp. 23–36;

for critics of the use of the term 'slave' see Spoerer, *Zwangsarbeit*, p. 17; Spoerer, Fleischhacker, 'Forced Laborers,' pp. 169–204; Wolfgang Sofsky, *Die Ordnung des Terrors. Das Konzentrationslager* (Frankfurt am Main, 1997), pp. 193–9.

36 Tooze, *The Wages of Destruction*, p. 381.

37 For background on Carl Krauch, as well as IG Farben operations before and during the Third Reich, see Stephan Lindner, *Inside IG Farben: Hoechst during the Third Reich*, trans. Helen Schoop (New York, 2008); Peter Hayes, *Industry and Ideology: IG Farben in the Nazi Era* (Cambridge, 1987).

38 See Ruth Bettina Birn, 'Vaivara – Stammlager,' in Wolfgang Benz, Barbara Distel, *Der Ort des Terrors: Geschichte der nationalsozialistischen Konzentrationslager, Band 8* (Munich, 2005–9), pp. 131–83; Alfred Streim, 'Konzentrationslager auf dem Gebiet der Sowjetunion,' in Wolfgang Benz (ed.), *Dachauer Hefte. Studien und Dokumente zur Geschichte der nationalsozialistischen Konzentrationslager*, Vol. 5, *Die vergessenen Lager* (Dachau, 1989).

39 Cited in Herman Kruk, (Benjamin Harshav, eds), *The Last Days of the Jerusalem of Lithuania: Chronicles from the Vilna Ghetto and the Camps, 1939–1944*, trans. Barbara Harshav (London, 2002), pp. 660, 665, 672; see also Mark Dworzecki, *Jewish Camps in Estonia, 1942–1944* (Jerusalem, 1970).

40 For background on the use of slave labour in the Bor copper mine, see Sabine Rutar, 'Arbeit und Überleben in Serbien: das Kupfererzbergwerk Bor im Zweiten Weltkrieg,' *Geschichte und Gesellschaft* (January–March 2005), pp. 101–34.

41 Spoerer, *Zwangsarbeit*, p. 31; Herbert, 'Forced Laborers,' p. 205.

42 Raim, *KZ-Außenkommandos*, p. 243.

43 Ottosen, 'Arbeits- und Konzentrationslager,' p. 359; Robert Bohn, *Reichskommissariat Norwegen; 'Nationalsozialistische Neuordnung' und Kriegswirtschaft* (Munich, 2000), pp. 379–80; Marianne Soleim (ed.), *Prisoners of War and Forced Labour: Histories of War and Occupation* (Newcastle, 2010), pp. 1–17; for further background on Nazi-occupied Norway see Ulf Larsstuvold, 'Finding Traces: Soviet Prisoners of War in Northern Norway, 1941–1945,' in M. N. Suprun, *Voina v Arktike 1939–1945*, (Arkhangel'sk: Pomorskii gos. Universitet, 2001).

44 TNA WO 208/3225, paras 91–2, 183; for background see Erich Kosthorst, Bernd Walter, *Konzentrations- und Strafgefangenenlager im Dritten Reich. Beispiel Emsland. Zusatzteil: Kriegsgefangenenlager. Dokumentation und Analyse zum Verhältnis von NS-Regime und Justiz. Mit historisch-kritischen Einführungstexten sowie statistisch-quantitativen Erhebungen und Auswertungen zum Strafvollzug in Arbeitslagern*, Vol. 1 (Düsseldorf, 1983), pp. 946–73; Nikolaus Wachsmann, *Hitler's Prisons: Legal Terror in Nazi Germany* (London, 2004), pp. 252–5; Lars Westerlund, 'German Penal Camps in Finland, 1941–1944,' in Soleim, *Prisoners of War*, pp. 157–79.

45 BArchL B 162/42181, Gefangenenlager Nord und dessen Teillager, pp. 306–10.

46 See Chapter 4.

47 Karin Orth, *Das System der nationalsozialistischen Konzentrationslager: eine politische Organisationsgeschichte* (Hamburg, 1999), p. 350; Buggeln, *Arbeit und Gewalt*, pp. 200–1.
48 Examples include Buggeln's *Arbeit und Gewalt*; see also Marc Buggeln, 'Building to Death: Prisoner Forced Labour in the German War Economy – The Neuengamme Subcamps 1942–1945,' *European History Quarterly*, Vol. 39, No. 4 (2009), pp. 606–32; for a detailed analysis of concentration camps in the final year of the war see Stefan Hördler, *Ordnung und Inferno. Das KZ-System im letzten Kriegsjahr* (Göttingen, 2015).
49 For background see Norbert Frei, Jose Brunner, Constantin Goschler (eds), Die Praxis der Wiedergutmachung: Geschichte, Erfahrung und Wirkung in Deutschland und Israel (Göttingen, 2009); Mark Spoerer, Jochen Fleischhacker, 'The Compensation of Nazi Germany's Forced Labourers: Demographic Findings and Political Implications,' in *Population Studies*, Vol. 56, No. 1, (2002), pp. 5–21.
50 Spoerer, *Zwangsarbeit*, pp. 71–3; see also Tooze, *The Wages of Destruction*, pp. 522–3; Christian Gerlach, *The Extermination of the European Jews* (Cambridge, 2016), pp. 223–34; Karel Berkhoff, *Harvest of Despair: Life and Death in Ukraine under Nazi Rule* (Cambridge, MA, 2004), pp. 90–113.
51 Figures for OT workers in occupied Soviet territory given by Speer's OT deputy, Xaver Dorsch, in Singer, *Quellen*, pp. 480, 512; for concentration camp prisoner totals see Wachsmann, *KL*, p. 627. The chart shows a peak of 714,211 inmates on 15 January 1945.
52 BArchB R 3/1808, Die Beschäftigten im Bereiche der OT Einsatzgruppen 30 September 1944.
53 Max Domarus, *Hitler: Reden und Proklamationen 1932–1945*, Band 1 Triumph, Zweiter Halbband 1935–1938 (Wiesbaden, 1973), p. 904.
54 Adolf Hitler, *Mein Kampf* (Munich, 1933), p. 136; for further background on this topic see Alan Bullock, *Hitler: A Study in Tyranny* (Reading, 1962); also Jost Dülffer, Jochen Thies, Josef Henke, *Hitlers Städte. Baupolitik im Dritten Reich. Eine Dokumentation* (Köln, Wien, 1978); Jochen Thies, 'Hitler's European Building Programme,' *Journal of Contemporary History*, Vol. 13, No. 3 (1978), pp. 413–31; for background on Hitler's imperial ambitions see Mazower, *Hitler's Empire*; Shelley Baranowski, *Nazi Empire. German Colonialism and Imperialism from Bismarck to Hitler* (Cambridge, 2011).
55 Authoritative studies on the Nazi war economy include Richard Overy, *War and Economy in the Third Reich* (Oxford, 1994); Tooze, *The Wages of Destruction*; Götz Aly, *Hitler's Beneficiaries: Plunder, Racial War, and the Nazi Welfare State* (New York, 2006); for an insight specifically into the construction sector and implications for the OT see also Christiane Botzet, 'Ministeramt, Sondergewalten und Privatwirtschaft. Der Generalbevollmächtigte für die Regelung der Bauwirtschaft,'

in Rüdiger Hachtmann, Winfried Süß, *Hitlers Kommissare. Sondergewalten in der nationalsozialistischen Diktatur* (Göttingen, 2006), pp. 115–37.

56 For example, Hitler's 2 September 1943 decree setting out OT functions, or Speer's powers as head of the OT; see respectively BArchB R 3/1637, ALLPROZ 6/12.

57 For example, Speer's directives empowering the OT to take over technical operations in occupied eastern territories following Hitler's 9 June 1942 decree; see BArchB R 3/1313, R 50 I/387.

58 For a comprehensive study of the WVHA and the slave-labour programme see Jan Erik Schulte, *Zwangsarbeit und Vernichtung: Das Wirtschaftsimperium der SS. Oswald Pohl und das SS-Wirtschafts-Verwaltungshauptamt 1933–1945* (Paderborn, 2001).

59 Studies include Karin Orth, *Die Konzentrationslager-SS. Sozialstrukturelle Analysen und biographische Studien* (Munich, 2004); Michael Thad Allen, *The Business of Genocide. The SS, Slave Labor, and the Concentration Camps* (Chapel Hill, NC, 2002); Klaus-Michael Mallmann, Gerhard Paul (eds), *Karrieren der Gewalt: nationalsozialistische Täterbiographien* (Darmstadt, 2004); Mark Roseman, 'Beyond Conviction? Perpetrators, Ideas and Actions in the Holocaust in Historiographical Perspective,' in Frank Biess, Mark Roseman, Hanna Schissler (eds), *Conflict, Catastrophe and Continuity: Essays on Modern German History* (New York, 2007), pp. 83–103; Harald Welzer, *Täter: Wie aus ganz normalen Menschen Massenmörder werden* (Frankfurt am Main, 2005) Michael Wildt, *An Uncompromising Generation: The Nazi Leadership of the Reich Security Main Office*, trans. Tom Lampert (Madison, WI, 2009); Christopher Dillon, *Dachau and the SS: A Schooling in Violence*, (Oxford, 2015); Alexander Haslam, Stephen Reicher, 'Beyond the Banality of Evil: Three Dynamics of an Interactionist Social Psychology of Tyranny,' *Personality and Social Psychology Bulletin*, Vol. 33, No. 5 (2007), pp. 615–22; Mark Roseman, 'The Lives of Others – Amid the Deaths of Others; Biographical Approaches to Nazi Perpetrators,' *Journal of Genocidal Research*, Vol. 15, No. 4 (2013), pp. 443–61; Dirk Riedel, *Ordnungshüter und Massenmörder im Dienst der "Volksgemeinschaft": Der KZ-Kommandant Hans Loritz* (Berlin, 2010).

60 For example, Christopher Browning, *Ordinary Men. Reserve Police Battalion 101 and the Final Solution in Poland* (New York, 1993); Daniel Goldhagen, *Hitler's Willing Executioners. Ordinary Germans and the Holocaust* (London, 1996). Goldhagen's book has been strongly criticised by leading historians, including Raul Hilberg, Ruth Bettina Birn and Sir Richard Evans, for errors of fact and selective use of evidence; see Raul Hilberg, 'The Goldhagen Phenomenon,' *Critical Inquiry*, Vol. 23, No. 4 (1997), pp. 721–8; Ruth Bettina Birn, Volker Riess, 'Revising the Holocaust,' *Historical Journal*, Vol. 40, No. 1 (1997), pp. 195–215; Richard Evans, *Rereading German History: From Unification to Reunification 1800–1996* (London, 1997), pp. 149–81.

61 TNA WO 208/5042
62 For background see Nicholas Bethell, *The Last Secret: Forcible Repatriation to Russia 1944-7* (London, 1976).
63 BArchL B 162/9063 Die Jugoslawische Kriegsverbrechens-Kommission.
64 The Wiener Library in London is one institution offering access to the International Tracing Service (ITS) archive.
65 Zwangsarbeit 1939-1945 archives: www.zwangsarbeit-archiv.de.
66 The project was funded by the foundation Erinnerung, Verantwortung und Zukunft and coordinated by the Institut für Geschichte und Biographie at the Fernuniversität Hagen.
67 For background on issues surrounding testimony provided by both survivors and perpetrators see Christopher Browning, *Collected Memories: Holocaust History and Postwar Testimony* (Madison, WI, 2003) and *Remembering Survival: Inside a Nazi Slave-Labor Camp* (New York, 2010); see also Jürgen Finger, Sven Keller, Andreas Wirsching (eds), *Vom Recht zur Geschichte: Akten aus NS-Prozessen als Quellen der Zeitgeschichte* (Göttingen, 2009).
68 Speer, *Erinnerungen*. His other books include *Spandauer Tagebücher* (Berlin, 1975) and *Der Sklavenstaat. Meine Auseinandersetzungen mit der SS* (Stuttgart, 1981).
69 BArchB R 3/1637 Letter from Hitler to Speer, 21 April 1944; IMT, Vol. 16, Speer testimony, p. 520; Trials of War Criminals before the Nuernberg Military Tribunals (NMT), Vol. 2, Walter Schlempp statement to Jägerstab, pp. 555-6; NMT, Vol. 2, Fritz Schmelter testimony, p. 582; Boelcke, *Deutschlands Rüstung*, pp. 346-7, 357-9.
70 Giesler published his own post-war memoirs, which showed no change of heart by this committed Nazi and Hitler loyalist; see Hermann Giesler, *Ein anderer Hitler: Bericht seines Architekten – Erlebnisse, Gespräche, Reflexionen* (Leoni, 1977).
71 Dorsch gave evidence as a defence witness in the trial of Erhard Milch at Nuremberg in 1947.
72 See, for example, Magnus Brechtken, *Albert Speer: eine deutsche Karriere* (Munich, 2017); Martin Kitchen, *Speer: Hitler's Architect* (New Haven, CT/London, 2015); Joachim Fest, *Speer: The Final Verdict* (London, 2001); Gitta Sereny, *Albert Speer: His Battle with Truth* (London, 1995); Matthias Schmidt, *Albert Speer: Das Ende eines Mythos. Speers wahre Rolle im Dritten Reich* (Bern/Munich, 1982).
73 Brechtken, *Albert Speer*, p. 9.

Chapter 1

1 Dr Henry Picker, *Hitlers Tischgespräche im Führerhauptquartier 1941-42* (Bonn, 1951), p. 98, entry for 8 June 1942; Dülffer, Thies, Henke, *Hitlers Städte*, p. 87.
2 British intelligence estimated 75 per cent of Todt's *Autobahn* workers transferred to the Westwall, TNA WO 208/5042, p. 165; Speer's team for rebuilding Berlin,

known as Construction Staff Speer (Baustab Speer), was incorporated into the Organisation Todt in 1942.

3   For the pre-war figure see TNA WO 208/5042, 'Handbook of the Organisation Todt, March 1945,' p. 46; for the higher wartime total see BArchB R 3/1808, Die Beschäftigten im Bereiche der OT Einsatzgruppen 30 September 1944.

4   Thies, 'Hitler's European Building Programme,' pp. 413–31; see also Dülffer, Thies, Henke, *Hitlers Städte*, pp. 85–7.

5   Goebbels recorded his reaction in a diary entry for 25 April 1941; Joseph Goebbels, *Die Tagebücher von Joseph Goebbels; im Auftrag des Instituts für Zeitgeschichte und mit Unterstützung des Staatlichen Archivdienstes Rußlands*, Elke Fröhlich (ed.), T. 1, Bd. 9 (Munich, 1998), p. 270.

6   Thies, 'Hitler's European Building Programme,' pp. 416–18; Helmut Weihsmann, *Bauen unterm Hakenkreuz: Architektur des Untergangs* (Vienna, 1998), pp. 185–6.

7   Domarus, *Hitler*, Bd. 1, p. 904; see also TNA WO 208/5042 pp. 6–7.

8   The Reichswerke 'Hermann Göring' came into existence in 1937 as a state concern to exploit domestic iron ore.

9   Hitler's disagreements with leaders of his military forces have been well documented. Conflicts with his generals led to almost half of those in top positions being dismissed, transferred or disciplined in the course of the war; see, for example, Karl Dietrich Bracher, *The German Dictatorship: The Origins, Structure, and Consequences of National Socialism*, trans. Jean Steinberg (London, 1971), pp. 499–500; Bullock, *Hitler*, pp. 665–9.

10 Hitler's comments on 18 July 1938 showed he used the term 'Organisation Todt' in private discussions with his staff well before his public pronouncement at Nuremberg; Gerhard Engel, Hildegard von Kotze (ed.), *Heeresadjutant bei Hitler 1938–1943: Aufzeichnungen des Majors Engel*, (Stuttgart, 1974), p. 27.

11 Seidler, *Fritz Todt*, pp. 166–7.

12 TNA WO 208/5042 The 'Westwall' (Siegfried Line) pp. 45–6.

13 Seidler, *Fritz Todt*, p. 168.

14 Seidler, *Fritz Todt*, pp. 17–33.

15 BArchB NS 26/1188 Letter from Todt to the NSDAP in Munich, 26 October 1931.

16 Seidler, *Fritz Todt*, pp. 30–3; although Todt emphasised the job-creating aspect of his scheme, its actual effect in this regard was limited. See Tooze, *The Wages of Destruction*, pp. 45–7.

17 Volker Schneider, *Waffen-SS, SS-Sonderlager 'Hinzert', Das Konzentrationslager im 'Gau Moselland' 1939–1945: Untersuchungen zu einem Haftstättensystem der Organisation Todt, der Inspektion der Konzentrationslager und des Wirtschafts- und Verwaltungshauptamtes der SS* (Nonnweiler-Otzenhausen, 1998), p. 84.

18 Gabriele Lotfi, *KZ der Gestapo; Arbeitserziehungslager im Dritten Reich* (Stuttgart/Munich, 2000), pp. 58–69, 323; IfZ ED 901/9 H. Auerbach, 'Arbeitserziehungslager

1940–1944,' in *Gutachten des Instituts für Zeitgeschichte* (Stuttgart, 1966), pp. 196–201; Benz, Distel, *Ort des Terrors*, Vol. 5, pp. 9–29; IfZ NO 2124 Hans Schmidt statement, 19 February 1947.
19 IfZ MA 414 Hermann Pister, 'Bericht über Aufbau und Führung der am Westwall befindlichen Polizeihaftlager und dem SS-Sonderlager Hinzert,' attached to letter dated 23 July 1940.
20 Orth, *Die Konzentrationslager-SS,* pp. 297–8. Pister was condemned to death by an American military court in 1947, but died of an acute heart condition in prison in 1948 before the sentence was carried out.
21 BArchB NS 26/1188 Letter to Himmler, 9 October 1941. Todt's letter was prompted by an SS directive affecting SS officers working for the OT on the front line, which said they should not wear field-grey uniforms unless they were members of the Waffen-SS. Field-grey uniforms were worn by *Sonderführer* in the OT.
22 BArchB NS 26/1188, Der Generalinspektor für das deutsche Straßenwesen, 4 September 1939.
23 Wachsmann, *KL*, pp. 101–4.
24 John Guse, 'Nazi Technical Thought Revisited,' *History and Technology*, Vol. 26 (2010), pp. 3–38; see also Konrad Jarausch, 'The Perils of Professionalism: Lawyers, Teachers, and Engineers in Nazi Germany,' *Historical Social Research/Historische Sozialforschung*, Supplement No. 24, Contemporary History as Transatlantic Project: The German Problem, 1960–2010 (2012), pp. 157–83.
25 For background see Jeffrey Herf, *Reactionary Modernism: Technology, Culture and Policies in Weimar and the Third Reich* (Cambridge, 1984).
26 BArchB NS 26/1188 Aussprüche Dr. Todt.
27 John Guse, 'Nazi Ideology and Engineers at War: Fritz Todt's "Speaker System"', *Journal of Contemporary History*, Vol. 48 (2013), p. 154; Guse, 'Nazi Technical Thought Revisited,' p. 13.
28 Guse, 'Nazi Technical Thought Revisited,' p. 13.
29 BArchB NS 26/1188, Speech by Dr Todt at Plassenburg, 31 August 1940.
30 Seidler, *Fritz Todt*, p. 312.
31 IWM FD 3063/49 File 66, p. 3, interrogation of Walter Rohland 18–19 October 1945.
32 BArchB NS 26/1188 Aussprüche Dr. Todt.
33 Sereny, *Albert Speer,* p. 268. Todt made a number of trips to the Eastern front, see for example IWM AL 2538/3/3 Box E7, Todt letter to Hans Blunk, 19 July 1941.
34 IfZ ED 99/9 'Einstellung von Todt und Speer zum Kriege,' Walter Rohland statement, Kransberg, 3 November 1945; Tooze, *The Wages of Destruction*, pp. 434, 507.
35 Kitchen, *Speer*, pp. 118–19; Fest, *Speer*, pp. 127–32; Sereny, *Albert Speer*, pp. 282, 460.
36 Brechtken, *Speer*, pp. 156–7; Tooze, *The Wages of Destruction*, pp. 508–9; Richard J. Evans, *The Third Reich at War* (London, 2008), pp. 321–2.

37 Tooze, *The Wages of Destruction*, p. 333.
38 IWM AL 2547/1 Box E8, Hitler decree of 17 March 1940 in Reichsgesetzblatt.
39 Seidler, *Fritz Todt*, p. 9.
40 Botzet, 'Ministeramt, Sondergewalten und Privatwirtschaft,' pp. 115–28; Tooze, *The Wages of Destruction*, p. 292
41 BArchB NS 26/1188 Aussprüche Dr. Todt.
42 Seidler, *Fritz Todt*, pp. 104–6.
43 For background see Lothar Gall (ed.), *Krupp im zwanzigsten Jahrhundert. Die Geschichte des Unternehmens vom Ersten Weltkrieg bis zur Gründung der Stiftung* (Berlin, 2002).
44 Tooze, *The Wages of Destruction*, pp. 349–52, 496–7, 508–9.
45 Alan Milward, 'The End of the Blitzkrieg,' *Economic History Review*, Vol. 16 (1964), pp. 499–518; Tooze, *The Wages of Destruction*, pp. 347–52; Neil Gregor, 'Big Business and the "Blitzkriegswirtschaft"; Daimler-Benz AG and the Mobilisation of the German War Economy, 1939–42,' *Contemporary European History*, Vol. 6 (1997), pp. 193–208.
46 BArchB R 3/1736, Rudolf Wolters Chronik, 14 February 1942.
47 Speer, *Erinnerungen*, pp. 210–13.
48 TNA WO 208/5042, p. 11.
49 Brechtken, *Speer*, p. 36.
50 Speer, *Erinnerungen*, p. 209.
51 Kitchen, *Speer*, p. 254.
52 BArchB 3100/F0022, Xaver Dorsch file.
53 Benz, Distel, *Ort des Terrors*, Vol. 2, pp. 355–8; Benz, Distel, *Ort des Terrors*, Vol. 6, p. 462; RAFA 2174/E/Ec/Ecj/L0071, List of firms provided by Allgemeine Ortskrankenkasse Berlin, 10 March 1943.
54 Singer, *Quellen*, p. 12.
55 See Chapter 3.
56 Tooze, *The Wages of Destruction*, p. 560.
57 BArchB R 3/1736, Rudolf Wolters Chronik, 14 February 1942.
58 Brechtken, *Speer*, p. 118.
59 BArchB NS 26/1188, *Gauleiter* Conference, 24 February 1942, in Munich.
60 Boelcke, *Deutschlands Rüstung*, p. 5.
61 BArchB R 3/1736, Rudolf Wolters Chronik, 14 February 1942; BArchB R 50 I/3a Neugliederung der OT, 18 February 1942; see also IfZ MA 251, Umorganisation der Aufgaben innerhalb des Reichsministeriums Dr. Todt, 23 February 1942.
62 IfZ MA 251 Umorganisation der Aufgaben innerhalb des Reichsministeriums Dr. Todt, 23 February 1942; BArchB R 3/1313, Speer directives relating to occupied Eastern areas, 22 July 1942, 'Ausführungsordnung zum Erlaß des Führers über den Einsatz der Technik in den besetzten Ostgebieten vom 9.6.42'; BArchB R 50 I/387.

63 Tooze, *The Wages of Destruction*, pp. 552–66; Brechtken, *Speer*, pp. 210–13.
64 Overy, *Interrogations*, p. 138–40.
65 For example, Schmidt, *Albert Speer*; Heinrich Breloer, *Die Akte Speer: Spuren eines Kriegsverbrechers* (Berlin, 2006); Brechtken, *Speer*.
66 Kitchen, *Speer*, pp. 82–96, 156.
67 Kitchen, *Speer*, pp. 78–9; Breloer, *Die Akte Speer*, pp. 161–6.
68 Kitchen, *Speer*, p. 190; Breloer, *Die Akte Speer*, pp. 178–9.
69 Wachsmann, *KL*, p. 449.
70 Tooze, *The Wages of Destruction*, p. 628.
71 Brechtken, *Speer*, pp. 221–2.
72 Brechtken, *Speer*, pp. 262, 276, 67980 (note 9).
73 Sereny, *Albert Speer*, p. 402.
74 Overy, *Interrogations*, p. 256.
75 Fest, *Speer*, pp. 39–42, 66.
76 *IMT*, Vol. 16, p. 430.
77 Bullock, *Hitler*, pp. 30–1, 721.
78 Speer, *Erinnerungen*, p. 44.
79 Fest, *Speer*, p. 64; Seidler, *Fritz Todt*, p. 100.
80 For background on such networks in the concentration-camp system see Stefan Hördler, *Ordnung und Inferno. Das KZ-System im letzten Kriegsjahr* (Göttingen, 2015), pp. 63–107, 470–4; Orth, *Die Konzentrationslager-SS*, pp. 127–52; see also Sara Berger, *Experten der Vernichtung: Das T4-Reinhardt-Netzwerk in den Lagern Belzec, Sobibor und Treblinka* (Hamburg, 2013).
81 Singer, *Quellen*, p. 37.
82 Gliederung der OT Einsatzgruppen im Osten, Speer directive, 19 July 1944, 2.2.3.0/82362040-1, ITS Digital Archive, London; Brechtken, *Speer*, pp. 126, 229–30.
83 Anschriften der OT-Einsatzgruppen im Reich 2.2.3.0/82361554, ITS Digital Archive, London; Singer, *Quellen*, pp. 50–1.
84 Hitler in fact rejected Speer's proposal; see Kitchen, *Speer*, pp. 192–3; Speer, *Erinnerungen*, p. 349.
85 BArchB SS 0085 A; BArchB 3100/H0113.
86 BArchB SSO/085 A, Letter from Speer to Himmler, 15 July 1942.
87 BArchB SSO/085 A, Aktenvermerk SS-Obersturmführer Heckenstaller, 15 December 1942.
88 Dienststellen im Heimatkriegsgebiet 2.2.3.0/82361436, ITS Digital Archive, London; Sereny, *Albert Speer*, p. 403.
89 Breloer, *Die Akte Speer*, pp. 90–116; Brechtken, *Speer*, p. 150; Kitchen, *Speer*, pp. 82–96, 339. For a comprehensive study on the issue see Susanne Willems, *Der entsiedelte Jude: Albert Speers Wohnungsmarktpolitik für den Berliner Hauptstadtbau* (Berlin, 2000).

90 Runderlass, 2.2.3.0/82357621, ITS Digital Archive, London; Anschriften der OT Einsatzgruppen im Reich, 2.2.3.0/82361554, ITS Digital Archive, London; BArchB R 50 I/355; BArchB R 43 II/1020.
91 RAFA 3915/D/Db/L0001/0031, Report on interrogation of Aumeier, Akershus Prison, 10 August 1945.
92 Giesler, *Ein anderer Hitler*, pp. 318–60; Speer, *Erinnerungen*, pp. 158, 185–6.
93 See, for example, OT Einsatzgruppe West, OBL Normandie, circular 30 May 1942 on 'self-cost' contracts, 2.2.3.0/82360135–82360146, ITS Digital Archive, London; RAFA 2188/1/E/E5/E5e/L0010, OT Einsatzgruppe Wiking contract with Josef Hoffmann & Söhne AG, 7 June 1943; R 50 I/106 January 1943, OT guidelines on performance-based contracts.
94 BArchB R 3/1637, Erlass des Führers über die Organisation Todt, 2 September 1943.
95 Boelcke, *Deutschlands Rüstung*, p. 91.
96 Arbeitskräfte bei der O.T., 2.2.3.0/82360625-82360626, ITS Digital Archive, London.
97 Dorsch, in Singer, *Quellen*, p. 473; Helmuth Euler, *Als Deutschlands Dämme brachen: Die Wahrheit über die Bombardierung der Möhne-Eder-Sorpe-Staudämme 1943* (Stuttgart, 1975), pp. 206–8.
98 BArchB R 3/1637, Letter from Dr Lammers to Speer, 6 September 1943.
99 IfZ Akten der Parteikanzlei 10116816–10116822, Speer decree, 3 June 1944.
100 IfZ ED 9/99 Speer, Zum Fragebogen für Bauwesen, 22 August 1945; Singer, *Quellen*, p. 12.
101 TNA WO 208/5042, Foreword, p. 1.
102 TNA WO 208/5042, Table IV, pp. 1–7; see also TNA WO 208/3224.
103 Raim, *KZ-Außenkommandos*, pp. 284–5.
104 TNA WO 208/5042.
105 RAFA 2188/1/E/E5/E5a/L0059/0004 Dr Schmelter Tarifordnung, 12 December 1944; Circular by Xaver Dorsch on OT pay in occupied territory, 20 February 1942, 2.2.3.0/82360092–82360098, ITS Digital Archive, London; TNA WO 208/5042, pp. 116–17, 138, 165–7. Women were estimated to represent about 7 per cent of personnel.
106 TNA WO 208/5042, p. 53; Singer, *Quellen*, p. 4.
107 BArchL B 162/3571, Rom statement, 28 April 1960; TNA WO 208/5042, p. 53.
108 BArchL B 162/5110, Glöckle statement, 13 January 1961; BArchL B 162/5110, Schmid statement, 6 April 1961; BArchL B 162/3571, Wolf statement, 12 April 1960; BArchL B 162/3571, Schneider statement, 6 February 1961.
109 BArchL B 162/5110.
110 BArchL B 162/3571.
111 BArchL B 162/3571; TNA WO 208/5042.
112 Lemmes, 'Arbeiten für den Besatzer,' pp. 83–103.

113 Martin Moll (ed.), 'Führer-Erlasse' 1939–1945 (Stuttgart, 1997), pp. 274–5.
114 Botzet, 'Ministeramt, Sondergewalten und Privatwirtschaft,' pp. 115–38.
115 IfZ ZS 1432, Vernehmung des Zeugen Fritz Schmelter, 8 May 1947.
116 TNA WO 208/5042, p. C 52; *NMT*, Vol. VIII, p. 529; Ernst Klee, *Das Personenlexikon zum Dritten Reich: wer war was vor und nach 1945?* (Frankfurt am Main, 2003).
117 BArchB SSO/085 A, Henne, Schulbildung und Beruf.
118 TNA WO 208/5042, Annexe C. The list of senior OT personnel in the March 1945 British intelligence report consistently included these types of qualifications and showed that 570 out of 1,401, or 40.7 per cent, possessed them. Of these, 263 were qualified engineers or architects, while 234 had regional state administration titles which were mostly for civil engineers, surveyors, town planners or building inspectors. Other job titles in the list of OT personnel included the areas of transport, medicine, training, forestry and supply; a handful of women had responsibilities in areas like female welfare. The full list of OT staff included all ranking personnel identified by British intelligence up to January 1945. Various individuals of NCO (non-commissioned officer) rank were listed because of the responsibilities many of them held in directing labour gangs.
119 IfZ NG 1584, Schmelter statement, 22 May 1947.
120 Mitteilungsblatt der OTZ, 30 October 1942, 2.2.3.0/82359934, ITS Digital Archive, London; see also IWM FD 3063/49 File 69, Interrogation of Dr Fritz Schmelter, 30 August 1945, pp. 4–5, 8.
121 Botzet, 'Ministeramt, Sondergewalten und Privatwirtschaft,' p. 115–28.
122 Tooze, *The Wages of Destruction*, pp. 491–2.
123 Schulte, *Zwangsarbeit und Vernichtung*, p. 390.
124 BArchB R 50 I/106 Tarifregister Nr. 3812/1, issued by Dr Schmelter on 1 October 1942.
125 Mitteilungsblatt der OTZ, Arbeitseinsatz-Statistik, 20 August 1943, 2.2.3.0/82359936, ITS Digital Archive, London.
126 Merkblatt zur Arbeitseinsatz-Statistik, 2.2.3.0./82359944, ITS Digital Archive, London.
127 TNA WO 208/5042, pp. 1–2.
128 Eidesstattliche Erklärung, Heinrich Werner Courté, 1.1.0.1/0014/82345317-20, ITS Digital Archive, London; BArchB 3200/C0078; BArchB SSO/131.
129 BArchB NS 26/1188, Todt letter to SS-Gruppenführer Heydrich, 25 April 1941.
130 Allen, *The Business of Genocide*, p. 16.
131 Wachsmann, *KL*, p. 394.
132 Orth, *Die Konzentrationslager-SS*, pp. 205–8; Allen, *The Business of Genocide*, p. 17.
133 Ulrich Herbert, 'Zwangsarbeit im 20. Jahrhundert,' p. 35; Spoerer, *Zwangsarbeit*, p. 224.

134 BArchB R 3/1808, Die Beschäftigten im Bereiche der OT-Einsatzgruppen im Reichsgebiet und im Auslande nach dem Stande vom 30.9.1944. These figures for the OT workforce, given in German Armaments Ministry correspondence, did not explicitly include a total for foreign civilian labourers, who generally made up the bulk of foreign forced or slave labourers. However, the figure can be estimated at around 775,000 by subtracting totals given for prisoners of war (164,700) and other prisoners (140,000) from the overall figure for OT foreign labourers (1,079,618).
135 TNA WO 208/5042, p. 3.
136 TNA WO 208/5042, p. 3.
137 Lotfi, *KZ der Gestapo*, p. 58.
138 TNA WO 208/5042, pp. 16, 121–7, 165–6, 177.
139 TNA WO 208/5042, pp. 85–6; on OT medical facilities see for example RAFA 2174/E/Ec/Ecj/L0071 OT-Lazarette, Reviere und Ärzte in Narvik, 20 September 1943.
140 The Interior Ministry said it should be made clear what exceptions were to be made to the citizenship offer, including wives and children of those who joined up, although they had the prospect of being included after the end of the war; see IfZ Akten der Parteikanzlei 10100464–5, Der Reichsminister des Innern, 1 June 1943.
141 Merkblatt zur Arbeitseinsatz-Statistik, Dr Schmelter, 2.2.3.0/82359944, ITS Digital Archive, London.
142 RAFA 2188/1/E/E3/E3e/L0011/0001, Romanian '*Volksdeutsche*' in Einsatz Wiking, 20 February 1943.
143 Lemmes, 'Arbeiten für den Besatzer,' pp. 83–9; Herbert, *Hitler's Foreign Workers*, p. 283.
144 Fabian Lemmes, 'The Economics of the German Construction Programs in Occupied France and Occupied Italy, 1940–1945', in Scherner, White (eds.), *Paying for Hitler's War*, p. 202.
145 TNA WO 208/5042, pp. 170–7; Lemmes, 'Arbeiten für den Besatzer,' pp. 83–9.
146 See Kershaw, *The Nazi Dictatorship*, pp. 161–82, 243–8.
147 Monika Renneberg, Mark Walker, 'Scientists, Engineers and National Socialism,' in Renneberg and Walker (eds), *Science, Technology and National Socialism* (Cambridge, 1994), p. 9.
148 Guse, 'Nazi Technical Thought Revisited,' p. 4.
149 IfZ MA 251, Reichsminister Speer Nr. 741/44, 29 April 1944.
150 IfZ ED 99/9, Speer, Zum Fragebogen für Bauwesen, 22 August 1945.
151 For an authoritative overview of engineering and technology in the Nazi era see Karl-Heinz Ludwig, *Technik und Ingenieure im Dritten Reich* (Düsseldorf, 1974).
152 Jarausch, 'Perils,' pp. 166–73, 179–80.
153 IfZ Akten der Parteikanzlei 10110538–9, Der Reichsminister für Wissenschaft, Erziehung und Volksbildung, 1 March 1943.

154 Baranowski, *Nazi Empire*, p. 48. Further details in this section are drawn from this work; see also Richard Evans, *The Pursuit of Power; Europe 1815-1914* (London, 2016), pp. 654-7; Gerlach, *Extermination*, pp. 37-8.
155 Peter Longerich, *Holocaust: The Nazi Persecution and Murder of the Jews* (Oxford, 2010), pp. 179-91; Aly, *Hitler's Beneficiaries*, pp. 4, 156-70.
156 Gerlach, *Extermination*, p. 261-2.
157 Schulte, *Zwangsarbeit und Vernichtung*, p. 261.
158 Cited in Gerlach, *Extermination*, p. 185.
159 *Der Frontarbeiter*, 20 April 1942, OT – Ein Werkzeug des Feldherrn Adolf Hitler.
160 See Brechtken, *Speer*, pp. 188, 194, 649 (note 159). *Der Frontarbeiter* first appeared on 22 June 1940 and was initially printed in Belgium, being distributed to OT units in Nazi-occupied Europe.
161 Breloer, *Die Akte Speer*, pp. 145-50.
162 Boelcke, *Deutschlands Rüstung*, p. 183.

Chapter 2

1 Tooze, *The Wages of Destruction*, pp. 65, 99-134, 513-51, 659; Richard J. Evans, *The Third Reich in Power, 1933-1939* (London, 2005), pp. 322-77; Overy, *War and Economy*, pp. 177-204, 233-56; Gerlach, *Extermination*, p. 49.
2 Scherner, White (eds), *Paying for Hitler's War*, p. 3; Aly, *Hitler's Beneficiaries*, pp. 75-179.
3 See Chapter 4.
4 Tooze, *The Wages of Destruction*, pp. 530-1.
5 RAFA 2188/1/E/E5/E5a/L0059/0004 Kgf.Bez.Kdt. Norwegen, 3 June 1944.
6 RAFA 2188/1/G/G3/G3c/L0001/0002, Speer decree to all OT regional chiefs, 5 September 1942.
7 Tooze, *The Wages of Destruction*, pp. 530-1.
8 RAFA 2188/1/E/E5/E5a/L0059/0004 Kgf.Bez.Kdt. Norwegen, 3 June 1944.
9 RAFA 2188/1/E/E5/E5f/L0006/0003, Nachkalkulation Leistungsmeldungen OBL Narvik/OBL Drontheim 1943-1944.
10 Hammermann, *Zwangsarbeit für den 'Verbündeten'*, pp. 239-40.
11 Singer, *Quellen*, p. 19.
12 Spoerer, *Zwangsarbeit*, p. 55.
13 IfZ NI 4813, Letter from Hofmann, Stahlwerke Braunschweig, to Paul Raabe, Hermann Göring Works Berlin, 21 June 1940.
14 Tooze, *The Wages of Destruction*, p. 362.
15 Enric C., interviewed on 16 January 2006 (Archiv-ID ZA405), translated into German from Catalan, www.zwangsarbeit-archiv.de (accessed 9 December 2013).
16 Lemmes, 'Arbeiten für den Besatzer', pp. 88-91.

17 Spoerer, *Zwangsarbeit*, pp. 62–6.
18 Spoerer, *Zwangsarbeit*, p. 57; Ottosen, 'Arbeits- und Konzentrationslager,' p. 358; Bohn, *Reichskommissariat Norwegen*, p. 376; for background on the economic aspects of the Nazi occupation of Norway see Harald Espeli, 'The Economic Effects of the German Occupation of Norway, 1940–1945,' in Jonas Scherner, Eugene White (eds.), *Paying for Hitler's War. The Consequences of Nazi Hegemony for Europe* (New York, 2016), pp. 235–65.
19 BArchB R 50 I/94 Arbeitseinsatzstatistik 30 May 1944. The figures were valid as of 25 April 1944 and overall totals included the OT's land and maritime transport sections, *Transportgruppe Todt* and *Transportflotte Speer*.
20 RAFA 2188/1/E/E3/E3g/L0022/0007, Zahl der norwegischen Bauarbeiter auf deutschen Baustellen, 1 August 1944.
21 RAFA 2188/1/E/E3/E3e/L0011/0001, OT OBL Bergen correspondence on Cossacks with A/S Nordag 5 April 1944; RAFA 2188/1/E/E3/E3e/L0014, OT correspondence with Breidt & Daub, 2 January 1944; Note on French and Polish workers assigned to Ovre Aardal, 11 August 1943, 2.2.3.2./77191107, ITS Digital Archive, London; Bohn, *Reichskommissariat Norwegen*, p. 414.
22 RAFA 2188/1/E/E3/E3e/L0011/0001, OT correspondence on Danish workforce in Norway, 15 January 1944.
23 Joachim Lund, 'Building Hitler's Europe: Forced Labor in the Danish Construction Business during World War II,' *Business History Review* (Autumn 2010), p. 488.
24 Spoerer, *Zwangsarbeit*, p. 56.
25 The OT's Einsatzgruppe VII, set up in summer 1944 with seven other OT regions as the OT partially withdrew into the Reich and surrounding regions, was responsible for this task; see Speer's June 1944 decree, IfZ Akten der Parteikanzlei 10116815–10116822; see also Pohl, Sebta, *Zwangsarbeit*, p. 127.
26 Jaroslav S., interviewed on 10 November 2005 (Archiv-ID ZA453), translated into German from Czech, www.zwangsarbeit-archiv.de (accessed 13 January 2014).
27 Seidler, *Fritz Todt*, p. 231.
28 Dorsch, in Singer, *Quellen*, p. 480.
29 Ernst Klee, Willi Dreßen, '*Gott mit uns*': *Der deutsche Vernichtungskrieg im Osten 1939–1945* (Frankfurt am Main, 1989), p. 138.
30 Ottosen, 'Arbeits- und Konzentrationslager,' p. 358.
31 Wagner, *Produktion des Todes*, pp. 96–101; HLSL, Jägerstab meetings, 28 March 1944, 27 June 1944; IfZ NG 1584, ED 99/9, ZS 1432.
32 Dorsch's figures were presented to the Jägerstab by his representative at the forum, Walter Schlempp, who was responsible for general construction affairs; see HLSL, Jägerstab meeting, 26 May 1944, and IfZ ZS 1432, Schmelter statement, 9 December 1946, also IfZ MB 27/7.
33 Wagner, *Produktion des Todes*, pp. 96–101.

34 Nachschub von polnischen Arbeitskräften, Dr. Ertl message to Dr. Schmelter, 8 July 1943, 2.2.3.0/82361733, ITS Digital Archive, London (copies from BArchB R 50 I/109, fol. 1).
35 2.2.3.0/82361733-82361736, ITS Digital Archive, London; Dorsch, in Singer, *Quellen*, pp. 484–5; Boelcke, *Deutschlands Rüstung*, p. 241.
36 IfZ MA 211 Richtlinien für die Behandlung der Kriegsgefangenen im OT-Einsatz.
37 Tooze, *The Wages of Destruction*, p. 517.
38 Tooze, *The Wages of Destruction*, pp. 627–8; Wachsmann, *KL*, pp. 406–10, 448; Benz, Distel, *Ort des Terrors*, Vol. 2, p. 360.
39 Tooze, *The Wages of Destruction*, p. 532; see also Herbert, 'Zwangsarbeit', in Pohl, Sebta, *Zwangsarbeit*, p. 32; SS WVHA chief Oswald Pohl estimated the total number of concentration-camp prisoners at the end of 1944 at 600,000; see *Trials of War Criminals before the Nuernberg Military Tribunals*, Vol. 5 (Washington, 1950), pp. 445–6.
40 Tooze, *The Wages of Destruction*, pp. 117–28, 219, 410–25; Mazower, *Hitler's Empire*, pp. 290–1; Wachsmann, *KL*, pp. 343–7; Aly, *Hitler's Beneficiaries*, pp. 1–8, 75–84.
41 Willems, *Der entsiedelte Jude*, pp. 433–4. Before Transit Road IV became a reality, Fritz Todt declared that he harboured two lifelong goals in building *Autobahnen*: one was to construct a motorway to Vienna, on which work had begun, and the other was an *Autobahn* leading to the Caucasus; BArchB NS 26/1188 Aussprüche Dr. Todt.
42 For background on Sweden's trade with both Germany and Allied countries during the Second World War see Eric Golson, 'Sweden as an Occupied Country? Swedish-Belligerent Trade in World War II,' in Scherner, White (eds), *Paying for Hitler's War*, pp. 167–95.
43 Tooze, *The Wages of Destruction*, p. 219.
44 IWM AL 2538/3/2 Box E7, Todt letter to Pleiger, 11 March 1940.
45 Overy, *War and Economy*, pp. 93, 145, 317–321, 349–356.
46 Oberlandesgericht Stuttgart 5.1.0111/82326425-82326434, ITS Digital Archive, London; Ruth Bettina Birn, 'Vaivara – Stammlager,' in Benz, Distel, *Der Ort des Terrors*, Band 8, p. 131.
47 Hayes, *Industry and Ideology*, pp. 358–60.
48 Tooze, *The Wages of Destruction*, pp. 449–50.
49 Dorsch, in Singer, *Quellen*, pp. 490–1, 504; Tooze, *The Wages of Destruction*, p. 450. In November 1944 Hitler emphasised the importance of holding on to bauxite supplies from the Lake Baloton area to ensure the maintenance of aluminium production – see Boelcke, *Deutschlands Rüstung*, p. 427.
50 Dorsch, in Singer, *Quellen*, p. 504.
51 Dorsch, in Singer, *Quellen*, pp. 502–4.
52 Bohn, *Reichskommissariat Norwegen*, pp. 383–422; Tooze, *The Wages of Destruction*, pp. 449–50.

53 Bohn, *Reichskommissariat Norwegen*, pp. 409–10.
54 Tooze, *The Wages of Destruction*, pp. 380–1.
55 Bohn, *Reichskommissariat Norwegen*, p. 131.
56 Dorsch, in Singer, *Quellen*, p. 495; Boelcke, *Deutschlands Rüstung*, p. 104; Bohn, *Reichskommissariat Norwegen*, p. 361.
57 Riedel, *Ordnungshüteri*, pp. 297–314; Bohn, *Reichskommissariat Norwegen*, pp. 179–80.
58 Bohn, *Reichskommissariat Norwegen*, pp. 355, 363–70.
59 Bohn, *Reichskommissariat Norwegen*, pp. 361–70.
60 Dorsch, in Singer, *Quellen*, p. 499.
61 Dorsch, in Singer, *Quellen*, p. 491.
62 NMT, Vol. 9, pp. 1461–4.
63 Boelcke, *Deutschlands Rüstung*, pp. 242–3.
64 Dorsch, in Singer, *Quellen*, pp. 503–4.
65 Boelcke, *Deutschlands Rüstung*, p. 243.
66 Dorsch, in Singer, *Quellen*, p. 504.
67 Boelcke, *Deutschlands Rüstung*, p. 303.
68 Dorsch, in Singer, *Quellen*, p. 509.
69 Dorsch, in Singer, *Quellen*, p. 481.
70 Longerich, *Holocaust*, p. 319; Pohl, Sebta, *Zwangsarbeit*, pp. 195–213; Singer, *Quellen*, pp. 33–44; see also Thomas Sandkühler, *'Endlösung' in Galizien. Der Judenmord in Ostpolen und die Rettungsinitiativen von Berthold Beitz 1941–1944* (Bonn, 1996), pp. 137–48.
71 Oberlandesgericht Stuttgart 5.1.0111/82326425-82326434, ITS Digital Archive, London; Birn, 'Vaivara – Stammlager', pp. 131–83; Geoffrey P. Megargee (ed.), *Encyclopedia of Camps and Ghettos, 1933–1945*, Vol. 1, Pt. B (Bloomington, Ind., 2009), pp. 1492–5; Boelcke, *Deutschlands Rüstung*, p. 286.
72 BArchB R 6/417 Anlage Nr. 4, Monatsbericht Wi Stab Ost, 1–30 September 1944.
73 Auszüge aus dem Bericht der Deutschen Revisions- und Treuhand-AG Berlin, 5.1.0111/82326426-82326434, ITS Digital Archive, London; Birn, in Benz, Distel, *Ort des Terrors*, Band 8, pp. 131–83; Megargee, *Encyclopedia*, pp. 1492–5.
74 Dorsch, in Singer, *Quellen*, pp. 511–12.
75 Boelcke, *Deutschlands Rüstung*, p. 363.
76 Boelcke, *Deutschlands Rüstung*, pp. 240–1.
77 Bohn, *Reichskommissariat Norwegen*, p. 371.
78 Cruickshank, *The German Occupation*, p. 188. The Channel Islands are dependencies of the British Crown but autonomous on domestic policy.
79 J. E. Kaufmann, H. W. Kaufmann, Aleksandr Jankovič-Potočnik, Vladimir Tonič, *The Atlantic Wall: History and Guide* (Barnsley, 2012), pp. 68–87; Lemmes, 'Arbeiten für den Besatzer', p. 85; TNA WO 208/5042, pp. 46–7; see also Colin Partridge, *Hitler's Atlantic Wall* (Guernsey, 1976).
80 Dorsch, in Singer, *Quellen*, p. 455.
81 Singer, *Quellen*, pp. 42–3.

82 Wachsmann, *KL*, pp. 444–51.
83 Boelcke, *Deutschlands Rüstung*, p. 240.
84 Kaufmann, *The Atlantic Wall*, pp. 239–41.
85 IfZ MA 265, Hitler directive regarding weapons, including the Tausendfüßler programme, 1 November 1943.
86 Kaufmann, *The Atlantic Wall*, pp. 247–8; Boelcke, *Deutschlands Rüstung*, pp. 290–1, 366; Dorsch, in Singer, *Quellen*, p. 490.
87 The programme took the name of the senior Armaments Ministry official who headed it, Edmund Geilenberg.
88 Herbert, 'Forced Labourers,' pp. 204–5; Gerlach, *Extermination*, pp. 113–15.
89 See Hördler, *Ordnung und Inferno*.
90 See Raim, *KZ-Außenkommandos*.
91 NMT, Vol. 2, Dorsch testimony in the Milch case, p. 591.
92 Raim, *KZ-Außenkommandos*, pp. 156–7.
93 BArchB R 3/1808 Die Beschäftigten im Bereiche der OT-Einsatzgruppen im Reichsgebiet und im Auslande nach dem Stande vom 30.9.1944.
94 Bohn, *Reichskommissariat Norwegen*, p. 378.
95 Raim, *KZ-Außenkommandos*, pp. 165–8.
96 Benz, Distel, *Der Ort des Terrors*, Band 2, pp. 442–5.
97 Benz, Distel, *Ort des Terrors*, Band 2, pp. 355–7; one especially feared Kapo was Christoph Knoll, who brutally beat Jewish prisoners and was transferred to the OT camp at Karlsfeld on 14 July 1944 before being sent to Mühldorf on 17 February 1945. He was sentenced to death at the main Dachau trial in 1945 and executed the following year; see also Knoll testimony at 1945 Dachau trial, 5.1./82310885, ITS Digital Archive, London.
98 Benz, Distel, *Ort des Terrors*, Band 2, pp. 314–15.
99 Benz, Distel, *Ort des Terrors*, Band 2, pp. 380–1.
100 Wagner, *Produktion des Todes*, p. 118.
101 Wagner, *Produktion des Todes*, p. 116.
102 Wagner, *Produktion des Todes*, pp. 235–41, 262.
103 For background see Glauning, *Entgrenzung*; Benz, Distel, *Ort des Terrors*, Vol. 6, pp. 55–63, 71–4, 163–7; Boelcke, *Deutschlands Rüstung*, p. 286.
104 IfZ NO 3901, Minutes of talks on oil-shale works attended by Oswald Pohl, 21 November 1944.
105 Before its takeover by the OT, the project had been under the steering committee for construction in the Armaments Ministry, which appointed its own on-site operator, Schlesische Industriegemeinschaft AG; see Benz, Distel, *Ort des Terrors*, Band 6, pp. 461–7.
106 Ifz ED 99/9 Speer Interrogation, Appendix 1, zu der Denkschrift an A.H. vom 19 April 1944.
107 Benz, Distel, *Ort des Terrors*, Band 6, pp. 461–7.
108 Benz, Distel, *Ort des Terrors*, Band 6, pp. 461–7.

109 IfZ Akten der Parteikanzlei 10800296–10800301, Speer letter to Bormann and all Gauleiter, 27 May 1944, Organisation zur Regelung der Bauwirtschaft und Gliederung der Organisation Todt im Reichsgebiet.
110 Cited in Buggeln, *Arbeit und Gewalt*, pp. 239–40.
111 Benz, Distel, *Ort des Terrors*, Vol. 5, pp. 372–5, 379–81; Buggeln, *Arbeit und Gewalt*, p. 234.
112 OT-Oberbauleitung Unterweser, Bremen-Farge 2.2.3.0/82361665-82361672, ITS Digital Archive, London. The files are copies of records from BArchB R 501/48 and listed workers from camps including an OT 'Foreigners' Camp' at Humannstr., contributing 737 labourers, the OT Camp Osterort, contributing 468, and the Neuenkirchen II and Heidkamp Camps 1 and 2, which provided by far the largest number of workers, totalling 4,222.
113 Cited in Lund, 'Building Hitler's Europe,' p. 489.
114 Cited in Tooze, *The Wages of Destruction*, pp. 652–3.
115 Megargee, *Encyclopedia*, Vol. 1, Pt. B, pp. 1448–1550, 1482–4.
116 Hördler, *Ordnung und Inferno*, pp. 250–2.
117 Benz, Distel, *Ort des Terrors*, Band 6, pp. 237–9, 351–3, 369–71, 438–43.
118 Goebbels, *Die Tagebücher*, T. II, Bd. 12, p. 137; Christian Gerlach, Götz Aly, *Das letzte Kapitel: Realpolitik, Ideologie und der Mord an den ungarischen Juden 1944/1945* (Stuttgart, 2002), p. 440.
119 Gerlach, Aly, *Das letzte Kapitel*, p. 415; Baranowski, *Nazi Empire*, p. 348.
120 Euler, *Als Deutschlands Dämme brachen*, p. 208.
121 Boelcke, *Deutschlands Rüstung*, p. 265.
122 Boelcke, *Deutschlands Rüstung*, p. 352.

Chapter 3

1 Brechtken, *Speer*, pp. 239–47; Kitchen, *Speer*, pp. 186–97.
2 Speer, *Erinnerungen*, pp. 339–40; Kitchen, *Speer*, p. 191.
3 IfZ Akten der Parteikanzlei, 10800082–10800093, Albert Speer, Hohenlychen, 29 January 1944.
4 Speer, *Sklavenstaat*, p. 317.
5 Brechtken, *Speer*, pp. 241–6.
6 IfZ NO 2602 Affidavit by Dr Friedrich Koch, 12 March 1947.
7 Boelcke, *Deutschlands Rüstung*, pp. 350–3; see also Lutz Budraß, *Flugzeugindustrie und Luftrüstung in Deutschland 1918–1945* (Düsseldorf, 1998), pp. 794–5.
8 Gregor Janssen, *Das Ministerium Speer; Deutschlands Rüstung im Krieg* (Berlin, 1968), pp. 160–1.
9 Fest, *Speer*, pp. 206–12; Sereny, *Albert Speer*, pp. 426–30.
10 See IfZ Akten der Parteikanzlei 10800296–10800301, Speer's letters on 27 May 1944 and 6 June 1944.

11 Kitchen, *Speer*, pp. 236–7.
12 For background see Kershaw, *The Nazi Dictatorship*, pp. 47–92; Peter Hüttenberger, 'Nationalsozialistische Polykratie', in *Geschichte und Gesellschaft* (1976), pp. 417–42.
13 Franz Neumann, *Behemoth. The Structure and Practice of National Socialism* (London, 1942).
14 Renneberg, Walker, 'Scientists, Engineers and National Socialism', pp. 2–3.
15 Schulte, *Zwangsarbeit und Vernichtung*, pp. 111–25; Wachsmann, *KL*, pp. 160–71.
16 Schulte, *Zwangsarbeit und Vernichtung*, p. 180.
17 Allen, *The Business of Genocide*, p. 72.
18 BArchB R 3/1313 Hitler decree, 9 June 1942.
19 Singer, *Quellen*, p. 40.
20 Schulte, *Zwangsarbeit und Vernichtung*, pp. 332–78.
21 Schulte, *Zwangsarbeit und Vernichtung*, p. 212.
22 BArchB NS 26/1188 Speer at Gauleiter-Tagung, 24 February 1942, München.
23 Wachsmann, *KL*, p. 392.
24 Wachsmann, *KL*, pp. 403–6.
25 Schulte, *Zwangsarbeit und Vernichtung*, p. 398.
26 IfZ Akten der Parteikanzlei 10116815-10116822, Speer decree, 3 June 1944.
27 Schulte, *Zwangsarbeit und Vernichtung*, pp. 379–425; Wachsmann, *KL*, pp. 392–410, 448–51.
28 Hördler, *Ordnung und Inferno*, pp. 291–2; Wachsmann, *KL*, p. 608.
29 Hördler, *Ordnung und Inferno*, p. 376.
30 Evidence from Obergefreite Georg Preukschat and Bruno Zietlow to British interrogators, 24 May 1945, TNA WO 311/12.
31 Statement by Leo Ackermann, 2 June 1945, TNA WO 311/12.
32 Former Sylt camp inmate Wilhelm Wernegau identified the Jew as a Russian army major who had managed to conceal his Jewish background. See Steckoll, *Alderney*, p. 81; Fings, *Krieg, Gesellschaft and KZ*, p. 203.
33 Pantcheff, *Alderney Fortress Island*, pp. 31–2.
34 Gruner, *Jewish Forced Labor*, pp. 214–22; see also Gerlach, *Extermination*, pp. 208–9.
35 IfZ MA 328 Prützmann to Brandt, 15 June 1943; Longerich, *Holocaust*, p. 353.
36 Kaienburg, *Die Wirtschaft der SS*, pp. 448–9.
37 Hayes, *Industry and Ideology*, p. 354. In June 1940 Hoechst was assigned 200 workers from the Westwall by the OT and promised a further 380 Polish workers, of whom Hoechst 'wanted only to take on 200'. See Lindner, *Inside IG Farben*, p. 225.
38 Raim, *KZ-Außenkommandos*, pp. 106–7.
39 NMT, Vol. 7, pp. 14–59; Wachsmann, *KL*, pp. 609, 775.
40 NMT, Vol 7, p. 957; Krauch wielded special powers through his position as general plenipotentiary for the chemical industry production plan.
41 NMT, Vol. 8, pp. 426–9; Hayes, *Industry and ideology*, p. 354.
42 NMT, Vol. 8, pp. 525–7.

43 Tooze, *The Wages of Destruction*, p. 445.
44 Wachsmann, *KL*, p. 346.
45 See Chapter 4.
46 Boelcke, *Deutschlands Rüstung*, p. 369.
47 Glauning, *Entgrenzung*, p. 401; Buggeln, *Arbeit und Gewalt*, p. 103.
48 Tooze, *The Wages of Destruction*, pp. 349–52.
49 NMT, Vol. 9, pp. 1412–16; Werner Abelshauser, 'Rüstungsschmiede der Nation? Der Kruppkonzern im Dritten Reich und in der Nachkriegszeit 1933 bis 1951,' in Gall (ed.), *Krupp*, pp. 375–99.
50 NMT, Vol. 9, pp. 753–5; memorandum on 14 October 1944 by Bernhard Weiss of the Flick concern after a visit to Krupp's Bertha works at Markstaedt.
51 NMT, Vol. 9, pp. 1165, 1417, 1450. Müller was tried with other top executives of Krupp before the Nuremberg Military Tribunal in 1948. He was sentenced to twelve years' imprisonment for plunder, war crimes and crimes against humanity in connection with slave labour. Abelshauser, in Gall (ed.), *Krupp*, pp. 465–72.
52 Michael Neufeld, *The Rocket and the Reich: Peenemünde and the Coming of the Ballistic Missile Era* (Cambridge, MA., 1996), p, 148.
53 Hans Mommsen, Manfred Grieger, *Das Volkswagenwerk und seine Arbeiter im Dritten Reich* (Düsseldorf, 1996), pp. 27–49, 803–29, 859–69.
54 Mommsen, Grieger, *Das Volkswagenwerk*, pp. 38–9, 608–9.
55 Tooze, *The Wages of Destruction*, pp. 134, 155.
56 TNA WO 208/5042, p. 53.
57 TNA WO 208/5042, pp. 9, 53–62; Tooze, *The Wages of Destruction*, p. 565.
58 Buggeln, *Arbeit und Gewalt*, pp. 227–34; Hördler, *Ordnung und Inferno*, p. 298; Glauning, *Entgrenzung*, pp. 215–16, 407.
59 Buggeln, 'Menschenhandel,' pp. 119–218.
60 Boelcke, *Deutschlands Rüstung*, pp. 250–1.
61 Singer, *Quellen*, p. 33.
62 TNA WO 208/5042, p. 27.
63 IfZ ED 99/9, Willi Nagel, Der Krieg des Transportwesens, p. 3.
64 IfZ MA 795, Letter from Reichskommissar für das Ostland, 28 August 1944; B 162/5123, Statement by Wilhelm Föhles, 12 July 1966.
65 IfZ NOKW 2085, Armeeoberkommando 16 an Oberkommando Heeresgruppe Nord, 31 July 1943; AOK 18 an Obkdo H.Gr.Nord, 2 August 1943; OT Russia-North Liaison Officer Klugar to Army Group HQ North, 2 August 1943.
66 RAFA 2188/1/G/G3/G3c/L0002/0007, Henne letter to Oberst Kiehl, 3 November 1942.
67 DOBN Box 8, Letter from Oberst Hörst, Deutscher Oberbefehlshaber Norwegen, to Commander Allied Land Forces Norway, 4 September 1945.
68 IfZ Akten der Parteikanzlei 10800265, Letter from Speer to General von Hengl, 11 October 1944.

69 IfZ Akten der Parteikanzlei 10111073–5, File note on state secretaries' meeting on 'Total War', 9 December 1944.
70 TNA WO 208/5042, p. 51; Gerlach, *Extermination*, pp. 195, 209.
71 UNWCC, United States v. Franz Auer et al., Review and Recommendations, 1 February 1948; Raim, *KZ-Außenkommandos*, pp. 104–5.
72 Seidler, *Fritz Todt*, p. 318.
73 Schulte, *Zwangsarbeit und Vernichtung*, p. 154.
74 Seidler, *Fritz Todt*, p. 186.
75 BArchB R 50 I/350, OT Einsatzgruppe IV 'Kyffhäuser' – Frontführung, 27 October 1944.
76 BArchB NS 26/1188 Letter to Himmler 9 October 1941.
77 BArchB SSO/085 A, Aktenvermerk SS-Obersturmführer Heckenstaller, 15 December 1942.
78 Kitchen, *Speer*, pp. 150–1.
79 Kitchen, *Speer*, p. 199.
80 Fest, *Speer*, p. 222.
81 Brechtken, *Speer*, pp. 266–7; Speer, *Spandauer Tagebücher*, pp. 283–4.
82 IfZ Akten der Parteikanzlei, 10800341–10800358, Speer letter to Kraus, copied to Bormann, 26 January 1944.
83 TNA WO 208/5042, p. 27.
84 Singer, *Quellen*, p. 39; the head of OT's Russia-South was Professor Walter Brugmann, the head of Russia-Central was Robert Meffert and the head of Russia-North was Professor Hermann Giesler. The OT chief based in Oslo working in Terboven's administration in occupied Norway was SS-Standartenführer Willi Henne.
85 Bohn, *Reichskommissariat Norwegen*, pp. 8, 43, 59.
86 Bohn, *Reichskommissariat Norwegen*, pp. 179–80, 361, 377.

Chapter 4

1 Arie P., interviewed on 26 September 2005 and 6 October 2005, translated into German from Hebrew (Archiv-ID ZA 109), in 'Zwangsarbeit 1939–1945, Erinnerungen und Geschichte, ein digitales Archiv für Bildung und Wissenschaft,' www.zwangsarbeit-archiv.de (accessed 9 December 2013); Itzhak gave his brother's formal name of Ludwig to be recorded the second time he presented himself for the labour transport, instead of Arie, the name he and his close family habitually used.
2 Raim, *KZ-Außenkommandos*, p. 243.
3 BArchL B 162/16432, Einstellungsverfügung, September 1976, p. 205.
4 Cited in Raim, *KZ-Außenkommandos*, p. 260.

5 BArchL B 162/16489, see for example Abram Grünstein statement 18 December 1967; see also summary of witness statements.
6 Arie P. (Archiv-ID ZA 109).
7 Arie P. (Archiv-ID ZA 109).
8 Arie P. (Archiv-ID ZA 109).
9 Cleve-Olsen letter dated 25 November 1949, CC Dachau, Kommando Kaufering, 1.1.6.0./82105389-93, ITS Digital Archive, London.
10 Selection of sick prisoners for extermination by the OT's Dr Erika Flocken has already been mentioned, see Raim, *KZ-Außenkommandos*, pp. 230–40. An indirect form of selection consisted of OT staff responding to firms' complaints about exhausted workers' performance by alerting the SS, who then despatched those 'unfit for work' to death camps; see, for example, Benz, Distel, *Ort des Terrors*, Vol. 2, p. 366.
11 Johan Galtung, 'Violence, Peace and Peace Research,' *Journal of Peace Research*, Vol. 6, No. 3 (1969), pp. 167–191); see also Buggeln, *Arbeit und Gewalt*, pp. 23, 481; Mark Vorobej, 'Structural Violence,' *Peace Research*, Vol. 40, No. 2 (2008), pp. 84–98.
12 There is wide consensus among historians that this was the case in the Third Reich's concentration-camp system, with the important exception of the extermination camps, such as Auschwitz-Birkenau and Majdanek. See Buggeln, *Arbeit und Gewalt*, pp. 23, 131–66, 200; Wagner, *Produktion des Todes*, pp. 469–91; Orth, *Die Konzentrationslager-SS*, p. 31; Orth, *Das System*, p. 350; Wachsmann, *KL*, pp. 169, 346, 422.
13 Zoltan B., interviewed on 1 June 2005 and 6 June 2005 (Archiv-ID ZA266), translated from Romanian into German, www.zwangsarbeit-archiv.de (accessed 9 December 2013).
14 Stjepan Pištignjat, interviewed on 23 July 2005 (Archiv-ID ZA359), translated into German from Serbian, www.zwangsarbeit-archiv.de (accessed 13 January 2014).
15 See Mühldorf trial evidence presented in this book, as well as numerous examples given in survivor accounts.
16 See Raim, *KZ-Außenkommandos*, p. 293; Benz, Distel, *Ort des Terrors*, Band 2, p. 393.
17 BArchL B 162/16489, Abram Grünstein statement, 18 December 1967.
18 BArchL B 162/16503, Abraham Katz statement, 21 October 1976.
19 BArchL B 162/16485, International Tracing Service Area 5 HQ, 16 August 1950; Hördler, *Ordnung und Inferno*, p. 359.
20 Arie P. (Archiv-ID ZA 109).
21 Gerhard Buschmann statement, 6 December 1944 in Case 000–50-105 in National Archives and Records Administration (NARA) RG 338, cited in Benz, Distel, *Ort des Terrors*, Vol. 2, p. 366; Hördler, *Ordnung und Inferno*, pp. 294–5.
22 Benz, Distel, *Ort des Terrors*, Vol. 2, p. 366; Raim, *KZ-Außenkommandos*, p. 238.
23 Arie P. (Archiv-ID ZA 109).
24 BArchL B 162/16432, Kaufering Lager III.

25 Statement by Elois Eisenhändler, cited in Benz, Distel, *Ort des Terrors*, Vol. 2, pp. 392–3.
26 Zoltan B. (Archiv-ID ZA266).
27 Review and Recommendations of the Acting Deputy Judge Advocate for War Crimes, 1 February 1948, United States v. Franz Auer et al., https://www.legal-tools.org/doc/173b55 (accessed 4 February 2014 via UNWCC website).
28 Raim, *KZ-Außenkommandos*, pp. 292–6, 237.
29 Zoltan B. (Archiv-ID ZA266). Zoltan names the camp as Landsberg, which was also known as Kaufering I.
30 Benz, Distel, *Ort des Terrors*, Band 6, p. 462.
31 Zoltan B. (Archiv-ID ZA266).
32 See Wachsmann, *KL*, pp. 347–9; Wagner, *Produktion des Todes*, pp. 359–500.
33 Hartog P., interviewed on 18 October 2005 (Archiv-ID ZA173), translated into German from Dutch, www.zwangsarbeit-archiv.de (accessed 7 November 2015).
34 Cited in Glauning, *Entgrenzung*, p. 259.
35 Jacek Z., interviewed on 19 January 2006 (Archiv-ID ZA247), translated from Polish into German, www.zwangsarbeit-archiv.de (accessed 9 November 2015).
36 Glauning, *Entgrenzung*, pp. 202–11.
37 Cited in Glauning, *Entgrenzung*, pp. 212–13.
38 Birn, in Benz, Distel, *Ort des Terrors*, Band 8, pp. 149–83.
39 Testimony of Bernard Zalkindson: Kruk, *The Last Days*, p. 665; see also Vernehmungsprotokoll vom 3 Oktober 1944 des Zeugen Markus Gardon, 1.2.7.4/82173222-82173224, ITS Digital Archive, London.
40 Account by Sholem Shub in Kruk, *The Last Days*, pp. 671–2.
41 B 162/30816, Weismann statement, 20 May 1974.
42 BArchL B 162/5109, Gurwicz statement, 5 November 1962. Gurwicz gives a phonetic spelling of the name as 'Peiniger'.
43 BArchL B 162/5117 Leichter statement, 17 April 1963.
44 BArchL B 162/5117 Alwin statement, 17 September 1962.
45 Benz, Distel, *Ort des Terrors*, Band 8, pp. 131–83; Megargee (ed.), *Encyclopedia*, pp. 1492–5.
46 BArchL B 162/5117, Leichter statement, 17 April 1963; Benz, Distel, *Ort des Terrors*, Band 8, pp. 152–5.
47 BArchL B 162/5117, Leichter statement, 17 April 1963; Benz, Distel, *Ort des Terrors*, Band 8, pp. 153–4; Megargee (ed.), *Encyclopedia*, pp. 1498.
48 BArchL B 162/5110, Schmid statement, 6 April 1961.
49 BArchL B 162/5110, Hefele statement, 5 March 1961.
50 BArchL B 162/5110, Hanke statement, 20 January 1960.
51 BArchL B 162/5110, Hanke statement, 20 January 1960.
52 Konstantins C., interviewed on 29 August 2005 (Archiv-ID ZA141), translated into German from Russian, www.zwangsarbeit-archiv.de (accessed 15 April 2014).

53 Longerich, *Holocaust*, p. 319; Pohl, Sebta, *Zwangsarbeit*, pp. 195–213; Singer, *Quellen*, pp. 33–44.
54 Kaienburg, *Die Wirtschaft der SS*, pp. 448–51; Andrej Angrick, 'Forced Labor along the Straße der SS,' United States Holocaust Memorial Museum Symposium, *Forced and Slave Labor in Nazi-Dominated Europe* (Washington, 2004), pp. 83–92.
55 Wolters diary entries on 30–31 May 1942; see Breloer, *Die Akte Speer*, pp. 163–4.
56 Cited in Willems, *Der entsiedelte Jude*, p. 434; see also Sandkühler, '*Endlösung*' in *Galizien*, p. 148.
57 Org. Todt., received from Zentrale Stelle Ludwigsburg, 2.2.3.0/82362040-82362089, ITS Digital Archive, London; further analysis of the figures is problematic, since the instruction to separate Jews and prisoners of war was not always followed.
58 BArchB R 50 I/130, OT Einsatzgruppe Kaukasus report, 20 November 1942.
59 Ottosen, 'Arbeits- und Konzentrationslager,' p. 359.
60 TNA WO 208/3225, War Crimes in Norway, Appendix A.
61 TNA WO 208/3225, War Crimes in Norway, Appendix A.
62 Kaufmann, *The Atlantic Wall*, p. 215.
63 Boelcke, *Deutschlands Rüstung*, p. 177.
64 Fjodor A. described how he and other Soviet POWs were repeatedly exhorted by their German captors to join the anti-Stalinist Vlasov army after they were deported to Lillehammer in Norway in 1942. See Fjodor A., interviewed on 11 and 12 February 2006 (Archiv-ID ZA018), translated into German from Russian, www.zwangsarbeit-archiv.de (accessed on 13 January 2014). Another former Soviet POW in Norway, Ivan Pasjkurov, wrote a memoir of his experiences entitled 'Lost Years'; see Larsstuvold, 'Finding Traces,' p. 93.
65 TNA WO 331/24, Preliminary report on legal matters pertaining to Camp Mallnitz (Skitbotn) investigation, Captain P. H. Gallagher, 27 June 1945; Major Dycker note on 'Delays apprehending German war criminals', 15 June 1945.
66 TNA WO 331/13, Appendix D(ii).
67 TNA WO 331/24, Conditions among Russian POWs in Mallnitz Camp, Skibotn, northern Norway.
68 RA/S-1681/D/Db/L0014, Displaced Persons, Repatrieringskontoret.
69 Ottosen, 'Arbeits- und Konzentrationslager,' p. 359; Benz, Distel, *Ort des Terrors*, Band 9, pp. 440–2.
70 BArchL B 162/9066 Ermittlungsverfahren gegen Ernst Heindl u.a. wegen Mordes; TNA 208/3225, para. 183.
71 Schulte, *Zwangsarbeit und Vernichtung*, p. 398.
72 BArchL B 162/9066, p. 335.
73 Stjepan Pištignjat (Archiv-ID ZA359).
74 Riedel, *Ordnungshüter und Massenmörder*, p. 306.
75 Stjepan Pištignjat (Archiv-ID ZA359).
76 BArchL B 162/9063, Hilmo statement, 12 March 1947.

77 Baurat Schmidt figures in OT correspondence as responsible for the Mo i Rana area in northern Norway in November 1942; see RAFA 2188/1/G/G3/G3c/L0002/0007.
78 RAFA 2188/1/E2b/4, Bauer report, 17 August 1942.
79 RAFA 2188/1/E2b/4; Baurat Köhling appears on lists of OT personnel as head of the Oberbauleitung in Narvik, see RAFA 2174/E/Ec/Ecj/L0071.
80 Boelcke, *Deutschlands Rüstung*, p. 224.
81 BArchL B 162/9066, Beck statement, 28 October 1974; RAFA 2188/1/E2b/4, Bauer report, 17 August 1942.
82 Stanko Diklic, ITS questionnaire on Korgen, 17 May 1950, 1.1.0.7./87769492, ITS Digital Archive, London.
83 Stjepan Pištignjat (Archiv-ID ZA359).
84 BArchL B 162/9063, Avdo statement in 11 March 1947 police report.
85 Stjepan Pištignjat (Archiv-ID ZA359); B 162/9063.
86 RAFA 2188/2/H/Ha/Haa/L0047/0001, Einsatz der Kriegsgefangenen, 28 March 1945.
87 TNA WO 208/3225 paras 107, 111, 115.
88 This section draws on Rutar, 'Arbeit und Überleben in Serbien,' pp. 101–34.
89 IfZ NG 5629, Sonnleithner message, 23–4 February 1943.
90 Nándor H., interviewed on 10, 11 and 22 July 2005 (Archiv-ID ZA363), translated from Hungarian into German, www.zwangsarbeit-archiv.de (accessed 6 November 2015).
91 Milan Pantoviç, interviewed on 24 March 2005 (Archiv-ID ZA358), translated from Serbian into German, www.zwangsarbeit-archiv.de (accessed 6 November 2015).
92 Jaroslav S., interviewed on 10 November 2005 (Archiv-ID ZA453), translated into German from Czech, www.zwangsarbeit-archiv.de (accessed 13 January 2014).
93 BA/MA RW 4/625 D, Ausbau und Verteidigung der englischen Kanalinseln, 20 October 1941.
94 Uroš Majstorović (Archiv-ID ZA 137).
95 TNA WO 208/3225, para. 82.
96 Uroš Majstorović (Archiv-ID ZA 137).
97 BArchL B 162/42181, UNWCC case R/N/206, charges list dated 27 September 1946.
98 Uroš Majstorović (Archiv-ID ZA 137).
99 RAFA 2188/2/F/Fa/Faa/L0111/0001, Müller-Altvatter accounts, 9 October 1942 to end March 1943.
100 BArchL B 162/9066, Christian Schrade statement. Schrade was questioned in West Germany in the 1970s, having been released early from a ten-year jail sentence imposed by a Belgrade court in 1946 on charges relating to his time at Ørlandet; see also BArchL B 162/9066, OT-Angehörige, p. 53. For the full list of the Belgrade court judgments see BArchL B 162/9063, Die Jugoslawische Kriegsverbrechens-Kommission. Schrade was one of five OT members convicted by the Belgrade court, which also sentenced five members of the Wehrmacht for crimes committed at Ørlandet.

101 Majstorović was later sent to a third camp, Persaunet, on the fringes of Trondheim; Uroš Majstorović (Archiv-ID ZA 137).
102 Uroš Majstorović (Archiv-ID ZA 137).
103 A total of 160 inmates died at Ørlandet under OT and Wehrmacht control; BArchL B 162/9066, p. 371.
104 BArchL B 162/9066, p. 366; see also Max Kraft statement, 29 October 1974.
105 TNA WO 208/3225, para. 196.
106 Interview with Albert Eblagon, a survivor of Norderney camp, in Solomon Steckoll, *Alderney Death Camp* (London, 1982), p. 93. Norderney camp was run by the Organisation Todt and the guards escorting Eblagon and the other Jews may have been from the OT Schutzkommando guard unit. Other former camp inmates have spoken of its deputy commander directing their transfer from the port on arrival around this time; see Madeleine Bunting, *The Model Occupation: The Channel Islands under German Rule 1940–45* (London, 2004), pp. 183–4.
107 Theodore Pantcheff, *Alderney Fortress Island; The Germans in Alderney 1940–1945* (London, 1981), pp. 6–7.
108 The OT and SS overlapped only partly on Alderney and comparative death rates for identical periods are lacking, but overall prisoner death rates were 11 per cent in OT camps and 10.6 per cent in the SS-run Sylt camp. These figures were calculated using maximum total strengths of 3,054 in OT camps and 946 in the SS-run camp, with total deaths of 337 at the former and 100 at the latter. Real strengths fluctuated considerably, and actual death tolls were almost certainly higher than the number of identifiable graves. The period with the highest number of fatalities in OT camps was October–December 1942, when 158 inmates died. This occurred before the SS arrived in March 1943. The worst three-month period in the SS-run Sylt camp was fifty-six prisoner deaths in April–June 1943. Comparative death rates for OT camps and the SS-run Sylt camp for these two three-month periods were 5.2 per cent and 5.9 per cent respectively. Unpublished 2013 dissertation by the author, 'Slave Labour under the SS and Organisation Todt on Nazi-Occupied Alderney'; see Brian Bonnard, *Alderney at War* (Dover, NH, 1993), p. 129; Charles Cruickshank, *The German Occupation of the Channel Islands* (London, 1975), pp. 204–5; Pantcheff, *Alderney Fortress Island*, pp. 7–10, 27, 74; Karola Fings, *Krieg, Gesellschaft and KZ: Himmler's SS-Baubrigaden* (Paderborn, 2005), p. 212.
109 The lower figure is cited in Bonnard, *Alderney at War*, p. 129, the higher one in Bunting, *The Model Occupation*, p. 291.
110 Interview with Kirill Nevrov in Bunting, *The Model Occupation*, pp. 165–6; for similar survivor accounts see Cohen, *The Jews in the Channel Islands*, p. 149.
111 Bunting, *The Model Occupation*, p. 182.
112 Bunting, *The Model Occupation*, p.293; Peter King, *The Channel Islands War 1940–1945* (London, 1991), p. 179.

113 For a comparative analysis of factors affecting death rates in Neuengamme subcamps, including the urgency of projects, see Buggeln, *Arbeit und Gewalt*, pp. 238–43.
114 Ulrich Herbert, 'Labour and Extermination: Economic Interest and the Primacy of Weltanschauung in National Socialism,' *Past and Present*, No. 138 (1993), pp. 144–95.
115 Orth, *Das System*, p. 240.
116 Wagner, *Produktion des Todes*, pp. 575–9; Gerlach, *Extermination*, pp. 160–6.
117 See Buggeln, *Arbeit und Gewalt*, pp. 238–334, 658–74; Buggeln, 'Building to Death,' pp. 606–32; Wachsmann, *KL*, pp. 474–9; Hördler, *Ordnung und Inferno*, pp. 364–78; Gerlach, *Extermination*, pp. 184–214.
118 Herbert, *Hitler's Foreign Workers*, pp. 187–8.
119 Wagner, *Produktion des Todes*, p. 152.
120 See Chapter 5.
121 For background see Spoerer, *Zwangsarbeit*, pp. 89–107; Herbert, 'Zwangsarbeit im 20. Jahrhundert,' p. 25.
122 BArchL B162/5117, Alwin statement, 17 September 1962.
123 Birn, 'Vaivara – Stammlager,' in Benz, Distel, *Der Ort des Terrors*, Vol. 8, p. 132.
124 BArchL B 162/30816, Goldstein statement, 21 August 1967; see also Josef Schneider statement in which he explains that prisoners named all OT personnel 'Meister', regardless of rank, and lists personnel in Trucksäss who held OT ranks.
125 Lemmes, 'Arbeiten für den Besatzer,' pp. 83–103.
126 Prisoners at OT camps on Alderney, who suffered high death rates in 1942, represented an exception. Along with the Slavs on that island were 700 French Jews, and the graves of eight of them have been identified. The relatively few deaths among Jews, who were so ruthlessly persecuted under Nazism, may partly be explained by the fact that they were only on Alderney for a comparatively short time, when a large part of the heavy construction work had been done; see Frederick Cohen, *The Jews in the Channel Islands during the German Occupation 1940–1945* (St Helier, 2000), pp. 130–4, 152–3.
127 Pohl, Sebta, *Zwangsarbeit*, p. 14.
128 Enric Casañas (Archiv-ID ZA405).
129 Lemmes, 'Arbeiten für den Besatzer,' pp. 83–7.
130 Joaquín Gálvez, interviewed on 27 January 2006 (Archiv-ID ZA407), translated into German from Spanish, www.zwangsarbeit-archiv.de (accessed 13 January 2014).
131 Alexander von Plato, 'It Was Modern Slavery: Some Results of the Documentation Project on Forced Labour,' in Alexander von Plato, Almut Leh, Christoph Thonfeld (eds), *Hitler's Slaves: Life Stories of Forced Labourers in Nazi-Occupied Europe* (New York, 2010), pp. 466–7.

132 See Spoerer, Fleischhacker, 'Forced Laborers,' pp. 173–4, on categories of foreign workers according to whether they had any voice in complaining about work conditions.
133 RAFA 21889/1/E/E3/E3e/L0011/0001, OT Einsatzgruppe Wiking in Oslo to OBL Kirkenes, Italienische Arbeitskräfte, 27 August 1942; Paul Stephan to OBL Kirkenes, 12 September 1942, Stellungnahme zum Brief der Org. Todt, Einsatzgruppe Wiking, Oslo; italienische Arbeitskräfte; Organisation Todt Oslo, 5 October 1942, Einsatz ital. Arbeitskräfte in Kirkenes; OTZ Berlin, Einsatz italienischer Militärinternierter, 12 October 1943.
134 RAFA 21889/1/E/E3/E3e/L0011/0001, From OT-Oslo (Janssen) to OT OBL Kirkenes, 28 August 1944; OT Einsatz Dänemark to OT Drontheim, Arbeitsanwerbung in Dänemark, 13 June 1944; Sager & Woerner to OT Drontheim, Klagen dänischer Arbeiter, 3 May 1944; OT Wiking Oslo Reichskomissar für die besetzten norweg. Gebiete, Klagen dänischer Arbeiter, 19 June 1944; NSKK-Gruppe Todt, Beschwerde des dän. Kf. Larsen, 20 January 1944.
135 RAFA 21889/1/E/E3/E3e/L0011/0001, Duben statement enclosed in OTZ letter, Beschwerde des Dipl. Ing. Franz Duben, 25 April 1944; OT EG Wiking, Einsatzleiter Stumpp, Urlaub, Beschwerde des Dipl. Ing. Duben, 10 July 1944.
136 See Wagner, *Produktion des Todes*, p. 578; Buggeln, *Arbeit und Gewalt*, pp. 238–334.
137 Maurice V., interviewed in French on 4 August 2006 (Archiv-ID ZA091), www.zwangsarbeit-archiv.de (accessed 9 December 2013).
138 Paul R., interviewed in French on 13 June 2006 (Archiv-ID ZA087), www.zwangsarbeit-archiv.de (accessed 13 January 2014).
139 Paul R. (Archiv-ID ZA087).
140 Paul R. (Archiv-ID ZA087).
141 Stefan K., interviewed on 18 and 19 June 2005 (Archiv-ID ZA211), translated into German from Polish, www.zwangsarbeit-archiv.de (accessed 9 December 2013).
142 Herbert, *Hitler's Foreign Workers*, p. 283.
143 Gabriele Hammermann, *Zwangsarbeit für den 'Verbündeten': Die Arbeits- und Lebensbedingungen der italienischen Militärinternierten in Deutschland 1943–1945* (Tübingen, 2002), p. 400.
144 Gabriele Hammermann (ed.), *Zeugnisse der Gefangenschaft: Aus Tagebüchern und Erinnerungen italienischer Militärinternierter in Deutschland 1943–1945*, trans. Friederike Hausmann, Rita Seuß (Berlin, 2014), pp. 10, 149.
145 Roughly half the deaths occurred when they were disarmed in 1943, and the rest while the Italians were subsequently prisoners and forced labourers. See Hammermann, *Zeugnisse der Gefangenschaft*, p. 18.
146 Hammermann, *Zeugnisse der Gefangenschaft*, p. 163; Italy's Marshal Pietro Badoglio concluded the armistice with the Allies on 3 September 1943.

147 Giovanni Bonotto, interviewed on 24 November 2005 (Archiv-ID ZA119), translated into German from Italian, www.zwangsarbeit-archiv.de (accessed 13 January 2014).
148 Spoerer, *Zwangsarbeit*, pp. 82–3.
149 Lemmes, 'The Economics of the German Construction Programs', p. 205.
150 BArchB R 3001/24367, Der Vorstand der Strafgefangenenlager Nord, 29 September 1942.
151 Kosthorst, Walter, *Konzentrations- und Strafgefangenenlager*, Vol. 2, p. 1455; Wachsmann, *Hitler's Prisons*, p. 254.
152 TNA WO 208/3225, paras 91–2, 183.
153 Wachsmann, *Hitler's Prisons*, p. 254.
154 Sierpinski, Johann, 2.3.1.2./78541661, ITS Digital Archive, London.
155 TNA WO 331/60, Happe statement, 3 July 1945.
156 TNA WO 331/60, Happe statement, 3 July 1945; RAFA 2188/2/F/Fg/Fga/L0001, Abrechnung über Beschäftigungsvergütung 1.9.44–28.2.45, Strafgefangenenlager Nord.
157 RAFA 2188/1/E/E3/E3e/L0014, Tomasz Staniak, born on 24 November 1900, and Janusz Staniak, born on 9 October 1927, were listed among forty-four workers, all Poles, who had arrived on 16 May 1944 having been shipped via the Danish port of Aarhus. They were described simply as 'workers' among labourers aged between sixteen and forty-nine, whose trades included carpenter, mechanic, bricklayer and truck driver. They had been allocated to the Plihal firm under OT Oberbauleitung (OBL) Fauske as Troop '1', Transport Nr. 112.
158 Gefolgschaftsmitglieder der Firma Arch. Richard Plihal, 2.2.3.2./77191038, ITS Digital Archive, London. Tomasz Staniak's entry states that he ended work on 31 May 1944 and was arrested in Bodø.
159 Soleim, *Prisoners of War*, pp. 9–10.
160 Zecharja S., interviewed on 11 October 2005 and 23 November 2005 (Archiv-ID ZA113), translated from Hebrew into German, www.zwangsarbeit-archiv.de (accessed 6 November 2015).
161 Zecharja S. (Archiv-ID ZA113).
162 Pohl, Sebta, *Zwangsarbeit*, p. 105; see also Benz, Distel, *Ort des Terrors*, Band 4, pp. 175–85.
163 Liviu B., interviewed on 15 June 2005 (Archiv-ID ZA267), translated into German from Romanian, www.zwangsarbeit-archiv.de (accessed 9 December 2013).
164 Liviu B., interviewed on 15 June 2005 (Archiv-ID ZA267).
165 Liviu B. (Archiv-ID ZA267).
166 Pohl, Sebta, *Zwangsarbeit*, p. 283.
167 Peter Demetz, interviewed in English on 16 December 2005 (Archiv-ID ZA573), www.zwangsarbeit-archiv.de (accessed 9 December 2013); Demetz gave a similar

account of his experiences in a post-war memoir, *Prague in Danger; The Years of German Occupation, 1939–45: Memories and History, Terror and Resistance, Theater and Jazz, Film and Poetry, Politics and War* (New York, 2008).

168 Gruner, *Jewish Forced Labor*, pp. 83–102.
169 Demetz (Archiv-ID ZA573).
170 Demetz, *Prague in Danger*, pp. 218–223; Demetz, (Archiv-ID ZA573)
171 Ziffermässige Erfassung der Lagerinsassen des Lagers Lenne nach Rassenzugehörigkeit und Nationalitäten. Stand vom 30.12.1944, 2.2.3.0/82362252, ITS Digital Archive, London.
172 Mommsen, Grieger, *Das Volkswagenwerk*, p. 871.
173 Ausscheiden nicht einsatzfähiger Juden, Mischlinge, Versippte, 2.2.3.0/82362261, ITS Digital Archive, London.
174 Abtransport der Juden aus dem Lager Lenne am 19.2.45 2.2.3.0/82362260, ITS Digital Archive, London. The Gestapo report on those being sent to Theresienstadt included Ernst Israel Fleischmann, who had been listed on 20 December 1944 after arriving in Lager Lenne as being in the Nazi racial category of 'privileged mixed marriage'. See 2.2.3.0/82362257, ITS Digital Archive, London.
175 Orth, *Die Konzentrationslager-SS*, p. 29.
176 Angrick, 'Forced Labor,' p. 89.
177 Hammermann, *Zwangsarbeit für den 'Verbündeten'*, pp. 378–9.
178 Hammermann (ed.), *Zeugnisse der Gefangenschaft*, pp. 163–7.
179 Jacek Z. (Archiv-ID ZA247).
180 November 1944 figure cited in Benz, Distel, *Ort des Terrors*, Band 2, p. 426.
181 Among subcamps administered by Allach was Karlsfeld OT for Jewish prisoners; see Benz, Distel, *Ort des Terrors*, Band 2, pp. 425–30.
182 Martin K., interviewed on 31 May 2006 (Archiv-ID ZA105), translated into German from Hebrew, www.zwangsarbeit-archiv.de (accessed 29 May 2015).
183 Andrej K., interviewed on 31 May 2006 (Archiv-ID ZA105), translated into German from Hebrew, www.zwangsarbeit-archiv.de (accessed 9 December 2013).
184 Andrej K. (Archiv-ID ZA105).
185 Andrej K. (Archiv-ID ZA105).
186 Ellis H., interviewed on 15 June 2005 (Archiv-ID ZA168), translated into German from Dutch, www.zwangsarbeit-archiv.de (accessed 13 January 2014).
187 Ellis H. (Archiv-ID ZA168).
188 Leszek Z., interviewed on 17 November 2005 (Archiv-ID ZA245), translated from Polish into German, www.zwangsarbeit-archiv.de (accessed 6 November 2015).
189 Raim, *Überlebende von Kaufering*, p. 15.
190 Raim, *KZ-Außenkommandos*, p. 165.
191 IfZ NO 030, Himmler note on 28 May 1944.
192 Wachsmann, *KL*, p. 477.

193　The five subcamps were Birnbäumel, Hochweiler, Kurzbach, Schlesiersee I and Schlesiersee II. Before evacuation, ten to twenty women were estimated to have died of hunger or exhaustion out of the original 1,000 in Birnbäumel (1–2 per cent); in Hochweiler there were twenty such deaths out of 900 prisoners (2 per cent); Kurzbach's death toll is unknown; in Schlesiersee I there were about thirty deaths out of 1,000 (3 per cent); and in Schlesiersee II there were thirty to forty deaths out of 1,000 (3–4 per cent). See Benz, Distel, *Ort des Terrors*, Band 6, pp. 237–9, 351–2, 369–71, 438–41. For the average death rate in Gross-Rosen women's subcamps and Riese see Andrea Rudorff, *Frauen in den Außenlagern des Konzentrationslagers Groß-Rosen* (Berlin, 2014), pp. 386–91.
194　Hördler, *Ordnung und Inferno*, p. 349.
195　Benz, Distel, *Ort des Terrors*, Band 6, pp. 237–9, 351–2, 369–71, 438–41; Rudorff, *Frauen*, pp. 386–91.
196　Rudorff, *Frauen*, pp. 386–91.
197　Wachsmann, *KL*, pp. 476–9.
198　Buggeln, *Arbeit und Gewalt*, pp. 274–82, 328–30.
199　For a detailed examination of the role of Stutthof as a hub for evacuated prisoners from the East who were either murdered there or redeployed as slave labour in the final year of the war see Hördler, *Ordnung und Inferno*, pp. 233–79.
200　Megargee, *Encyclopedia*, Vol. 1, Pt. B, pp. 1448–50.
201　Megargee, *Encyclopedia*, Vol. 1, Pt. B, pp. 1482–3; for details on the wider context of the Vistula River scheme see Lund, 'Building Hitler's Europe,' pp. 488–92.
202　Hördler, *Ordnung und Inferno*, p. 251; Botten, Argenau and Schirkenpass were SS-guarded Stutthof subcamps in the Thorn complex. Although conditions in two camps were catastrophic, Denzler identified one camp, led by an older *SS-Sturmscharführer*, as showing 'evidence of absolute cleanliness and order'.
203　Hördler, *Ordnung und Inferno*, p. 251. The English translation cited here is an excerpt from Denzler's statements in September 1945; the German originals were no longer available in NARA, RG 549, US Army Europe, Cases not tried, Case 000-50-56 (Stutthof), Box 533, Folder No. = Case No.
204　Daniel Blatman, *The Death Marches: The Final Phase of Nazi Genocide* (Cambridge, MA, 2011), pp. 117–25; Evans, *The Third Reich at War*, p. 692; Wachsmann, *KL*, p. 560.
205　Judith A., interview conducted in English on 16 October 2005 (Archiv-ID ZA570) www.zwangsarbeit-archiv.de (accessed 13 January 2014).
206　Judith A. (Archiv-ID ZA570).
207　BArchL B 162/5109, Lewin statement, 5 November 1962.
208　B 162/30816, Weismann statement, 20 May 1974. A post-war murder investigation by West German prosecutors into a former OT member called Schneider ruled out a suspect with the same last name, and the file was set aside in 1976.

209   BArchL B162/5117, Alwin statement, 17 September 1962.
210   BArchL B 162/5109, Molly Ingster letter, 27 October 1964.
211   UNWCC, United States v. Franz Auer et al., Review and Recommendations, 1 February 1948, accessed via UNWCC website www.legal-tools.org/doc/173b55/ on 4 February 2014.
212   See, for example, Jacek Z.'s description of fellow inmates working in summer clothes in winter, and having to go barefoot himself until he received shoes when another prisoner died. Jacek Z. (Archiv-ID ZA247).
213   For reports on OT personnel shooting prisoners see BArchL B 162/14312, Munich district court judgment in case of Diederich Scholz, sentenced on 10 April 1962 to four years' penitentiary for attempted murder; see also witness statements in the case of Winand Schneider, BArchL B 162/3571, Gareis statement, 4 January 1962; BArchL B 162/3571, Körtgen statement, 24 April 1960. See also report of Danish OT guards at Commando West, or Commando 'X', camp in France shooting dead a prisoner named Brennecke, who was said to have been 'shot during escape, hit in the neck': Kommando 'X' France, 1.1.3.34.0/82147390-1, ITS Digital Archive, London.
214   Pohl, Sebta, *Zwangsarbeit*, pp. 13–18.
215   Raim, *KZ-Außenkommandos*, p. 243.
216   Benz, Distel, *Ort des Terrors*, Band 6, pp. 461–7.
217   Glauning, *Entgrenzung*, pp. 13, 260–1.
218   Ottosen, 'Arbeits- und Konzentrationslager,' p. 359; Bohn, 'Zwangsarbeiter,' pp. 293–5.

Chapter 5

1   BArchL B 162/3571, 2 AR-Z 94/60.
2   BArchL B 162/3571, 2 AR-Z 94/60, Anzeigesache gegen Winand Schneider, 28 April 1960.
3   BArchL B 162/3571, Gareis statement, 4 January 1962.
4   BArchL B 162/3571, Schneider statement, 6 February 1961.
5   BArchL B 162/3571, Schmitz statement, 16 March 1962.
6   BArchL B 162/3571, Letter from Dortmund to Ludwigsburg Zentrale Stelle der Landesjustizverwaltungen, 21 February 1967.
7   For background on the debate on 'annihilation through labour', a term Jens-Christian Wagner criticises as misleading, see Wagner, *Produktion des Todes*, pp. 499–500; Blatman, *The Death Marches*, pp. 45–50; Gruner, *Jewish Forced Labor*, pp. 289–93; Tooze, *The Wages of Destruction*, pp. 531–4; Herbert, 'Labour and Extermination,' pp. 144–95.

8   Blatman, *The Death Marches*, pp. 92–5.
9   West German investigators stated in April 1960 that their inquiries had shown that SS-Führer Grave was dead. See BArchL B 162/3571, 2 AR-Z 94/60, Anzeigesache gegen Winand Schneider, 28 April 1960.
10 For background on the participation of Lithuanians and Latvians in German-organised killings see Gerlach, *Extermination*, pp. 69–71; Mazower, *Hitler's Empire*, pp. 174–6; Ruth Bettina Birn, Volker Riess, 'Revising the Holocaust,' *The Historical Journal*, Vol. 40, No. 1 (1997), pp. 207–8.
11 BArchL B 162/3571, Abenstein statement, 26 April 1960.
12 Gerlach, *Kalkulierte Morde*, p. 1136.
13 BArchL B 162/3571, Abenstein statement, 26 April 1960.
14 BArchL B 162/3571, Frantzen statement, 20 April 1960.
15 BArchL B 162/3571, Körtgen statement, 24 April 1960.
16 BArchL B 162/3571, see statements by Körtgen, Abenstein, Peter Fröbus (15 April 1962). Schneider said in his statement he 'saved' Jewish workers at the time of the 1943 shootings, but could not say what became of them.
17 Pohl, Sebta, *Zwangsarbeit*, pp. 129–33, 156.
18 Longerich, *Holocaust*, p. 346.
19 Gerlach, *Kalkulierte Morde*, p. 1139; see also Tooze, *The Wages of Destruction*, p. 525.
20 BArchL B 162/3571, Körtgen statement, 24 April 1960.
21 BArchL B 162/3571, see statements by Frantzen, Abenstein.
22 BArchL B 162/3571, Horn statement, 16 March 1962.
23 Rom said Schneider was often in contact with a man called Schmidt, whom Schneider said in his statement was the *Gebietskommissar* in Wilejka. BArchL B 162/3571, Rom statement, 28 April 1960.
24 BArchL B 162/3571, Körtgen statement, 24 April 1960.
25 BArchL B 162/3571, Schneider statement, 6 February 1961. Schneider said he was expelled from the party in 1938, but a document confirming his exclusion, issued by the NSDAP in Köln-Aachen, was dated 30 January 1942. Schneider could not explain the discrepancy, nor why the order should have been backdated.
26 BArchL B 162/3571, Schneider statement, 6 February 1961.
27 BArchL B 162/3571, Rollmann statement, 5 April 1960.
28 See Browning, *Ordinary Men*, pp. 47–8.
29 Molly Harrower, 'Rorschach Records of the Nazi War Criminals: An Experimental Study after Thirty Years,' *Journal of Personality Assessment*, Vol. 40, No.4 (1976), pp. 341–51; see also Welzer, *Täter*, pp. 7–17; Harrower, one of the ten experts to whom the verbatim Rorschach records were sent in 1946, wrote thirty years later of her misgivings at the time. She said she and colleagues had implicitly believed in 1946 that the Rorschach tests on the Nazi defendants 'would reveal an idiosyncratic psychopathology, a uniform personality structure of a particularly repellent kind'. Her own follow-up tests, using some of the Nazi defendants' Rorschach

data, provided evidence in 1976 to show how misguided this view had been. Harrower concluded that 'well integrated, productive and secure personalities are no protection against being sucked into a vortex of myth and deception, which may ultimately erupt into the commitment of horror on a grand scale. It is an over-simplified position to look for an underlying common denominator in the Rorschach records of the Nazi prisoners.'

30 Milgram conducted studies of obedience in which 'teachers' proved willing to deliver electric shocks up to a simulated 450 volts to another person posing as a 'learner'. Results of his research were first published in 1963. In the Stanford Prison experiment, Philip Zimbardo and colleagues assigned college students to be either guards or prisoners in a simulated prison; results of the study were published in 1973. See Haslam, Reicher, 'Beyond the Banality of Evil,' p. 616.

31 Mallmann, Paul, *Karrieren der Gewalt*, pp. 1–23; Roseman, 'Beyond Conviction?,' pp. 83–103; Welzer, *Täter*, pp. 7–17; Wildt, *An Uncompromising Generation*, pp. 3–18; Dillon, *Dachau and the SS*, pp. 1–9; Haslam, Reicher, 'Beyond the Banality of Evil,' pp. 615–22; David Cesarani, *Becoming Eichmann: Rethinking the Life, Crimes, and Trial of a 'Desk Murderer'* (Cambridge, MA., 2006).

32 Haslam, Reicher, 'Beyond the Banality of Evil,' p. 619.

33 Michael Thad Allen, 'The Banality of Evil Reconsidered: SS Mid-Level Managers of Extermination through Work,' *Central European History*, Vol. 30, No. 2 (1997), p. 259.

34 Allen, 'The Banality of Evil Reconsidered,' p. 283.

35 Allen, 'The Banality of Evil Reconsidered,' p. 294.

36 Richard Evans, *Rereading German History: From Unification to Reunification 1800–1996* (London, 1997), pp. 159–60; Dillon, *Dachau and the SS*, pp. 13–14.

37 BArchL B 162/3571, Schneider statement, 6 February 1961.

38 BArchL B 162/3571, Rollmann statement, 5 April 1960.

39 BArchL B 162/3571, Wolf statement, 12 April 1960.

40 BArchL B 162/3571, Jehlen statement, 12 May 1960.

41 BArchL B 162/3571, Löhrer statement, 13 February 1962.

42 BArchL B 162/3571, Fröbus statement, 15 March 1962.

43 Dillon, *Dachau and the SS*, pp. 13–14.

44 BArchL B 162/3571, Schneider statement, 6 February 1961.

45 Examples include a notoriously brutal OT commander of two camps on the Channel Island of Alderney, Truppführer Karl Tietz, who was court-martialled and sentenced to eighteen months' penal servitude and a 200 RM fine in April 1943 on charges connected to black-market dealing. See BA/MA RW 60/3881; Pantcheff, *Alderney Fortress Island*, pp. 7, 14.

46 Wachsmann, *KL*, pp. 383–7.

47 Haslam, Reicher, 'Beyond the Banality of Evil,' p. 615; Dillon, *Dachau and the SS*, p. 7.

48 BArchL B 162/9066, Beck statement, 28 October 1974.
49 BArchB R 50 I/101a, Merkle 'Bericht über die Entwicklung des Bahnbaues im Bereich der OBL Fauske', 8 March 1945.
50 BArchB R 50 I/101a, Merkle Bericht.
51 BArchB R 50 I/101a, Merkle Bericht.
52 BArchB R 50 I/101a, Merkle Bericht.
53 RAFA 2188/2/H/Hg/0032, Renner confidential file note, 31 March 1944.
54 RAFA 2188/1/E/E3/E3g/L0022/0007, Stand des Arbeitereinsatzes im September 1943.
55 RAFA 2188/2/O/Oc/L0002/0007, Kgf.-Programm Bahnbau 1944, 18 April 1944.
56 Hayes, *Industry and Ideology*, p. 382.
57 Alf Lüdtke, 'People Working: Everyday Life and German Fascism,' *History Workshop Journal*, No. 50 (2000), pp. 74–92.
58 Alf Lüdtke, 'The Appeal of Exterminating "Others"; German Workers and the Limits of Resistance,' *Journal of Modern History*, Vol. 64 (1992), pp. S46–S67.
59 IWM AL 2538/3/1 Box E7, Todt letter backing von Gottstein for an academic post in Graz, 20 February 1939; see also IWM AL 2538/3/2 Box E7, Todt letter to Schönleben, 25 October 1940.
60 Overy, *Interrogations*, pp. 198–9, 374
61 BArchL B 162/14312, Munich district court judgment in case of Diederich Scholz, sentenced on 10 April 1962 to four years' penitentiary for attempted murder. Details in this section are taken from the judgment; see also RAFA 3182.
62 BArchL B 162/14312.
63 BArchL B 162/14312.
64 *IMT*, Vol. 1, pp. 97–100. Apart from the SS and Gestapo, the leadership corps of the NSDAP was also classed as a 'criminal organisation'. The prosecution's request for the Reich Cabinet, the SA and the General Staff and High Command of the German Armed Forces to be put in the same category was rejected. For a comprehensive study on the Nuremberg trials see Kim Christian Priemel, *The Betrayal. The Nuremberg Trials and German Divergence* (Oxford, 2016).
65 For an analysis of organisations in the Nazi era see Stefan Kühl, *Ganz normale Organisationen. Zur Soziologie der Holocaust* (Berlin, 2014).
66 Kühl, *Ganz normale Organisationen*, p. 326.
67 See Browning, *Ordinary Men*; Goldhagen, *Hitler's Willing Executioners*.
68 Kühl, *Ganz normale Organisationen*, pp. 38, 299–307.
69 Raul Hilberg, *The Destruction of the European Jews*, Vol. 3 (New York, 1985) p. 1011.
70 Klee, Dressen, *'Gott mit uns,'* p. 114; Glauning, *Entgrenzung*, p. 210.
71 Raim, *KZ-Außenkommandos*, p. 231.
72 Kühl, *Ganz normale Organisationen*, pp. 245–6.
73 RAFA 2188/2/H/Hg/0032, Confidential Speer circular to all OT regional chiefs, 25 November 1943.

74 Disziplinarstrafordnung der Organisation Todt, 2.2.3.0/82359952, ITS Digital Archive, London.
75 Dienststellen im Heimatkriegsgebiet, 2.2.3.0/82361436, ITS Digital Archive, London.
76 Beschäftigung von Kunstmalern, 2.2.3.0/82359939, ITS Digital Archive, London.
77 *Der Frontarbeiter*, 14 March 1942, OT-Kriegsberichter Helmut Blenck; 21 March 1942, Frontarbeiter in der Polarnacht; Kultur in der Technik.
78 Brechtken, *Speer*, pp. 190, 649–50.
79 *Der Frontarbeiter*, written by Werner von Lojewski, 8 May 1943, cited in Brechtken, *Speer*, p. 199.
80 *IMT*, Vol. I, p. 332. In his trial testimony, Speer recounted how he planned to assassinate Hitler with poison gas in mid-February 1945, but recent research suggests his story was fabricated. The impractical plan involved putting poison gas into the ventilation system for the bunker under Hitler's Chancellery. Speer said he had intended to use the poison gas Tabun, but the scheme proved unworkable because the gas was only deadly if there was an explosion, so it was abandoned. See *IMT*, Vol. XVI, pp. 493–5; Kitchen, *Speer*, pp. 295–7; Brechtken, *Speer*, p. 267.
81 For background on the debate about the use by historians of evidence from trials in East European communist states after the Second World War see Dieter Pohl, 'Sowjetische und polnische Strafverfahren wegen NS-Verbrechen – Quellen für den Historiker?', in Jürgen Finger, Sven Keller, Andreas Wirsching (eds), *Vom Recht zur Geschichte; Akten aus NS-Prozessen als Quellen der Zeitgeschichte* (Göttingen, 2009), pp. 132–41; for background on general issues surrounding testimony provided by both survivors and perpetrators see Christopher Browning, *Collected Memories: Holocaust History and Postwar Testimony* (Madison, WI, 2003) and Christopher Browning, *Remembering Survival: Inside a Nazi Slave-Labor Camp* (New York, 2010).
82 Durth, *Deutsche Architekten*, p. 507; Weihsmann, *Bauen unterm Hakenkreuz*, pp. 650–1.
83 Raim, *KZ-Außenkommandos*, pp. 230–40; Dr Flocken statement as defence witness, 5 December 1945, in Dachau Prozess 5.1/0054/82310669-82310671, ITS Digital Archive, London.
84 UNWCC, United States v. Franz Auer et al., Review and Recommendations, 1 February 1948, accessed via UNWCC website https://www.legal-tools.org/doc/173b55/on, 4 February 2014.
85 Those sentenced were Karl Gickeleiter, who received twenty years, and Otto Sperling, who was condemned to death. See Raim, *KZ-Außenkommandos*, pp. 284–5.
86 BArchL B 162/9066, OT-Angehörige, p. 53.
87 BArchL B 162/9066, OT-Angehörige, pp. 53–4.
88 BArchL B 162/9063, Die Jugoslawische Kriegsverbrechens-Kommission. Leopold was listed as having the OT rank of *Haupttruppenführer* (*sic.*), working at a camp

dispensary near Trondheim from 1942 to 1945. OT records listing Trondheim staff in March 1943 include Truppführer Leopold in the medical section; see RAFA 2188/1/G/G3/G3a/L0037/0001, Geschäftsverteilungsplan der Oberbauleitung Drontheim vom 1.3.1943. OT Truppführer Max Leopold also featured in British military lists of German suspects held as part of investigations into ill treatment of prisoners at Ørlandet-Østraat; see TNA WO 331/25, HQ BLFN Casesheet, Case No. D/884.

89   BArchL B 162/9066, Fälle von vorsätzlicher Häftlingstötung, p. 53; Max Leopold was listed in the German Federal Archive in Ludwigsburg as belonging to Prisoner-of-War Labour Battalion 180.

90   BArchB R 50 I/88a, Dienststellenverzeichnis der OT-Einsatzgruppe Wiking, March 1944.

91   RAFA 2188/1/E/E5/E5a/L0059/0004, Henne letter to OT EG-Wiking, OBL Alta, 24 February 1943.

92   BArchL B 162/9066, Autenrieth statement, 25 August 1977.

93   Dieter Pohl, 'Sowjetische und polnische Strafverfahren wegen NS-Verbrechen – Quellen für den Historiker?', in Finger, Keller, Wirsching (eds), *Vom Recht zur Geschichte*, pp. 132–41. For background on tensions between Stalin and the Western Allies see Nicholas Bethell, *The Last Secret: Forcible Repatriation to Russia 1944-7* (London, 1976).

94   For the trial of Adler and Evers, see Bunting, *The Model Occupation*, p. 294; for Kabus, see Glauning, *Entgrenzung*, p. 210.

95   BArchL B 162/9066, Ermittlungsverfahren gegen Ernst Heindl u.a. wegen Mordes.

96   BArchL B 162/42181, Gefangenenlager Nord und dessen Teillager. OT records listing SGL Nord staff include the last names of some of those mentioned in the post-war West German investigation; see RAFA 2188/2/F/Fg/Fga/L0001, Abrechnung über Beschäftigungsvergütung 1.9.44–28.2.45; RAFA 2188/1/G/G2/G2b/L0005/0001, Abrechnung über Reisekosten und Beschäftigungsvergütung für Reg.Med.Rat Dr. Thurn.

97   Mallmann, Paul, *Karrieren der Gewalt*, pp. 5, 17–18.

98   Wagner, *Produktion des Todes*, pp. 116–18.

99   On former OT in Kammler's team see Courté, 1.1.0.1/0014/82345317-20, ITS Digital Archive, London; on Speer see Schulte, *Zwangsarbeit und Vernichtung*, p. 413.

100 Raim, *KZ-Außenkommandos*, p. 293.

101 Glauning, *Entgrenzung*, p. 405.

102 For a review of the historiography on this see Omer Bartov, 'German Soldiers and the Holocaust: Historiography, Research and Implications,' *History and Memory*, Vol. 9 (1997), pp. 162–88.

103 Browning, *Ordinary Men*.

Conclusion

1. This figure is calculated by taking the estimated death toll among foreign forced labourers in the Greater Reich during the Second World War (2.7 million dead out of more than 13.5 million: Spoerer, *Zwangsarbeit*, pp. 220–9) and working out the same proportion of deaths among the OT's foreign labour force in the three categories of foreign workers: prisoners of war, concentration-camp prisoners and *Arbeitsjuden*, and civilians. This division into categories allows a more accurate estimate than any calculation based on the combined average. The estimated overall death rates among foreign forced labourers in the Greater Reich in these categories were respectively 30 per cent (1.1 million deaths out of 3.7 million), 65 per cent (1.1 million out of 1.7 million) and 6 per cent (0.5 million out of 8.15 million). Comparison of overall figures with those of the OT is justified because the organisation was so well integrated into the slave-labour system as a whole. The OT's overall strength was nearly 1.5 million on 30 September 1944, but its foreign labourers totalled about 1.08 million without its German workers and core personnel (BArchB R 3/1808). These foreign workers were made up of 164,700 prisoners of war, 140,000 concentration-camp prisoners and *Arbeitsjuden*, and 775,000 civilian labourers. Applying the above death rates to the respective categories gives an estimated 49,410, 91,000 and 46,500 deaths – a total of 186,910. This figure is an underestimate, since it derives from calculations that were merely a snapshot of OT workforce totals taken at the end of September 1944. The actual number of foreigners who toiled for the OT between 1939 and 1945 would have been much higher.
2. Wachsmann, *KL*, pp. 607–13; Finger, Keller, Wirsching (eds), *Vom Recht zur Geschichte*, pp. 9–20; Ludwig Eiber, 'Nach Nürnberg. Alliierte Prozesse in den Besatzungszonen,' in Finger, Keller, Wirsching (eds), *Vom Recht zur Geschichte*, pp. 38–51; Edith Raim, 'Westdeutsche Ermittlungen und Prozesse zum KZ Dachau und seinen Außenlagern,' in Ludwig Eiber, Robert Sigel (eds), *Dachauer Prozesse. NS-Verbrechen vor amerikanischen Militärgerichten in Dachau 1945–1948. Verfahren, Ergebnisse, Nachwirkungen* (Göttingen, 2007), pp. 210–36; Claudia Kuretsidis-Haider, 'Die strafrechtliche Verfolgung von NS-Verbrechen durch die österreichische Justiz,' in Finger, Keller, Wirsching (eds), *Vom Recht zur Geschichte*, pp. 74–83.
3. Dorsch set up the firm of Reg. Baumeister Xaver Dorsch, Ingenieurbüro, which then became Dorsch Consult, based in Munich. The company continued to bear his name after his death in 1986, and the Dorsch Gruppe grew to employ around 2,000 people. See Karl Strute (ed.), *Who's Who in Technology 1984*, Vols 1–3 (Essen, 1984), p. 2611; see also https://www.dorsch.de/home/ (accessed 28 November 2018).
4. Ludwig, *Technik*, p. 515.
5. Gerd Hortleder, *Das Gesellschaftsbild des Ingenieurs. Zum politischen Verhalten der Technischen Intelligenz in Deutschland* (Frankfurt am Main, 1970), p. 140.

6 Mary Fulbrook, *A Small Town Near Auschwitz; Ordinary Nazis and the Holocaust* (Oxford, 2012), pp. 47, 122.
7 Sebastian Haffner, *The Observer*, London, 9 April 1944 https://www.newspapers.com/image/257854979 (accessed 30 May 2018); Sebastian Haffner, *Schreiben für die Freiheit; 1942 bis 1949: Als Journalist im Sturm der Ereignisse* (Berlin, 2001), p. 41.
8 Primo Levi, *The Drowned and the Saved*, (trans. Raymond Rosenthal) (London, 1988), p. 231.
9 David Rousset, 'Die Tage unseres Sterbens,' in *Die Umschau. Internationale Revue*, Jahrg. 1, Hft 1 (1946), pp. 33–41. Rousset published his camp experiences in *Les jours de notre mort*, 2 vols (Évreux, 1993).
10 For example, Wagner, *Produktion des Todes*, p. 582; Browning, *Ordinary Men*, pp. 188–9.
11 Evans, *The Third Reich at War*, p. 764; Aly, *Hitler's Beneficiaries*, p. 4.

Appendix: Organisation Todt ranks with Army equivalents

OT-Einsatzgruppenleiter	General
OT-Einsatzleiter	Major general
OT-Hauptbauleiter	Colonel
OT-Oberbauleiter	Lieutenant colonel
OT-Bauleiter	Major
OT-Hauptbauführer	Captain
OT-Oberbauführer	First lieutenant
OT-Bauführer	Lieutenant
OT-Haupttruppführer	Sergeant major
OT-Obertruppführer	Technical sergeant
OT-Truppführer	Sergeant
OT-Obermeister	n/a
OT-Meister	Corporal
OT-Vorarbeiter	Private first class
OT-Mann	Private

Source: RAFA 2188/1/E/E5/E5a/L0059/0004, Dr Schmelter Front-OT pay scales, 12 December 1944, Grundsätze für die Einstufung der Angestellten der Front-OT in die OT-Dienstränge und OT-Soldgruppen; TNA WO 208/5042, Table IV, OT ranks and equivalent assignments, uniforms and insignia

Bibliography

Archives

Bundesarchiv, Berlin

ALLPROZ 6/12
NS 26/1188
R 3/1313
R 3/1637
R 3/1736
R 3/1808
R 6/417
R 43 II/1020
R 50 I/3a
R 50 I/88a
R 50 I/94
R 50 I/101a
R 50 I/106
R 50 I/130
R 50 I/350
R 50 I/355
R 50 I/387
R 3001/24367
3100/F0022
3100/H0113
3200/C0078
SSO/085 A
SSO/131

Bundesarchiv/Militärarchiv, Freiburg

RW 4/625 D
RW 60/3881

Bundesarchiv, Ludwigsburg

B 162/14312
B 162/16432
B 162/16485
B 162/16489
B 162/16503
B 162/30816
B 162/3571
B 162/42181
B 162/5109
B 162/5110
B 162/5117
B 162/5123
B 162/9063
B 162/9066

Imperial War Museum, London

AL 2538/3/1
AL 2538/3/2
AL 2538/3/3
AL 2547/1
FD 3063/49

Institut für Zeitgeschichte, Munich

Akten der Parteikanzlei 10100464-5; 10110538-9; 10111073-5; 10116815-10116822; 10800082-10800093; 10800265; 10800296-10800301; 10800341-10800358
ED 99/9
ED 901/9
MA 211
MA 251
MA 265
MA 328
MA 414
MA 795
MB 27/7
NG 1584
NG 5629
NI 4813
NO 030

NO 2124
NO 2602
NO 3901
NOKW 2085
ZS 1432

International Tracing Service (ITS Digital Archive, Wiener Library, London)

1.1.0.1/82345317-20
1.1.0.7./87769492
1.1.34.0/82147390-1
1.1.6.0/82105389-93
1.2.7.4/82173222-82173224
2.2.3.0/82357621
2.2.3.0/82359934
2.2.3.0/82359936
2.2.3.0/82359939
2.2.3.0/82359944
2.2.3.0/82359952
2.2.3.0/82360092-82360098
2.2.3.0/82360135-82360146
2.2.3.0/82360625-82360626
2.2.3.0/82361436
2.2.3.0/82361554
2.2.3.0/82361665, 82361671-2
2.2.3.0/82361733-82361736
2.2.3.0/82362040-82362089
2.2.3.0/82362252, 82362257, 82362260-61
2.2.3.2/77191038, 77191107
2.3.1.2/78541661
5.1/82310885
5.1/0054/82310669-82310671
5.1/0111/82326425-82326434

The National Archives in Britain (TNA)

WO 208/3224
WO 208/3225
WO 208/5042
WO 311/12

WO 331/13
WO 331/24
WO 331/25
WO 331/60

Riksarkivet (The National Archives of Norway)

DOBN Box 8
RAFA 2174/E/Ec/Ecj/L0071
RAFA 2188/1/E2b/4
RAFA 2188/1/E/E3/E3e/L0011/0001
RAFA 2188/1/E/E3/E3e/L0014
RAFA 2188/1/E/E3/E3g/L0022/0007
RAFA 2188/1/E/E5/E5a/L0059/0004
RAFA 2188/1/E/E5/E5e/L0010
RAFA 2188/1/E/E5/E5f/L0006/0003
RAFA 2188/1/G/G2/G2b/L0005/0001
RAFA 2188/1/G/G3/G3a/L0037/0001
RAFA 2188/1/G/G3/G3c/L0001/0002
RAFA 2188/1/G/G3/G3c/L0002/0007
RAFA 2188/2/F/Fa/Faa/L0111/0001
RAFA 2188/2/F/Fg/Fga/L0001
RAFA 2188/2/H/Ha/Haa/L0047/0001
RAFA 2188/2/H/Hg/0032
RAFA 2188/2/O/Oc/L0002/0007
RAFA 3182
RAFA 3915/D/Db/L0001/0031
RA/S-1681/D/Db/L0014

'Zwangsarbeit 1939–1945, Erinnerungen und Geschichte, ein digitales Archiv für Bildung und Wissenschaft' www.zwangsarbeit-archiv.de

Fjodor A. (Archiv-ID ZA018)
Judith A. (Archiv-ID ZA570)
Giovanni Bonotto (Archiv-ID ZA119)
Liviu B. (Archiv-ID ZA267)
Zoltan B. (Archiv-ID ZA266)
Konstantins C. (Archiv-ID ZA141)
Enric Casañas (Archiv-ID ZA405)
Peter Demetz (Archiv-ID ZA573)
Joaquín Gálvez (Archiv-ID ZA407)

Ellis H. (Archiv-ID ZA168)
Nándor H. (Archiv-ID ZA363)
Stefan K. (Archiv-ID ZA211)
Andrej K. (Archiv-ID ZA105)
Martin K. (Archiv-ID ZA105)
Uroš Majstorović (Archiv-ID ZA 137)
Arie P. (Archiv-ID ZA 109)
Hartog P. (Archiv-ID ZA173)
Milan Pantoviç (Archiv-ID ZA358)
Stjepan Pištignjat (Archiv-ID ZA359)
Paul R. (Archiv-ID ZA087)
Jaroslav S. (Archiv-ID ZA453)
Zecharja S. (Archiv-ID ZA113)
Maurice V. (Archiv-ID ZA091)
Jacek Z. (Archiv-ID ZA247)
Leszek Z. (Archiv-ID ZA245)

OT publications

Der Frontarbeiter
Mitteilungsblatt der Organisation Todt-Zentrale

Electronic sources

Harvard Law School, Nuremberg Trials Project: http://nuremberg.law.harvard.edu
Jewish Virtual Library: www.jewishvirtuallibrary.org
International Criminal Court: https://www.legal-tools.org/
Online newspaper archive: www.newspapers.com
Dorsch Group website: https://www.dorsch.de/home/

Printed sources

Abelshauser, W., 'Rüstungsschmiede der Nation? Der Kruppkonzern im Dritten Reich und in der Nachkriegszeit 1933 bis 1951,' in Gall, L., (ed.), *Krupp im zwanzigsten Jahrhundert. Die Geschichte des Unternehmens vom Ersten Weltkrieg bis zur Gründung der Stiftung* (Berlin, 2002).

Allen, M. T., 'The Banality of Evil Reconsidered: SS Mid-Level Managers of Extermination through Work,' *Central European History*, Vol. 30, No. 2 (1997), pp. 253–94.

Allen, M. T., *The Business of Genocide. The SS, Slave Labor, and the Concentration Camps* (London, 2002).

Aly, G., *Hitler's Beneficiaries: Plunder, Racial War, and the Nazi Welfare State* (New York, 2006).

Angrick, A., 'Forced Labor along the "Straße der SS"', United States Holocaust Memorial Museum Symposium, *Forced and Slave Labor in Nazi-Dominated Europe* (Washington, DC, 2004).

Baranowski, S., *Nazi Empire. German Colonialism and Imperialism from Bismarck to Hitler* (Cambridge, 2011).

Bartov, O., 'German Soldiers and the Holocaust: Historiography, Research and Implications,' *History and Memory*, Vol. 9 (1997), pp. 162–88

Benz, W., Distel, B., (eds) *Der Ort des Terrors. Geschichte der nationalsozialistischen Konzentrationslager*, Vols 1–9 (Munich, 2005–9)

Berger, S., *Experten der Vernichtung; Das T4-Reinhardt-Netzwerk in den Lagern Belzec, Sobibor und Treblinka* (Hamburg, 2013).

Berkhoff, K., *Harvest of Despair; Life and Death in Ukraine under Nazi Rule* (Cambridge, MA, 2004).

Bethell, N., *The Last Secret: Forcible Repatriation to Russia 1944–7* (London, 1976).

Birn, R. B., Riess, V., 'Revising the Holocaust,' *The Historical Journal*, Vol. 40, No. 1 (1997), pp. 195–215.

Birn, R. B., 'Vaivara – Stammlager,' in Wolfgang Benz, Barbara Distel (eds), *Der Ort des Terrors: Geschichte der nationalsozialistischen Konzentrationslager*, Band 8 (Munich, 2005–9).

Blatman, D., *The Death Marches: The Final Phase of Nazi Genocide* (Cambridge, MA, 2011).

Boelcke, W., *Deutschlands Rüstung im Zweiten Weltkrieg: Hitlers Konferenzen mit Albert Speer 1942–1945* (Frankfurt am Main, 1969).

Bohn, R., *Reichskommissariat Norwegen: 'Nationalsozialistische Neuordnung' und Kriegswirtschaft* (Munich, 2000).

Bohn, R., 'Zwangsarbeiter und Zwangsarbeiterinnen im Reichskommissariat Norwegen; Fakten und Erinnerungen,' in Pohl, D., Sebta, T. (eds), *Zwangsarbeit in Hitlers Europa*, pp. 293–300.

Bonnard, B., *Alderney at War* (Dover, NH, 1993).

Botzet, C., 'Ministeramt, Sondergewalten und Privatwirtschaft. Der Generalbevollmächtigte für die Regelung der Bauwirtschaft,' in Rüdiger Hachtmann, Winfried Süß (eds), *Hitlers Kommissare. Sondergewalten in der nationalsozialistischen Diktatur* (Göttingen, 2006), pp. 115–37.

Bracher, K., *The German Dictatorship: The Origins, Structure, and Consequences of National Socialism*, trans. Jean Steinberg (London, 1971).

Brechtken, M., *Albert Speer: eine deutsche Karriere* (Munich, 2017).

Breloer, H., *Die Akte Speer: Spuren eines Kriegsverbrechers* (Berlin, 2006).

Browning, C., *Ordinary Men. Reserve Police Battalion 101 and the Final Solution in Poland* (New York, 1993).

Browning, C., *Collected Memories: Holocaust History and Postwar Testimony* (Madison, WI, 2003).

Browning, C., *Remembering Survival: Inside a Nazi Slave-Labor Camp* (New York, 2010).
Budraß, L., *Flugzeugindustrie und Luftrüstung in Deutschland 1918–1945* (Düsseldorf, 1998).
Buggeln, M., 'Were Concentration Camp Prisoners Slaves? The Possibilities and Limits of Comparative History and Global Historical Perspectives,' *International Review of Social History*, No. 53, (2008), pp. 101–29.
Buggeln, M., 'Building to Death: Prisoner Forced Labour in the German War Economy – The Neuengamme Subcamps 1942–1945,' *European History Quarterly*, Vol. 39, No. 4 (2009), pp. 606–32.
Buggeln, M., *Arbeit und Gewalt: das Außenlagersystem des KZ Neuengamme* (Göttingen, 2009).
Buggeln, M., '"Menschenhandel" als Vorwurf im Nationalsozialismus. Der Streit um den Gewinn aus den militärischen Großbaustellen am Kriegsende (1944–1945),' in Heusler, A., Spoerer, M., Trischler, H. (eds), *Rüstung, Kriegswirtschaft und Zwangsarbeit im "Dritten Reich"* (Munich, 2010).
Bullock, A., *Hitler: A Study in Tyranny* (Reading, 1962).
Bunting, M., *The Model Occupation: The Channel Islands under German Rule 1940–45* (London, 2004).
Cesarani, D., *Becoming Eichmann: Rethinking the Life, Crimes, and Trial of a 'Desk Murderer'* (Cambridge, MA, 2006).
Cohen, F., *The Jews in the Channel Islands during the German Occupation 1940–1945* (St Helier, 2000).
Cruickshank, C., *The German Occupation of the Channel Islands* (London, 1975).
Demetz, P., *Prague in Danger: The Years of German Occupation, 1939–45. Memories and History, Terror and Resistance, Theater and Jazz, Film and Poetry, Politics and War* (New York, 2008).
Dillon, C., *Dachau and the SS: A Schooling in Violence* (Oxford, 2015).
Domarus, M., *Hitler: Reden und Proklamationen 1932–1945*, 4 vols (Wiesbaden, 1973).
Dülffer, J., Thies, J., Henke, J., *Hitlers Städte. Baupolitik im Dritten Reich. Eine Dokumentation* (Köln, Wien, 1978).
Dumett, R., 'Africa's Strategic Minerals during the Second World War,' *Journal of African History*, vol. 26 (1985), pp. 381–408.
Durth, W., *Deutsche Architekten: Biographische Verflechtungen 1900–1970* (Munich, 1992).
Dworzecki, M., *Jewish Camps in Estonia, 1942–1944* (Jerusalem, 1970).
Eiber, L., 'Nach Nürnberg. Alliierte Prozesse in den Besatzungszonen,' in Finger, Keller, Wirsching (eds), *Vom Recht zur Geschichte*, pp. 38–51.
Engel, G., von Kotze, H. (eds), *Heeresadjutant bei Hitler 1938–1943: Aufzeichnungen des Majors Engel*, (Stuttgart, 1974).
Espeli, H., 'The Economic Effects of the German Occupation of Norway, 1940–1945,' in Scherner, White (eds), *Paying for Hitler's War*, pp. 235–65.
Euler, H., *Als Deutschlands Dämme brachen: die Wahrheit über die Bombardierung der Möhne-Eder-Sorpe-Staudämme 1943* (Stuttgart, 1975).

Evans, R., *Rereading German History: From Unification to Reunification 1800–1996* (London, 1997).
Evans, R., *The Third Reich in Power 1933–1939* (London, 2005).
Evans, R., *The Third Reich at War 1939–1945* (London, 2008).
Evans, R., *The Pursuit of Power: Europe 1815–1914* (London, 2016).
Fest, J., *Speer: The Final Verdict* (London, 2001).
Finger, J., Keller, S., Wirsching, A. (eds), *Vom Recht zur Geschichte: Akten aus NS-Prozessen als Quellen der Zeitgeschichte* (Göttingen, 2009).
Fings, K., *Krieg, Gesellschaft and KZ: Himmler's SS-Baubrigaden* (Paderborn, 2005).
Frei, N., Brunner, J., Goschler, C., (eds), *Die Praxis der Wiedergutmachung: Geschichte, Erfahrung und Wirkung in Deutschland und Israel* (Göttingen, 2009).
Fulbrook, M., *A Small Town Near Auschwitz: Ordinary Nazis and the Holocaust* (Oxford, 2012).
Galtung, J., 'Violence, Peace and Peace Research,' *Journal of Peace Research*, Vol. 6, No. 3 (1969), pp. 167–91.
Gerlach, C., *The Extermination of the European Jews* (Cambridge, 2016).
Gerlach, C., Aly, G., *Das letzte Kapitel: Realpolitik, Ideologie und der Mord an den ungarischen Juden 1944/1945* (Stuttgart, 2002).
Gerlach, C., *Kalkulierte Morde: die deutsche Wirtschafts- und Vernichtungspolitik in Weißrußland 1941 bis 1944* (Hamburg, 1999).
Giesler, H., *Ein anderer Hitler: Bericht seines Architekten – Erlebnisse, Gespräche, Reflexionen* (Leoni, 1977).
Ginns, M., *The Organisation Todt and the Fortress Engineers in the Channel Islands* (St John, Jersey 2006).
Glauning, C., *Entgrenzung und KZ-System: Das Unternehmen 'Wüste' und das Konzentrationslager in Bisingen 1944/45* (Berlin, 2006).
Goebbels, J., *Die Tagebücher von Joseph Goebbels: im Auftrag des Instituts für Zeitgeschichte und mit Unterstützung des Staatlichen Archivdienstes Rußlands*, Elke Fröhlich (ed.), T. 1–3, (Munich, 1987–2008).
Goldhagen, D., *Hitler's Willing Executioners. Ordinary Germans and the Holocaust* (London, 1996).
Golson, E., 'Sweden as an Occupied Country? Swedish-Belligerent Trade in World War II,' in Scherner, White (eds), *Paying for Hitler's War*, pp. 167–95.
Gregor, N., 'Big Business and the "Blitzkriegswirtschaft"; Daimler-Benz AG and the Mobilisation of the German War Economy, 1939–42,' *Contemporary European History*, Vol. 6 (1997), pp. 193–208.
Gruner, W., *Jewish Forced Labor under the Nazis: Economic Needs and Racial Aims, 1938–1944* (Cambridge, 2006).
Guse, J., 'Nazi Technical Thought Revisited,' *History and Technology*, Vol. 26 (2010), pp. 3–38.
Guse, J., 'Nazi Ideology and Engineers at War: Fritz Todt's "Speaker System",' *Journal of Contemporary History*, Vol. 48 (2013), pp. 150–74.

Haffner, S., *Schreiben für die Freiheit: 1942 bis 1949: Als Journalist im Sturm der Ereignisse* (Berlin, 2001).

Hammermann, G., *Zwangsarbeit für den 'Verbündeten': Die Arbeits- und Lebensbedingungen der italienischen Militärinternierten in Deutschland 1943–1945* (Tübingen, 2002).

Hammermann, G. (ed.), *Zeugnisse der Gefangenschaft: Aus Tagebüchern und Erinnerungen italienischer Militärinternierter in Deutschland 1943–1945*, trans. Friederike Hausmann and Rita Seuß (Berlin, 2014).

Harrower, M., 'Rorschach Records of the Nazi War Criminals: An Experimental Study after Thirty Years,' *Journal of Personality Assessment*, Vol. 40, No. 4 (1976), pp. 341–51.

Haslam, A., Reicher, S., 'Beyond the Banality of Evil: Three Dynamics of an Interactionist Social Psychology of Tyranny,' *Personality and Social Psychology Bulletin*, Vol. 33, No. 5 (2007), pp. 615–22.

Hayes, P., *Industry and Ideology: IG Farben in the Nazi Era* (Cambridge, 1987).

Herbert, U., 'Labour and Extermination: Economic Interest and the Primacy of Weltanschauung in National Socialism,' *Past and Present*, No. 138 (1993), pp. 144–95.

Herbert, U., *Hitler's Foreign Workers: Enforced Foreign Labor in Germany under the Third Reich* (Cambridge, 1997).

Herbert, U., 'Forced Laborers in the Third Reich: An Overview,' *International Labor and Working-Class History*, No. 58 (2000), pp. 192–218.

Herbert, U., 'Zwangsarbeit im 20. Jahrhundert: Begriffe, Entwicklung, Definitionen,' in Pohl, Sebta (eds), *Zwangsarbeit in Hitlers Europa*, pp. 23–36.

Herf, J., *Reactionary Modernism: Technology, Culture and Policies in Weimar and the Third Reich* (Cambridge, 1984).

Hilberg, R., *The Destruction of the European Jews*, Vols 1–3 (New York, 1985).

Hilberg, R., 'The Goldhagen Phenomenon,' *Critical Inquiry*, Vol. 23, No. 4 (1997), pp. 721–8.

Hitler, A., *Mein Kampf* (Munich, 1933).

Hördler, S., *Ordnung und Inferno. Das KZ-System im letzten Kriegsjahr* (Göttingen, 2015).

Hortleder, G., *Das Gesellschaftsbild des Ingenieurs. Zum politischen Verhalten der Technischen Intelligenz in Deutschland* (Frankfurt am Main, 1970).

Hüttenberger, P., 'Nationalsozialistische Polykratie,' in *Geschichte und Gesellschaft* (1976), pp. 417–42.

Janssen, G., *Das Ministerium Speer: Deutschlands Rüstung im Krieg* (Berlin, 1968).

Jarausch, K., 'The Perils of Professionalism: Lawyers, Teachers, and Engineers in Nazi Germany,' *Historical Social Research/Historische Sozialforschung. Supplement*, No. 24, Contemporary History as Transatlantic Project: The German Problem, 1960–2010 (2012), pp. 157–83.

Kaienburg, H., *Die Wirtschaft der SS* (Berlin, 2003).

Kaufmann, J. E., Kaufmann, H. W., Jankovič-Potočnik, A., Tonič, V., *The Atlantic Wall: History and Guide* (Barnsley, 2012).

Kershaw, I., *The Nazi Dictatorship: Problems and Perspectives of Interpretation*, fourth edition (London, 2010).

King, P., *The Channel Islands War 1940–1945* (London, 1991).

Kitchen, M., *Speer: Hitler's Architect* (New Haven, CT/London, 2015).

Klee, E., Dreßen, W., '*Gott mit uns': Der deutsche Vernichtungskrieg im Osten 1939–1945* (Frankfurt am Main, 1989).

Klee, E., *Das Personenlexikon zum Dritten Reich: wer war was vor und nach 1945?* (Frankfurt am Main, 2003).

Kosthorst, E., Walter, B., *Konzentrations- und Strafgefangenenlager im Dritten Reich. Beispiel Emsland. Zusatzteil: Kriegsgefangenenlager. Dokumentation und Analyse zum Verhältnis von NS-Regime und Justiz. Mit historisch-kritischen Einführungstexten sowie statistisch-quantitativen Erhebungen und Auswertungen zum Strafvollzug in Arbeitslagern*, Vols I-3 (Düsseldorf, 1983).

Kruk, H., (Harshav, B., ed.), *The Last Days of the Jerusalem of Lithuania: Chronicles from the Vilna Ghetto and the Camps, 1939–1944*, trans. Barbara Harshav (London, 2002).

Kühl, S., *Ganz normale Organisationen. Zur Soziologie der Holocaust* (Berlin, 2014).

Kuretsidis-Haider, C., 'Die strafrechtliche Verfolgung von NS-Verbrechen durch die österreichische Justiz,' in Finger, Keller, Wirsching (eds), *Vom Recht zur Geschichte*, pp. 74–83.

Larsstuvold, U., 'Finding Traces: Soviet Prisoners of War in Northern Norway, 1941–1945,' in M. N. Suprun, *Voina v Arktike 1939–1945* (Arkhangel'sk, 2001).

Lemmes, F., 'Arbeiten für den Besatzer: Lockung und Zwang bei der Organisation Todt in Frankreich und Italien 1940–1945,' in Pohl, Sebta (eds), *Zwangsarbeit in Hitlers Europa*, pp. 83–103.

Lemmes, F., 'The Economics of the German Construction Programs in Occupied France and Occupied Italy, 1940–1945,' in Scherner, White (eds), *Paying for Hitler's War*, pp. 198–231.

Levi, P., *The Drowned and the Saved*, trans. Raymond Rosenthal (London, 1988).

Lindner, S., *Inside IG Farben; Hoechst During the Third Reich*, trans. Helen Schoop (New York, 2008).

Longerich, P., *Holocaust: The Nazi Persecution and Murder of the Jews* (Oxford, 2010).

Lotfi, G., *KZ der Gestapo: Arbeitserziehungslager im Dritten Reich* (Stuttgart/Munich, 2000).

Lüdtke, A., 'The Appeal of Exterminating "Others": German Workers and the Limits of Resistance,' *Journal of Modern History*, Vol. 64 (1992), pp. S46–S67.

Lüdtke, A., 'People Working: Everyday Life and German Fascism,' *History Workshop Journal*, No. 50 (2000), pp. 74–92.

Ludwig, K-H., *Technik und Ingenieure im Dritten Reich* (Düsseldorf, 1974).

Lund, J., 'Building Hitler's Europe: Forced Labor in the Danish Construction Business during World War II,' *Business History Review* (Autumn 2010), pp. 479–99.

Mallmann, K.-M., Paul, G. (eds), *Karrieren der Gewalt: nationalsozialistische Täterbiographien* (Darmstadt, 2004).

Mazower, M., *Hitler's Empire: Nazi Rule in Occupied Europe* (London, 2008).
Megargee, G. P. (ed.), *Encyclopedia of Camps and Ghettos, 1933-1945*, Vol. 1, Pt. B (Bloomington, IN, 2009).
Milward, A., 'The End of the Blitzkrieg,' *Economic History Review*, Vol. 16 (1964), pp. 499-518.
Moll, M. (ed.), *'Führer-Erlasse' 1939-1945* (Stuttgart, 1997).
Mommsen, H., Grieger, M., *Das Volkswagenwerk und seine Arbeiter im Dritten Reich* (Düsseldorf, 1996).
Neufeld, M., *The Rocket and the Reich: Peenemünde and the Coming of the Ballistic Missile Era* (Cambridge, MA, 1996).
Neumann, F., *Behemoth. The Structure and Practice of National Socialism* (London, 1942).
Orth, K., *Das System der nationalsozialistischen Konzentrationslager: eine politische Organisationsgeschichte* (Hamburg, 1999).
Orth, K., *Die Konzentrationslager-SS. Sozialstrukturelle Analysen und biographische Studien* (Göttingen, 2001).
Ottosen, K., 'Arbeits- und Konzentrationslager in Norwegen 1940-1945,' in Robert Bohn (ed.), *Neutralität und totalitäre Aggression. Nordeuropa und die Großmächte im Zweiten Weltkrieg* (Stuttgart, 1991).
Overy, R., *War and Economy in the Third Reich* (Oxford, 1994).
Overy, R., *Why the Allies Won* (London, 1995).
Overy, R., *Interrogations. The Nazi Elite in Allied Hands, 1945* (London, 2001).
Pantcheff, T., *Alderney Fortress Island: The Germans in Alderney 1940-1945* (London, 1981).
Partridge, C., *Hitler's Atlantic Wall* (Guernsey, 1976).
Picker, H., *Hitlers Tischgespräche im Führerhauptquartier 1941-42* (Bonn, 1951).
Plath, T., '"Schonung", "Menschenjagden" und Vernichtung. Die Arbeitseinsatzpolitik in den baltischen Generalbezirken des Reichskommissariats Ostland 1941-1944,' in Pohl, Sebta, *Zwangsarbeit in Hitlers Europa*, pp. 63-82.
Plato, A. von, 'It Was Modern Slavery: Some Results of the Documentation Project on Forced Labour,' in Plato, A. von, Leh, A., Thonfeld, C., (eds), *Hitler's Slaves: Life Stories of Forced Labourers in Nazi-Occupied Europe* (New York, 2010), pp. 466-7.
Pohl, D., Sebta, T. (eds), *Zwangsarbeit in Hitlers Europa: Besatzung, Arbeit, Folgen* (Berlin, 2013).
Priemel, K. C., *The Betrayal. The Nuremberg Trials and German Divergence* (Oxford, 2016).
Raim, E., *Die Dachauer KZ-Außenkommandos Kaufering und Mühldorf: Rüstungsbauten und Zwangsarbeit im letzten Kriegsjahr 1944/45* (Landsberg am Lech, 1992).
Raim, E., 'Westdeutsche Ermittlungen und Prozesse zum KZ Dachau und seinen Außenlagern,' in Eiber, L., Sigel, R., (eds), *Dachauer Prozesse. NS-Verbrechen vor amerikanischen Militärgerichten in Dachau 1945-1948. Verfahren, Ergebnisse, Nachwirkungen* (Göttingen, 2007), pp. 210-36.

Raim, E., *Überlebende von Kaufering: Biografische Skizzen jüdischer ehemaliger Häftlinge, Materialien zum KZ-Aussenlagerkomplex Kaufering* (Berlin, 2008).

Renneberg, M., Walker, M., 'Scientists, Engineers and National Socialism,' in Renneberg, Walker (eds), *Science, Technology and National Socialism* (Cambridge, 1994).

Riedel, D., *Ordnungshüter und Massenmörder im Dienst der "Volksgemeinschaft": Der KZ-Kommandant Hans Loritz* (Berlin, 2010).

Roseman, M., 'Beyond Conviction? Perpetrators, Ideas and Actions in the Holocaust in Historiographical Perspective,' in Biess, F., Roseman, M., Schissler, H. (eds), *Conflict, Catastrophe and Continuity: Essays on Modern German History* (New York, 2007), pp. 83–103.

Roseman, M., 'The Lives of Others – Amid the Deaths of Others: Biographical Approaches to Nazi Perpetrators,' *Journal of Genocidal Research*, Vol. 15, No. 4 (2013), pp. 443–61.

Rousset, D., 'Die Tage unseres Sterbens,' in *Die Umschau. Internationale Revue*, Jahrg. 1, Hft 1 (1946), pp. 33–41.

Rutar, S., 'Arbeit und Überleben in Serbien: das Kupfererzbergwerk Bor im Zweiten Weltkrieg,' *Geschichte und Gesellschaft* (January–March, 2005), pp. 101–34.

Sandkühler, T., *'Endlösung' in Galizien. Der Judenmord in Ostpolen und die Rettungsinitiativen von Berthold Beitz 1941–1944* (Bonn, 1996).

Scherner, J., White, E. (eds), *Paying for Hitler's War. The Consequences of Nazi Hegemony for Europe* (New York, 2016).

Schmidt, M., *Albert Speer: Das Ende eines Mythos; Speers wahre Rolle im Dritten Reich* (Bern/Munich, 1982).

Schneider, V., *Waffen-SS, SS-Sonderlager 'Hinzert', Das Konzentrationslager im 'Gau Moselland' 1939–1945: Untersuchungen zu einem Haftstättensystem der Organisation Todt, der Inspektion der Konzentrationslager und des Wirtschafts- und Verwaltungshauptamtes der SS* (Nonnweiler-Otzenhausen, 1998).

Schulte, J. E., *Zwangsarbeit und Vernichtung: Das Wirtschaftsimperium der SS. Oswald Pohl und das SS-Wirtschafts-Verwaltungshauptamt 1933–1945* (Paderborn, 2001).

Seidler, F., *Fritz Todt: Baumeister des Dritten Reiches* (Munich, 1986).

Seidler, F., *Die Organisation Todt: Bauen für Staat und Wehrmacht 1938–1945* (Koblenz, 1987).

Sereny, G., *Albert Speer: His Battle with Truth* (London, 1995).

Singer, H. (ed.), *Quellen zur Geschichte der Organisation Todt* (Osnabrück, 1987).

Sofsky, W., *Die Ordnung des Terrors. Das Konzentrationslager* (Frankfurt am Main, 1997).

Soleim, M. (ed.), *Prisoners of War and Forced Labour: Histories of War and Occupation* (Newcastle, 2010).

Speer, A., *Erinnerungen* (Frankfurt am Main., 1974).

Speer, A., *Spandauer Tagebücher* (Berlin, 1975).

Speer, A., *Der Sklavenstaat. Meine Auseinandersetzungen mit der SS* (Stuttgart, 1981).

Spoerer, M., *Zwangsarbeit unter dem Hakenkreuz. Ausländische Zivilarbeiter, Kriegsgefangene und Häftlinge im Deutschen Reich und im besetzten Europa 1939–1945* (Munich, 2001).
Spoerer, M., Fleischhacker, J., 'Forced Laborers in Nazi Germany: Categories, Numbers, and Survivors,' *Journal of Interdisciplinary History*, Vol. 33 (2002), pp. 169–204.
Spoerer, M., Fleischhacker, J., 'The Compensation of Nazi Germany's Forced Labourers: Demographic Findings and Political Implications,' *Population Studies*, Vol. 56, No. 1 (2002), pp. 5–21.
Steckoll, S., *Alderney Death Camp* (London, 1982).
Streim, A., 'Konzentrationslager auf dem Gebiet der Sowjetunion,' in Benz, W. (ed.), *Dachauer Hefte. Studien und Dokumente zur Geschichte der nationalsozialistischen Konzentrationslager*, Vol. 5, *Die vergessenen Lager* (Dachau, 1989).
Strute, K., (ed.), *Who's Who in Technology 1984*, Vols 1–3 (Essen, 1984).
Thies, J., 'Hitler's European Building Programme,' *Journal of Contemporary History*, Vol. 13, No. 3 (1978), pp. 413–31.
Tooze, A., *The Wages of Destruction: The Making and Breaking of the Nazi Economy* (London, 2006).
Trial of the Major War Criminals before the International Military Tribunal, 42 vols (Nuremberg, 1947–9).
Trials of War Criminals before the Nuernberg Military Tribunals under Control Council Law No. 10, 15 vols (Washington, DC, 1953).
Vorobej, M., 'Structural Violence,' *Peace Research*, Vol. 40, No. 2 (2008), pp. 84–9.
Wachsmann, N., *Hitler's Prisons: Legal Terror in Nazi Germany* (London, 2004).
Wachsmann, N., *KL: A History of the Nazi Concentration Camps* (London, 2015).
Wagner, J.-C., *Produktion des Todes: Das KZ Mittelbau-Dora* (Göttingen, 2001).
Waterford, V., *Prisoners of the Japanese in World War II: Statistical History, Personal Narratives and Memorials Concerning POWs in Camps and on Hellships, Civilian Internees, Asian Slave Laborers and Others Captured in the Pacific Theater* (Jefferson, NC and London, 1994).
Weihsmann, H., *Bauen unterm Hakenkreuz: Architektur des Untergangs* (Vienna, 1998).
Welzer, H., *Täter: Wie aus ganz normalen Menschen Massenmörder werden* (Frankfurt am Main, 2005).
Westerlund, L., 'German Penal Camps in Finland, 1941–1944,' in Soleim, *Prisoners of War.*
Wildt, M., *An Uncompromising Generation: The Nazi Leadership of the Reich Security Main Office*, trans. Tom Lampert (Madison, WI, 2009).
Willems, S., *Der entsiedelte Jude: Albert Speers Wohnungsmarktpolitik für den Berliner Hauptstadtbau* (Berlin, 2000).
Yap, F., 'Prisoners of War and Civilian Internees of the Japanese in British Asia: The Similarities and Contrasts of Experience,' *Journal of Contemporary History*, Vol. 47, No. 2 (2012), pp. 317–46.

Index

Abenstein, Jokob 165, 166–7, 169
Ackermann, Leo 89–90
Adam, Arnold 31, 120, 179
Adler, Adam 132
aircraft production 28, 58, 59
    Fi 103 93–4
    Messerschmitt Me-262 jet fighters 6, 7, 45, 71, 101
    raw materials 60, 61–2, 64–5
    underground factories 6, 7, 13, 56, 71, 78, 79, 81, 82–3, 88, 93–4, 101, 105, 190
    Volkswagen 93–4
    see also industry
Alderney 89, 129, 131–3, 181
Allen, Michael Thad 85, 173
aluminium 56, 61–2, 64
Alwin, Philipp 118, 134, 157
Ambros, Otto 92
Amt Bau-OT 34, 83, 88
Andrej K 149–51, 196
anti-Semitism 134, 143, 163, 171, 174, 180
antimony 65
Arbeitsjuden see Jewish labourers
architecture 17, 25, 29, 46, 48, 193
Arctic railway 61–5, 78, 103, 126, 177–9, 190
Arendt, Hannah 173, 175
Arie P. 105–8, 111, 112–13
armaments production 24, 31
    Fighter Staff 28, 39, 58, 70, 71, 72, 88, 89
    raw materials 60, 61–2, 64–5
    Speer and 24–7, 30
    Todt and 24
    underground factories 41–2, 59, 73, 88, 133
    'wonder weapons' 21, 45, 68, 69–70, 78
    see also aircraft production; industry; V1/V2 rockets
Atlantic Wall 6, 28, 34, 35, 55, 67–8, 78, 136

August Dohrmann 121
Aumeier, Hans 32, 71
Auschwitz
    conditions at 115
    Hungarian Jews 70, 93
    IG Farben and 61, 91–2
    labour shortage 58
    OT administration in 92
    reassignment to other camps 72, 75, 89, 105–6
    Speer and 27, 28
    Volkswagen and 93–4
Autenrieth, Fritz 188, 190
Autobahnen 24, 83, 94, 193
    Todt and 15, 21, 22, 24, 30, 46
Avdo, Cakic 126

Balkans
    Bor copper mine 7, 60, 61–2, 127–8, 152
    raw materials 7, 65
Baltics 36, 116
    Peenemünde test-site 69, 88
    Prora 16
    shale oil *see* Estonian shale oil
    see also Vaivara
Baltöl (Baltische Öl GmbH) 6, 66–7, 68, 116, 117, 135
Bartold Operation 77, 152, 153, 159
Bauer, Dr 125–6, 160
Bauer, Martin 143
bauxite 61
Beck, Walter 126, 177
Beernaert, Norbert 132
Beisfjord 124–5, 126, 127
Belarus *see* White Ruthenia
Biel, August 146
Bisingen camp 115, 116, 160
Bohemia and Moravia 56, 128, 138, 196
Bohr, Erwin 32
Bonotto, Giovanni 141
Bor copper mine 7, 60, 61–2, 127–8, 152

Bormann, Martin 81–4, 99, 100, 104
Breslau 139, 145, 196
British intelligence 2, 25, 41, 43
Brugmann, Walter 30, 31, 83, 179
Buchenwald 19, 41, 74, 88, 155–6, 176
Burma-Thailand railway 3
Buschmann, Gerhard 112

Camp Lenne 146
cannibalism 1, 123
Casañas, Enric 136
Caucasus oilfields 6, 30, 60
    transport links 65–6, 120
'Centipede' gun 69–70
Channel Islands 68
    see also Alderney
Christiani & Nielsen 56
chromium 65
civilian labourers 2, 74, 167, 184, 196
    Danes 56, 137–8, 159
    death rates 4
    foreign 43, 74, 120, 134, 159, 177, 196
    French 55, 136, 140, 159
    Germans 55, 74, 95
    Japan and 3
    Nazi racial hierarchies 44, 137, 138, 141, 159, 196
    Norwegians 56
    number of 3, 59, 134, 177
    OT control 137–42
    Soviet Union 54, 55, 77, 97, 121, 135
    terminology 5
    volunteers 6, 55, 56, 135–6, 142, 143, 159
Cleve-Olsen, H. 108
colonial possessions 47
compensation for victims 8, 12
concentration camps
    conditions in 122–7, 158–9
    death marches *see* death marches
    East Europe 116–21
    economic justification for 85–6
    German prisoners 142–7
    Greater Reich 111–16
    guards *see* guards
    Nazi racial hierarchies 57, 133–7
    North Europe 122–7
    OT control over sub-camps 110–33, 158–60

Southeast and Central Europe 127–9
    the SS and 19–20, 30, 59, 85–91, 119, 158
    SS Inspectorate 19–20, 87
    violence in 158–60
    Wehrmacht control 63, 129–30, 131
    and see individual camps by name
conscription 44, 45, 51, 56, 94
Construction Staff Speer 26
construction work 147, 151, 154
copper
    Bor mine 7, 60, 61–2, 127–8, 152
    Sweden 61
Courté, Heinrich 41–2

Dachau 13, 72–3
    trial 186–7
    see also Kaufering; Mühldorf
DAF (Deutsche Arbeitsfront) 34, 98
Dailmann 118
'Dambuster' raid 31, 34, 79, 137
Dautmergen 74, 115, 148, 160
de Martin, Franz 181–2
death marches 107, 158, 159, 195
    OT and SS collaboration 164–5
deaths 3, 4, 10–11
    in camps 7, 8, 56, 131–3, 142, 147, 194–6
    executions of prisoners 1, 106, 129, 143
    from ill-treatment/poor conditions *see* structural violence
    mass shootings *see* mass shootings
    racial categories and 4
    'selections' *see* 'selections'
    Soviet labourers 160
    women labourers 152–4, 155, 157
    Yugoslav labourers 160
defence lines *see* Atlantic Wall; East Wall; West Wall
Demetz, Peter 144–6
Denzler, Ludwig 154
DESt (German Earth and Stone Works) 85
Deutsch, Ervin 113
Dolp, Hermann 125, 126
Dorsch, Xaver 12–13, 18, 25–6, 31, 32, 34, 41, 57, 71, 78, 79, 81–4, 179, 197
Drohsin, Heinz 119
Duben, Franz 138, 196

East Wall 68–9
Eblagon, Albert 131
economy
    Four-year Plan 60–1
    Hitler and 47, 77–8, 103–4
    industry and OT in 91–5
    Nazi ideology and 133–4, 138
    OT role in 9–10
    raw materials for 6–7, 59–65, 61–2
    slave labour in 33, 38, 43–5, 51–8
    Speer and 26–7, 81, 83, 194
    SS and OT in 42, 84–91
    Todt and 24
Eichmann, Adolf 172–3
Einsatzgruppen (task groups) 26, 30, 31, 32, 34, 35–8, 194
    mass killings 26, 165, 187
Eisenhändler, Elois 113
Elie P. 137
Ellis H. 151
empire 2, 9–10, 29
    Germania 15, 16, 29, 30, 32, 46, 193
    Hitler's imperial ambitions 9, 15–17, 33, 46–7, 84, 193
    leader cities 16
    Lebensraum 2, 47, 60, 86
    new settlements 16, 47, 48, 76, 86, 87, 91
    the OT and 15–49
engineers 197–8
    anti-Semitism 134
    Nazi ideology and 38–43, 45–6
    qualifications 39–40
    rank 35
    as slave drivers 161–91
    status of 35
    technopolitical training 21–2
    Todt's 'engineers of the future' 21–4
Ereda 117–19, 134–5, 156–7
Ertl, Dr. 58
Estonian shale oil 6, 37, 61, 66–7, 68, 74, 92, 116, 117, 119, 135, 136, 160
    see also Vaivara
Evers, Heinrich 132
executions of prisoners 1, 106, 129, 143

Fi 103 93–4
Fieseler 93
First World War, the 2, 3, 198
    Versailles Treaty 44, 47, 51

Fighter Staff (Jägerstab) 28, 39, 58, 70, 71, 72, 88, 89
Flocken, Dr Erika 35–6, 110, 125, 158, 183, 187, 189
forced labourers
    Nazi racial hierarchies 135, 145
    skilled workers 149–51, 152
    terminology 5
    types of labour 147–52
    wages 5, 55, 136
foreign labourers
    categories of 3–4
    dependence on 3–5, 180–2
    number of 3–4, 43, 44, 59
    the OT and 43–5, 54–9, 180–2
    see also civilian labourers; prisoners of war; slave labourers
Four Year Plan 60, 81
France 37–8, 135, 136
    raw materials 61, 65, 93–4
Frank, Gerhard 32
Frank, Hans 76
Frantzen, Heinrich 166, 167, 169
Fröbus, Peter 175
Front-OT 36
front-worker enterprises 86–7
Der Frontarbeiter 48, 184, 185
frontline workers (*Frontarbeiter*) 24, 35, 36, 184, 185, 186
fuel
    Caucasus oilfields 6, 30, 60, 65–6, 120
    Geilenberg programme 70, 71, 74–5, 93, 190
    shale oil *see* shale oil
    shortage 60, 78
    underground refineries 7, 59, 70, 73, 74, 88, 133, 190

Galtung, Johan 108
Gálvez, Joaquín 136
Gareis, Elisabeth 162, 163, 169, 175
GBBau (Generalbevollmächtigter für die Regelung der Bauwirtschaft) 38, 40
Gebhardt, Karl 82
Geilenberg programme 70, 71, 73, 74–5, 93, 190
Gerlach, Christian 167
German Labour Front (Deutsche Arbeitsfront – DAF) 34, 98

Germania project 15, 16, 29, 30, 32, 46, 193
Gestapo 19, 20, 131, 146
Giesler, Hermann 12, 13, 29, 32, 33, 35, 68, 71, 91, 99, 179, 183
  trial 187, 189
Giesler, Paul 101
Gimple, Max 32
Goebbels, Joseph 16, 29, 98
Goecke, Wilhelm 124, 125
Gogia, Klementi 123
Goldstein, Baruch 135
Göring, Hermann 23, 38, 55, 60-1, 81-4, 96, 104
Griesinger, Wilhelm 99, 187
Gross-Rosen 75, 77, 114, 152-3, 157
  see also Riese (Giant) project
Grünstein, Abram 111
guards
  mass shootings 108, 109, 116, 118-19, 124, 155
  OT guards 7, 8, 10, 92, 93, 106, 119, 155, 167
  Riese 75
  Romanian policemen 144
  Schutzkommando 20, 55, 167
  SS Death's Head guards 41, 151
  SS Guards 75, 90, 94, 106, 108, 109, 116, 118-19, 124
  Ukrainian SS guards 41
  Vaivara 74, 119, 120
  violence 106, 112, 122, 158-60

Haffner, Sebastian 198
'Handbook of the Organisation Todt' 12
Hanke, Karl 100
Hanke, Paul 120
hard labour 108-10
Hartog P. 114-15
Hayes, Peter 179
Hefele, Otto 119
Heinkel, Ernst 94
Heinrich Köhler 36-7, 120
Henne, Willi 26, 31-2, 35, 39, 62, 63, 83, 98, 103, 122, 179, 183, 189
Hermann Göring Works 60-1
Heydrich, Reinhard 42
Hilmo, Terzic 124, 126
Himmler, Heinrich 20, 28, 31, 41, 42, 58, 82, 146, 176, 191

Speer and 84-6, 88
  see also SS
Hinkerohe, Josef 185
Hinzert 19-20, 41
Hitler, Adolf 2, 9, 10, 193
  assassination attempt 1944 101
  bomb-proof headquarters 75
  imperial ambitions 9, 15-17, 33, 46-7, 84, 193
  Nazi racial code and 133-4
  the OT and 2, 9, 33-4, 77-9, 81, 103-4
  polycratic system 84, 103
  Speer and 12-13, 29, 48, 81-3
  Todt and 17-18, 22-3, 25
  the Westwall and 17-18, 43-4, 68, 78, 79, 96
Hofmann, Franz 115
Horn, Johannes 168
Hornisse submarine works 54, 72, 75-6
Hungarian Jews 13, 44, 58, 78
  Bor copper mine 127-8
  deported to Auschwitz 70
  Kaufering 72, 113
  Mühldorf 72, 113
  Riese complex 75
  Volkswagen 93-4
  women 72, 152
  see also Jewish labourers
hydroelectric power 61, 64, 67, 86, 177

IG Farben 6, 91-2, 93, 103, 179, 194
  Auschwitz site 61, 91-2
  Nuremberg Tribunal 91-2, 197
  synthetic rubber 61, 91, 92
  see also Krauch, Carl
imperial ambitions *see* empire
industry 18, 27, 194
  the OT and 36-8, 49, 91-5
  relocation of key industries 2, 59, 69, 73, 78, 93
  the SS and 85, 86-8
  see also aircraft production; armaments production; raw materials; underground projects; *and individual companies by name*
information sources 11-13
Ingster, Molly 157
International Tracing Service (ITS) 12, 108
iron ore 6, 60, 62, 64

Italian military internees 57, 128, 137, 138, 141, 148, 151, 196

Jacek Z. 115, 148
Japan 3
Jaroslav S. 56, 128–9
Jehlen, Erwin 174–5
Jewish labourers
    Hungarian *see* Hungarian Jews
    number of 4
    skilled workers 93, 164, 165, 166–7
    status of 41
    Transit Road IV 66, 120–1
    use of 7
    women 58, 72, 76–7, 93, 120, 152–7
Jews
    anti-Semitism 134, 143, 163, 171, 174, 180
    evictions 27, 32
    Nazi racial hierarchies 4, 74, 134–5, 144–6
    'resettlement' 32
Josip, Jurisic 126
Jost, Jules 72
Judith A. 155–6
Junkers 56

Kammler, Hans 28, 41–2, 43, 59, 69, 73, 74, 88, 99, 151, 190
Karasjok 123–4, 126, 177, 181, 188
Katz, Abram 111–12
Kaufering 12
    death rates 7
    identifying victims 107–8
    jet-fighter production 71–2, 78, 89
    OT control over 110
    'selections' 112, 114
    survivor accounts 105–8, 111–13, 114
    women labourers 72, 152
Keitel, General Wilhelm 23, 34, 64, 95
Kelley, Douglas 172
Kerch Strait 30, 58, 66, 79
Kiefer, Fritz 125
Kleinecke, Baurat 170
Koch, Erich 102
Koch, Karl Otto 176
Konstantins C. 120
Kontinentale Öl AG 6, 66
Koppenberg, Heinrich 56, 61, 62

Korn, Alfred 116
Körtgen, Hermann 166, 167, 169–70, 174
Krauch, Carl 6, 61
    synthetic rubber 61, 91, 92
    trial 91–2
    see also IG Farben
Kraus, Erwin 101–2
Krupp 91, 93, 103, 194
    employment in 156
    Nuremberg Tribunal 197
    tungsten mining 65
Kühl, Stefan 182–3, 184

Lammers, Hans 46
Langleist, Walter Adolf 71
Larsen, Gunlaug 138
last-ditch defences 76–7
Laule-Kirchenbauer 138
leader cities 16
Lebensraum 2, 47, 60, 86
    see also empire
Leichter, Franz 118–19
Leitmeritz 56, 143–4, 151
Leonhard Moll AG 91, 107, 112
Leopold, Max 188
Leszek Z. 151
Levi, Primo 198
Lewin, Nora 156
Ley, Robert 34, 98
Lindhardtsen, Otto 138
Lindner, Oskar 188
List, Maximilian 90
Löhrer, Josef 175
Lohse, Hinrich 102
Loritz, Hans 63
Lütkemeyer, Albert 75

Majstorović, Uroš 1, 7, 10, 12, 129–31, 160
    see also Ørlandet
manganese 65
Martin K. 148–9
mass shootings
    Einsatzgruppen 26, 165, 187
    OT staff 108, 155
    in Poland 172, 191
    Radoskowice 37, 161–72, 176
    the SD and 164, 165
    SS guards 108, 109, 116, 118–19, 124
    typhus and 124–5, 158, 195

Index

Maurer, Gerhard 40
Maurice V. 139, 196
Meiners, Edo 54, 76
Messerschmitt Me-262 jet fighters 6, 7, 45, 71, 101
Messerschmitt, Willy 94
Milch, Erhard 83, 93
military internees *see* prisoners of war
mines
    conditions in 141
    see also raw materials
Mittelbau-Dora 28, 69, 94, 190
Monchieri, Lino 141, 148
Morgen, Konrad 176
motorways *see* Autobahnen
Mühldorf
    conditions in 113
    Dachau trial 12, 13, 186, 187
    death rates 7
    German workers 95
    jet-fighter production 71–2, 78, 89
    OT control over 110
    'selections' 36
    survivor accounts 113–14
    women labourers 72, 152
Müller-Altvatter 130
Müller, Erich 24, 93
munitions production *see* armaments production

Nagel, Willi 96, 101, 102
Nándor H. 127
Natzweiler 74, 85, 94, 190–1
    Bisingen 115, 116, 160
    conditions in 115–16
    Dautmergen 74, 115, 148, 160
    see also Wüste (Desert) project
Navy projects 97
    submarines 54, 72, 75–6, 95
Nazi Party
    ideology 38–43, 45–6
    the OT and 98, 99–103
    Speer and 25, 26, 31, 99–102
    Todt and 18, 31, 48
    war criminals 172–6
Nazi racial hierarchies 4, 15, 44, 55, 57, 133–7, 196
    civilian labourers 44, 137, 138, 141, 159, 196

flexibility of 133–4, 141, 159
forced labourers 135, 145
half-Jews 74, 144–6
Jews 4, 74, 134–5, 144–6
jüdisch Versippte 74, 146
Mischlinge 74, 144–6
Romanians/gypsies 144
Slavs 134, 135
'subhumans' 8, 57, 171
Nederlandsche Oost Bouw NV (N.O.B.) 87
Neuengamme 76, 89, 154
Neumann, Franz 84
Nevrov, Kirill 132
nickel 64
Nordische Aluminium AG (Nordag) 56
Norway
    aluminium 56, 61, 62
    Arctic railway 61–5, 78, 103, 126, 177–9, 190
    Atlantic Wall 68
    Beisfjord 124–5, 126, 127
    civilian labour 196
    conditions for slave labourers 122–7
    fortification projects 56
    iron ore 62
    Karasjok 123–4, 126, 177, 181, 188
    Nordag 56
    number of labourers 72
    Ørlandet 1, 12, 123, 129–33, 138, 160, 181, 188
    Reichsstrasse 50 62–3, 124, 177, 180
    SGL Nord 7, 98, 142–3, 189
    Soviet POWs 57, 98, 122–3
    transport scheme 62
NSBDT (National Socialist League of German Technology) 21
NSKK (National Socialist Motor Corps) 18, 96, 101–2, 138, 181
Nuremberg Tribunal 182, 197, 198
    IG Farben 91–2
    slave labour as war crime 5
    Speer trial 5, 13, 27, 29, 75, 172, 186, 189
    see also war crimes

oilfields
    Caucasus 6, 30, 60, 65–6, 120
    shale oil *see* shale oil
'ordinary men' 171, 175, 182–6, 191, 196–7

Organisation Todt (OT) 1–3
  1943 decree 34
  Amt Bau-OT 34, 83, 88
  as armed force auxiliaries 35, 87, 95, 104, 186
  attitude to labourers 73
  business model 52–9
  competition for labour resources 73, 74, 84, 86, 103
  camps in control of 110–33
  camps in sole control of 129–33
  doctors 44
  in Eastern Europe 65–7, 86, 116–21, 170–2, 196
  efficiency drive 53, 54, 176–9
  engineers *see* engineers
  female staff 35–6
  foreign labour and 43–5, 54–9, 180–2
  Front-OT 36
  frontline workers 24, 35, 36, 184, 185, 186
  German prisoners 142–7
  German workers 43–4
  in the Greater Reich 3, 4, 34, 52, 70–7, 111–16
  hard labour under 108–10
  Hitler and 2, 9, 33–4, 77–9, 81, 103–4
  in Hitler's empire 15–49
  industry and 36, 49, 91–5
  last-ditch defences 76–7
  low historical profile 8–9
  management of 52–9, 176–9
  mobile units 96
  naming of 15, 17
  Nazi Party and 98, 99–103
  in the Nazi system 81–104
  Nazi war criminals and 172–6
  NSKK and 101–2
  in occupied Europe 60–70
  operations 33–46
  'ordinary men' 171, 175, 182, 191, 196–7
  as 'ordinary' organisation 182–6
  as paramilitary organisation 20
  pay and allowances 35, 36, 40–1
  performance feeding 53–4
  as perpetrators of war crimes 186–9, 197
  plunder of occupied countries 51–79, 194, 197
  police detention centres 19, 20
  protests about practices of 98
  in Radoskowice 163–72
  records 11–12
  role of 5–8
  the SA and 38–9
  Schutzkommando 20, 55, 167
  'selections' by 108, 110, 164, 195
  the SD and 164, 168
  size of labour force 71–2
  Speer's leadership 5, 10, 25–33, 34, 38, 48–9, 53–4, 94, 99–102, 184, 185, 186
  the SS and 2, 7, 10, 20, 38–43, 79, 84–91, 103–4, 118–19, 123, 146, 165, 190, 194
  staff/personnel 35–6, 49
  structures 33–8
  task groups 26, 30, 31, 32, 34, 35–8, 194
  Todt's leadership 17–24, 36, 38, 42, 48–9, 54, 99
  transitions 46–9
  types of labour 147–52
  uniform 2, 31, 32, 36, 99–100
  Volksdeutsche staff 44, 45, 100
  war crimes trials 186–9
  the Wehrmacht and 34, 35, 43, 79, 86, 95–9, 103–4, 123, 129, 184, 194
  women under 76–7, 152–7
Ørlandet 1, 12, 123, 129–33, 138, 160, 181, 188
  see also Majstorović, Uroš
'OT stoves' 94

Pannicke, Kurt 117–18
Pantoviç, Milan 128
Paul R. 139–40, 196
Paul Stephan 137
Peenemünde test-site 69, 88
performance feeding 53–4
personal accounts *see* survivor accounts
Pister, Hermann 19, 20, 41, 42
Pištignjat, Stjepan 124, 126, 127
Plassenburg Castle 21–2, 42
plunder of occupied countries 51–79, 194, 197
Pohl, Oswald 41, 42–3, 74, 85, 87, 152
Polensky & Zöllner 91, 187

police detention centres 19, 20
Polish labourers 4, 55
  volunteers 143
polycratic system 84, 103
Ponzi, Giovanni 137
Porphyr project 74
Porsche, Ferdinand 94
Poschmann, Alois 31, 39
prisoners of war (POWs) 2-3, 43, 98
  Burma–Thailand railway 3
  compensation issue 8
  deaths 4, 8, 57
  Italian military internees 57, 128, 137, 138, 141, 148, 151, 196
  Soviet POWs 4, 7, 8, 57, 99, 103, 122-3, 134-5, 177
Prora 16
Prützmann, Hans-Adolf 90

racial hierarchies *see* Nazi racial hierarchies
Radoskowice 37, 161-72, 176
Raim, Edith 191
Ravensbrück camp 82, 85
raw materials
  Bor copper mine 7, 60, 61-2, 127-8, 152
  conditions in mines 141
  OT exploitation of 60, 61-2, 64-5
  shale oil *see* shale oil
  Sweden 60, 61, 62, 64
rearmament *see* armaments production
Rediess, Wilhelm 63, 125
Reich Castle of Technology 21
Reichsdeutsche Germans 44, 100
Reichsstrasse 50, 62-3, 124, 177, 180
Reserve Police Battalion 101, 172, 182
Riese (Giant) project 70, 75, 78, 114, 190
  see also Gross-Rosen
roads
  building/repairing 148, 149-50
  transit roads 65
  see also Autobahnen; Reichsstrasse 50; Transit Road IV
rockets *see* V1/V2 rockets
Rohland, Walter 23
Rollmann, Peter 171, 174
Rom 37, 163, 166, 167, 169, 170, 171, 174-5
Rom, Josef Peter 37, 169

Roma people 120
Rorschach test 172
Roscher, August 150
Rosenberg, Alfred 26-7, 48
Rousset, David 198
Russia *see* Soviet Union

SA (Sturmabteilung) 2, 41, 48, 191, 193
  the OT and 38-9
  Speer's membership 25, 39
  Todt's membership 18, 20, 39
Sager & Woerner 75, 91, 94, 137-8
Sauckel, Fritz 34, 40, 52, 57-8, 59, 77, 87, 88, 100
Saur, Karl Otto 26
Scharfetter, Erich 117
Schieber, Walther 27, 92
Schmelt, Albrecht 90
Schmelter, Fritz 31, 39, 40-1, 44-5, 57-8
Schmid, Otto 119
Schmiele, Arthur 93
Schmitz, Peter 163, 171
Schnabel, Helmut 117, 118, 157
Schneider, Winand 161-72, 174-6, 183
  see also Radoskowice
Scholz, Diederich 180-2, 186
Schrade, Christian 188
Schutzkommando guard units 20, 55, 167
SD (Sicherheitsdienst)
  mass shootings 164, 165
  the OT and 164, 168
  Radoskowice 161-2
  Schneider and 164, 168, 169, 174, 175
self-sufficiency 61, 91
'selections' 105, 114, 120
  children 157
  by Flocken 35-6, 110, 125, 158, 183, 187, 189
  by OT staff 108, 110, 164, 195
  by the SS 118, 158, 190
settlements, in occupied territory 16, 47, 48, 76, 86, 87, 91
SGL Nord 7, 98, 142-3, 189
shale oil
  Estonian 6, 36-7, 61, 66-7, 92, 116, 117, 119, 135, 136, 160
  Wüste project 74, 78, 92, 115, 116, 160, 190
  see also Natzweiler; Vaivara

Shub, Sholem 117
Siegfried Line *see* Westwall
Sierpinski, Johann 143
skilled workers
    forced labourers 149–51, 152
    Jewish labourers 93, 164, 165, 166–7
slave labourers
    business of 52–9
    cooperation between the OT, SS, and Wehrmacht 103–4
    dependence on 3–5, 180–2
    engineers as slave drivers 161–91
    hard labour 108–10
    Nazi racial hierarchies 4, 44, 55, 57, 133–7, 196
    number of 43, 59
    organisation under the OT 52–9
    OT control over camps 6, 43, 110–47, 158–60
    OT sole control over camps 6, 43, 129–33, 158
    POWs *see* prisoners of war
    terminology 5
    types of labour 147–52
    women 76–7, 152–7
Slavs
    Nazi racial hierarchies 134, 135
    persecution of 40, 55, 142–3
    as 'subhuman' 8, 57
    see also Soviet Union; Yugoslavia
Soviet Union
    Caucasus oilfields 6, 30, 60, 65–6, 120
    invasion of 6, 7, 47, 55, 60
    OT operations in 9, 44, 65–7, 96, 97, 176, 184, 196
    plunder of 57–9
    raw materials 60
    Soviet POWs 4, 7, 8, 57, 99, 103, 122–3, 134–5, 177
    Todt's statement to Hitler on 22–3, 24
    war crimes trials 188
Speer, Albert
    as 'apolitical technocrat' 13, 198
    architecture 9, 48
    as armaments minister 24–7, 45–6
    'armaments miracle' claims 24, 48
    assassination attempt on Hitler 1944 101
    Auschwitz and 27, 28
    Central Planning 27, 194
    control of war economy 27, 194
    on discipline 184
    efficiency drive 26, 53, 54, 61, 176
    engineering staff 45–6
    Fighter Staff 70, 72
    the *Gauleiter* and 26, 100–1
    Germania project 15, 16, 29, 30, 32, 46, 193
    Giesler and 32, 33
    Himmler and 84–6, 88
    Hitler's imperial ambitions 16–17
    leadership of OT 5, 10, 25–33, 34, 38, 48–9, 53–4, 94, 99–102, 184, 185, 186
    memoirs 12–13, 32, 101
    navy projects 75–6
    Nazi Party and 25, 26, 31, 99–102
    networks 30–3
    organisational abilities 26–7
    OT uniform 100
    political crisis 1944 81–4, 99, 104, 194
    relationship with Hitler 29, 48, 81–3
    SS/SA membership 25, 39
    Todt and 22, 23, 24, 31
    trial 5, 13, 27, 29, 75, 172, 186, 189
    use of slave labour 27–8, 194
    war crimes 11, 13
Speer Construction Staff East (Baustab Speer-Ostbau) 27
SS (Schutzstaffel)
    attitude to labourers 73
    competition for labour resources 73, 74, 84, 86, 103
    concentration camps 19–20, 30, 59, 85–91, 119, 158
    Death's Head guards 41, 151
    front-worker enterprises 86–7
    Lithuanian SS 166
    officers' uniforms 100
    the OT and 2, 7, 10, 20, 38–43, 79, 84–91, 103–4, 118–19, 146, 164–5, 190, 194
    private industry and 85, 86–8
    prosecutions post-war 197
    special detention units 19–20
    Speer and 28, 31, 194
    Todt and 20, 31, 194
    Waffen-SS 11, 20, 31–2, 41, 44, 87, 100, 183

the Wehrmacht and 43, 103–4, 187
WVHA 10, 40, 42, 69, 87, 173, 197
see also Himmler, Heinrich
Staniak, Janusz 143
Staniak, Tomasz 143
Starkens, Josef 188
Stefan K. 140
structural violence 108–9
  deaths from 8, 10–11, 109, 111–12, 113, 115, 118, 127, 195
Stutthof (Weichsel/Ostland camps) 77, 134, 153, 154–5
'subhumans' 8, 57, 171
submarine projects 54, 65, 72, 75–6, 95
  workforce 76
subterranean factories *see* underground projects
survivor accounts 12, 109–10, 132, 134
  Kaufering 105–8, 111–13, 114
  Mühldorf 113–14
  Vaivara 117–18
  violence 158, 160
swastika armband 2, 99–100
Sweden 60, 61, 62, 64
synthetic rubber 61, 91, 92

task groups *see* Einsatzgruppen
Terboven, Josef 63–4, 102–3
Tessenow, Heinrich 25
Texled 85
Thurn, Karl 189
Tiercelet iron-ore mine 93–4
Todt, Fritz 6, 103
  Arctic railway and 63
  armaments production 24
  Autobahnen and 15, 21, 22, 24, 30, 46
  character of 19, 22
  death of 5, 23
  'engineers of the future' 21–4
  Göring and 23
  Hitler's imperial ambitions 16–17, 193
  leadership of OT 17–24, 36, 38, 42, 48–9, 54, 99
  military service 18, 20, 99
  Nazi Party and 18, 31, 48
  NSBDT 21
  Plassenburg political school for engineers 21–2, 42
  powers 23–4

  relationship with Hitler 17–18, 22–3, 25, 29, 48
  SA membership 18, 20, 39
  Speer and 22, 23, 24, 31
  the SS and 20, 31, 194
  training for engineers 21–2
  on war with Soviet Union 22–3, 24
Transit Road IV 31, 60, 65–6, 96
  conditions for labourers on 120–1, 134, 160, 179
  death rates 133, 195
  OT and SS cooperation 66, 90–1
  Speer and 28
  women labourers 152
Trucksäss 36–7, 119, 120
tungsten 64–5
Turmalin project 74
typhus 114, 115, 121, 144, 159
  mass shootings and 124–5, 158, 195

Ukraine 27–8, 65, 66, 86, 90, 102, 121
underground projects 13, 70, 106, 193
  aircraft production 6, 7, 13, 56, 71, 78, 79, 81, 82–3, 93–4, 101, 105, 190
  armaments production 41–2, 59, 73, 88, 133
  conditions in 78, 133, 147–8
  deaths 70, 78, 133
  fuel refineries 7, 59, 70, 73, 74, 88, 133, 190
  Geilenberg programme 70, 71, 73, 74–5, 93, 190
  Porphyr project 74
  Riese complex 70, 75, 78, 190
  rocket production 28, 69, 71, 88, 93–4, 190
  Tiercelet iron-ore mine 93–4
  see also Kaufering; Mühldorf
unemployment 19, 55, 135, 147, 174

V1/V2 rockets 42, 45, 69–70, 74
  Fi 103 93–4
  Mittelbau-Dora 28, 69, 190
  Peenemünde test-site 69, 88
  Tiercelet iron-ore mine 93–4
  underground factories 28, 69, 71, 88, 93–4, 190
  see also 'wonder weapons'
Vaivara 6, 32, 66, 74, 92, 116–20

conditions in 117–18
Ereda 117–19, 134–5, 156–7
guards 74, 119, 120
Jewish and Slavic inmates 134–5
subcamps 97, 117–18
survivor accounts 117–18
women labourers 152, 156
see also Estonian shale oil
Valentin submarine works 54, 72, 75–6, 95
Vereinigte Stahlwerke 23
Versailles Treaty 44, 47, 51
violence 10–11, 194–5, 197
    beatings 90, 106, 108, 116, 118
    in the camps 158–60
    camps under OT control 108, 110–33, 158–60
    camps under sole OT control 129–33, 158
    executions of prisoners 1, 106, 129, 143
    functionaries 197–8
    guards *see* guards
    mass shootings *see* mass shootings
    prosecutions for 197–8
    the SS and 159
    structural *see* structural violence
    systemic violence 197–8
    see also war crimes
Vistula River 76–7, 141, 153, 154
Volksdeutsche Germans 44, 45, 100
Volkswagen 93–4
voluntary workers 6, 55, 56, 135–6, 142, 143, 159
von Braun, Wernher 69
von Falkenhorst, Nikolaus 63, 64
von Gottstein, Ernst 180–1
von Rundstedt, Gerd 96
von Stauffenberg, Claus 101

Wagner, Jens-Christian 73
war crimes 11, 131, 163, 182
    British investigations 1, 7, 123, 143, 160, 189
    Dachau trial of Mühldorf case 12, 13, 89, 186, 187
    Nazi perpetrators 172–6
    OT perpetrators 186–9, 197
    Radoskowice mass shootings 161–72
    slave labour as war crime 5
    Soviet prisoners 123
    Speer trial 5, 13, 27, 29, 75, 172, 186, 189
    starvation 127
    see also Nuremberg Tribunal
Wehrmacht 5, 7, 24, 38, 42, 60, 104
    camps under control of 63, 129–30, 131
    competition for labour resources 86, 103
    the OT and 34, 43, 79, 86, 95–9, 103–4, 129, 184, 194
    the OT as auxiliaries of 35, 87, 95, 104, 186
    'slave hunts' 141–2
    slave labour and 103–4, 141–2, 194
    the SS and 43, 103–4, 187
    violence 10, 57, 131, 191
Weiß, Karl 34, 35, 67
Weismann, Eta 117, 157
Weiss, Martin 89
Wendtland, Bruno 188
Westwall 15, 26, 31
    building operations 18, 48, 101
    Hitler and 17–18, 43–4, 68, 78, 79, 96
    labour force 44, 59, 94
    Speer and 48
    Todt and 19–21
    work stopped on 34
Weustenfeld, Karl 131
White Ruthenia 102, 161
    Radoskowice *see* Radoskowice
Wilhelm II 47
Wolf, Ferdinand 174
Wolters, Rudolf 32, 121, 184
women
    Bartold operation 77, 152, 153, 159
    death rates 152–4, 155, 157
    Gross-Rosen 77, 152–3, 157
    Hungarian Jews 72, 152
    Jewish women 58, 72, 76–7, 93, 120, 152–7
    Kaufering 72, 152
    Mühldorf 72, 152
    as OT staff 35–6
    slave labour 76–7, 152–7
    Stutthof (Weichsel/Ostland camps) 77, 134, 153, 154–5
    survival chances 152
    under the OT 76–7, 152–7
    Vaivara 152, 156

'wonder weapons' 21, 45, 68, 69–70, 78
    see also V1/V2 rockets
work education camps 20
Wüste (Desert) project 74, 78, 92–3, 115–16, 160, 190–1
    see also Natzweiler; shale oil
WVHA 10, 40, 42, 69, 87, 173, 197

Yugoslavia
    Bor copper mine 7, 60, 61–2, 127–8, 152
    Yugoslav labourers 7, 63, 98, 123–4, 126, 129–30, 160, 181

Zalkindson, Bernard 117
Zoltan B. 113–14, 148

www.ingramcontent.com/pod-product-compliance
Lightning Source LLC
Chambersburg PA
CBHW051805230426
43672CB00012B/2645